Touch and

A History of Professional Rugby League in London

By Dave Farrar and Peter Lush with Michael O'Hare

LONDON LEAGUE PUBLICATIONS

Touch and Go

A History of Professional Rugby League in London

A CIP catalogue record for this book is available from the British Library.

First published in Great Britain in August 1995 by:

London League Publications
144, St Leonards Road
London E14 0RA

ISBN 0 9526064 0 2

Design by: Stephen McCarthy Graphic Design,
                       23, Carol Street, London NW1 0HT

Printed and bound by: Juma Printing & Publishing,
                       44, Wellington Street, Sheffield S1 4HD

Cover photos: George Nepia - courtesy of Les Hoole
                       John Gallagher - David Stevens
                       Fulham v Wigan - Ken Coton

Dedicated to the supporters of Fulham, London Crusaders and the London Broncos; and to Bob Brown and Hemel Hempstead RLFC, the pioneering spirits of the sport.

The Authors

Dave Farrar has been watching Rugby League for over 30 years. He is aged 41, was born in Salford, and his parents watched the original Red Devils (Salford RLFC) in the 1930s.

He is a member of the *London Calling* Editorial Board, London's only Rugby League magazine, and has watched Rugby League in the capital since the birth of Fulham in 1980. He is a member of the NUJ, and works as a consultant in public relations, administration and industrial relations.

Peter Lush is the only born and bred Londoner writing for this book. He had never been to a Rugby League match until taken to Fulham v York by Dave Farrar in October 1980. Since then he has attended around 95% of Fulham and London's home matches. He is also an avid football supporter, having a season ticket at West Ham, a soft spot for Brentford, and spent much of his youth supporting Hendon FC.

Has now retired from active participation in sport, but writes occasional articles for fanzines. He works as the co-ordinator for a housing co-operative, and also does freelance training and consultancy work.

Michael O'Hare originally hails from Cleckheaton, West Yorkshire. He is a full-time journalist with *New Scientist* magazine, having previously worked on titles as diverse as *Autosport* and *Video Trade Weekly*. He freelances as a Rugby League writer for various publications including *Open Rugby*. He now lives with Sally in Northwood, Middlesex and is, sadly, a closet Huddersfield supporter.

Huw Richards has reported on Rugby League in London since 1983, first for the *Rugby Leaguer* and more recently for *League Express*. He was editor of the Fulham programme in 1985-6 - the season covered in his chapter in Dave Hadfield's *XIII Winters* (1994) - and was a regular contributor to the *Rugby League Yearbook*.

He also writes on Football (supporting Swansea City), and Rugby Union. During the production of this book, he went to South Africa to cover the Rugby Union World Cup for the *Financial Times*. He works for the *Times Higher Education Supplement*.

Dave Farrar and Peter Lush would like to thank the following:

Michael O'Hare and Huw Richards have given us invaluable help, and their knowledge and experience have made our work on the book much easier. Also, Sandra, Pete and Kath gave their advice and support. Apart from them, we would like to thank the following people for either contributing material used in the book, agreeing to be interviewed, or helping in the production (in alphabetical order):

Association of Sports Historians
Phil Babbs
Chris Blanchard
Rachel Burkitt
Louis Burgess
Garry Clarke
Roy and Barbara Close
Ken Coton
Trevor Delaney
Harry Edgar and *Open Rugby*
John Evans
Friends of London Rugby League
Robert Gate
Harold Genders
Les Hoole
Trevor Howard
Tim Lamb
Michael Latham
Richard Lawton
League Express
Roy Lester

Lloyds Bank
London Broncos RLSC
London Calling
David Mace
Tom Mather
Robbie Moore
Neil Robinson
Rugby League Supporters Assn
Rugby Leaguer
Dennis Samuels
Irvin Saxton
Mike Stephenson
David Stevens
Ron, Mo, Kevin and
Michelle Snares
Sportspages
Harry Stammers
Tower Hamlets Libraries
Tower Hamlets UNISON
Barry and Gwen Warren
Mike and Sylvia Waite

and everyone who subscribed to the book in advance.

Michael O'Hare:

My utmost thanks go to the following without whom there would almost certainly have been no finished product: Sally Manders, Les Hoole, Tom Mather, Trevor Delaney, Robert Gate, Raymond Fletcher, Mike Bondy & MJB Research, Harry Edgar and Open Rugby, Louis Burgess, Chris Allen, Association of Sports Historians, Keith and Joyce O'Hare.

Preface

The very idea of this book has been met with bemusement in certain Rugby League areas and indeed amongst non Rugby League people in the capital. "Oh, it'll be three pages long" was one comment from a Cumbrian visitor to Copthall, which underlined this view.

The breadth and scope of this book will, hopefully, finally show that not only has London a League history to be proud of, but also that there is a potential League constituency as big if not bigger than anywhere else in the world. The attendances for the recent Australian and New Zealand international matches at Wembley have included up to 15,000 spectators from London and the South East.

Rugby League is rightly proud of its heritage, especially in its centenary year and this history is a part of that tradition and is a tribute to the supporters and players who over the years have kept the League flag flying in London.

The supporters have always played a key role in professional Rugby League in London. There were active supporters clubs in the short-lived 1930s ventures, and since the birth of Fulham, there has always been an active and committed supporters' group.

We may not have the length of history of clubs in the north, but we still have our own memories and heroes. Ian Van Bellen and Tony Karalius from the first season; Roy Lester, both as a player and as a manger; Steve Mills and Charlie Jones, who stayed loyal to the club through uncertain times; and Tony Gordon, who both kept the club alive in 1993-4, and managed to create a team playing the most attractive Rugby League ever seen from a London team. And there were Adrian Cambriani and Hussein M'Barki, our first real "stars" who had not come from another Rugby League club.

Add on numerous Australasians, and the Londoners who represented the club, and there is a rich selection for supporters to remember. And each supporter will have their own highlights, be it the first game, or beating Bradford Northern in the challenge match at Craven Cottage, or the Premiership Final at Old Trafford, just to name three possible choices.

We hope League fans everywhere will enjoy this book and hope it has captured the true spirit of the game. Many people have helped us with this project, and given it their support. We are grateful for this, but naturally, any mistakes are our responsibility.

Dave Farrar and Peter Lush

Contents

Introduction: The development of Rugby League outside its traditional heartlands

"What a wonderful, superb, heart-warming, cracking game this Rugby League is - the best football, in my opinion, for spectators in the world. I know this is an old unavailing complaint, but why the professional league game flourishes only in Yorkshire, Lancashire and Cumberland, I shall never understand. I hope against hope that the old saying 'What Lancashire thinks today, London thinks tomorrow', will come true in the sporting sense."

Daily Mirror writer Peter Wilson's response to the 1961 Challenge Cup Final, quoted in Vince Karalius's memoirs, sums up the history of Rugby League in London - a story which mixes hope with frustration, and ambition with mystification. Fulham in 1980 and their predecessors of the 1930s were formed in belief that enough of London's millions would agree with Wilson that League was irresistible entertainment. Their story has been one of frustration that, a few enthusiasts apart, London and its inhabitants have found the game all too resistible.

London has always mattered much more to League than League has to London. A game largely concentrated in towns too small to support successful league football - Leeds and Huddersfield are not the only traditional Rugby League cities to have won the Football League, but the only ones to have sustained First Division status for more than a few seasons - at the wrong, poorer end of the country, has been well aware of what it loses if absent from the capital. Any doubters need only look at the strength, financial backing and media presence Australian League has drawn from its dominant position in Sydney - which, while the largest city in Australia, although not the capital, scarcely looms over national life the way London does in Britain.

The most recent and spectacular manifestation of London's importance came in the formation of the Super League. The promotion of London Broncos to the Super League over the heads of nine clubs who had finished higher in the League, and several more who attract consistently higher gates reflected the belief of the game's authorities that a capital presence, however unjustified in terms of playing, attendance or financial performance, was indispensable to their new venture.

The dream of making the game work in London is little more than a decade younger than the schism that created the Northern Union in 1895. As

1

Michael O'Hare records elsewhere in this volume, the capital has been hosting international matches since they were invented. And that first Australian test in 1908 was followed almost immediately by a proposal to set up a club in the capital. Historian Graham Williams, writing in the Rugby League heritage journal *Code 13*, records that a group of "Northern businessmen" interested in setting up a club organised an exhibition match between Wakefield Trinity and Warrington at the Memorial Gardens, West Ham - then the ground of London Welsh RUFC. But this early outbreak of rugby ecumenicism got no further, a Leeds delegate carrying the day at the subsequent Northern Union AGM with his argument that the code "ought to make sure that they were safe at home before forming clubs in London and other southern districts." Some of the arguments of that time have a familiar ring as well.

But such ambitions and their frustration, are not exclusive to London. What science fiction writer John Wyndham termed "the outward urge" has been a consistent theme of the game's history. At the same time as the game's rulers were taking tests to Stamford Bridge and White City they were also taking them elsewhere. Of the nine tests played pre 1914 only one, at Leeds, was played within the heartlands. As well as London, Birmingham (twice), Newcastle (twice), Edinburgh and Cheltenham were also exposed to the game. And that exhibition game in West Ham was paralleled by others in Plymouth, Bristol and Scotland between 1909 and 1911.

History can inspire in several ways. Those who seek inspiration from the story of League's outward urge must draw from it evidence of enthusiasm, commitment and vision. Those who only look for success must seek it elsewhere, as the failures massively outweigh the successes.

There has been international progress - many British fans have spent the last 15 years rather regretting that Australia took to the game quite so well - but the boundaries of the British game remain recognisably those of 1895. There have been only two solid advances, up the Cumbrian coast in the years after 1945, and into South Yorkshire, initially from the early 1950s and with much greater conviction over the last decade. Both are regions bordering on the traditional heartlands, growth into them essentially incremental.

London's story fits into those of League's attempts to branch out further afield, and here the record is one of persistent failure. Early optimism has consistently turned into disillusionment as poor results, insufficient crowds and financial adversity have worn clubs down. Over the last 15 years numerous observers, myself included, have asked "Why have Fulham and their successors been so unsuccessful?" A fair question. But it is equally reasonable to ask "How on earth have they survived so long?" The 1995-6 season is their 16th. The previous endurance record for clubs outside the heartlands was held by Ebbw Vale, with five seasons.

While wanting expansion, the Rugby League has rarely been too sure how to go about it. One reason for this has been the ambivalence of its established clubs. Most have welcomed development in principal. But another league club, wherever located, is a competitor - a potential rival for league funds and league points. The more parochial have complained about the travelling - when a second's reflection might remind them that the journey they resent as an annual expense is a fortnightly cost for their far-flung opponents. And the ambivalence becomes still greater when, as in the late 1980s and after, when the League could be argued to be discriminating in favour of the newcomers - loosening import quotas and ignoring infringements of them, putting League funds indirectly into the London club and then promoting them on potential rather than performance.

For many years, the tendency was to test the water by putting on an exhibition game or an international. Understandable perhaps in the days before television coverage made League familial across the whole of the UK, but hardly a reliable indicator of the real size of the potential market. The number of people willing to turn out for a one-off novelty, particularly one of a high standard, is considerably greater than those willing to turn up every other week for a rather inferior product.

Opportunism rather than strategy has been a governing factor in British expansion - a policy summed up as recently as the early 1990s as "Put a club anywhere there's a businessman prepared to front the money." And once those clubs are established, the League's attitude has often been summed up by Winston Churchill's famous order: "Send all support short of actual assistance." It took until the late 1980s for the game to appoint anyone with specific responsibility for national expansion - and then the initiative came from the British Amateur Rugby League Association rather than the Rugby Football League.

This opportunism has had three phases. Before 1914 it tried to capitalise on disputes over professionalism within Rugby Union - triggering off the bids in South Wales after 1907 and Coventry from 1911. Since then the impetus has come from other sports with ground owners looking for a second source of income from their expensive capital assets. In the interwar years it was greyhound tracks - since 1980, football clubs. Common to both has been the problem that they are not interested in Rugby League for its own sake. Carlisle United FC were the target, but Rugby League PRO David Howes could have been speaking of any number of RL's disillusioned entrepreneurs when he said: "The Carlisle board seemed to view Rugby League club like a publican might view a jukebox. Install it. Watch it twinkle. Enjoy the music, but take it out the moment it shows signs of loosing money."

The approach has too often been top down, attempting to establish the game as a paying proposition before it has any serious roots in a community. Even Gary Hetherington, whose Sheffield Eagles have been by far the most successful of the 1980s expansion clubs, said: "If I was starting again I'd do it from the bottom up. Get the game into the schools, start up amateur clubs. And only then try to set up a professional club." Clubs that have no real roots in their communities lack staying power. The last decade has seen the likes of Bramley, Hunslet and Leigh survive apparently insuperable financial problems precisely because of these roots, while Scarborough, Bridgend and Southend Invicta died.

Both Cumbria and South Yorkshire have drawn on an established local base. Clubs like Kells and Hensingham made Cumbria a formidable league nursery, long before Workington Town were founded in 1945, while Doncaster had its own league for 25 years before a professional club was set up in the town. And although Sheffield development officer Tim Butcher said "when we started we might as well have been in London or Truro for all Sheffield knew or cared about Rugby League" they were able to draw on nearby hotbeds such as the Wakefield district. And in each case the club has been an independent organisation, tied to no other game.

History repeats itself - and looking at the handling of the Super League, the cynic might be tempted to add Karl Marx's comment: "The first time as tragedy, the second time as farce." It was no fluke that London, Cardiff and Newcastle should be three British areas outside the heartlands that figured in discussions of the new set up. London, south Wales and the north-east are the three regions that have provided the focus for the game's longer distance expansionary ambitions throughout history. South Wales was attractive for its similarity to Yorkshire and Lancashire in having a mass industrial population which followed rugby enthusiastically, and generated an endless flow of talent for the game. While the north-east may not have been quite so fertile a source of players, it had the advantage of relative proximity.

The 20 seasons between the formation of the Northern Union in 1895 and the outbreak of the First World War in 1914 were characterised by fluctuation and instability. The game experienced its first Super League breakaway in 1901, lost its first champions when Manningham decided only seven years after taking the title to convert to soccer as Bradford City, and briefly flew the flag in communities such as Millom, Birkenhead and Lancaster. But by the mid-1900s the pattern familiar to fans ever since had crystallised with clubs grouped in what is now known as the M62 corridor. It was indeed a game of three counties - no Cumberland as yet, but Peter Wilson forgot Cheshire. The northern outposts of west and east were to be found at Barrow and York, both playing by the beginning of the century, and the southern border at Warrington and Widnes.

The first serious attempt to break the pattern came in 1901, and should have served as a warning of the difficulties which would afflict expansion clubs, South Shields, deprived of their best fixtures by the schism of 1895, opted to change code. Then they changed their mind. Then they changed back, attracted by the possibility of joining the new Super League, which declined to admit them, and forced them to spend a year marking time playing friendlies. Winning admission to the newly-formed Second Division in 1902, their trajectory was all too prophetic of the fortunes of subsequent pioneers. A promising start was rapidly negated by poor results, with gates dropping to around 1,000 and debts mounting. Nor were established clubs invariably supportive - there were complaints about the cost of travelling to Tyneside. When they finished their second season in the re-election zone, they were voted out. The club's demise was completed when an hotelier won a court judgment against them for an unpaid bill. Historian Graham Williams argues that the failure was down "partly to the weakness of the club and partly to the financial problems of other clubs in the Second Division."

Similar frustrations attended the next English development club, Coventry, formed in 1910 when the town's Union club split following accusations of professionalism. They lasted three seasons, but showed even less signs of establishing themselves than South Shields. Their final year was one of unmitigated playing failure, concluding with a 102-0 defeat at Leeds. But in the years of opportunism, the main focus of attention was South Wales. While the middle-class rugby of the south and west of England was likely to be immune to the attractions of professionalism, no such assumptions could be made of an industrial area whose working population provided the bulk of the game's players and followers in the district. The Welsh Rugby Union never operated the professionalism clauses with quite the puritanical zeal of their English and Scottish counterparts - inducing a memorable row when their flexibility extended to raising a testimonial for Arthur Gould of Newport, the Welsh game's first authentic giant. And there were persistent allegations that the pay-for-play was much more pervasive than that at many clubs. By 1907 Ebbw Vale secretary William Evans was arguing for adherence to the Northern Union saying that it was "The more honest way of doing business."

The east Wales valleys were the focus of this first burst of activity. In May 1907 E. H. Rees announced the creation of a Northern Union club at Aberdare, coupling his announcement with allegations of widespread professionalism within union and claims, subsequently justified, that an important match had been fixed in 1905.

On New Year's Day 1907, an exhibition match pulled in a crowd of between 15,000 and 20,000 at Aberdare and by 1908-9 there were six Welsh clubs with Ebbw Vale and Aberdare joined by Merthyr Tydfil, Mid Rhondda, Treherbert and Barry. By 1912 they were all gone. Some made their mark - Mid Rhondda were the first club to play the first Kangaroos in 1908, going down 20-6 in front of 7,500 spectators. Ebbw Vale's Jenkins went out on the first Great Britain tour of Australia while Merthyr forward D. Jones was capped against New Zealand in 1907-8.

There were early moments of promise too - Merthyr finished eighth in their first season and attracted a crowd of more than 3,000 for the visit of Huddersfield while their union neighbours could pull in only 500 to watch Swansea. But within three seasons, Merthyr were so impoverished that they could only fulfil away fixtures if their rail fare was paid for them. The club collapsed at the end of 1910, but had already outlived four of its compatriots - Aberdare, Barry and Mid Rhondda lasted only a single season while Treherbert staggered into a second in which they lost all 12 games they played and drew three-figure crowds.

The last survivors were Ebbw Vale, who were attracting crowds of more than 4,000 in their early days. But they too were close to three figures by the time they closed at the end of 1911-12, having suffered the humiliation of a Challenge Cup defeat by non-league Beverley - the last such reverse for a professional club for 83 years until the same Humberside amateur team defeated Highfield.

With valley economies booming - 1913 would see the peak of

employment and production in the South Wales coalfields - Wales undoubtedly looked promising. But it was an illusion. Gareth Williams, Wales's leading rugby historian, argues that there was no space for League alongside Union and soccer, fast establishing itself in Wales during the same period. If it had, he says: "professionalism would have come as night follows day; the trick was to balance various factors in such a way as to keep the game on for the whole community. This meant a mixture of rigidity over their own rules and compromise, as over Gould, in the face of a social reality very different from elsewhere."

The promise of copious playing talent was similarly illusory. The very best Welsh players, when attracted to League, were still likely to opt for the better quality competition on offer in the North - even with a local option on offer, 18 Welsh players still "went North" between 1909 and 1914. Gareth Williams argues that League's first Welsh experiment was brought down by "The failure to build an administrative base, the sheer distance separating South Wales from the North of England, the paucity of professional clubs and their poor playing record."

Nor would the inter-war period be any more successful. Drawing on Robert Gate's estimate that for every international who "went North", there were 12 other players, Williams reckons that no fewer than 900 Welsh players, including 70 internationals, signed for League between 1919 and 1939 - the high-point of what Phil Melling has called "One of the greatest migrations of sporting talent in history." As Gareth Williams says: "The alluring power of the north of England itself continued to draw the ablest players who were so minded away from Wales and this factor, combined with the distances involved in fulfilling fixtures in Yorkshire and Lancashire, and low attendances at home, condemned the professional game (occasional showpieces apart) to a lingering death in Wales itself."

Not that there was anything terribly lingering about the death of Wales's only inter-war venture. Encouraged by the 22,000 crowd for the Wales v England match at Pontypridd in 1926, local promoters set up a club in the town. There was a crowd of 10,000 for the opening game against Oldham, which was lost 33-15, and a further five figure crowd for the visit of the New Zealand tourists. But poor results soon drove the crowds away, and they lasted only eight matches into their second season.

Quite why, in spite of that international gate, the promoters believed South Wales had the spare money to support a new sporting venture amid the social devastation visited on the region - still heavily dependent on coal - following the defeat of the General Strike and the 1926-7 miners strike, is a mystery. Between 1927 and 1934 Merthyr Tydfil and Aberdare lost their league soccer clubs and Cardiff City declined from cup winners to re-election candidates. For Rugby Union, these were years of desperation, with several valleys clubs going under.

But if that was another failed venture up a familiar blind alley, an even more short-lived launch a couple of years later held the shape of things to come. Launched simultaneously with Carlisle United's entry into the Football League, Carlisle City Rugby League Club shared the Harraby Park stadium, and its alleged 38,000 capacity, with greyhound races. It was a logical move for the greyhound companies, promoting their new sport against the scepticism of often puritanically-minded local authorities, to both spread their costs, and acquire a little respectability by association with new sporting partners. For the nascent league it solved the problem of finding a new ground to go with a squad of players. But as the next decade was to show, it was rarely a happy association.

Carlisle, admitted in June 1928 with only Featherstone and Leeds voting against, argued in support of their application that they would be able to draw on a region famous for producing tough forwards. It was unhappily rather less productive of supporters - there were only 2,000 present for the opening match against Wigan Highfield, and crowds had fallen to 450 by the time they met Warrington in late October. The team was not without colour - it included James Peel, formerly of Flimby & Fothergill and a descendant of huntsman John Peel, but was almost entirely unsuccessful. They won only once, against Keighley, in 10 outings. Reasoning, correctly in the light of subsequent history, that the coastal towns offered better prospects than Cumberland's ancient capital, they applied to move to Maryport, but were turned down by the League and closed down on 8 November. Professional League would take 17 years to return to Cumberland, and 53 years to reappear in Carlisle.

Subsequent chapters in this book tell the story of the three greyhound linked ventures in London which followed in the early and mid-1930s. They had almost run their course by the time the next dog-track joint-tenants were launched upon the world with the appearance of the Newcastle club in 1936. League was by now learning a healthy distrust of greyhound promoters. Historian Trevor Delaney records that one of the factors weighing against

Newcastle was distrust induced by broken promises of Streatham & Mitcham and Acton & Willesden, but the RFL were won over by the chance to bid again for an area with a "dense population and undoubted presence of a rugby-loving public and rugby-playing ability."

Advert for
Streatham & Mitcham
v Newcastle,
September 1936

Their election, on 13th May 1936, may have done London League a service as it ensured an even number of clubs would compete in 1936-7 - Keighley had already proposed that, if no new clubs were forthcoming, Streatham and Mitcham should be excluded to produce even numbers.

But the pattern of Newcastle's existence was to be a depressingly familiar one, as an inadequate squad reeled from defeat to defeat - they lost their first 15 matches, although may have felt the wait worth it, as they toppled champions Hull 5-0 in their 16th game - and rapidly ran into debt. Moving to Gateshead's White City Stadium for 1937-8 was no more successful as results stayed uniformly depressing and only 4,000 saw the visiting Australians win 37-0 in late September. This season too had its miraculous result, as Halifax were held 14-14 at Thrum Hall, but Newcastle had to borrow £2,000 to complete the season. With Newcastle heavily in debt Rugby League secretary J. Wilson told the AGM: "I don't think it is possible for Newcastle to complete the season. I am not in a position to advise you to accept Newcastle as members of the League for another season" and they were duly voted out 15-6.

Delaney's verdict could serve equally well for several other failed development clubs: "No attempt was made to introduce junior Rugby League into the area either before or during the establishment of the senior club -

recruitment locally was concentrated on the apparently rich seam of Rugby Union talent... There is clear evidence that the sporting public of the north east will watch good quality Rugby League - unfortunately Newcastle were unable to produce the goods on the field to sustain latent interest."

Newcastle also found that even if they produced prime talent, they could not necessarily retain it. Local product Dennis Williams, only 18, made an immediate impact and attracted the attention of Wigan. As Delaney records: "He was keen to swap the red and white of Newcastle for the more famed cherry and white of Wigan." Williams made 48 senior appearances for Wigan before his career was terminated by the war - a reminder, as Fulham subsequently found with Andrew Mighty, that however worthy the ambitions of development clubs, the best young players will naturally want to play for the best clubs.

The early post-war years produced unquestioned success in the establishment of Workington Town, inspired by Gus Risman to a series of trophies within years of joining the League, and Whitehaven, followed by the rather shakier entry of Doncaster and Blackpool Borough.

And there was one more Welsh failure, as Cardiff emerged from the nine team Welsh League for a disastrous year in the senior ranks in 1951-2. Liverpool City's spectacular awfulness saved them from finishing bottom, but only 13,000 spectators for 13 home games - including 98 for the visit of fellow-newcomers Doncaster - told its own story.

Welsh Rugby Union attitudes to League were as uncompromising as ever - WRU president Rowe Harding, who had caused a stir 20 years earlier by describing his Cambridge University XV as effectively full-time rugby players - told the 1950 AGM that Welsh League was "only an infant, but it wants strangling." Nor did the success of the short-lived Bridgend League club in outbidding the town's old-established Union club for their Brewery Field ground, driving them into exile for eight years, do much to soften Welsh attitudes.

The quarter of a century between the demise of Belle Vue Rangers - founder members fallen on hard times and greyhound-track sharing in 1955 - and the arrival of Fulham in 1980 was a period of unprecedented stability for League. Liverpool City became Huyton, Bradford Northern went under for half a season and the League shifted twice to two divisions and back once, but the personnel remained the same.

Even so, the game changed importantly during this period. The introduction of limited tackles, first four then six, began the shift towards the fast, aesthetic game on show today. Television coverage, hosted idiosyncratically by Eddie Waring, meant that audiences outside the heartland became familiar with the game, its clubs and big names. At my primary school in Shropshire in the 1960s, a good 100 miles from the nearest League club, a skied shot at the soccer goals in the playground was invariably greeted with the cry: "And it's two points to Wigan!." Increased disposable income and travel opportunities threatened the place of traditional pursuits like League in some communities, but made the possibility of trying out new districts plausible again.

It was this much-changed world that Fulham entered in 1980. Their early success inspired the most regionally diverse crop of new clubs in the history of the game. The 15 years since have seen six more new clubs - of whom Sheffield Eagles and Carlisle survive as League members - plus the reincarnation of Blackpool Borough as first the wandering tribe of Lancashire then League's first exponents of binary fission.

The list might have been much longer - Portsmouth FC went as far as holding a referendum among their fans, who turned the idea down by a 15 to 1 margin, Stockport County were turned down by the League and other football clubs to look into the possibility of launching the sport included Colchester, Grimsby, Rangers and Heart of Midlothian.

All of the newcomers except Sheffield started life as the offshoot of football clubs, and suffered in the same way as their greyhound-based predecessors of the 1930s. Most had odd moments of glory - Carlisle emulated Fulham in winning immediate promotion with a squad of case-hardened pros, Cardiff turned Welsh union flanker Tom David into the game's highest-scoring prop, Mansfield won seven of their first eight games and even Kent Invicta claimed a Try of the Season trophy when Peckham builder Frank Feighan - later a Fulham favourite - slalomed unstoppably through the Castleford defence in a John Player Trophy tie. And they have shown much greater staying power than their predecessors. Scarborough were the only one-season wonders. Mansfield may in their second incarnation as Nottingham City have launched a sustained assault on the game's all-time worst season records, but they had still lasted nine seasons - comfortably ahead of Ebbw Vale's pre-1980 record - before being ejected in the 1993 restructuring of the game.

Kent Invicta would have been a bizarre idea even without the presence of Paul Faires, while yet another failure in Cardiff should perhaps lead League to reconsider its obsession with east Wales. Ystradgynlais were the best supported of the post-war Welsh league clubs and the revived Wales international XIII has drawn better gates in Swansea - a city with a hinterland at least as large as Cardiff's and arguably much more rugby-conscious. Yet none of the nine clubs who have competed in the Rugby League, lasting a total of 21 seasons, has been any further west than Bridgend.

Carlisle and London have survived. And Sheffield have done much better than that. They had undoubted advantages over other clubs - the proximity of the heartlands ensuring that they could put out an adequate side from the start without spending vast amounts of money.

But what has really distinguished Sheffield from other development clubs has been strategic vision. Sheffield have always been a free-standing League operation - though forced to share with first a greyhound track, then soccer clubs, they were tenants rather than subsidiaries. They recognised the importance of building from the bottom up. Hetherington and his team recognised that the end-product of schools development work is not players, but supporters. Only a tiny minority in any community will have the talent or motivation to play at professional level - and will take years to come through. But the youngster who is coached during the week by Daryl Powell is quite likely to want to see him play at the weekend.

The lesson of Sheffield, seen against that of other modern development area clubs, is that the trickle-down theory of League - starting with the professionals and slotting in grassroots and commercial development when you can - does not work. Sheffield have shown that the grassroots work is not an option but an integral part of development. It does not guarantee success or make league communities overnight - Hetherington said after five years, with his team pushing for promotion: "If I was in Rochdale or Huddersfield I'd spend £30,000 on the right player, knowing that a better team would bring in the crowds. Here I can't be certain." But its absence vastly increases the odds against a club establishing itself. Where so much League development has been myopic - relying entirely on short-term, on-field playing success - Sheffield have been in it for the long term, prepared to build on a number of fronts over a long period. Their reward has been that nobody could possibly question their right to a Super League place. London will have to learn from their example if their status is ever to become as unquestioned.

Part 1:

International matches in London and the first Wembley Cup Final

by Michael O'Hare

1   The Successes   1990 to 1994

The old Empire Stadium had never seen the like. People pushing off the packed Metropolitan Line trains at Wembley Park clutching Union Jacks; a mass of replica shirts shuffling through the ticket barriers before plunging down through the infamous station tunnel and out onto Olympic Way, blinking in the sunlight. On the afternoon of 27 October 1990, a crowd of 54,569, a test match record for this country, was about to witness the arrival of big time international Rugby League in London.

While it was not the first time that Great Britain had played an international match in London, nor the first time they had appeared at Wembley, it was the first time that such a match had attracted such attention from the country's sporting public and from the national media. In 1973, the last time a test had been played at Wembley Stadium, Rugby League had shuffled out of town almost unnoticed, not even 10,000 having turned up to watch Britain defeat Australia. Rugby League had been embarrassed and 17 years elapsed before it was prepared to risk another visit. But this time the sport was ready.

It is fair to say the seeds of the successful 1990 Wembley experiment were sown as far back as 1982. As all British Rugby League supporters are aware, that was the watershed year. The game in this country was taught a footballing lesson by Australia that it would never forget. The Invincibles tore through their British opposition, establishing a legend that remains undiminished even now.

By their return in 1986, some people thought that Great Britain were ready to match Australia once again and interest in the Ashes series was unprecedented. The Rugby Football League took the first test of that series away from an established Rugby League ground, to Old Trafford, home of Manchester United FC. They were rewarded, if not by the result, with a record test crowd of 50,583. For the first time in its history, the BBC *Grandstand* programme left London and was hosted live from the venue. Rugby League was rising in the nation's sporting consciousness.

Four years later and the RFL had a point to prove. Rumours regarding a test at Wembley were already rife. Indeed, some Australian tour companies were selling Ashes holidays using a match in London as one of their selling points. National interest in Rugby League was at its peak and the pinnacle of the sport had always been the Ashes series between Great Britain and Australia. The League reckoned that the nation's top sports venue should host the game's top event and, if people outside of Rugby League's traditional heartlands would not turn out to watch the best, then maybe there was no future for expansion at domestic level. It was time to test the waters and the RFL took the plunge. The decision was no doubt bolstered by the fact that Britain had taken a test off the Australians on the 1988 antipodean tour and the public were now aware that Britain could match their rivals on the one-off occasion.

Les Bettinson, the British manager that day, writing in his book *In the Lions Den*, noted that "with half an hour to kick off there were still some gaps in the stadium, and David Oxley, the chief executive [of the RFL], was prowling about looking more than a little anxious. He above all others knew how important it was for the whole venture to be successful... there would be a heavy price to pay in terms of prestige."

Oxley and the RFL were to be vindicated. The regular international matches taking place at Wembley today are the direct result of the RFL's bold and successful move in 1990. The first test of that series, the 103rd between the two nations, on that sunny autumn afternoon rekindled hopes of Rugby League one day becoming a national sport. And it rewarded those who made the journey, from the north, from Wales, from Australia, from Russia and, of course, from London, with a day to remember.

The Australians, naturally, had been a major part of the publicity campaign in the week running up to the match and had played their part in a photo-call on the Wembley pitch with *Neighbours* soap star Jason Donovan. Nonetheless, the photographs failed to make the major daily newspapers. Team captain Mal Meninga also appeared on TV in the *Good Morning Britain* show, some proof that Rugby League was making the mainstream.

But it wasn't the visitors' pre-match publicity that made people take notice by the time Saturday's match came around, it was the performance of the home team on the pitch. The British win that afternoon was one that those present and those watching on TV would never forget. While not a complete shock it was certainly against the odds and one that was to capture the imagination of both public and press. The 19-12 scoreline erased memories of the 3-0 home series whitewashes of 1982 and 1986 as the famous Wembley atmosphere sparked Great Britain to one of their greatest ever performances.

Australia, who prior to the test trained at Crystal Palace, then home of

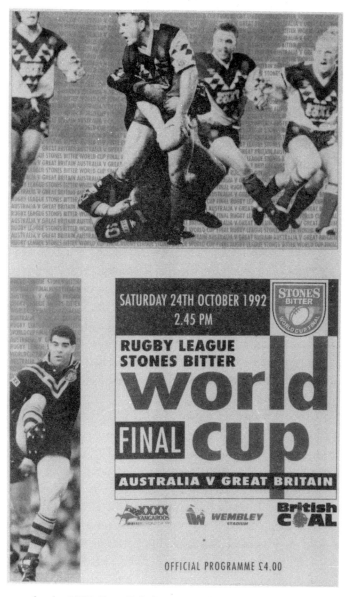

Programme for the 1992 Great Britain v Australia match (Published by the RFL)

professional League in London, opted to play Ricky Stuart, normally a scrum-half, at stand-off with Allan Langer in the number 7 shirt. Many have since seen this as their tactical downfall that day because, with Stuart moving to scrum-half for the second and third tests, Australia took the series 2-1. But that would be to detract from Great Britain's magnificent performance at Wembley.

The teams came out to the strains of Land of Hope and Glory from the Philharmonia Chorus and the contrasting effects on Britain and Australia were quite noticeable, as the Kangaroos visibly wilted in the face of the intense barrage of noise and song from the home support. The game remained tied at 2-2 at half-time with Paul Eastwood and Mal Meninga having swapped penalties. But the deadlock was to be broken by British captain and loose-forward Ellery Hanley. His powerful run and subtle kick over Gary Belcher the Australian full-back, took him to within inches of the line. The ball was whipped out to the right wing and Eastwood crashed home in the corner to put Britain 6-2 ahead. "It was a quick piece of thinking which got the ball out to me in the corner, and I knew I would have to burrow down under the tackles to be sure of getting the ball down. The Aussies went over the top and I was able to slide underneath," recalls Eastwood, in Ray French's *The Match of my Life*.

Australian captain Meninga levelled the scores when he touched down in the left corner after a typically powerful drive but Hanley and Britain were not to be denied. The British captain put up a bomb which fell to Belcher at the side of the posts. Hanley and Daryl Powell hit Belcher as he collected (some Australians claimed it was just before) and the ball bounced free to Martin Offiah to score Britain's second try. Eastwood converted and Schofield added a drop-goal to open up a 7-point gap.

Australia didn't go down without a fight and, when centre Mark McGaw shrugged off four British tackles to score a rampaging and Meninga-converted try with 15 minutes left, the signs for Britain were ominous. It was left to the sublime skills of Britain's stand-off Garry Schofield to make the game safe. His chip over the Australian defensive line put him into space and he linked cleverly with centre Powell who supplied Eastwood with his second try in the right-hand corner. Eastwood's 78th-minute penalty gave Britain the 7-point lead they needed and took his personal tally to 14 points. The Australians left the field to the chants of "Easy, easy" from the stands.

Australian coach Bob Fulton had a lot to say about the refereeing decisions of Alain Sablayrolles of France, pointing to a 17-7 penalty count against his team and disagreeing with some interpretations of the laws, but he conceded that Britain played a great game. "I don't want this to sound like sour grapes or take anything away from Great Britain or Ellery Hanley who had a superb game," he said. "We're not playing mugs here. We're playing Great Britain and there's some tremendous players out there." Meninga added: "It's not a nice feeling to lose a test match on foreign soil."

British coach Malcolm Reilly was delighted at Britain's first home win since 1978. "We were the underdogs," he said, in Adrian McGregor's book *Simply the Best*. "They take a lot of stopping." But he pointed out that "the series isn't over and there is still a lot of work to do. I know what Bobby [Fulton] is like, he'll fire the bastards up for this next one." Phil Larder, director of coaching in Britain, said the Australians "didn't do their homework. They thought they could just play good football and beat us. Used to, not anymore." In his biography, *Doing my Block*, Australian prop Steve Roach admitted as much. "The Poms were better than we anticipated," he said.

But, while successful on the field, had the experiment in taking the game to the capital scored success with the national media? Response was good, although it was short-term. Jim White, writing in the *Independent on Sunday*, complained that the game was over-hyped although he added that the victory "was magnificent, a triumph of substance over marketing." This paper also gave Britain the full back page, an honour not usually reserved for Rugby League matches. *The Sunday Correspondent* did the same but the tabloids, the most influential newspapers among the sporting public, hid the reports inside their southern editions.

The match programme, however, showed the growing stature of Rugby League in the mainstream consciousness of the country, carrying advertisements from such big name companies as Panasonic, *The Daily Telegraph*, Sharp and CIS. And expansion into southern England was not the only potential benefit to come from the event. The first ever Russian touring squad played a curtain raiser against an amateur London XIII before the big match, indicating that international development was also on the agenda.

Television provided the nation with the best coverage as the BBC screened the whole game live, showing millions of people the spectacle that is international Rugby League. The BBC even presented Mal Meninga with their Overseas Sports Personality of the Year award at the end of the year - the first time such a prestigious trophy has been awarded to a League player. The 1990 Ashes series went on to produce a record aggregate crowd of 133,684, beating the 1948 mark of 114,883 and, despite the fact that Great Britain went on to lose the Ashes, the Wembley experiment was clearly considered a success. So much so, that when the cumbersome four-year, five-nation Rugby League World Cup came to its final match in 1992 - Australia and Great Britain topping the table - the RFL and the International Board opted to return to Wembley.

The record for an international attendance in Britain was to fall again as Rugby League made its most high-profile visit to the capital ever. Rugby League was now staking an even bigger claim for the attention of the British public and one of its stars, Martin Offiah, was used in sports equipment company Nike's advertisement campaign that year, appearing on billboards next to the legend "The hand can't catch what the eye can't see."

1992 was also the year of the famous Offiah poster on the London Underground as the RFL took its publicity to the capital's population. The campaign cost nearly £20,000 but 1,000 advertising sites on the Underground escalators were flooded with the striking figure of Offiah, his heels ablaze under the heading "Can the Aussies catch Offiah at Wembley?." Unfortunately for Britain the answer was yes.

But off the field the marketing campaign was a success. The RFL Public Affairs Executive, David Howes, remarked that he had "never known a poster make such an impact." One fifth of the ticket sales for the 73,631 crowd, a record for an international match, came from the south of England - a clear indication of just what Rugby League could achieve in the region under the right conditions.

So, after such a build-up it came as something of a shame that the match, while thoroughly absorbing with the result always in doubt, was such a defensive and stifling affair. Great Britain were content to sacrifice expansive play for containing the Australians and then relying on a strong kicking game from scrum-half Deryck Fox to keep their opponents under pressure.

Fox had been devastated at originally being left out of the previous season's tour to the Antipodes and had believed his international chance gone. However, he was called into the tour party after Bobby Goulding was suspended. The Featherstone man so impressed coach Reilly that, by the time the World Cup Final came around, he was a key member of the team. "I had to look after Langer at the scrums and pin the Australians back near their line and make them play in their own half." he recalled in *The Match of My Life*. The plan relied on Fox's accurate kicking and a strong and stifling tackling game to keep the Australians from playing an open attack.

20

The photo for the Martin Offiah poster (Photo: Oliver Stothert)

This approach appeared to be paying dividends because, just prior to half-time Britain lead 6-4, by virtue of three Fox penalties to two by Mal Meninga, once again Australia's captain. Fox had been practising his goal-kicking at Wembley the day before the match. "I had been kicking them from all angles and distances," he said, and it appeared as the second half wore on that his boot and Britain's determination would be good enough to keep the home team in front.

However, in the 67th minute. Alan Hunte, the St Helens right-wing, took the ball up on the first tackle, driving towards the 25. Inexplicably the ball bounced from his grasp as Australian scrum-half Langer moved in. It was a moment that Hunte admitted in an *Independent on Sunday* interview in 1994, that would haunt him for the rest of his playing career. One seen, of course, by the millions watching on television with the BBC and around the world.

Another player who is similarly haunted is British substitute centre John Devereux. As the ball was moved out to the left following Hunte's mishandle, it came to Australian centre Steve Renouf. Devereux found himself half a yard out of position and could only lunge at Renouf who found the way to the line opening up in front of him. His try was converted by Meninga from the touchline and the score was 10-6. Britain were forced to open up play and both substitute full-back Alan Tait and captain Garry Schofield went close but the game was lost.

For the vast number of people new to the sport at Wembley that day, the game was something of a disappointment. Inspired by the Offiah posters on the Underground they must have been bemused to see him hardly receive a pass and then, instead of watching him on a lap of the stadium with his team mates, see him leave the stadium. "I took that more personally than any defeat I'd ever experienced in the game," he said in David Lawrenson's book *Offiah: A Blaze of Glory*. "I could imagine a lot of people new to Rugby League, who had got caught up in the whole marketing thing, thinking, 'What was all the fuss about? Nothing really happened.' Even though people said it was wrong for me to take this so personally, I couldn't help it."

All of which might have gone some way to explaining the tabloid newspaper reaction the following morning. "Booed Off-iah, Rugby Shame" crowed the *Sunday Mirror*, alongside "Offiah in new storm" from the *News of the World*. Whereas in 1990 the newspaper reports were positive, Rugby League did not come out of the 1992 World Cup Final with as much media credibility. The tabloids were wrong to pick Offiah's early departure as the main talking point of the afternoon, but it was only to be expected.

The broadsheet newspapers were more circumspect and, while both the *Independent on Sunday* and *The Sunday Times* were of the view that Rugby League was struggling to capture the nation, both *The Observer* and *The Daily Telegraph* offered positive reporting. *The Telegraph*'s Mark Bailey said the Final was "a great sporting occasion" and "utterly compelling." *Sunday Telegraph* writer Michael Crossley hit the nail on the head when he wrote: "It was so tantalisingly close that just one fatal British error meant there is still no sign of an end to Australia's 17-year reign as world champions." As David Hopps wrote in *The Guardian* the following Monday: "Will the Australians ever catch Offiah at Wembley? Will we ever know?"

However, despite the intense disappointment, nobody could fail to notice that a crowd of 73,000 represented a great marketing success. But while the RFL was now committed to Wembley as an international test venue the Australians were not set to tour Britain again until 1994. However, the impetus for international Rugby League had been established in London and it was vital that interest was not allowed to wane. Harry Edgar of *Open Rugby* magazine called for regular international matches to be played at Wembley as the specialist media attempted to capitalise on the successes of 1990 and 1992.

The tourists in 1993 were the New Zealanders, rapidly becoming a strong force on the international League scene and keen to challenge Britain for their number two spot behind Australia. The Kiwis were not the big draw that Australia represented and it might have been an easy option to play all three tests in the north. But the RFL realised that, with Australia returning in 1994, the impetus had to be maintained. The public is a creature of habit and missing out on playing a test in London in 1993 would see it quickly forget the sport. The first test of the Kiwi tour was to be played at Wembley.

It wasn't the first time New Zealand had played international matches in the capital. The Kiwis, touring under the name of A. H. Baskerville's "All Golds" had the distinction of taking part in Rugby League's first true international match against Wales on 1 January 1908, and also the first ever match against the British Northern Union the same year at Chelsea. And New Zealand teams had also played two matches against Empire and Commonwealth XIIIs in the fifties and sixties.

But the sporting climate was very different in 1993. The Wembley matches of the previous years and national television coverage meant that League was no longer the alien sport in the south that it once was. Again the

RFL ran a campaign on the London Underground, although it received some criticism; a cartoon of a Lion savaging a sheep did not have the same impact as the 1992 Offiah poster. Some predicted a poor turnout at Wembley - especially as the tourists had already lost to a club side, Bradford Northern - others hoped to better the 1990 Australian Test match attendance.

In the event 36,131 turned up for the match, the third best crowd for a Britain-New Zealand test. The RFL had kept the momentum going and were rewarded with an attendance nearly equal to that for the England versus Canada Rugby Union international which was held at Wembley the previous season. This was good news for League because union, rightly or wrongly, is always perceived as the nationwide code.

The match itself was a superb advertisement for the effectiveness of a sound team performance and the coaching ability of Malcolm Reilly. Britain wore New Zealand into the ground, denying them any scoring opportunity, and

The programme for the 1993 New Zealand match (Photo: Peter Lush)

took the match 17-0. The Kiwis were disappointed with their performance that afternoon, but in truth, Britain held all the cards and punished New Zealand for any defensive lapses. "Technical precision", was how Dave Hadfield, writing in *Open Rugby*, described it.

That the game never truly opened up was a testament to British organisation and, during the few moments of match-winning inspiration, a new British hero came to the fore to stamp his mark on the game and ensure the spoils went Britain's way. Jason Robinson's first try came in the 17th minute. Shaun Edwards, playing at scrum-half, put through a perfectly weighted kick. Wigan wing Robinson showed his speed by overtaking Sean Hoppe on New Zealand's left flank, and lunged at the ball in-goal to touch down. It was a remarkable effort that required determination and strength. Yet, only minutes later, from a Gary Connolly kick through, Robinson did the same again, leaving the hapless Hoppe trailing. Britain had the game in their grasp and although Jonathan Davies, playing at full-back, could not convert either try, he added a penalty to take Britain to a half-time lead of 10-0.

In the 52nd minute the game was over. Morvin Edwards, the Kiwi full-back, already a criticised selection, failed to take a towering Davies kick by his own posts. The ball fell loose to Britain's other wing, John Devereux, and he had the simplest job to touch down by the posts. Davies converted, and later added a drop-goal to seal the victory. Many said that New Zealand failed to perform that afternoon, including their coach Howie Tamati who said: "That's probably the worst performance from a side I've been in charge of. We were the authors of our own downfall." But that would be to detract from a fine British performance. The Lions were in no mood for losing.

So what of the media reaction to the event? Once again the BBC covered the whole match live and Robinson's first try was shown repeatedly at the start of numerous editions of the *Grandstand* programme. The national newspapers again turned out in force and seemed determined to draw conclusions from the size of the crowd rather than the quality of the match.

As for match coverage, the tabloids as always concentrated on other sports, despite the fact that 36,000 people represented one of the weekend's largest crowds. The worst culprits were the *Mail on Sunday* and the *Sunday Mirror*. The *Mirror* hid its report five pages from the back, while the *Mail*'s report was tucked away in one corner alongside large reports of the Rugby Union matches between Wales and Japan and the North versus London and South-East.

The Welsh attendance was given as 15,000, yet it was the 36,000 at Wembley that received the negative coverage. Simon Barnes, writing in *The Times* on the Monday after the game, said the match "was a great triumph of showmanship. In other words it was a failure." And he explained the presence of cheerleaders as showing "beyond all doubt that something has gone terribly wrong."

These comments came as something of a surprise after the quality newspapers had all given the game positive feedback the day before and all bar *The Sunday Times* had featured the match in full colour. Still, 10 years previously, this amount and standard of coverage in national newspapers would have been unthinkable, especially as many chose also to feature the curtain raiser involving the superb Junior Kiwis who narrowly defeated the British Academy team 30-22.

The Australians were set to return in 1994 and, based on the successes of tours since 1990, it was impossible that the first test venue could have been anywhere other than Wembley. The afternoon of 22 October 1994 was one of torrential rain and blustery wind and it did not bode well for what was to come. However, nobody could have predicted the outcome of the Ashes opener and none of the 57,034 who were present, nor the millions watching on television will ever forget what they saw.

The Australians had cut a swathe through their opening tour games causing commentators to fear an avalanche of points against the British at Wembley. Many people considered the Australians to be better than their 1982 and 1986 counterparts who both destroyed the British opposition, winning both series 3-0. Headlines such as "Can these supermen fall to earth?" and "How and why the Australian Rugby League team is ahead of the game" appeared in the newspapers in the days prior to the match. But interest was running high and the RL authorities extended their London Underground advertising campaign and also took sites on London's buses.

So it was with trepidation that another test record crowd (bettered only by the World Cup Final attendance of 1992) assembled at the Empire Stadium that afternoon. By the end the majority were hoarse with delight after witnessing the finest international to take place in the capital and one of the most dramatic ever.

The three key figures for the home team were the recently installed Great Britain coach, Ellery Hanley, his new captain, Shaun Edwards, and the British full-back Jonathan Davies.

Many doubted Hanley's ability to mould a successful Great Britain team in the time available. The previous coach, Malcolm Reilly, had departed his position just six weeks before the Wembley test when he took a post coaching Newcastle Knights in Australia. Hanley, who was still a player with Leeds and had never coached a team before, although he was well-respected, had replaced the previous British captain, his Leeds club-mate Garry Schofield, with the Wigan scrum-half Shaun Edwards, a move that had led to many column inches in the newspapers.

The downpour didn't prevent singer Cliff Richard from opening the afternoon's entertainment and his energetic performance set the tone for the drama to follow. "Rugby League, the rock 'n' roll of sport," he announced. The match proved him right.

The first 25 minutes saw some tense play and scoring opportunities had been minimal save for a relatively simple penalty missed by Jonathan Davies. Chinks had just begun to open and play was becoming slightly more expansive when the incident that was to turn the whole match occurred. The Australians ran the ball on the fifth tackle and Australian full-back Brett Mullins and second-row Bradley Clyde fashioned an overlap. Clyde stepped inside Edwards with the try line opening up. Edwards was wrong-footed, realised he had to attempt the tackle and jumped to his right with his arm outstretched. Clyde took a sickening blow to the jaw and slumped to the ground.

The tackle was a terrible one and referee Graham Annesley had no hesitation in sending Edwards from the field. If the task had been regarded as difficult before the odds were now certainly stacked against the Lions. Stand-off Daryl Powell was already off the field with an injury and, for seven minutes, the British had no recognised half-back to call the shots.

Yet, while the British prepared for the introduction of Bobby Goulding, the substitute scrum-half, Davies put them into the lead with a penalty.

Goulding had been on the field for only five minutes when, feeding a scrum in his own half, he broke on the left and moved the ball to centre Alan Hunte. Hunte got the ball to Offiah in space but the wingman chose to cut inside and was wrapped up by the Australian defence.

Two key moments then won the match for Great Britain. Australian full-back Mullins allowed himself to become involved a brief altercation with Hunte at the play-the-ball and he failed to return immediately to his defensive position. Then the ball was moved quickly right by Britain to Denis Betts who fed full-back Jonathan Davies, moving quickly into the line. Davies dummied, and stepped inside the Australian defensive line, leaving only Mullins to beat.

But Mullins was struggling to get back into position and, despite his speed, Davies just beat him to the corner. The stadium erupted and Britain led 6-0. That Davies had forged the opening was in itself superb rugby. That he beat Australia's finest full-back to the touchdown meant his try was set to become one of British sport's golden moments of the year. It was repeated on opening sequences for BBC sports programmes for months, so well known that newspapers and television merely referred to it as " that try."

The second half was always going to be tense as Britain's 12-man defence was stretched by the Australians but it took until the 72nd minute before Steve Renouf scored on the left to make the score 6-4. David Furner missed the conversion, Goulding notched a penalty for Britain in the dying seconds and the Lions were home 8-4.

It was an astounding and totally unexpected victory, evoking comparison with the successful 10-man British effort in the Rorke's Drift Test of 1914 at Sydney Cricket Ground. "You can't deny them their superb defensive work," said Australian coach Bobby Fulton. "We were beaten by a better side. If Edwards had stayed on we might have got away with the game, but we dropped down a peg. I think the sending off aided and abetted Britain more than us."

Hanley's surprise appointment was, for the moment, vindicated. "Everyone expected us to lose today but we had a quiet confidence in ourselves," he said. Britain's vice-captain Phil Clarke added: "I am sure that will go down in the history of test rugby as one of Britain's finest ever victories." It almost certainly would, despite the fact that Britain failed to clinch the series once again, going down to defeats in Manchester and Leeds.

Sadly, but perhaps predictably, southern editions of the national tabloid newspapers missed the point a little. "GBH - Edwards sent off for horror tackle" screamed *The People*. And it wasn't only the tabloids, *The Daily Telegraph* on the Monday after the match gave nearly the whole of the front page of its sports section to a picture of the Edwards foul and an editorial from David Welch condemning the player and calling for the toughest penalties. It all seemed to be an overreaction.

But the sport could pride itself on the coverage it received elsewhere. "Twelve good men and true," said *The Times*, "A tremendous match that

Jonathan Davies on his way to scoring "that try." (Photo: Sporting Pictures UK)

fulfilled all expectations," wrote Ken Jones in *The Independent*. And *The Sunday Express* led with "Britain's Wembley Wonders."

Rugby League had surely arrived in the national consciousness even if it still didn't have club teams in many of Britain's major cities. The kind of wall-to-wall coverage enjoyed by the 1994 test match at Wembley, and the eulogies that followed could not have been expected a mere five years earlier and were almost certainly the direct result of the decision to take international matches to the country's most important venue. This decision, coupled with the excellence of the players and their sport, meant that more and more people throughout the nation were seeing Rugby League in a new light. Possibly as a direct consequence of this new awareness Wigan Rugby League team were voted as the BBC's Sports Team of the Year only weeks after the 1994 Ashes series.

And the RFL seem determined to keep the momentum going. 1995 is Rugby League's Centenary year and, despite the ramifications of the new Rupert Murdoch-inspired Super League, the World Cup in autumn will see the opening match, England versus Australia, and the final take place at Wembley. It is an opportunity to take the game even further and one which the sport will surely embrace. Indeed, it seems unthinkable that World Cup matches would not be played in the capital, and this only a few years since supporters of the game's expansion were crying out for a missionary policy in London. The RFL were so often accused of impotence when attempting to spread the game beyond it's northern confines in the years before 1990 that it seems surprising that such an expansion policy was vigorously pursued in the early days of Rugby League, or the Northern Union as it was then known.

2   The Pioneers: 1908 to 1939

The early years of the Northern Union saw the game's rulers struggling for a foothold outside the counties of its birth. Taking international matches to the nation at large was one way to achieve this aim, and the authorities were not slow to arrange two test matches in London in 1908, two of the very first Rugby League internationals ever.

Since the inception of the Northern Union in 1895 the authorities had been looking for ways in which to make the game attractive to a wider public. Indeed, the survival of the sport at that point depended on a rapid expansion both in Britain and abroad. No headway had been made outside these shores until the sport came to the attention of Albert Henry Baskerville, a postal department worker in Wellington, New Zealand.

He was so inspired by the activities of the radical Northern Union that, in co-operation with George Smith, a former Rugby Union All Black, he organised a tour of England and Wales by New Zealand. None of the 26 tourists had played Northern Union rules before and the New Zealand press dubbed the team the "All Golds" because of their newly professional status. The tourists were accused of bringing no honour to their country and four former All Blacks in the squad had had to sign assurances that they "would do nothing contrary to the laws and spirit of Rugby Union."

Despite the negative reaction the New Zealanders set out for Britain via Australia where they acquired the services of the most famous Australian rugby player of his day, Dally Messenger, to join them - a coup indeed for the emerging sport.

On arrival at Folkestone in late September 1907, the tourists learned that they would receive 70 per cent of gate receipts from the 35 matches they were to play. They also learned that, in the spirit of pioneers, they would be expected to play a role in spreading the gospel of their new code: their second test against the British Northern Union, after also playing an international against the Welsh, would be at Stamford Bridge, Chelsea.

The tourists had lost the first test at Headingley by 14-6, yet an estimated 14,000 Londoners turned up on 8 February 1908 to see the Kiwis level the series 18-6, a remarkable turnout considering the absence of mass media attention at the time, and contemporary reports of "the counter attraction of the [Rugby Union] international proper at Richmond."

Unfortunately, reports insist the standard of play was not of the highest quality, although the journalist pseudonymed Steala Way wrote "there was not a dull moment" adding that "It was the first Northern Union match played in London, and I for one hope that we may see some more. The result [of rule changes] is a game tremendously fast and interesting to watch. Incidents sparked like facets of a diamond at every turn."

However, the quality of play may have contributed to the poor attendance at Park Royal for the visit of the Australians later in the year. The early stages of the match were characterised by a powerful kicking game from the British, which put the New Zealand backs under pressure, but also upon which the home team failed to capitalise. In fact New Zealand were the first to score, counter attacking with speed to put George Smith in under the posts, Messenger converting. Bert Jenkins of Wigan fashioned the opening for his club-mate and winger Jim Leytham to score, the same player missing the conversion opportunity.

In the second half, however, the tourists began to show the open play for which they were noted. Ably prompted by stand-off Lance Todd, he of Challenge Cup Final Man-of-the-Match trophy fame, the Kiwis took control. First the famous Kiwi, William "Massa" Johnston, was set up by Messenger and scored an unconverted try, and then Todd himself ran half the length of the field to score beneath the posts after Smith had evaded four opponents to create an opening. Messenger's conversion was successful as was his kick after the final New Zealand try scored by Johnston.

Britain had the small consolation of closing the scoring when winger Eccles took a pass from Tom Llewellyn to score a simple touchdown. Contemporary newspaper reports bemoaned the British inability to play to their usual standard, a fact which led to their defeat in the final test - and the series - at Cheltenham.

So impressive were the tourists, that both Todd and Johnston were to sign for Wigan the following season. Incidentally, both become involved in a bribery scandal. They were asked by an Edward Croston to throw a match against Hunslet. Both refused and Croston was convicted.

However, the Chelsea experiment had proved moderately successful and with the news that a section of Australian rugby had also broken away, were playing Northern Union rules, and were set to tour Britain, the authorities were keen to return to the capital as soon as possible. They were to get their chance sooner than they expected.

As a consequence of the All Golds' visit to Australia *en route* to Britain, interest had been kindled in New South Wales and later in that same watershed year of 1908, the New South Wales Rugby Union decided to adopt the new Northern Union rules, begin its own competition with eight clubs and send a touring team to Great Britain to follow in the footsteps of the New Zealanders.

Sadly, the pioneer who gave Rugby League its international dimension, A. H. Baskerville was not to see the second tour depart from the southern hemisphere. He contacted pneumonia while returning from Britain and died in Brisbane, never to see his native New Zealand again.

Dally Messenger was to return as captain on the first Australian tour, alongside the man who still holds the British record with 80 tries in a season for Huddersfield, Albert Rosenfeld. The Rugby League tourists arrived in Europe at the same time as their Rugby Union counterparts, the Wallabies. In order to create a distinction, the League players became known as the Kangaroos, a name still held in high esteem today.

The Northern Union was determined to promote the game outside its established boundaries, a policy which led to fierce criticism, some of which can still be heard in the 1990s when suggestions are made to play big matches outside the north. It was, perhaps, not the policy of taking matches to the nation-at-large which was flawed, but the administrational blunders which led to them proving unsuccessful.

The first test against the Australians was scheduled for Park Royal in London, home of Queen's Park Rangers FC, on 12 December 1908. Encouraged by the crowd figure for the New Zealand test at Stamford Bridge, the organisers failed to note that Chelsea were at home to Newcastle United in a vital football match and that the Rugby Union Varsity match was being played at Kensington, both on the same day.

The result was a dismal crowd of only 2,000, an inauspicious start for what was to become Rugby League's most eagerly awaited international challenge. The game itself, however, was a different matter. It was an outstanding match which finished 22-22 and, according to one reporter, "no better match could have been offered for the attraction of the Metropolitan public." That Britain should have won the game appears to be not in doubt, but the Australians showed strength of spirit to nearly snatch victory for themselves.

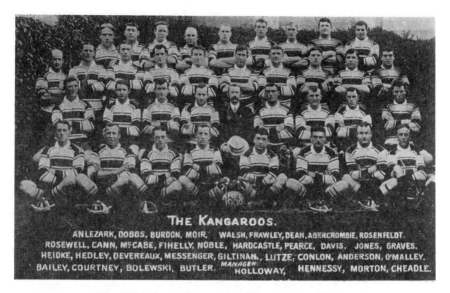

THE KANGAROOS.

ANLEZARK, DOBBS, BURDON, MOIR, WALSH, FRAWLEY, DEAN, ABERCROMBIE, ROSENFELDT.
ROSEWELL, CANN, McCABE, FIHELLY, NOBLE, HARDCASTLE, PEARCE, DAVIS, JONES, GRAVES.
HEIDKE, HEDLEY, DEVEREAUX, MESSENGER, GILTINAN., LUTZE, CONLON, ANDERSON, O'MALLEY.
BAILEY, COURTNEY, BOLEWSKI, BUTLER. MANAGER: HOLLOWAY, HENNESSY, MORTON, CHEADLE.

The 1908 Australian tourists (Courtesy Les Hoole)

Messenger received most of the plaudits that afternoon and Australia "owed their level share of the points to the individual brilliance" of the player, although he was also admonished for over-physical play during the game. Needless to say, Messenger was the very first scorer in an Ashes test, landing a penalty, before Britain began to take command. Johnny Thomas, the British scrum-half, had the distinction of scoring the opening try when he scooped up a loose ball and Britain extended their lead when Hunslet wing, Billy Batten, completed a fine passing movement.

Jimmy Devereaux replied for Australia, but further tries by Batten and stand-off Ernie Brooks put Britain 14-5 ahead at the interval. Unfortunately, goal kicking was to prove decisive for the home team. Brooks converted only one of the Lions' first-half tries and was also unsuccessful shortly after the break when George Tyson scored in the right-hand corner.

The final 20 minutes were quite remarkable. Devereaux scored again and was followed 3 minutes later by Butler. Messenger added the goals and the Australians were within 2 points of the British, before the Lions scored the best try of the match. Full-back Harry Gifford of Barrow, opened up play before feeding Bert Jenkins, Brooks and Batten who put Billy Jukes over.

Again the kick failed.

With five minutes remaining Messenger took an interception in his own half before the alert Devereaux, backing-up well, took the ball from a difficult pass to score the first test hat-trick. The conversion was successful and the scores were tied 20-20. But before long, the Kangaroos had their first taste of the lead, Messenger's penalty setting up a riveting finale which saw a disputed obstruction penalty awarded to Great Britain. Brooks atoned for his earlier misses to level the scores at 22-22 and ensure the very first meeting between the two nations would end in a draw. The British ultimately went on to record a 2-0 series win.

"Colonials fighting efforts" read the newspapers the following week. And, comparing the Northern Union game to Rugby Union, one correspondent wrote: "It is not too much to say that their [Great Britain's] passing was a perfect eye-opener to those used to watching Rugby as played in the south." However, the same journalist wrote: "as a missionary enterprise it was a complete failure." How often has Rugby League been described in this way? Today we still read of what a superb sport the game is, yet it still struggles to capture converts from outside its traditional areas.

The Australians were to return for the 1911-12 season and, while the Northern Union were still hoping to use their visit to promote the game outside its traditional areas it seems that, following the poor attendance at Park Royal, they were wary of staging a test in London. Newcastle, Edinburgh and Birmingham were the chosen venues and the Kangaroos won what was to be their first and only Ashes series in Britain for 51 years by 2-0.

The game in the Antipodes had progressed apace since 1908, benefiting from a Northern Union tour, and, even without Dally Messenger, the Australian team (which contained five New Zealanders) was a force to be reckoned with. Despite, not taking an official test to London, the Northern Union wished to build on the promotional matches played three years earlier, if only to let the capital know the game still existed. Rugby League would return on a more permanent basis to Fulham's Craven Cottage nearer the end of the century with the formation of Fulham RLFC but, in 1911, the stadium received its first taste of the game, when it was chosen as the venue for a promotional representative match between England and the touring Kangaroos on Wednesday 18 October.

Official statistics give the crowd as 6,000, but that is disputed by contemporary newspaper reports which hint at around 5,000 paying spectators.

All seem certain that taking the tourists to a football stronghold was not a wise move. "The attendance at Fulham compared most unfavourably with the Socker [sic] seen on the ground, even in midweek matches," wrote one correspondent.

The game too was something of a disappointment, not least for the home support, as Australia ran out 11-6 winners. *The Sportsman* wrote: "The game was not a brilliant example of the professional code," and another report said that "The most enthusiastic Northern Unionists could not have felt satisfied with the football played. It [the match] could make no converts either from Twickenham or elsewhere."

Australia were worthy winners in a match which also drew criticism for violent aspects of play, the newspapers drawing on this in their reports. Of the players, Bill Farnsworth, playing at stand-off for Australia, was influential in the middle of the field, despite picking up a ligament injury late on in the game. Harold Wagstaffe and Jim Lomas, the English centres, were the home team's most impressive performers, with the half-backs, Fred Smith and Tom White, failing to dominate play.

The English put themselves immediately under pressure by kicking dead from the kick-off and set the tone for the first-half. Sustained attacking from Australia saw the home line under siege and it was no surprise when Bob Craig, the Australian forward, scored from a scrum near the line. Then Bill Farnsworth broke through poor English tackling to score by the posts, "Bolla" Francis adding the conversion, and the tourists found themselves with an 8-point lead.

England were finally spurred into action. A succession of penalties put them near the Australian line, and Wagstaffe sold an outrageous dummy to crash over, despite the attention of the Australian tacklers. The English kept up the pressure at the beginning of the second-half with a string of missed penalties and drop-goal attempts which would have seen them back into contention.

However, it was to be the tourists who scored next to put the match out of reach for the English, with the game's best try. Intricate passing saw Craig, Russell and Viv Farnsworth (brother of Bill) fool the English defence for the latter to score. While Billy Kitchen scored the game's last try for the home team, it was a more comprehensive victory than the 5-point margin suggests.

It had proved a disappointing day for the Northern Union, both in terms of the result and also in attracting the kind of publicity they desired. Those who criticised the wisdom of taking the sport to a wider audience appeared vindicated. The authorities were made to reconsider the decision to play matches in London and it would be a full decade before the capital witnessed Rugby League again.

That 1921 tour by the Kangaroos saw for the first time all three test matches against Great Britain played at established northern Rugby League grounds. As in 1911, however, the tour organisers wanted a match to be played in London as a promotional venture, but once again they were to be disappointed, not by the more encouraging attendance figure of 12,000, but by the standard of football on display.

The Arsenal football ground at Highbury provided a high-profile venue for another England versus Australia clash and among the many commentators witnessing Rugby League for the first time was "Ubique", union correspondent for *The Sportsman*. He wrote: "Rugby Unionists in plenty were gathered at Highbury yesterday, being attracted there out of curiosity in order to satisfy themselves how the Northern Union game compared with their own... some of our impressions, which I give below, are not made with any feeling of bias whatever.

"We had been led to believe that the NU game was played at so fast a pace that it was quite unsuitable for amateurs. Well, as regards the speed we were frankly disappointed. The game seemed to be a continual succession of scrimmages and free-kicks. As regards tackling, most of it was of the neck-grabbing order... while the passing itself was of a speculative order, much of it being of the 'sky-rocket' type." Particular criticism was reserved for the lack of a line-out as a means of restarting play and opening up the field.

Ubique concluded: "I rather fancy that the Rugby Union followers came away contented that their own laws... made for as fast and spectacular game as they could wish for." These comments will sound familiar for followers of the League code, for they are claims often applied today in criticism of the union code.

Innovations new to the London crowd included the numbering of jerseys which allowed new supporters the opportunity to recognise players whom they may have read about, but never seen. Nonetheless, the game at Highbury on 10 October 1921 was a dour affair, which was a shame for an exhibition match of this nature.

Very few fluid passing movements were apparent and the only

encouragement that could be drawn for the Northern Union, apart from the reasonable crowd figure, was that England won 5-4. The Northern Union correspondent of *The Sportsman* lamented that it was the Australians' only poor showing of the tour, with only the half-back Duncan Thompson and full-back Norman living up to their potential. The English forwards laid the solid groundwork for victory, controlling play at all stages of the match, yet it was Australia who took the lead in the 15th minute with a penalty from Thompson.

The English struck back before the break in the game's best movement. Slick handling by half-backs Jonty Parkin and Brittain fed Todd of Halifax. The centre still had three opponents to beat, but clever footwork and a dummy before the line saw England take a 3-2 half-time lead.

Yet again it was the tourists who took the advantage. Thompson had already missed a penalty when Gray took the kicking duties from a difficult position near the touchline. His penalty was successful and the tourists had a 1-point lead. But 2 minutes later the English were to regain the lead they never lost. Contemporary reports said the attempt "was as fine a goal as ever was kicked in a representative contest" and it earned Tommy Clarkson, the Leigh full-back, all the after-match plaudits. His carefully judged kick was on the halfway line and only 10 yards in from touch, but its success brought a huge roar of approval from the crowd and England were home 5-4 despite a strong finish from the tourists.

The following day's headline read: "A keen but unscientific contest." And the text "The spectacular side of Northern Union football was so limited as to be practically negligible," was a sad reflection on a bold venture. The report went on to say that the poor game "was much to be regretted from the [Northern] Union's point of view, for obviously one of the reasons for playing the match in London was the presenting of the Northern Union code in its most attractive form." As the Northern Union was only set to benefit from the match in promotional terms because its share of the gate money was to be given to the Russian Famine fund, it was a shame that this charitable gesture was not rewarded with a game of higher quality.

Nonetheless, the Rugby League authorities persevered with their experiments in the capital and in December of the following year England met Wales at Herne Hill Stadium in south London on 11 December. The event was a failure. Anyone who has visited Herne Hill (and its stadium still exists as a cycle track) will realise it is an inaccessible part of the capital, some distance from the Underground system. The event suffered from a severe lack of pre-match publicity and a high entrance fee. Both these factors were out of the RFL's hands as they were organised by the southern promoters, but Rugby League received no benefit from a meagre crowd of around 3,000. The match was kicked off by Sir F. H. Sykes MP and he presented gold medals, a gift from Lord Colwyn, to the victors England, who defeated the Welsh 12-7. Under the heading: "Game that failed" *The Daily News* reported that the Rugby League kept their part of the bargain by merely turning up to play and that the local promoters were at fault for the poor attendance.

The *News* described the game as a "moderate contest" and criticised the excessive kicking saying how this kind of play would not win any converts. Nonetheless "it was a keen and well-contested affair" wrote the reporter, but the respected Welsh backs Shea, Johnny Rogers and Williams were never allowed the possession to make an impact.

It was a surprise then, when Wales took a half-time lead of 7-6 thanks to a try by Edgar Morgan from Jim Bacon's inside pass. Jim Sullivan converted but, after tries by Billy Stone and Bob Taylor, the latter following a clever kick by Tranter, it took a penalty by Sullivan before half-time to give Wales the interval lead. While the English suffered from poor goal-kicking, none of Stone's or Tommy Clarkson's attempts proving successful, the second half saw their forwards gain the upper hand.

However, it was not until late into the game that Stone secured the English victory with a try described by the *Leeds Mercury* as "the effort of a master of opportunism." The Welsh scrum-half Rogers dropped a pass and wingman Stone, lurking unexpectedly infield, scooped up the ball to race into the clear and score. Shortly afterwards, man-of-the-match and English captain and stand-off, Jonty Parkin capitalised on a high kick and chase when the Welsh defence spilled the ball to score England's fourth try and take the score to 12-7.

Despite the poor crowd, those locals who did attend were said to be impressed, 'Yorkist' in the *Leeds Mercury* overhearing one spectator describing the match as "the best game of 'Rugger' he had seen for many years." As an exhibition 'Yorkist' considered the game an "illumination" for the London people although he said "there always seemed something missing... the atmosphere was foreign." *The Daily News* correspondent, however, wrote from the standpoint of an outsider saying "followers of the amateur code could not but be struck with the fine physique, speed, agility and cleverness of the teams."

Unfortunately the size of the crowd was the factor by which the authorities would judge the success of the venture. It simply wasn't big enough to warrant a return to the capital the following year.

Sadly, Rugby League looked set to return to the confines of its northern heartlands until a startling proposal was presented to the Rugby League Council. The council had officially renamed the sport as Rugby League, dispensing finally with the Northern Union tag, and it was searching for a permanent home for the showpiece event of its calendar, the Challenge Cup Final. The 1924 final at Rochdale had provided an attendance of 42,000 which had proved difficult for police and ground stewards to handle, as were the crowds at the 1927 and 1928 finals at Wigan. It was clear that none of the northern stadiums could accommodate the growing number wishing to attend the final.

John Leake, the chairman of the RFL's Welsh Commission suggested that the League should take a look at venues in London, including Crystal Palace, White City and the new Wembley Stadium, completed in 1923 and home to football's FA Cup Final. John Wilson, a proponent of the switch to London and secretary of the RFL, visited the capital but was deterred by the high cost of Crystal Palace. It appeared the investigations would come to nothing but Sir Arthur Elvin of Wembley Stadium saw the opportunity to benefit from bringing the final to his venue and lowered his required percentage cut of the gate. The outcry from northern traditionalists was as angered as it was expected but the RFL rode the storm and in May 1929 Dewsbury were defeated by Wigan in front of 41,500 people in Rugby League's first ever Wembley final.

The move was one of the RFL's most successful and, for a while in the early thirties, interest in London was kindled for the sport. In 1932 Leeds played Wigan under floodlights at White City, which the following year became the home venue for the London Highfield Club. On the back of this interest other clubs at Acton & Willesden and Streatham & Mitcham were to follow.

The potential was such that, only eight years after seeing a paltry 3,000 spectators at Herne Hill, Rugby League felt confident to take two international matches back to the capital. Both involved the Kangaroo tourists and their manager, Harry Sunderland, was instrumental in urging the RFL to play the games at Wembley. In both matches Wales were to fall victim to the tourists.

The 1929 Australian Tourists (Courtesy Les Hoole)

Originally scheduled for Cardiff, the first match on 18 January 1930 was switched to Wembley to avoid a clash with the England versus Wales Rugby Union match at the Arms Park. It attracted 16,000 spectators, a small figure by today's standards but one that allowed the tourists to return to Australia with record profits. The crowd also included Mr Clynes, the Home Secretary; the Earl of Birkenhead and a number of prominent London sportsmen as Rugby League tried to promote itself to a wider audience. *The Daily Mail* also supplied a Challenge Bowl to the victorious Kangaroos which was presented by Mr Clynes. Both the bowl and Harry Sunderland were returned to Australia by Bert Hinckler, the famous aviator, who also had the distinction of kicking off the match.

Hinckler's countrymen proved too strong for their Welsh opponents, especially in the second half, and scored six tries in a powerful 26-10 victory. This was a small compensation for the fact that they had lost the test series with Great Britain in an unscheduled fourth and deciding test at Rochdale after the initial three-match series controversially ended all-square with a drawn match at Swinton.

Most reports comment on how quiet Wembley Stadium was for that

41

first international in 1930, with the local crowd unfamiliar with the rules of Rugby League, but the first half was a dour affair which did not encourage audience participation. The Welsh were strong in the scrum and the Australian stand-off Fred Laws failed to set his backs in motion, leading to a stifled game. The Australians took the lead through a Bill Shankland penalty but Wales responded with a try by Stephen Ray who beat a clutch of defenders to score by the posts. A contemporary newspaper report described the try as "capital." Jim Sullivan added the goal, but George Treweeke's try, a strong run by the second-row Australian, ensured the sides were level at half-time, 5-5.

The Australians changed their tactics for the second half. Laws, always proving too slow at half-back, found the ball from scrum-half Joe Busch bypassing him *en route* to the centres, and the tourists began to run the game. Initially Wales stayed with the Kangaroos and, after Bill Spencer had scored a try to give Australia a 3-point lead, the Welsh scored the game's best try, clever passing leading to Swinton stand-off Billo Rees selling Frank McMillan an outrageous dummy before feeding try scorer Mel Rosser. Jim Sullivan's conversion gave Wales a 10-8 lead. But from there on in, it was all Australia.

The final 30 minutes saw the tourists run in four tries with three of them converted by Shankland. Spencer, the Australian right wing, ran his Welsh counterpart Johnny Ring ragged as he notched two of the tries. The Welsh trio of Rosser, Rees and Ray did their utmost in defence but were unable to stop the Australian flow, the remaining two tries being scored by the forwards Snowy Justice and Wally Prigg.

The *Western Mail* put the tourists' success down to "speedy combination, in which the whole team participated." The report went on to say that "the Australians were a fine side" who "showed conclusively that they knew the value of the wind," a reference to the fact that the Australians won the toss and elected to play with the wind behind them in the second half, using strong kicking to their advantage.

The crowd of 16,000 may have appeared small in the vast bowl of the new Wembley Stadium, but the standard of play did impress those who were there. Reports state that "the Home Secretary commented on the cleanness of the game. He stated that both teams had shown the spirit of goodwill, and had afforded the spectators many fine instances of the best examples of football that could be found in any part of the Empire." Inspiring words indeed and all part of the positive feedback that led to a return fixture between the two nations at the same venue three years later.

The *Daily Mail* trophy was up for grabs again and Wales were confident that they could defeat Australia this time around. The Kangaroos had been whitewashed in the three-match Ashes series with Great Britain and the Welsh were fielding seven former Rugby Union internationals. Unfortunately their confidence was misplaced and the tourists, stung by their defeats to the British side exacted revenge in a stunning 51-19 victory.

"Wales crushed at Wembley" was the headline in the *Newport Football Argus*, while a contemporary report told how Wales who "looked strong enough to test the Australians to the full was swept aside in the most contemptuous fashion." The tourists' points total fell only 2 short of their record against a club side on that 1933 tour against Bramley.

Welsh full-back Jim Sullivan and his centre Gus Risman were the only two players to put up any form of stern resistance to the Australians, but their skill was restricted to good tackling stints and kicking to relieve pressure. The Welsh side struggled from a perennial problem which still existed until the 1994 ruling on grandparent qualification for international selection - that of

Programme for Wales v Australia at Wembley 1933
(Courtesy Les Hoole)

possessing a weak pack. The scrum was a troublesome area against the strong Australian forwards and the Welsh could make no headway up the middle with the backs seeing little of the ball.

Nonetheless, the Australians were impressive. The newspapers wrote: "Give the Australians credit for a very fine and intelligent display. Their forwards gave them the opportunities and the backs as well as the forwards took them. One or two of their tries were cut so brilliantly that the best of defences would have been left helpless, and some of the movements which did not produce tries were masterpieces." All of which has a very familiar ring to watchers of international League in the nineties.

Cliff Pearce, fed by Wally Prigg, scored the opening try under the posts after only eight minutes and from there on in it was one-way traffic. Jim Sullivan responded with two penalties but first Doyle, and then Jack Why with two tries in a minute followed by Pearce notching a second and Dave Brown converting four of the tries took Australia up to half-time with a 23-4 lead.

Wales rallied briefly at the start of the second-half and Norman Fender powered over from close to the line. Sullivan's conversion left the score at 23-9 but Frank Gardner, with a run from his own half taking him through the Welsh defence, restored Australia's dominance as did Vic Hey who scored shortly afterwards. The Welsh tackling became woeful as first Pearce, then Brown, Why and "Cire" Smith all scored for the tourists and Brown's nine goals gave him a tour points record. His final total of 285 may never be beaten by a tourist.

The 10,000 crowd, a poor showing given the attendance for the 1930 match and subsequent Challenge Cup Finals, had something to cheer when Wales notched tries through Jack Morley and Isaac but in all departments the Welsh were outgunned. Sullivan's total of five goals still left the Welsh with a staggering 32-point deficit. After the presentation of the cup the *Newport Football Argus* tells us that "the Australian team placed the trophy on the turf, surrounded it, and again gave their war cry."

The Observer added that "the London weather was not of the best, and from the attendance point of view it was evident that the morning mist and rain would ruin the match." The crowd applauded the tourists' superb display and it was a shame that international Rugby League would not be seen in the capital for another 16 years.

44

3 The Failures: 1945 to 1973

A combination of the outbreak of the Second World War and the end of Rugby League's brief boom in the capital in the early thirties, when the London-based professional teams were disbanded, meant that it would be 12 March 1949 before internationals returned to London, this time with new faces in attendance as the French made their first, and so far only, visit to Wembley to play England.

In 1931 the four British Isles members of the Five Nations Rugby Union Championship banned the French from entering the competition, citing foul play and professionalism. Several French clubs had been threatening to split from the French Union in much the same way as the north of England clubs went alone in 1895 and, with the banning of the French national union team, the door was open for Rugby League. In 1933 French clubs met British RL officials in London and a British XIII played Australia in Paris on 31 December 1933 in an exhibition game, the day after Wales had played Australia at Wembley.

The French were obviously impressed and toured England briefly in early 1934 before making their international debut at the Stade Buffalo Velodrome, Paris in April 1934, losing 32-21 to England. French League flourished under such pioneers as Jean Galia and by 1939 France had become European champions. Despite a ludicrous and still talked about ban on the French RL by the Nazi puppet Vichy Government during the Second World War, League continued to grow in the villages and towns away from German influence and by the late 1940s and early 1950s the French RL team was at its most dominant, winning the European Championship three times.

One of the matches which led to the first of those three European Championships was the Wembley game in the year after the International Board had been set up in Bordeaux. The international game was now on an official footing and the French were early and eager pioneers, keen to establish European and World Championship competitions. They were not, however, expected to beat the English on home soil.

But, as Eddie Waring pointed out in the *Rugby League Review*, the French victory at Wembley in 1949 was one of a number of surprises. The way the visitors had turned their performance around after recent defeat by Australia impressed many in the modest crowd of 12,382, and the French were

45

The programme for England v France, Wembley March 1949 (Courtesy LesHoole)

46

dominant in most departments.

The crowd was one of the disappointments that afternoon as the RFL had banked on at least 20,000 with some optimists hoping to double that. The supporters were also surprised, and many a little angry, at the late change of venue, the game originally scheduled for Leeds.

The *Rugby League Review* ran a scathing article condemning the switch, editor Stanley Chadwick writing "spasmodic propaganda such as this impresses no one, least of all Londoners familiar with the showmanship of Bertram Mills circus and the Lord Mayor's Parade." Chadwick saw the match as "a betrayal and an affront to the thousands of loyal followers of the code in the counties of its home and birth."

But the RFL were keen to capitalise on the post-war boom in sports crowds and saw the match as a means of attracting new support for the game outside its traditional areas. A newspaper report previewing the game, however, pointed out that "little time was allowed for giving the England v. France match the necessary publicity." Yet the same report went on to say that "this is a better opportunity to see the game played in an attractive style than will be the Cup Final on the same ground in May." The report was confident that England would win and take the championship title but added that "the volatile Frenchmen would pass the ball at all costs." The writer assured Londoners that "nothing like it has ever been seen at Twickenham."

The French did indeed throw the ball around and, against all the odds, secured a famous victory that ultimately led to them taking the European Championship from England and Wales. "At no time were England on top," wrote Eddie Waring, suggesting that the absence of Wigan's in-form Martin Ryan and the fact that the English had recently played in Challenge Cup matches were significant factors.

A further surprise was the decision of the BBC to televise the game in London, the journalist Bob Pemberton writing "the match seemed even more thrilling 'looking in' than 'looking out'." This was despite the fact that the match contained 60 scrums, a figure that would be considered ludicrous today.

"English slower and less decisive," wrote *The Manchester Guardian*, which also complained that the game was too "esoteric" for the uninitiated. The same newspaper also praised the French full-back Puig-Aubert for his "high technical polish" and, indeed, the famous French captain was chaired from the pitch by jubilant team mates at the end.

The opening minutes of the game had hinted, however, at the predicted

English victory. Gordon Ratcliffe was put in the clear by Ernie Ashcroft and the Wigan winger scored in the corner. But the English were not to score another try and within a minute Robert Caillou, the French centre, had kicked ahead for Lespes to win the chase to the ball. Puig-Aubert failed with the conversion, but his drop-goal (in the days of the two-pointer) from 35 yards and a further penalty gave France a half-time lead which, with the possession and territory they had held, was well-deserved.

England played with more vigour in the second-half and an Ernest Ward penalty gave them hope at 7-5, but poor tackling allowed the French to keep to their expansive game. From a weak English drop-out the French kept the ball alive through Dejean whose pass to Calixte gave the French a match-winning try. Puig-Aubert's second drop-goal in the last minute secured a 12-5 success for the visitors.

The French were justifiably proud of their achievement for the English team contained 11 Great Britain test match players. Reports insisted that "there was no doubt about the superiority of the elusive and fleet-footed Frenchmen", the best of whom, forward Paul Bartoletti, won the Jean Galia Memorial Trophy for the man-of-the-match awarded by the press. The *Rugby League Review* still insisted that "this international match in London was the biggest flop of all post war sport", a harsh assessment indeed for a brave experiment, but one that deterred the English RFL more than it did the French. Indeed, it was a golden age for Rugby League in France which led to them being hosts to the first World Cup tournament in 1954. But, after the 1950s, French RL would never achieve the same heights again and its national team has, to date, never returned to play in London.

Because of the barrage of criticism, which included calls for the Challenge Cup Final to return north, the next true international match would not be staged in the capital until 1963 when Great Britain met Australia in that year's Ashes series. There were two other games, however, which carried an international element in the fifties and sixties, both involving New Zealand.

The first came on the back of the Kiwis' tour to Britain and France over the winter of 1951-2. The series with Great Britain had produced some close results but had ended in a 3-0 whitewash against the tourists. Crowds had been good, however, and the New Zealanders had agreed to play a promotional match against a British Empire XIII. Surprisingly, the match was scheduled after the French leg of the tour and on the day before the tourists were to sail for home, 23 January 1952. The New Zealanders therefore insisted that the match be played in London and used as a missionary exercise.

Both the RFL and the tourists had profited from the first part of the tour and were expecting to make a loss as Stamford Bridge prepared for its second taste of international Rugby League. The crowd of 6,800 looked a little lost inside Chelsea's famous stadium, but the match itself, despite being thrown together in some haste, remains memorable for its excellent standard of play and for one other thing: the ball.

Because the game was televised and kicked-off on a dull London afternoon, two other factors which mitigated against a large crowd, the ball was coloured white - the first time for a match not played under floodlights. Alfred Drewry wrote: "the real star of the Rugby League missionary match was the white ball... it was always so easy to follow." It was an auspicious beginning for something that is taken for granted today.

The French leg of the Kiwis' tour had proved to be a tough exercise and, with their thoughts on the return journey to New Zealand, the tourists proved to be no match for a powerful and skilful Empire XIII. Besides the ball, the other star of the afternoon was Huddersfield's Australian wingman Lionel Cooper who bagged three of the Empire's six tries. At half-time, with the score at 6-2 to the Empire, it looked as though openings would be few and far between but, when Cliff Johnson, the Kiwi prop went off injured with 25 minutes remaining, the Empire ran riot, notching a further 20 points to chalk up a 26-2 victory.

Drewry wrote: "If this exhibition had been given before a 30,000 crowd at Headingley, it would have been written down as a rattling good game, particularly in the second half when both sides showed brilliant ideas in attack."

The Empire's attack consisted of dazzling passing and movements covering the full width of the pitch, but the Kiwis were on their game too and the Empire defence had to be exemplary to stop the strong running and swift passing of Haig, Charlie McBride, Atkinson and Eastlake.

Cooper was the first player to register a try when he dived over in the corner and his second plus Desmond White's penalty (one of only six in the whole game) for the tourists gave the half- time scoreline. But it was only after Johnson's injury that the Empire team pushed home their superior skill. Cooper completed his hat-trick before any other player registered a try; his second score coming after he beat three men down the touchline, his third when he scooped up a dropped ball in his own half and ran 75 yards.

By now the tourists were spent and first Australian Brian Bevan and then his countryman Trevor Allan followed by Dave Valentine, the future British 1954 World Cup winning captain, took the Empire's try total to six, these last two tries well worked by the dominant Empire stand-off Broome. Ernest Ward's four goal tally gave the Empire the winning 26-2 scoreline.

Gerard Walter, writing in the *News Chronicle*, while positive about the standard of play was more critical about the decision to stage the match in London. "The poor attendance emphasises that there is very little interest in the 13-a-side game in the South," he wrote in a report headlined "Rugby League takes beating down south" that did little to popularise the game to new potential new supporters. Other writers had conflicting views and the *Rugby Leaguer*, keen to record how the game was taken by the national press, published a page of media reaction in its 2 February 1952 issue.

The *Sunday Graphic* wrote: "The biggest sports mystery of all time is why Rugby League football has not wiped the Rugby Union version off the map of Britain." It's a question still being asked today. The report went on to say that "fair-minded Union fans admit Rugby League provides a better spectacle... There is a good reason for it. League playing rules are deliberately framed to bring out the maximum in spectator appeal.

"Here then is a sport seeming to have everything for the masses: colour, spectacle, top-grade craft, thrills and an administration aiming all the time to please the public... Last weekend's Twickenham maul between England and Wales, in many respects the negation of all that is admirable in Rugby Union, drew 75,000 spectators, nearly all of whom behaved and sounded as if they were having the Rugby time of their lives. A few days later, the vast spaces of Stamford Bridge swallowed almost without noticing the mere 6,000 people who turned out to watch the cream of the Empire's Rugby League stars and the Kiwis gave an exposition of Rugby which made Twickenham stuff seem shoddy. There seems no explaining this indifference to Rugby League, especially in the south." The correspondent could have been writing these words 40 years later.

Peter Wilson also raised an argument often aired today by writing: "It is inevitable that the Southerner, accustomed to Rugby Union, should try to compare the two codes. But it is as impossible as trying to compare badminton with lawn tennis." However, he also went onto describe League as monotonous and added: "At the best, Rugby League can never be more than an honest utility model compared with the richer tapestry of the older game.

The Times correspondent praised Lionel Cooper, describing him as "a wing of the first magnitude" and also noted that League had gone a long way to reducing the endless kicking of the Union game. Unfortunately, Vivian Jenkins of the *News of the World* argued that League had gone too far in reducing the number of times the ball was kicked and it had "gone from one extreme to the other. Too much passing can become as much a bore as not enough of it." Pat Marshall of the *Daily Express* also felt cheated by not being able to enjoy Rugby Union's "thundering foot-rush." He too was unstinting in his praise of Cooper but also wrote that "Rugby Union really has nothing to fear from its professional cousin apart from the odd Union man changing codes for a tempting bundle of banknotes." Marshall missed the line-outs and the forward rush and abhorred the play-the-ball rule, three of the very things League had altered in order to attract more spectators.

But the most fascinating comments and, indeed, astounding when read today, were those from *The People*'s hockey correspondent, Maurice Smith, who, when asked how League could be made more popular, wrote: "It can't. Rugby League on this showing will never have wider box-office appeal than club hockey. An afternoon out for the enthusiast - that's all."

Opinions clearly differed on the entertainment value of Rugby League but, by the time the second quasi-international in London involving New Zealand was played on 18 August 1965, it was clear that attendances were of serious concern. The game was part of a festival of sport at Crystal Palace, that also included a Rugby League 7-a-side tournament.

The game was, once more, a promotional tool for RL in the capital, with the three tests between the touring Kiwis and Great Britain to be played later in the north. The tourists were to lose the series 2-0, with the final test at Wigan producing a 9-9 draw.

However, of far more concern than the New Zealanders lacklustre test performances was the fact that this last test at Central Park was played out in front of only 7,919 spectators. The 1960s had produced a huge decline in attendances at all sports events following the post-war boom and the finger was being pointed firmly at television. The first televised Rugby League match in the north of England was Great Britain versus New Zealand at Swinton in 1951, with the first televised Challenge Cup Final being the following year's Featherstone Rovers against Workington Town clash.

By the sixties, attendances were falling rapidly as - or so the argument ran - people stayed at home to watch sport rather than venture out. In 1965, the

51

BBC's Floodlit Trophy was introduced, to cash in on the TV boom and, while the competition provided much-needed revenue, new support was needed if League was to survive as a spectator sport.

It is also fair to say that unlimited tackles in Rugby League had, by the 1960s, produced an uninspired and dull game, with safety-first football becoming the norm. Innovations such as substitutions (introduced in 1964), and the limited-tackle rule (only four consecutive play-the-balls were allowed from 1966) attempted to spice up the game as the RFL looked to attract new areas of support.

This go-ahead attitude to reform saw the opening match of that 1965 Kiwi tour played at Crystal Palace as the RFL tried once again to show the sport to a wider audience. They had little luck for only 1,200 people turned up to see a Commonwealth XIII take on the tourists at what was to become one of the many homes of professional Rugby League in London in the 1980s and nineties. The Central Council for Physical Recreation would not have benefited much from the decision to offer them the match receipts. However, the fixture did bring Rugby League enthusiasts in London together, resulting in the relaunch of an amateur league in the south.

Those spectators who did turn out saw a game with an exciting conclusion for, although the New Zealanders won the match 15-7, they did not take the lead until 10 minutes from the final whistle, taking advantage of a tiring Commonwealth side who were one man down from shortly after the interval.

The New Zealanders' defence was tight throughout, but it was the Commonwealth who took the lead on the 25th minute when Huddersfield's Fijian forward John Ravitale took the ball after a superb break and pass by Fogerty. He knocked off two tackles in a 35-yard rush to the line. James missed the conversion, but his penalty goal in reply to a New Zealand try by Emery gave the Commonwealth a 5-3 half-time lead which was extended shortly afterwards when James landed a second penalty.

But the New Zealanders always looked to have the upper hand and when Dolton, the Wakefield prop, left the field with a chest injury their dominance grew, although it still took until the 70th minute before they were ahead. But they played a stunning last 10 to score two tries through wingman Reidy and loose-forward Mattson, with Jack Fagan landing three goals. Substitutes were, at that time, only permitted before the interval and the Commonwealth were unable to replace Dolton, leading to their sluggish second-half performance, but the Kiwis were worthy of their victory without being spectacular. Alfred Drewry wrote that the Kiwi management's claim that "they will turn out to be a much better team [than their 1961 predecessors] remains to be seen." His doubts, borne out by a defeat in the forthcoming test series, were well founded.

This match was not, however, the only Rugby League representative international to be played in the capital in the 1960s. Only two years earlier in 1963, the two biggest names in international Rugby League had clashed at Wembley Stadium in only the second Ashes encounter to be played in the capital, and the first since that superb inaugural Lions versus Kangaroos match at Park Royal in 1908.

Great Britain had won the Ashes in Australia the previous year and were favourites to hold them at home. The Australians were keen to play in London and the British administration obliged, intent on a new propaganda campaign for the south.

With typical bad luck, the day of the match turned out to be dreadful and only 14,000 turned out on a cold and wet Wednesday evening in October to see the first test of the series. Bill Fallowfield, the secretary of the RFL, recalled that: "We had the Duke of Edinburgh there and it was all set to be a successful do; possibly setting a pattern for subsequent tours. But it did nothing but pour with rain." Fallowfield was not to know it but, by the 1990s, the first test of the Ashes series would find a home at Wembley.

To rub salt into the RFL's wound, Britain were outplayed under the Wembley floodlights (the first time lights were used for a Rugby League test) and Australia rattled up a 28-2 victory in search of their first Ashes win on British soil since 1911. It was a target they were to achieve when they won the second test at Swinton 50-12, before a bad-tempered match at Headingley saw Britain avoid a whitewash.

The British had to play a man short from early in the first half when Dave Bolton's shoulder was injured in a tackle and Alec Murphy at scrum-half played nearly the whole match with a broken nose, but the Australians were the better side, exploiting all of the home team's mistakes. At the time of Bolton's departure the scores were level at 2-2 with Neil Fox and Graeme Langlands having traded penalties, but the Lions were not to score again as the Australian forwards began to exert control.

The home team held out until the 34th minute when the Kangaroos' full-back Ken Thornett took a fine pass from Barry Muir to stride over.

Langlands missed the conversion but then scored a fine try in the corner from a British mistake and landed the kick himself to give the tourists a half-time lead of 10-2.

Britain raised their game after the break but, when Australia added to their lead in the 50th minute after Johnny Raper and Thornett fashioned a superb converted try for Reg Gasnier, there was no looking back. Gasnier completed a memorable hat-trick - the first man to score two in Anglo-Australian tests, and Ken Irvine notched a try after another British mistake to leave the final score at 28-2, Langlands kicking five goals in all to give him a 13-point tally.

The RFL, and indeed the supporters and media, once again looked on the Wembley test as a failed venture, but Eddie Waring wrote: "Some called it a flop. I didn't, at least not from an experimental viewpoint, though from a playing point of view it probably was. Torrential rain affected the gate, a poor British team was selected and the Australians ran away with victory."

The RFL were brave not to be deterred by the crowd figure and the critical reaction, especially in light of the embarrassing 1,200 who turned up at Crystal Palace in 1965 for the Commonwealth match, and returned to the capital with the Ashes series in 1967. Another evening match, this time on a Friday in November and this time at the now demolished White City Stadium in West London, saw Australia attempting to level the series after a first test loss at Headingley.

The British were trying to reclaim the Ashes but suffered a bizarre pre-match blow. Bill Burgess the Barrow winger failed a fitness test on a leg injury on the morning of the match which meant his place fell to Jordan, the travelling reserve from Featherstone. With mounting panic, the British management realised they couldn't locate him and sent out an emergency call to Bill Francis of Wigan who travelled 200 miles on the afternoon of the game to take the left-wing place.

Both his and the RFL's endeavours were rewarded with a crowd approaching 20,000 and a winning Australian display which suggested that they could wrest the Ashes back in the decider at Swinton the following month, an achievement which they duly completed 11-3.

Prime Minister Harold Wilson, who for so long represented Huyton, a constituency with an infamous Rugby League connection, met the teams before the game. Journalist Peter Marson wrote that Wilson's roots lay "deep in the heart of the country in which the Northern code first struggled for recognition." Unfortunately his presence was not to inspire Britain that evening.

Australia trailed at White City until 17 minutes from the end but, according to journalist Alfred Drewry, "they always looked the faster and more polished side." The tourists were without both Reg Gasnier and Johnny Raper, both injured in the Headingley test, but showed no lack of form as a result. Indeed, Raper's replacement Ron Coote, played a key role in the Kangaroos' victory, performing a number of try-saving tackles and running with pace. Along with Graeme Langlands the Australian kicking centre, these two players made the Australian attack a cutting and penetrative one, ably led by third choice captain Peter Gallagher of the Brisbane Brothers.

The Great Britain half-backs Tommy Bishop and Roger Millward were the pick of the home side but too often they found themselves on the back foot as Australia piled home their attack. It took superb last-ditch tackling by Arthur Keegan, the Lions' full-back, to keep the half-time score level at 2-2, after a Langlands penalty and a Bishop drop-goal.

Against the run of play it was Great Britain who reopened the scoring after 12 minutes of the second half. Bishop played the ball himself and dived on it in the in-goal area before the Australian defence could react. With Neil Fox converting, Britain led 7-2, a lead that Langlands alone eradicated. His penalty goal in the 66th minute cut the lead to three and then, from Tony Branson's pass, he cut inside the British defence to score by the posts. The scores were level but, amazingly, Langlands missed the simple conversion.

When Fox goaled for Britain, it looked as though Langlands's mistake might prove costly, but it was Britain who were to falter at the end. With 10 minutes remaining, Bill Holliday returned a towering kick from Australian full-back Les Johns. However, on his 25-yard line he sent out a weak pass to Ian Brooke. The ball was greasy for rain had started to fall and, hitting him on the shoulder, the pass squirmed away. The St George wing, Johnny King, pounced on the ball and dived over. Langlands's conversion was matched by another Fox penalty to leave Australia 3 points ahead. But any doubt was removed when, despite British protests that the ball was not grounded, Coote crashed over. "Never was a player more fittingly rewarded," wrote Drewry. Langlands's conversion gave Australia a 17-11 victory.

Journalist Harold Mather was surprised by Britain's poor showing: "They had their moments... but by and large they were well beaten," he wrote. Peter Marson wrote how the crowd, despite not being natives to the game, backed Britain to the hilt, Bishop's drop-goal being greeted by a roar which "rose up out of the arena as a single spontaneous shout." And Bob Pemberton of the *Daily Telegraph* described the game as "a splendid open match... and the 20,000 crowd were wildly enthusiastic as move after move kept the result in doubt until Australia settled matters three minutes from the end."

The RFL, despite Britain losing both game and series, should have been pleased with the media and public reaction to the White City game, but they left a gap of six years before returning to play a test in the capital. It was far too long and any chance the 1967 game offered to push home the message that League was a game for London was lost. It would take until 1990, and the series of regular games that took place from then before crowds and a suspicious media began to accept international League as a regular item on the London sporting agenda.

Even the match that took place in 1973 at Wembley was at the insistence of the Australian tour management who, convinced that the many antipodeans resident in the capital would turn up in numbers, forced the RFL into a late change of heart after Central Park had originally been the scheduled venue. Live television and a lack of pre-match publicity provided Rugby League with one of its most embarrassing off-field afternoons as a mere 9,874 rattled around the vast terraces of Wembley Stadium to witness a British victory in the first test.

The low crowd may have also been influenced by a poor World Cup in 1970 which was hosted by Britain. Poor crowds had watched mediocre matches, including a bad-tempered final which saw the Kangaroos beat Britain 12-7. Britain regained the World Cup in 1972 in Lyon, with Clive Sullivan scoring a memorable touchline try, but Rugby League in this country was, by the early seventies, at possibly its lowest ebb. David Oxley had yet to arrive as secretary of the RFL and crowds and entertainment value were dwindling.

On-field, however, that particular Wembley afternoon couldn't have been more exciting. The British had, against all the odds, taken the Ashes in Australia in 1970, losing only one match, the first test in Brisbane, in the whole of their tour of Australia and New Zealand. To date, it is the last Ashes series they were to win. But Britain came into that first 1973 test determined to hang onto their tag as Ashes holders and world champions.

Six tackles had now replaced the four, substitutes were allowed at any time, the drop-goal was only worth one point and the timekeepers had taken the place of the referee's watch. The game was attempting to update and, if the on-field performance that day was anything to go by, it had improved dramatically. Robert Gate, writing in *The Struggle For The Ashes* described it as "a magnificent contest worthy of its grandiose setting."

The Lions took the lead in only the fourth minute and never surrendered it despite a determined fightback midway through the second-half from Australia. Great Britain were on the offensive from the first minute when captain Clive Sullivan's pass to Charlton went to ground, after the full-back seemed certain to score but, shortly afterwards, Phil Lowe was put through a gap by Castleford's Brian Lockwood to give the British a 3-point lead. A Graeme Langlands penalty for Australia and a Steve Nash drop-goal for Britain gave a half-time score of 4-2 to the home side.

The second half was far more open and Britain stormed into an apparently unassailable lead through two quick and well-worked tries. Ray Batten forged a clever opening for Colin Clarke before Brian Lockwood (fouled by Tom Raudonikis in the process of scoring) found his way to the line, courtesy of fine play by George Nicholls and David Topliss. Both were converted by Terry Clawson.

But Australia were not finished. In the 56th minute Ray Branighan scored in the corner after Artie Beetson, playing a powerful and inspirational game at prop, held off the English defence. Langlands was successful with the difficult kick and also four minutes later when Bobby Fulton, the Australian stand-off later to taste defeat at Wembley as an Ashes coach, took a kick that should rightly have been British three-quarter Syd Hynes's, and dived over. Australia were back in the game at 14-12.

Fortunately for Britain their nerve held and Clawson's 65th minute penalty, following further indiscretion by Raudonikis, gave the home side a 4-point breathing space. The result remained in doubt, however, until the 72nd minute when Lowe's strong running brought his second try, duly converted by Clawson. The goalkicking Oldham prop had a barnstorming game for Britain and it had been his power, combined with that of Lowe, that had finally worn down Australia's resistance, with David Topliss at stand-off being the architect who fashioned the openings. It was a shame that fewer than 10,000 people were there to witness it. Worse was to follow for the British as Australia took the remaining two tests to claim the Ashes.

Eddie Waring described the crowd as "meagre" and "virtually lost in the Empire Stadium vastness, while Keith Macklin in *The Story of Rugby League* described the Australians' insistence that the antipodean population of

London would fill Wembley as a plan that "misfired."

The criticism wasn't lost on the RFL. Their experiment had been a failure and Rugby League looked less likely than ever to win a truly national audience. Save for an under-24 international match at Craven Cottage in 1980, played on the back of the interest generated by the arrival of Fulham RLFC, which saw a New Zealand team featuring the likes of Dane O'Hara, Gary Kemble, Fred Ah Kuoi, Howie Tamati and Graeme West defeat Britain, international Rugby League was lost to Londoners. It was to take 17 years of confidence building from the Wembley 1973 match before they felt ready, once again, to bring international Rugby League to the capital. In 1990 things were to be markedly different.

4   The first Wembley Cup Final

It was the Super League controversy of its day. Until the arrival of Rupert Murdoch's News Corporation onto the Rugby League stage in 1995, the decision to take the Challenge Cup Final to London in 1929 was the most momentous and far-reaching the Rugby Football League (RFL) had ever taken. And then, as now, the move was made amid acrimony, recrimination and opposition.

The critics were legion, many predicting catastrophic failure. Hindsight has proved those who made the decision to be visionaries, the Challenge Cup Final at Wembley - at least until the arrival of the Super League - now has a major place in the British sporting calendar and is played before capacity crowds and millions on television. But, back in 1929, success was not guaranteed and the decision to move the final from its home in the north was one taken with some trepidation. It remains to be seen what riches the Super League has in store, but the men who ensured that the Challenge Cup Final had a permanent home at Wembley can rest assured that their bold step was one of the most significant the sport has ever made.

Throughout the twenties the Challenge Cup Final was proving to be a major attraction. The north of England did not possess a stadium capable of coping with the huge crowds that the event was generating. The finals of 1927 and 1928 at Central Park, Wigan had both exceeded 33,000, and the 42,000 who turned up at Rochdale in 1924 to see Wigan beat Oldham had proved very difficult for the police to handle. Clearly, the authorities needed an alternative venue.

The new 100,000 capacity Empire Stadium at Wembley had staged football's FA Cup Final for the first time in 1923, but when this prestigious venue, which would allow Rugby League's showpiece to reach a much wider audience, was mooted as a possible home for League's big final, it was received with much scepticism. There had been calls for some time for the match to be taken to the capital, but these had always been defeated by the pro-north supporters in the Rugby Football League. Fortunately, for those with a progressive attitude, the stadium problem forced their hand. The Challenge Cup Final had simply outgrown any northern venue. Bradford Northern's huge ground at Odsal, which would house Rugby League's record crowd for the 1954 Cup Final replay, had not yet been built.

The chairman of the League's Welsh Commission, John Leake, raised the proposal at the League's annual conference in Llandudno in 1928. Welshman Leake, one of 13 delegates to back the vote which won a slender majority of three, had a number of venues in mind and officials were dispatched to London. Their brief was to find a site that would make the final a major annual event which would encourage as many people as possible to see the sport. They also had to bear in mind the RFL's requirement that their choice should "make it easy in a financial sense and convenient from a travelling point of view to get there."

Wembley was only one of two prospective choices. Ironically, considering its future role in professional Rugby League, Crystal Palace was the other. White City, home of the 1908 Olympic Games, was considered to possess inferior facilities. The Rugby League Council adopted the proposal to take the match to London in Leeds on 3 October 1928 although the venue was not finalised until League secretary John Wilson visited Wembley and Crystal Palace in November.

His first choice was Crystal Palace, but the stadium owners had harsh terms in mind. They wanted one third of all gate money, including all cash taken at the turnstiles before noon on matchday. Wilson reckoned that northern supporters would be arriving in the capital on the morning of the game and would travel straight to Crystal Palace, arriving well before midday - the deal would see the RFL make a loss. Fortunately, both for Wilson and the future of the sport, Sir Arthur Elvin, the proprietor of Wembley Stadium, saw the potential that League had. He struck a deal, offering use of his stadium for only 7.5 per cent of the gate.

The deal was met with dismay in some quarters. Rugby League belonged to the north claimed many. Why should its biggest match be played in London? The RFL was swayed but stuck to its guns and opted, bravely, for Wembley. Turnstile entry was set at 2 shillings (10p) with the most expensive tickets at 10/6 (52p). And applications were received from not only Lancashire, Yorkshire, Cumberland and the capital, but from the Midlands, the South-west and from Wales. The RFL, in a move years ahead of its day, had carried out an extensive advertising campaign and it was proving to be a success.

The match itself did not prove to be as exciting as the occasion deserved. Dewsbury had a team based on local players with only Welshman

The London Transport poster advertising the Final
(Courtesy London Transport Museum)

On Wigan's line: Wilf Hodder, Jim Sullivan, Jack Woolmore, J.Rudd, Roy Kinnear,
C.Smith, "Plonk" Rhodes, Tom Bailey   (Courtesy Les Hoole)

Jack Davies at full-back not hailing from Yorkshire. They had surprised the sport by defeating Warrington and Castleford to reach the final. They were to meet hot favourites Wigan, with their team of former Rugby Union stars and internationals and, as ever, the Riversiders were in no mood for a surprise.

It has been alleged that Dewsbury were told to play expansive rugby to impress the southern crowd, a game that was alien to their usual defensive, stifling style and one that gave them no chance of overcoming Wigan's attacking strength. What is certain is that, in an unprecedented move, League chairman Mr Kennedy visited the dressing rooms before the kick-off to tell the teams to behave in a sportsmanlike fashion as the game was on show before the nation. The *Dewsbury Reporter* commented that "in other circumstances such an appeal would have been regarded as official interference, but on Saturday the general desire was that the code's first Wembley venture should create a favourable impression. One is able to add that the appeal did not fall on deaf ears."

Although Dewsbury went into the match with many believing they could tackle Wigan out of the cup, an apparent fear of showing the game in a poor light meant they did not play to their strengths, and it was Wigan's Syd Abram, the only Englishman to score that afternoon, who took the distinction of scoring the first try at Wembley after a 40-yard dash to the line. This, added to Jim Sullivan's earlier penalty and a drop-goal from Dewsbury's Davies, gave Wigan a 5-2 interval lead. In the second half the Lancashire team took complete command. Lou Brown, the New Zealand international winger, scored Wigan's second while Roy Kinnear scored the Sullivan-converted match-winner 10 minutes from time. Kinnear was a former Scottish Rugby Union centre who later died playing Union in an RAF match, and was the father of Roy, the TV comedian. His contribution to the match was outstanding and brought praise from all sections of the media.

Captain Sullivan received the Challenge Cup from Lord Daresbury and, after the match, chairman Kennedy was moved to say: "The council has been satisfied with the experiment which will almost certainly be repeated." This was not a surprise. The crowd of 41,500 was just 331 short of the 1924 final record but receipts of £5,614 4s 6d bettered the highest takings by £2,000. Rugby League was not going to look back.

However, in 1929 the game was still a novelty outside the counties of its birth and was viewed with detached interest by the national media. The capital too, as a venue for a major Rugby League match, was an enigma to many northern supporters and it is fascinating to see just how the sport, the final and the interaction of northerners and Londoners was perceived by the newspapers of the day.

The *Dewsbury Reporter* certainly went to town, devoting many column inches to previews, reports and reactions and superbly capturing the essence of a twenties small town's slice of fame.

In the days leading up to the match the paper reported that "the journey to London will be begun next morning [Friday] - the team, officials and others leave Dewsbury LNER Station at 10.14 and King's Cross will be reached at 1.35 pm. The party will proceed to Wembley immediately on arrival at the Metropolis and a photograph of the team to represent Dewsbury will be taken. The party will later proceed to the Grand Central Hotel, the headquarters for the weekend, and in the evening a visit will be paid to the Lyceum theatre."

The itinerary for matchday was just as busy with a visit to the Cenotaph (it was only a decade since the end of the First World War and many families were still deeply affected by the aftermath) followed by a trip around the House of Commons, and lunch at the hotel, all prior to the game, before the team headed to Windsor on the Sunday.

Of the opposition the newspaper added: "the Wigan players will leave Wigan next Friday afternoon, arriving in London about 9 o'clock. They will make the First Avenue Hotel their headquarters. The Rugby League headquarters... will be the Hotel Metropole, and the Yorkshire officials will leave for London next Friday mid-day. Despite the poor state of trade at Wigan, eight special trains, together with numerous motor-coaches, will leave the Lancashire town for the final, and it is estimated that Wigan's share of the crowd will be approximately 4,000. Dewsbury's representation will probably exceed 1,000."

The teams' approach to the big day also differed: "While Dewsbury players are to undergo strict training for the cup final, the Wigan players are to content themselves with country walks and games of golf."

The reporter was at pains to point out that supporters could travel on the day: "Owing to the publicity given to the fact that only ticket-holders can be admitted to Wembley on the occasion of the FA Cup final today, there appears to be a general misapprehension that the same conditions will apply in the case of the Rugby League final. The Wembley Stadium authorities make it clear that this is not so." Of course, this is not the case today as the following

63

comment also illustrates: "Congestion... is unknown at Wembley."

And, as the big day approached, the newspaper became packed with anecdotes to fuel readers' desire to know everything that surrounded such a major occasion. "The Rev F. H. Chambers has been definitely selected by the BBC, after a trial, to broadcast a running commentary of the final. He will thus have the distinction of being the first minister to broadcast a Rugby football match," the *Reporter* announced. It went on to tell us that "Mr Bob Robinson of Bradford, who will referee the final, states that he has had the same watch and whistle for the whole of his refereeing career, which must extend over 25 years. The pea is a wooden one, and it has never been changed."

There was also the story of H. H. Townend, a Wigan miner, who called in at the *Reporter* office in the week before the final to "explain that he was on his way to Wembley. He was wearing... one of Jim Sullivan's jerseys, and he had in front of him a card on which was printed the words 'Rugby Cup Final. Wigan v. Dewsbury. I am walking from Wigan to Wembley.' The gentleman was hoping to take a break in Peterborough..."

Readers were even told that Mr Herman Day of the USA, formerly of Warwick Road, Batley, and a Batley supporter had written to say that "he hopes that when the result is received in New York, Dewsbury's name will be first." There were very few in either Dewsbury or Wigan who were unaware of the approaching final. Indeed, many of them were intending to be there.

The newspaper's journalist pseudonymed "Old Hand" followed the supporters to London, no doubt taking advantage of the LMS day return train fare of 15s 6d (78p). The train departed Dewsbury at 1.25 am on Saturday morning, took five hours and returned from St Pancras at 1.10 am the following day.

This meant that Old Hand was in the capital by early morning to witness the tumultuous activity. "Both before and after the match, the scenes beggared description," he wrote. Another of the newspaper's writers followed supporters throughout the morning of the match, writing: "From the very earliest hours of Saturday morning it was quite apparent that there was something in London which was attracting crowds of northerners. Special trains began to arrive from midnight onwards, and from that time parties could be seen travelling around the Metropolis, sporting favours of the two teams and speaking in dialects that were quite strange to many of the Cockneys.

"The cheery badinage of the visitors was generally countered by an equally witty remark from the Londoner, and there were many humorous incidents. Parties from the North, and many from the South of England, too, who had been attracted by the novelty of the event, travelled around the Metropolis, visiting the various places of interest, and greeting each other with some friendly word or humorous chaff." Very little, save for the dated tones of the journalist, has changed in 65 years.

Old Hand was in Whitehall in the early morning and was amazed at the number of northern supporters at the Cenotaph. The locals were also surprised: "This was a new and lively experience for them", he wrote. "Boat race crowds and Association crowds they know, but a North of England Rugby crowd are different. Hundreds and hundreds of folk from the Heavy Woollen District made a special point of being in Whitehall by 9.45 am to watch the laying of wreaths on the Cenotaph. It was at this period of the day that the fun and shouts of the partisans subsided... except for the noise of passing traffic there were periods of impressive silence."

Dewsbury laid a commemorative wreath first and the players were surrounded by well-wishers as they made their way to the memorial. The Wigan team arrived shortly afterwards and Jim Sullivan laid flowers in the club's colours, followed by supporters of many different teams. Supporters today might find it difficult to understand that, after the match itself, the Cenotaph was the most important stop on a visit to London, but to those coming to the capital for that first final it was a must.

Of the event itself, the reporter wrote: "Buses, char-a-bancs and trains brought the crowds", and "so far as the visitors to the final were concerned, it was plain to be seen that many Northerners had never seen the stadium before, and amazement at the colossal size of this great temple of sport could be gauged by the many comments that could be heard in Northern tongues." "A never-to-be- forgotten sight," added Old Hand.

And the southern editions of the national newspapers were there in force too, to witness the arrival of an alien sport in their territory. The *Daily News and Westminster Gazette* wrote: "There is always something appealing to the sporting enthusiast about a Cup Final, no matter under whatever code it may be played. The Rugby League Cup Final... is the first of its kind ever to be staged in London, and as one who intends to be present, I expect it to prove a thrilling sequel to the big game of the dribbling persuasion which drew nearly a hundred thousand spectators to Wembley a week ago.

"Some Rugby Union conservatives profess to regard the Rugby League game as neither fish, fowl nor good red herring, but that is mere

65

unthinking prejudice. For my part I shall go to Wembley with an open mind, remembering that the late A. O. Jones, who knew both games well, once told me that the Northern Union experts could give a Rugby Union international team 20 points and a beating!"

What a shame that such comments are still few and far between in the national papers today. Still, the writer felt fit to reassure Union supporters that the match "does not indicate the cloven hoof of propaganda, but the urgent necessity for playing the Final at a venue which can accommodate all who wish to see it." He was also aware that while Wigan were regarded as favourites "the White Rose brigade will, no doubt, proclaim its sympathy with the usual confidence characteristic of the county."

The *Daily Herald* also previewed the game telling readers that "there will be another invasion of London by Northern football enthusiasts today, when the Rugby League Cup final is to be played at the Wembley Stadium. The competing teams are Dewsbury and Wigan, and they are expected to provide the fastest game of Rugby ever seen in the South." The writer anticipated that many Union supporters would attend the match as there were no Union matches in the south that weekend.

The newspaper also took time to describe some of the different rules of League one of which was that "after an unconverted try or a touch-down the ball is dropped out at the 25 line."

Even the *Daily Telegraph* in its inimitable style was present, commenting "this match, which is the greatest annual sporting event in the North, has been brought to Wembley this year to find adequate accommodation for the increasing crowds which flock to see it in the home of thirteen-a-side Rugger." Keen, as always, on the social side of events the *Telegraph* told readers that the cup would be presented by Lord Daresbury who with "the High Commissioner for Australia, where thirteen-a-side Rugby is very popular, will watch the match from the Royal box."

Of course, the Dewsbury supporters were to be disappointed at the outcome. The *Dewsbury Reporter* told us that "in the morning, Dewsbury partisans would not hear of defeat at the Stadium and in the evening, though watching the Wigan supporters wave miniature cups high in the air when strolling through Leicester Square, Piccadilly, or other famous parts of the city, they were a most lively lot. Few discarded their colours, and often one could hear the observation, 'It's nobbut t'League o' Nations that bet us'. This was a pointed reference to the fact that the members of the victorious side had been drawn from various parts of the world." The same comments are still being made decades later.

Wigan were indeed a fine team, representing the best that the sport had to offer but Dewsbury were accused of not playing to their strengths which led to a one-sided final. However the local newspaper defended its team saying "some of the Southern writers severely criticised Dewsbury's play, and while it is not possible to speak of it in laudatory terms, there were features which the regular follower of the game could not but admire."

Indeed, the southern-based nationals were very critical, the *Daily Telegraph's* special correspondent writing: "In the crowd of 41,500 which witnessed Wigan beat Dewsbury for the Rugby League Cup at Wembley Stadium on Saturday by 13 points to 2 were a great many followers of the amateur Rugby code, who had been attracted to this match between professionals out of curiosity to see how the game compared with the one which is more familiar to Southern crowds.

"They must have been disappointed in the game as a spectacle... there was far too much aimless kicking; the handling of the ball, except in a few instances, was crude, clumsy and obvious, and very rarely was a movement carried through with finish and artistry." It was stinging criticism but, of the match, probably a fair assessment.

Another writer added: "It was Rugger with the fun missing", while others said: "This was Rugby Union football with the soft pedal and with the hazards of a manly game eliminated" and "The play-the-ball rule will not make converts in the South or in the West. The men who play, especially if they be local products like the Dewsbury team, are sound stuff, and I wish we could draw on them, especially when a pack is being drawn up to represent England."

Perhaps typically, the *Telegraph* sought out a former Rugby Union star for praise: "The outstanding player, however, not only among the three-quarters but among the two teams, was Kinnear, the former Scottish Rugby Union international." There is no doubt that Roy Kinnear had a fine match but Rugby League supporters know only too well the praise heaped upon former union stars at the expense of homegrown League talent. The practice obviously has a long history.

Still, there can be no escaping the fact that the match was no classic. The *Daily News* wrote: "There were many Rugby Union enthusiasts present in the crowd of 41,500... I doubt whether they went away converts. The Rugby Union man, who is admittedly a very conservative person and very much opposed to change as a rule, missed a lot in this League game." The football supporter too left feeling unfulfilled: " 'Quite a good game, but I didn't understand it', said a professed Soccer fan at Wembley."

However, the writer, Astral, went on to say that: "I enjoyed the match immensely. Its speed and sustained animation and variety of movement are undeniable. Some of the passing is very clever, and I fancy that it is supported more intensively than in the older game. The tackling, too, is very good.

As a game it has many bright features... and I will readily admit there are fewer dull patches than in our Rugger. Yet - and I hate to think it may be mere prejudice that influences the view - I prefer the older stuff. In the desire to make the League play faster and more spectacular, something seems to have been taken out of the game, something more full blooded and satisfying, although I would not for a moment suggest that the League game is in the least bit emasculated. It is not. It is vigorous and strenuous enough to suit the most exacting."

Astral went on to praise the play-the-ball, suggesting that it led to far less scrummaging and a general tidying up of the game. He also commented on the sportsmanship of the players. The *Daily Herald* too took time to point out the better aspects of the game, its writer qualifying the stilted play by saying: "To Londoners who rarely have an opportunity of judging the merits of the Rugby League code, the game might have been a disappointment inasmuch as the players generally concentrated upon 'stopping' so that there was nothing like the amount of open play which is a feature of ordinary Rugby League games."

As The *Daily News* writer had noted, the match was a clean game and the *Dewsbury Reporter* journalist at the game spotted that "Lyman had a few words to say to his men about the necessity for a strict observance of the rules, a warning that appeared necessary in view of Sullivan's prowess as a goal-kicker." The same writer, once inside the stadium, commented that "at first glance the attendance seemed poor, but when a little calculation was made it could be seen that the crowd fell little short of 50,000." It is a problem that perennially plagues an unfilled Wembley. Even at 75 per cent capacity today the stadium still has 20,000 empty seats which, to the uninitiated, can make it look only half full.

The order of events, too, was somewhat different from the norms established today. The players entered side-by-side and walked to the Royal Box to have their photographs taken but there were no further formalities until after the match, when once again the teams were photographed before the national anthem was played - a strange way in which to counter the post-match euphoria. Jim Sullivan, after being chaired from the field carrying a huge good luck horseshoe, collected the cup from Lord Daresbury.

Both Sullivan and Lyman came out of the match with enhanced reputations despite the latter having a quiet game. The *Dewsbury Reporter* wrote that "One of the big surprises was the subjection of Lyman. He was occasionally in the limelight, but at no time was he able to control his side's play as in previous cup-ties. It was not a good match for Dewsbury's captain... it would have been a crowning triumph if Lyman had been able to add the Rugby League cup medal to his two Yorkshire cup medals. He was one of the most disappointed men at the failure to lift the cup, but in his great disappointment he did not forget the honour that was due to the victors. Many Londoners commended the excellent grace with which the defeat was accepted, and Lyman was hailed as a prince among sportsmen for the alacrity with which he congratulated Sullivan."

Immediately after the game Lyman had sought out the opposition captain to shake his hand.

The cup winning Wigan Team. (Courtesy *The Rugby Leaguer*)

The same writer commenting on the disappointment in the Dewsbury camp wondered whether "Dewsbury could have used the wind to better advantage" and "whether they were obliging the Rugby League authorities by playing, or attempting to play pretty football. Perhaps if Dewsbury had played at Headingley they would have been seen in a more assertive mood. One wondered if the players were too far away from the crowd." It was, of course, all supposition and, for whatever reasons, Sullivan and Wigan were worthy winners of the first Wembley final.

The authorities were aware that there would be many people unable to attend the final and arranged coverage of the match by BBC radio. The *Dewsbury Reporter* even covered in detail the nature of the Reverend Chambers's commentary. "It was a wise choice to select such an authority on the game", the paper wrote. "Mr Chambers commenced with a very illuminating and instructive address on the difference between the Rugby League game and the Rugby Union game for the especial benefit of the Southerners."

The nature of radio listening has obviously altered over the years and the medium was a far cry from today's sports broadcasts on national Radio 5. Apparently, as the game proceeded, "by means of the familiar voice over the wireless, listeners, with the aid of marked charts were able to follow the position of the game." Whether the charts were a success is not recorded, but one would not expect a radio company to distribute similar props today.

The *Reporter* writer was also impressed by the commentary following the game as it progressed rather than waiting for movements to be completed and then describing them retrospectively. Whether this was a new style is not clear but it obviously set a precedent for it would be a strange commentary today that did not keep the listener fully informed as play continued. Chambers had a few problems with player identification but considering no other means other than observation from the stands was available to him his mistakes were kept to a minimum.

Chambers's radio position was obviously in the open, among the crowd, as listeners could clearly hear a Dewsbury supporter in the background shouting: " 'Now Dews!' 'Come on Dews' but this 'clarion call' at first a very enthusiastic cry, gradually dwindled until it became almost a wail." The reporter told us that "with Wigan's third try, the cry seemed to disappear, as if the gentleman, who seemed to be broadcasting almost as much as Mr Chambers, had lost heart. Mr Chambers and the Dewsbury supporter, whoever he might be, are to be thanked for providing a very entertaining, exciting, and interesting afternoon."

The BBC's broadcast was provided at a number of locations back in the north for the benefit of supporters without wireless although the excitement of children at the Majestic Cinema in Dewsbury apparently made following the game difficult. Nonetheless, colour sellers around Dewsbury Town Hall did a roaring trade until news of their team's imminent defeat came through.

But nobody in Dewsbury or Wigan that afternoon and, of course, none of those who made the trip to see the game live, would deny that the Challenge Cup Final had been a huge success. It had been a popular event before but it had now become a special occasion, a game played at the finest stadium in the country. Any opposition, in the face of such overwhelming evidence, found it difficult to raise support and, even in its leanest years, the Rugby League Cup Final retained its place as a major event on the national sporting calendar. Had it remained in the north, it might have taken the sport many more years to come to the attention of the mass of the nation. Those who chose its destiny in the late 1920s made a decision which ensured that, at least once a year, Rugby League had the sporting stage to itself.

DEWSBURY V WIGAN, 4 May 1929, Wembley

Dewsbury 2   **Wigan 13**

Dewsbury: J. Davies, H. Coates, H. Hirst, C. Smith, T. Bailey,
J. W. Woolmore, J. Rudd, P. Brown, W. Rhodes,
J. A. Hobson, H. Bland, J. Malkin, J. Lyman (capt).

Wigan: J. Sullivan (capt), J. Ring, T. Parker, R. M. Kinnear,
L. Brown, S. Abram, A. Binks, W. Hodder,
J. Bennett, T. Beetham, F. Stephens, J. Sherrington,
L. Mason.

Dewsbury: Drop goal: Davies

Wigan: Tries: Kinnear, Brown, Abram, Goals: Sullivan 2

Half time: 2-5

Referee: R. Robinson (Bradford)

Attendance: 41,500

Part 2: The first try

London Highfield 1933-1934

Acton & Willesden 1935-1936

Streatham & Mitcham 1935-1937

Interlude 1937 to 1979

By Dave Farrar and Peter Lush

5   London Highfield 1933-4

The creation of London Highfield in 1933 has many parallels with the setting up of the Fulham club nearly 50 years later. The short-lived Rugby League boom of the 1930s was launched on the back of the rapid expansion of greyhound racing, and was seen as a way of maximising the use of the greyhound stadiums. So as Fulham RLFC were to cohabit with Fulham Football Club, so the thirties clubs lived -and died- on the back of the dogs.

Modern greyhound racing had started at Belle Vue in Manchester in 1926. During the late 1920s, nineteen new tracks were established in Britain, including six in London. Unlike football and cricket, the greyhound promoters were there primarily to make money, and, as Ernie Clay of Fulham was to realise later, the owners aimed to maximise the use of their stadiums. Sports promoter and journalist Tom Stenner, writing about the pioneers of greyhound racing, described Brigadier-General A. C. Critchley, the creator of the London Highfield Rugby League Club, as deserving "full marks for enterprise".

This was the age of the sports entrepreneur. With no competition from television, huge crowds by today's standards could be attracted to events. Rugby League was an attraction for both Brigadier-General Critchley, and later Sydney Parkes, because entry could be obtained to the top competition immediately, unlike football, and there were no other Rugby League clubs in London. While some money could have been earned hiring out the stadiums to Rugby Union clubs; club Rugby Union in London has never had large crowds, and little profit could have been made.

Sports such as ice hockey, and the new motorcycle sport of speedway, as well as greyhound racing, were growing quickly. For example, Chelsea FC's Stamford Bridge ground staged both greyhound racing and speedway in the 1930s and, at Wembley, Sir Arthur Elvin promoted both these sports using the stadium, and ice hockey in the Wembley Pool.

The possibility of Rugby League being one of the different sports to be played in the greyhound stadiums was bolstered with the arrival in London of the Challenge Cup Final. The first, in 1929, between Wigan and Dewsbury, was played at Wembley where it remains to this day, and it proved an important catalyst for the foundation of a Rugby League club in the capital.

For what was seen as a new club, London Highfield inherited a long pedigree by taking over Wigan Highfield, the Lancashire town's less successful professional side. Highfield had been a leading junior side in the last century and had turned professional in 1922. Their ground at Pemberton in Wigan, was used for the new London club's reserve games. Highfield was purchased lock, stock and players.

Unfortunately, Highfield's London sojourn did not last beyond a season, and since then Highfield have had many metamorphoses, including Liverpool Stanley, Liverpool City, Huyton, Runcorn Highfield, and finally today's long suffering Highfield, now based in Prescot. At the time of the move to London, it is believed that their finances were so precarious that they may not have survived anyway. Mr Green, the Club Chairman, was reported as saying: "he could not see the club carrying on... A few people had been carrying the club on their shoulders, and money was owing to tradesmen."

The new owner, Brigadier-General A. C. Critchley CMG, DSO, was surely one of the most incongruous men ever to be associated with the sport, especially in the thirties when the game was even more entrenched in its working class roots. His past included being an oil prospector in Mexico, a Canadian Mountie, a Tory MP , and editor of the Government's strike-breaking *British Gazette* newspaper during the 1926 General Strike. In the 1920s, he set up the Greyhound Racing Association, which managed various tracks.

Critchley's concern, the White City Greyhound Company, purchased Wigan Highfield. After discussion with the Rugby League, a meeting of the League clubs agreed that Wigan Highfield could play in London. The vote was 20-3, with 4 abstentions.

Initially, the delegates were sceptical but were won over when Captain Walsh, one of Critchley's fellow directors, outlined the company's plans and declared that in the next five years they would have one of the strongest teams in the country. Highfield also agreed to fund the travelling expenses of the other clubs on their trips to London.

Highfield R.F.C.	HIGHFIELD R.F.C.
Offer From London Syndicate	To Play in London.
ACCEPTED BY MEMBERS	BIG MAJORITY IN FAVOUR.

Newspaper headlines covering London Highfield's formation

London Highfield was based at the famous White City Stadium in west London, which was demolished in the late 1980s. The leasehold, and later the freehold, had been purchased for greyhound racing. Although the venue had been used for the 1908 Olympic Games, the new company had to renovate a derelict stadium. Midweek floodlit soccer was tried there, but it had flopped, despite the 40 million candle power floodlights, which were then considered both luxurious and state-of-the-art. A report in the *Wigan Examiner* said that the London ground could hold 120,000 (surely an overestimation), and "surpasses any ground of its kind in Europe for all amenities." Although the stadium was very impressive, the greyhound track meant that the fans were a long way from the pitch, which reduced the atmosphere at matches.

Critchley was no stranger to innovation. He had attempted to introduce cheetah racing into the country, surely one of the most bizarre events to take place on a Rugby League ground. Unfortunately for him, the exotic animals were more interested in having the bookmakers for lunch, and refused to race. A more germane innovation was the sale of a 20-page booklet (for one penny) explaining the rules of Rugby League. The matchday programme was 18 pages long and printed in the club's colours of blue and yellow, a parallel with today's London Broncos colours. The club had uniformed ball-boys and ironically, a greyhound for a mascot.

As a taster for the London public, an exhibition game between Wigan and Leeds was staged at the stadium on 14 December 1932. It featured a startling innovation, whitewashed rugby balls. A decent crowd of 10,000 saw Wigan win 18-9.

Obviously Critchley was encouraged by this gate, but his plans were that Rugby League would always play second fiddle to greyhound racing, and games were scheduled to be played under the floodlights on Wednesday nights. Most matches at this time were played on Saturdays, so Wednesday nights avoided competition with football, especially as floodlit football did not start until the 1950s.

The League reversed a ruling that did not allow competitive matches under floodlight, so the new club could play their fixtures.

The new venture was met with outright opposition from not only Rugby Union but also the pro-Union southern press. The Union authorities threatened to ban *sine die* any player who played for the fledgling club, even if they played only as an amateur, and also threatened to ban any Union player

77

who even went along as a spectator.

This was not really a problem for the club, as they had targeted football spectators as potential new supporters for the game in London. The London-based newspapers sent along their Union correspondents to London Highfield's home games and, not surprisingly, these scribes gave the new club a baptism of fire. Presumably some of them could still remember the original schism between League and Union in 1895.

On the playing side, the Rugby Union boycott was not really a problem because the club had bought the whole of the original Wigan Highfield playing squad. The club did, however, manage to sign two leading Union internationals. Eddie Richards came from Plymouth Albion, and was an England half-back, and W. B. Welsh, a back or loose-forward from Hawick in Scotland also joined. The squad for the start of the season was:

William Dysart: Wigan Highfield player. Forward
Joe Fairhurst: Wigan Highfield player. First captain
Robert Fraser: Full-back, signed from Widnes
Mick Griffin: Signed from Leigh. Forward
E. C. Hill: Signed from Wigan Old Boys
H. Hunter: Wigan Highfield player
Robert Ilsley: Signed from Wigan
Jack Maloney: Signed from Halifax. Winger or centre
Eddie Richards: Union player signed from Plymouth
H. Salmon: Signed from Swinton. Half-back
Jimmy Walker: Wigan Highfield player. Winger, centre or loose-forward
W. B. Welsh: Former Hawick and Scotland Union player
Tom Winstanley: Wigan Highfield player. Half-back
Harry Woods: Wigan Highfield forward. Later played for Great Britain, and toured Australia.

For the players, still based in the north, the regular trips to London caused problems. Interviewed by Michael Latham, Harry Woods recalled for home matches taking the afternoon off work, then catching the train to Euston. After the match, he would catch the midnight train home, and arrive in Wigan at 4.30 am. He had to start work an hour or so later.

There was only one division in Rugby League at this time, with 28 teams, which was split into Yorkshire and Lancashire Leagues. Each team played 38 matches, including all the teams in their own county league, and some from the other county. The championship was decided by a play-off between the top four teams at the end of the season, so the team that finished top of the table were not necessarily declared "champions". London were put into the Lancashire League, a similarity to the 1980s Fulham club that was to play in the Lancashire Cup, and for so long trained in Lancashire. So London faced a tough programme, including visits from some of the best teams. In 1932-3, Wigan Highfield had only won six league games out of 38.

Of course, many features of the modern game were not present. A try was only worth three points, a drop goal was worth two, there were no substitutes, no limit on the number of tackles, and the feed of the ball at the scrum was (usually) towards the hooker, unlike scrums today.

After an initial trial game, the first three games were all away. Ironically, the first game on 2 September was at Wigan, another parallel with the Fulham club nearly 50 years later. Wigan were far superior and ran out winners 43-11 in front of 7,000 spectators. Hunter had the distinction of scoring the club's first try with Bob Fraser kicking four goals. The *Wigan Examiner* reported that London "for the most part were engaged defending their line", although it noted half-back Salmon's "brilliant play". The team on that historic day was:

Fraser, Hill, Walker, Hunter, Maloney, Salmon, Winstanley, Fairhurst, Dysart, Ilsley, Griffin, Woods and Stock.

The second game was at Dewsbury, where the team recorded its first victory, 18-6, with Salmon scoring two tries. Next came defeat at Halifax. This was not a bad start because Wigan and Halifax finished second and fourth respectively that season.

The first home game at White City was played on 20 September 1933, and the visitors were Wakefield Trinity. Unfortunately, despite the Londoners scoring two tries to one, the Yorkshiremen took the points by 9-8, having led 2-0 at half-time. London's tries were scored by Walker and Gordon. The result was disappointing, as the London club would finish eight places above Wakefield in the final league table.

The attendance was reported as 4,000 in one paper, and a reasonable 6,000 in another. It was swelled by a trainload of 600 Wakefield supporters. One report said that "The northern spectators were naturally pleased at the result, but the rest of the crowd despite their comparative ignorance of the game, obviously found the play both entertaining and satisfying."

The return at Wakefield followed and, not surprisingly, Highfield again went down, Jimmy Walker scoring two tries for London. The club's first

London Highfield team at Dewsbury (Courtesy Les Hoole)
Back row: Fraser, Belshaw, Griffin, Fairhurst, Dysart, Collier, Gray, Woods
Front row: Walker, Salmon, Gordon, Maloney, Hunter

TEAMS & SCORING SHEET.—Saturday, September 30th, 1933.

HORNETS			London Highfield		
Selected from	SCORE. Goals Tries		Selected from	SCORE. Goals Tries	
Full Back			*Full Back*		
1 W. Gowers			1 Fraser or A. N. Other		
Threequarter Backs			*Threequarter Backs*		
2 A. C. Falwasser			2 Walker		
3 A. L. Davies			3 Haigh		
4 R. Gaunt			4 Hunter		
5 T. Tolan			5 Maloney		
Half Backs			*Half Backs*		
7 J. Belmo			7 Gordon		
6 C. J. Aynsley			6 Salmon		
Forwards			*Forwards*		
8 E. D. Milne			8 Ilsley		
9 R. Lister			9 Fairhurst or A. N. Other		
10 R. Thompson					
11 B. Walker			10 Oakley		
12 G. E. Mills			11 Griffen		
13 L. V. Armbruster			12 Woods		
14 M Campbell			13 Welsh or Gray		
Referee: Mr. A. S. Dobson, Featherstone.			Kick off at 3.30		

The teams in the programme for the match at Rochdale

80

cup game was at Rochdale in the Lancashire Cup. They had taken Wigan Highfield's place in the competition. London went down 19-10 with Walker and Gordon again scoring tries.

The Londoners' first home league win was against a powerful Halifax side on 4 October. Despite being 6-5 down at half-time, London stormed the second-half with tries from Walker (2), Jack Maloney and William Belshaw. The game was watched by an encouraging 8,000 fans. Two more home victories followed, and an away win at Featherstone, with Welsh scoring a debut try. St. Helens Recs were the next visitors, and they too were overcome in front of a record 9,000 supporters. At this time there were two clubs from St. Helens in the league.

Home and away defeats to Leeds, who were to finish third that season, followed. However, a home win over Dewsbury on 15 November secured a first league double. London Highfield were now thirteenth, with 14 points from 13 matches.

London played hosts to the 1933 Australian tourists on 22 November. The Kangaroos were playing their 25th game in a gruelling 37 match tour. This tour was used in part to promote the sport, and part of this was bringing this fixture to the capital. The match programme said that the tourists had "worthily maintained the high tradition established by their predecessors."

London Highfield v Australians programme

Despite some tough tackling from the London team, the visitors ran in four tries and triumphed 20-5. London's only reply was a try from the prolific Jimmy Walker and a goal from Oakley. Consolation for the club was the excellent gate of 14,500 and receipts of more than £1,000.

One report was headlined: "Dazzling floodlight rugby - masterly play by Aussies", and described the Australians as "wonderfully versatile", saying that their "handling was always superior to that of their opponents". Another said that the tourists "were easily the better side in physique, speed and tactical skill" - which sounds strikingly similar to the modern Australian touring teams.

The teams were:

London: Fraser, Walker, Belshaw, Merritt, Maloney, Haigh, Richards, Unwin, Griffin, Fairhurst, Sherrington, Woods and Oakley.

Australia: McMillan, Ridley, Brown, Why, Gardner, Mead, Doonar, Folwell, Madsen, Stehr, S. Pearce, Gibbs and Prigg.

The Londoners then lost at Swinton, which did not bode well for what was to follow, a match at home to Salford, who were leading the league, and were to finish at the head of the league table, and runners up in the Championship.

This match, however, was one of the achievements of London's year, a victory over a team that only lost six matches all season. Despite being down by 3-10, two tries from Jack Maloney, and one from Hunter saw them home. However, Salford were without five of their stars that afternoon.

Unfortunately the victory over Salford was followed by London losing the next four games. An improved display saw a win at lowly Barrow, followed by victory over Widnes at home by two points. Next came a narrow defeat by one point to Oldham, a game that the Londoners should have won, as they had controlled most of the match.

Then, on 31 January, at home in front of a 7,000 crowd, including 500 Wigan supporters, London pulled off a shock win. Wigan were to finish second in the league table, and included Jim Sullivan, one of the game's all time greats and a member of the Hall of Fame.

However, the home side played sparkling rugby and won comfortably 30-12. After London had taken an early lead, Wigan hit back with two tries. Two goals from Oakley and a drop-goal from Oster gave London a narrow half-time lead. Wigan were nilled in the second-half as the London players again showed they could rise to the big occasion. The six London tries were scored by Maloney (2), Haigh, Stock, Belshaw and Mick Griffin, with Oakley kicking five goals and Oster a drop-goal. The *Wigan Examiner* said that this result caused "great surprise" in Wigan. It noted the "great enthusiasm" among the London supporters. It claimed that some Wigan players had problems catching passes under the floodlights.

London Highfield were now confident, and won their first Challenge Cup tie against amateurs Hull St. Mary. The attendance of 1,000 was low because the Saturday afternoon kick-off meant that the club were competing directly with soccer. The amateurs went into an early lead, but the first hat-trick of tries for the club from Walker saw the home side through.

An away defeat by Widnes in a dour game was followed by the second round of the Challenge Cup, and the visit of Warrington. Again the game was played on a Saturday afternoon, but this time the attendance was an acceptable 5,000. The cup was clearly bringing out the best of the team, who swept home 19-5. London's try scorers were Griffin, Walker, Stock, Maloney and Hunter.

In a return to the league, bottom club Featherstone were beaten, giving London their second double. The next game, on 3 March, was very different, at high-flying Salford. The Londoners were 21-5 behind at the interval, but tough tackling kept the final score down to 26-5. Unlike the first game against Salford, this match went true to form.

The third round of the cup saw London drawn at cup-holders Huddersfield. In a tumultuous game, three players were sent-off, and London could only manage an Oakley penalty as they lost 21-2.

The next two league games saw victories against St. Helens at home, and at Batley, where London only snatched the lead in the last five minutes with a try from Maloney. The Londoners' programme described the win against St. Helens as "a delightful exhibition of constructive football", and said that the team "fully merited their success."

In another development initiative, London Highfield had the honour of staging a game against the newly formed French Rugby League side on 21 March. The French were led by former Rugby Union great Jean Galia, the French Rugby League pioneer, and a close game was in prospect. The 6,000 fans were not disappointed as the score swung to-and-fro. London took the lead with a try from Mick Griffin, but the French took control and led at half-time 17-11. One report said that at the end of the first-half "the French seemed to be improving with every stride."

Only tiredness from the French *treizistes* allowed the home side back to score two tries in the last five minutes. Welsh scored his second try on the final whistle, and Oakley's touchline conversion from 40 yards out allowed London to pull "the match...out of the fire in thrilling fashion", as one reporter wrote. London won 19-17.

The sides were:

London: Maddock, Walker, Maloney, Hunter, Belshaw, Oster, Richards, Oakley, Stott, Davies, Woods, Griffin and Welsh

France: Cassagneau, Samatan, Barbazanges, Amila, Lambert, Mathon, Carrere, Blanc, Pettit, Duhau, Dechavanne, Galia, and Rechacorde.

The French game pepped up the season as London then extended their winning run to seven games. This run ended abruptly away at mid-table St. Helens. Then came the first league home defeat since early January, as Batley triumphed by two points. A dramatic game at St. Helens Rec saw the club record their last ever away win in front of a 3,000 crowd. Salmon scored in the dying seconds, with Oakley converting to see London taking the points with a 17-16 victory.

London Highfield v France Programme

On Challenge Cup Final eve Bramley were the final visitors for a league game at White City on 4 May 1934. They were to finish two places from the bottom of the league, and London Highfield turned on their best display, scoring 13 tries with Oakley kicking a club record 10 goals. Welsh created another record by scoring four tries and, according to one account of the match "played probably his finest game since becoming professional." The other tries were by Eddie Richards (3), Hunter (2), Belshaw, Oster, Haigh and Salmon, with one journalist commenting that "the backs handled and ran in a fashion far superior to anything their opponents could show." At half-time the Londoners led 29-4, which by the end had risen to 59-11. It was Bramley's heaviest defeat of the season. The attendance was 3,000.

The final London Highfield team was:
Belshaw, Stock, Haigh, Hunter, Salmon, Oster, Richards, Woods, Griffin, Oakley, Hitchen, Davies and Welsh.

Despite all the assurances given by Brigadier-General Critchley and the White City Board, they decided to pull the plug after only one season. Losses had totalled £8,000 but Critchley had said that he was prepared for a loss in the first season. However, he had probably not envisaged such a large amount. Gates had averaged 6,000, far more than many teams in the north. In truth, the idea of floodlit games on Wednesday evenings in midwinter was always going to be problematical.

HIGHFIELD'S BEST

BRAMLEY OVERWHELMED :
OAKLEY KICKS 10 GOALS

London Highfield 59 pts., Bramley 11 pts.

LONDON HIGHFIELD, in their last match, put up their best Rugby League score of the season when they beat Bramley under floodlight at the White City last night by 59 points to 11.

Their forwards got the ball from most of the scrums, and the backs handled and ran much better than their opponents.

Welsh, among the Highfield forwards, played probably his finest game since becoming professional, and behind the scrum Oster in the unusual position of centre-three-quarter, Hunter and Richards and Salmon, the halves, played splendidly.

Highfield led at half-time by 29 to 4, Haigh, Salmon, Hunter, Welsh (2), Oster, and Richards getting tries. Oakley kicked four goals, while Litt kicked two penalty goals for Bramley. The visitors, though overplayed, fought pluckily.

Litt began the second half with a penalty goal. Welsh, Richards, and Hunter added tries for Highfield, all of which Oakley improved. Telford, a strong runner, crossed for the visitors. Afterwards Welsh, Belshaw, and Richards, tries, and Oakley, three goals, scored for Highfield. Litt kicked Bramley's fourth goal.

Report of the London Highfield v Bramley match

85

Midweek evening sport was still a novelty, with people working longer hours than today, and with less transport available. Presumably, the income did not compensate for the costs of bringing the teams down to London, and of staging matches at White City.

The playing side of the operation was relatively successful with wins against France, and three of the league's top sides Salford, Wigan and Halifax. London had continued to improve as the season progressed, and finished a respectable 14th. The final league record was:

Played	Won	Drawn	Lost	For	Against	Points
38	20	0	18	509	489	40

It must have been apparent to Critchley that only the best would appeal to the general London sporting public. This would entail a greater degree of expenditure. The small attendances for the Challenge Cup games on Saturdays showed that competition with soccer would have been futile. But the Australia game had shown that 14,500 people were prepared to watch a match in the capital. It was a pity that the White City Company did not continue with their vision of establishing the game in London as the Highfield players, under coach Jimmy Green, returned north to become Liverpool Stanley and in the next two seasons finished in the top four, winning the Lancashire Cup and League double in 1935-6 to show London what might have been. Rugby League in London could have had the winning team at the top level of the sport it has always needed.

6   Acton & Willesden 1935-6

As with London Highfield, the driving force behind the setting up of two new clubs in 1935 was a greyhound racing entrepreneur. Sydney E. Parkes was the millionaire proprietor of the Wandsworth Greyhound Stadium, and had seen the 1934 Wembley Challenge Cup Final between Hunslet and Widnes. The new clubs were Acton & Willesden, based near White City in north west London, and Streatham & Mitcham, based in south London.

Parkes was a visionary and believed that more than one team was necessary to develop a League culture in London. He approached the Rugby League and, after further discussions, his two new clubs joined the League by 19 votes to 8, in the spring of 1935. He guaranteed that the clubs would run for at least two years. His original idea however, was far more radical as he had intended to set up a separate league, based in the south. When this fell through, he opted to join the Rugby Football League.

He was also a shrewd businessman, and saw that he could use the setting up of the infant League clubs as a Trojan Horse to set up new dog tracks. Greyhound tracks had to be licensed, and Parkes believed that if he established the stadium for another sport, he could then apply for a greyhound licence. The original planning permission for both stadiums was only listed as accommodating Rugby League, not greyhound racing.

A consortium of London businessmen under the aegis of Parkes was created, which proposed to form the two clubs. One major difference with London Highfield was that, by playing on Saturday afternoons, the new teams would be competing directly for support with football clubs.

Reports said that Parkes put up £16,000 of his own funds, but even more daring was his plan to build the two stadiums from scratch.

Acton Stadium was built on the old Park Royal Stadium site, a shrewd move as greyhound racing had taken place there before, and Parkes was confident of obtaining a licence. Both stadiums had capacities of 30,000, and cost in the region of £100,000 each. Both had main grandstands able to seat 10,000 people, with a smaller one holding 5,000.

Mitcham Stadium was built on waste ground between Eastfields Road and Sandy Lane. Unlike Highfield, players moved to the capital, and were employed to build the grounds. Most were living in London by the end of May.

The players earned £2.10s per week while building the stadiums before the season started. Once the season started, some players (the ones with Rugby League experience) preferred to draw the dole and match fees, which was the accepted practice in the north.

The *West London Observer* reported that the players had "started their training a week earlier than any other Rugby League players in the country. They are leaving nothing to chance." Part of the reason for the extra training was that "a number of the players... are new to the professional code, and the differences between the thirteen a side game and Rugby Union football have had to be mastered by the new professionals."

Acton signed nine Welshmen, including Con Murphy, a Rugby Union international from Cross Keys, and two schoolboy internationals. Six players joined from northern Rugby League clubs. Nearly all the players were under 30, with most being in their early twenties. Cyril Braund was appointed as secretary-manager. He was a former Leigh player, and had appeared in their 1921 Challenge Cup Final team.

The squad at the start of the season was:

J. Addison: Full-back, formerly with Batley. Said to be "splendid in defence and a constructively attacking full back

G. Atherton: Front-row forward from Liverpool Stanley, 23 years old

Jack Avery: Forward from Aberavon RUFC, 22 years old. Described as having the same kicking style as Jim Sullivan: "takes no more than two paces before kicking the ball"

J. Cayzer: Second-row forward signed from Liverpool Stanley. 24 years old

D. Elward: Second-row forward from Cardiff

R. G. Forbes-Bassett: "One of the fastest forwards of southern Rugby (Union) football." Had played Rugby Union for Richmond, Rosslyn Park and Hampshire. (Never actually played for the Club)

Dai Jenkins: 21 years old, had been Cardiff RUFC's scrum-half for two years, and captain of the Welsh Rugby Union schoolboy team. Had "speed, a very deceptive dummy and gives great service from the scrum"

Ken Jones: Full back, formerly with Crumlin RUFC, "noted for his positional play"

Dennis Madden: Outside half, signed from Aberavon RUFC. The *West London Observer* commented: "Has great burst and thrust away and is very fast; was a Welsh Powderhall sprinter and one of the most sought after men by Rugby League." 20 years old

Gil Morgan: Second-row or loose-forward, formerly with Halifax. 26 years old

Con Murphy: Hooker, signed from Cross Keys RUFC, Welsh Rugby Union international

J. Phillips: Scrum-half, described by the *West London Observer* as "an elusive man on the field, and full of tricks, should make a name for himself"

J. Pritchard: Full-back, formerly with Crumlin RUFC

F. Ribby: Centre three-quarter, had played for Glamorgan and Bridgend at Rugby Union

S. Roberts: Centre, from Maesteg, signed after "keen competition for his services by Rugby League clubs in the north", 26 years old

P. Sutcliffe: Signed from Featherstone Rovers

E. Thomas: Signed from Salford, had played Rugby Union in Wales for Mountain Ash. Former Welsh Powderhall sprinter

Arthur Veysey: Welsh wing three-quarter, had played Rugby Union for Abercarn and Monmouth

Illtwyd Williams: Utility player, could play at hooker, scrum-half or outside-half. 20 years old, had played Rugby Union for Bridgend RUFC and the Wales schoolboy side. Said to have "a fine pair of hands." 20 years old

Ironically, while the stadiums were being built the players trained in Mill Hill Park, not far from the site of the current Copthall Stadium, home of the London Broncos.

The first game was on 11 May 1935. A joint London side (playing as Streatham & Mitcham) met Broughton Rangers (from Salford) at Crystal Palace in a friendly, the Lancastrians winning 17-13. This venue was later to be the home of Fulham and the London Crusaders for some seasons in the 1980s and 1990s.

After the completion of the Park Royal Stadium, the first of the two grounds to be built, a public trial game was held on 24 August 1935, one week before the season began. It drew a promising crowd of 4,000 spectators.

By now, local interest was growing. In the spring, before the new clubs had even played, supporters clubs had been set up, recruiting around 1,000 fans. They were boosted by contingents of northern exiles who were working at Ford's Dagenham plant. The subscription fees were two shillings (10p) for gentlemen, one shilling (5p) for ladies and one shilling for boys under 18.

The *West London Observer* reported that: "the first home match is, however, of major importance to Londoners, and the tussle between Acton & Willesden and the York team promises to be a stiff one." It outlined that: "during the week players have attended conferences with their manager, Mr

Local newspaper advert for the first match

Sydney E. Parkes - founder of the two new London clubs

Braund and their trainer, at which they have discussed in the fullest detail the moves and tactics they will try against York."

The match at Park Royal on 31 August 1935 attracted between 5,000 and 6,000 spectators. The Royals, as Acton were nicknamed, were soon behind and were losing 14-5 at half-time. A spirited second- half performance saw the home side clinch a 17-17 draw in the closing stages. This was a creditable result with a team who would finish in seventh place. The *News Chronicle* said that "the Royals played with a splendid enthusiasm that more than counter-balanced their defects." Acton's points came from tries by Madden, Roberts and Morgan and four goals from Addison. Acton's team that day was: Addison, Veysey, Bibby, Roberts, Williams, Madden, Phillips, Walton, Murphy, Atherton, Morgan, Sutcliffe, and Cayzer.

One innovation was a running commentary throughout the match to explain the action and rules of the game. The *News Chronicle* report concluded that "If Acton keep up this form they should have a good following."

A week later, Acton recorded their first win, against Featherstone, who would finish the season at the bottom of the league. The return match at Featherstone, a couple of days later, was controversial. The home side had two players dismissed, yet were still winning in injury time. A dramatic late try from Bibby saw the Royals take the spoils by 15-13, giving Acton their first away win. Bibby's late try was his second, with another from Cayzer and three goals from Addison. The *News Chronicle* commented that the match "finished amid a storm of protest." However, the *West London Observer*, maybe reflecting Acton's point of view, said that "The Featherstone men indulged in spoiling tactics, just as they had done two days earlier at Park Royal, and thus somewhat marred the game."

Acton & Willesden had been put into the Yorkshire Rugby League, and Streatham & Mitcham into the Lancashire League, so that even numbers were maintained, and the additional travelling evenly shared. After three games Acton were top of the Yorkshire table, the first London team to do this. They were also second in the overall championship table.

In the Yorkshire Cup, the Royals lost at mid-table Hunslet by 10 points. The *West London Observer* magnanimously outlined that "Hunslet deserved their success. The forwards were usually quicker in obtaining possession of the ball than the visiting team, the Acton three-quarters having less opportunity to show the attacking powers they used to such effect against Featherstone last week." However, an impressive away win at St Helens followed this defeat, the Londoners winning 5-2.

Acton were now challenging for the top-of-the-table spot and attracted a record crowd of 17,841 for the visit of Batley. Acton, playing in their usual cherry and white, raced into a 21-point lead, but were pulled back by Batley in the last quarter. The Royals just held on, Madden scoring a hat-trick of tries, with others from Addison and Jenkins. James kicked two goals with one from Addison, the final score being 21-14 to the Londoners. The *News Chronicle* report said that "Batley were well beaten by a superior side." Acton were now top of the overall championship table, a great achievement for a club that was less than a month old. They were the first southern side to top the table, and the *West London Observer* proclaimed proudly that "No other new Rugby League club has ever played five opening matches without losing one." Given the inexperience of many of the players who were recruited from Rugby Union, it was indeed a major achievement.

Unfortunately, the team now hit a difficult patch with a defeat at York, and a 7-7 draw at Barrow. At York, Acton were leading 7-6 until 10 minutes from the end. Apparently the Acton team impressed the York crowd so much that they were cheered the whole way to their dressing room. At Barrow, Cutbush had been concussed, and had to come off at half time. Even so, the Royals had been winning 7-2, and Barrow only equalised with a penalty two minutes from time.

Three further defeats followed at Hull Kingston Rovers, by two points, at home to cup-holders Castleford, in front of 12,000 fans, by four points, and at Batley. There were also mitigating circumstances. The team's train had been delayed by gales on the way to Hull. The players changed on the train, but the game kicked off 20 minutes late, and was played in a 60 mph gale. Dennis Madden had missed the Castleford game, because he was playing in France.

More ominous for the Royals, however, was the application for a licence for greyhound racing at Park Royal. Rugby League was now set to become a poor relation to dog racing. The London County Council granted the licence in November.

Nonetheless, more than 9,000 saw the next home game, despite foul weather. The Royals beat Keighley with a try from Veysey, scored "after a race down the touchline at an amazing pace for such a heavy ground." But Acton then suffered a defeat at Castleford, although the game was noticeable for "the brilliance of the handling movements of both sides."

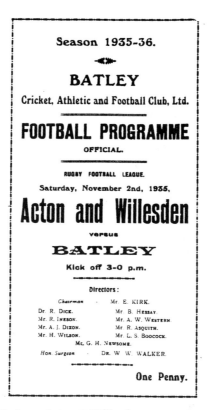

Season 1935-36.

BATLEY

Cricket, Athletic and Football Club, Ltd.

FOOTBALL PROGRAMME
OFFICIAL.

RUGBY FOOTBALL LEAGUE.

Saturday, November 2nd, 1935,

Acton and Willesden

versus

BATLEY

Kick off 3-0 p.m.

Directors:

Chairman -	Mr E. KIRK.
Dr. R. DICK.	Mr B. HESSAY.
Mr. R. INESON.	Mr. A. W. WESTERN.
Mr. A. J. DIXON.	Mr. R. ASQUITH.
Mr. H. WILSON.	Mr. L. S. BOOCOCK.
Mr. G. H. NEWSOME.	
Hon. Surgeon -	DR. W. W. WALKER.

One Penny.

Batley v Acton & Willesden programme

Wakefield were dispatched at home with the help of a spectacular try from Jack Cutbush, but defeat at Hull, who were to go on to win the championship followed. Even in defeat, the Royals were worth watching. This match was described as "as fast, sporting and spectacular an exhibition of Rugby football as anyone could wish to see."

At the start of December, Acton's form went into sharp decline, with defeat at home to Bradford by two points in a London "pea-souper" fog. By the end no player could be recognised. The conversion for the Royals' try in the last minute missed by inches. The *West London Observer* commented that "When they were visible, which was seldom, Cutbush and Roberts, the home side's three-quarters, were seen putting in fine passing movements and great defensive work."

Spirits were lifted with a home win against lowly Leigh, just before

93

Christmas. But with gates now down to 2,000, Sydney Parkes decided to transfer all games to the Mitcham Stadium where match attendances had been higher. Coincidentally the London County Council had refused a licence for greyhound racing at Mitcham. At the beginning of January, greyhound racing was advertised at Park Royal Stadium for the first time.

The first derby game between the two new London clubs took place on Christmas Day 1935. Acton won, despite fine play from George Nepia, Streatham's Maori full-back. Cutbush, Murphy and Cayzer scored for Acton and 10,000 attended the game at Mitcham, which was Streatham's home game.

Acton followed this by their first "home" defeat at Mitcham, when Hull KR won 10-8. A heavy defeat followed at Leeds, but Acton then produced good form to see off Rochdale at Mitcham before losing at Keighley.

Following representation from the supporters club, Parkes agreed to return matches to Park Royal. The crowd did improve to 3,000 for the visit of St. Helens, in which the home side triumphed 5-0. A narrow defeat at Wakefield at the beginning of February was caused mainly by the sending-off of two of Acton's forwards.

The next game was Acton's first Challenge Cup match, at home to a strong Liverpool Stanley side. Liverpool still had six players from the 1933-4

The Acton home programme cover

94

London Highfield squad: Belshaw, Robinson, Maloney, Woods, Stock and Davies. Former Streatham player Shaw also appeared for the visitors. A 0-0 score was a good result for the "new" Londoners.

Then followed a disastrous run of six consecutive defeats, including a 3-29 loss to Liverpool in the cup replay. The home game against Huddersfield only attracted a paltry 1,000 fans to see Acton lose by four points. Things improved, but only slightly, at Hunslet where the Royals were 3-0 ahead at half-time but went down 3-10. A home win against struggling Dewsbury, inspired by the arrival of Turton from Streatham, raised spirits briefly for the club.

The second London derby saw Streatham triumph 21-12 at the Mitcham Stadium before 4,000 fans, despite this being Acton's "home" game. Presumably it was felt that a better crowd would attend at Mitcham. Acton had led with four minutes to go, but two late tries saw Streatham home. A draw at Leigh was the Royals' third draw of the season.

The rest of the season saw up and down performances from the team. The new Challenge Cup winners Leeds, who had won the trophy a week before, and displayed the cup in the stand at the match, smashed an Acton side fielding six reserves, 54-5 at White City. Eric Harris scored his 64th try of the season for the Yorkshiremen. Defeat at Rochdale was followed by the fourth draw of the season at Bradford, this time 18-18.

A third (and final) derby match of the season was played on May Day, at the neutral Wandsworth Stadium for the Sydney E. Parkes Hospital Trophy with Streatham winning by 33-19.

The very next day Acton played their last game, against Bramley. Ironically it was Bramley who had provided London Highfield's last opposition. Like Highfield, Acton beat their Yorkshire opponents, 20-11, with Johnson scoring a try and four goals. The last Acton side was:
James, Turton, Johnson, Cutbush, Avery, Bibby, Jenkins, Walton, Murphy, Atherton, Morgan, Sutcliffe and Cayzer.

The team finished 21st in the table, out of 30. Cutbush finished as Acton's top try scorer with 14, and Addison kicked 46 goals. The final league record was:

Played	Won	Drawn	Lost	For	Against	Points
38	13	4	21	382	529	30

So Acton were wound up, despite Mr Parkes's promises that the club would run for at least two years, and the best players joined Streatham, much to the dismay of the hard working supporters club.

Acton, (like Streatham), were set up to make maximum use of purpose built greyhound stadiums. After initial success, the crowds declined as the playing performances dived. Once the greyhound licence had been secured, the owners had no need to subsidise rugby from the proceeds of the greyhound racing. It was thought that by transferring all the players to Streatham, where crowds were better, a combined London side could succeed. Also, a greyhound licence had not been secured at Mitcham, and therefore rugby was the sole sport played at that stadium. In order to maximize crowd potential, the management arranged for buses to be laid on from Acton so that west London fans could still see some rugby. But it was still a rapid decline for a club that had promised so much.

7   Streatham & Mitcham 1935-7

The Streatham & Mitcham club was based at Mitcham Stadium, very close to the Tooting & Mitcham United Football Club. In 1956, when the Stadium was being demolished, Leyton Orient Football Club purchased one of the stands, to become the main stand at their Brisbane Road ground. Leyton Orient have plans to rebuild their ground, but at the moment, one part of London's Rugby League history still survives.

On 11 May 1935, the first game was played, a joint London side (playing as Streatham & Mitcham) against mid-table Broughton Rangers (from Salford) at Crystal Palace in a friendly, the Lancastrians winning 17-13. In reality, this was a trial game for the club's management as much as to introduce the game to the south London public. The report in the *South London Press* was headed: "Enter the New Football. Rugby League should draw big crowds", and said that between 300 and 400 were present. The reporter outlined that "Although Streatham & Mitcham lost, they played good, hard, open football, and considering this was the first time they had played as a team, they combined splendidly... If football as seen on Saturday is served up regularly, the game should soon have a big following."

In some ways the Streatham club was more glamorous than their cross-town rivals Acton. Not only did it sign experienced northern players such as Dewsbury's George Banks, but, after initial defeats, signed four New Zealand Rugby Union All Blacks including the world famous Maori full-back George Nepia for £500.

Streatham signed more northerners than their London rivals Acton. The squad at the start of the season included:

P. Barnes: Full-back, signed from St. Helens Recs, described in the club programme as "although rather slight, is a very clever and elusive full-back"

S. Crabtree: "Very strong, determined" front-row forward, signed from Halifax. Also, had a great reputation as a weightlifter

Tommy Egan: Stand-off, and the smallest player in the club. Signed from Oldham

C. Harling: Forward signed from Dewsbury

H. Hunter: Back. Signed from Liverpool Stanley. Formerly with London Highfield

A. Johnson: Signed from Leigh. Centre

Ike Jones: Former Aberavon RUFC loose-forward

B. Langford: Forward signed from Leigh

Arthur Lemon: Second-row forward and club captain, signed from St. Helens Played for Wales at Rugby League and Rugby Union. Described in the club programme as "A magnificent tireless forward"

J. McTiffin: Forward, signed from Welsh Rugby Union

K. Nicholson: Half-back, formerly with York

W. Shaw: Former Halifax player. The club programme said about him: "fast, exceedingly clever in the loose, and besides possessing a wonderful set of hands is a splendid place kicker"

J. Turton: Signed from St. Helens Recs. Right-winger

T. Walsh: Scrum-half

W. Whitworth: Another recruit from Oldham, played on the left-wing

C. Williams: Centre. Played Rugby Union in the army, fast sprinter

At the time, Sydney Parkes was warned about paying over the odds for the players, and it was thought that he could have signed some of them for a tenth of the fees he actually paid. He appointed Reg Farrar, a former Oldham player, as secretary-manager. The coach was Reg Jones, who was from Buckinghamshire, and the local paper reported that there were nine miners in the team.

Streatham had been placed in the Lancashire League half of the Rugby League Championship. The *South London Press* welcomed the new sport. In a report headed "Pro. Rugby starts its 'Big Push'", the paper said that "Tomorrow should be an important day in the history of South London sport, the newly formed Streatham & Mitcham Rugby League club play their first match." The report said that Mr Parkes expected to get support from northerners based in London. The writer had attended a joint dinner of the Acton & Willesden, and Streatham & Mitcham players, and said that ".. The teams I must confess, were the toughest guys I've seen for a long time... They seem very decent fellows and I liked the way each team toasted the other and wished them good luck for the season."

Initial results were not encouraging. The first game at Broughton Rangers saw the Hams, as they were known, beaten by 20 points. Barnes scored two goals. His first goal registered the first points scored in the whole Rugby League for that season. At half-time, the score was 2-2, but the loss of Egan through injury saw the Londoners wilt in the second-half. One report said that the new club "shaped well enough...to suggest that, with a little polishing up of the rough edges, they will hold their own."

The writer added that "Barnes gave a faultless display of fielding and kicking.... while at half-back Egan and Walsh seemed destined to strike up a profitable partnership."

The Streatham side that day was:

Barnes, Turton, Hunter, Whitworth, Nicholson, Walsh, Egan, Crabtree, McTiffin, Langford, Lemon, Shaw and I. Jones.

The first home game against Oldham, who had finished the previous season in 18th place, although disappointing in terms of the result, could be classed as a success, as a crowd reported as 15,000 in some papers, and 24,000 in others, came through the turnstiles that Saturday, 7 September 1935. With due ceremony, the Mayor of Streatham kicked off.

Streatham played well, and took the lead with a try from Walsh and a goal from Twose, who had been signed from Wigan just before the game. But an injury to Egan forced the home side to play with the scrum-half as a passenger on the wing. The Lancashire team took full advantage and won 10-5.

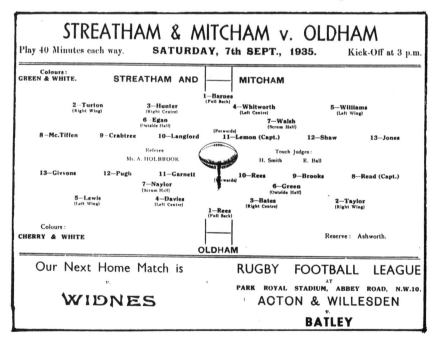

The team line up in the Streatham & Mitcham v Oldham programme

However, the one Oldham reporter did comment on the "gallant and spirited display" of the Streatham team.

The enthusiasm of the London crowd for the match was shown in the report in the *Oldham Evening Chronicle*. The reporter, "Cherry-White" quoted his cockney messenger boy saying "Lummy, Guv'ner, worra gime!", and said that the lions in Trafalgar Square must have heard the noise when Streatham went ahead. W. Sullivan reported in the *South London Press* that "this new sport is going to be a bigger danger to soccer than I thought", and pointed out that the crowd was bigger than those at any of the football league matches covered by the paper that day.

The next game saw a narrow loss in the Lancashire Cup at St. Helens. A further home defeat to Widnes, who would finish the season in third place, was played on a Thursday before a crowd of 2,000. Arthur Lemon, the Streatham captain was sent-off. The infant club was struggling in its first weeks, unlike London rivals Acton who were near the top of the table.

The next home game was, nevertheless, attended by a healthy crowd of 20,174 (although other reports gave a figure of 10,000), and they were not to be disappointed. Two tries from Hunter and four goals from Johnson gave the 'Majors'- a second nickname for the club- their first win, against Bradford Northern. The *South London Press* said that "they played as a team for the first time, and so reaped the reward they justly deserved." The Bradford local paper described Streatham's play as "handling freely but wildly." Their report described the Mitcham Stadium as "a place to admire, with its fine playing area and two magnificent covered stands."

To strengthen the playing squad, as well as the Kiwis, - George Nepia, MacDonald, Edward Holder and Charlie Smith, - who were due to arrive later in the season, Streatham signed Jack Avery, Francis Allan, Stanley Horsman and Ken Jones from neighbours Acton.

In their first visit to Yorkshire, Streatham were ahead early on at Bramley, but succumbed 14-7. A match report said that the Londoners' "best work was done in defence." Bramley were to finish a place below Streatham in the table, so this was a match that should have been won.

The home game that followed was no better, as Warrington took the honours before 16,000 fans, although the *South London Press* pointed out that there were five new players in the team, and "until a settled team is decided on, it would perhaps be as well to withhold criticism." One new recruit was hooker, George William Banks. Interviewed many years later, by Tom Mather for *Open Rugby*, Banks was clear why he signed for Streatham: "Money... They gave me a contract for £12/10 shillings (£12.50p) a week, which was good money in those days."

Banks had been paid around £9 to £10 a week at Dewsbury, which put him among the top earners in the northern based players. He made the move so he could give his family additional financial support. His pay at Streatham was usual for the contracts Sydney Parkes was offering northern players, to entice them to London. To put this in context, average players in the north earned £4 to £6 a week from the game. A salaried worker at this time would earn around £4 a week, and a skilled manual worker usually less than £4. A labourer was earning less than £3 a week. The maximum basic wage for a professional footballer was £8 per week.

The club parted with their secretary-manager Reg Farrar in early October, and Major T. V. O' Neill-Joyce was appointed to the post. A further defeat at lowly St. Helens Recs did nothing to raise morale, leaving Streatham bottom of the league. A further recruit to "Pro. Rugby" as the *South London Press* still called it, was 23-year-old E. M. Jones from London Welsh RUFC.

Local newspaper advert for Streatham & Mitcham v Warrington match

A rousing 44-8 home win against struggling Featherstone, described as "the weakest opposition they will ever encounter", at last brought some relief to the green-and-whites of Streatham, with the tries including a Nicholson hat-trick. The crowd of 15,278 showed the loyalty earned by the club. The next game was a trip to Wigan, who were too good for the Hams, and won 28-5 with Jim Sullivan kicking five goals.

At the beginning of November, Streatham beat St. Helens Recs, with tries from Hunter (2), Walsh and Shaw and 13,487 attended the game, including the president of the Rugby League. A draw at Barrow showed that Streatham were improving all the time, having led until late in the second-half.

Streatham now awaited the arrival of the major All Black signings who had set sail from New Zealand earlier in the season. They would be joined by another Kiwi, George Harrison, a six-foot forward. A further change occurred in November, when Captain Gee replaced O'Neill-Joyce to become the new secretary-manager.

All Black Charlie Smith scored a try on his home debut, a victory over Rochdale. A Wellington newspaper had described him as ".. a whizzer as an attacking player... a human thunderbolt..employs a useful hand-off and knows how to bump with his hips." This praise seemed to be borne out, with a report of the match highlighting the new recruit's "sustained exhibition of constructive, brainy play."

Despite All Black Edward Holder's debut in the return game, Streatham lost 31-5, followed by another loss at home to champions Salford, with the *South London Press* concluding that "It is hoped that the Hams will remember in future that their salvation lies in the open game. The forwards are only average, but their three-quarter line is one of the fastest in the league, and must be properly fed."

But further problems were looming when Sydney Parkes heard that his application to race greyhounds at the Mitcham Stadium was turned down.

The New Zealanders were finding life difficult in a struggling side, and, despite MacDonald's debut, Streatham lost at Featherstone, who would finish the season at the bottom of the league.

Nonetheless, the arrival of George Nepia brought an avalanche of publicity. Described as "The King of Maoridom", he had been a member of the all-conquering 1924-5 New Zealand Rugby Union touring team nicknamed the Invincibles, which won all their 30 games.

His first game, alongside fellow debutant Harrison, was against mighty Wigan. The *South London Press* previewed the game, reporter Olympian's article being headlined "World's finest Rugby full-backs clash at Streatham", and describing the match as "The Rugby treat of the year." Indeed, the duel between the full-backs Nepia and Sullivan was the highlight for the 15,000 crowd. Unfortunately for the new players, Wigan won 11-3 with MacDonald scoring the only Streatham try. The *Daily Despatch* highlighted the duel between the two full-backs, commenting on their "epic display" and "fine sportsmanship." The *South London Press* said that "Wigan played above themselves to give their best display of the season."

Nepia had enjoyed his first game of Rugby League, saying he found the game better than Rugby Union: "Although last Saturday's match against Wigan was my first in the 13-a-side game, I can honestly say that it is an improvement on ordinary Rugby. Individual players have so much more chance to show their skill... The League code is better for positional play, gives you more chance to work out schemes - in fact the general layout is much more chess-like."

On Christmas Day, London rivals Acton won the first London derby with Nepia kicking two goals for Streatham.

Nepia's drawing power was such that Sydney Parkes, *entrepreneur par excellence*, actually asked Streatham's opponents for 25 per cent of their gate if they wished Nepia to play, such was his fame.

At the end of December, despite having less than a month's experience of Rugby League, Nepia was appointed as acting manager and club captain. A 3-3 draw at home to St. Helens followed, with Streatham down to 12 men for most of the second-half. The team then lost narrowly at Leigh, in front of the home side's largest gate of the season, 6,000. Two away defeats, at mid-table Batley and Swinton, followed as the team, now under Nepia's control, failed to gel. At Batley, Nepia's first appearance in Yorkshire, he had been given a "rousing reception" by the crowd.

Another new signing, C. Hitchen, who had played for London Highfield, joined from Liverpool Stanley. He inspired Streatham to a home victory against Batley, but crowds were now beginning to fall, this game only attracting 6,000.

Batley had been beaten by Acton earlier in the season, and felt their long journey was to blame. This time, they travelled down the day before, stayed at the Strand Palace Hotel, went to a pantomime on the Friday night, and still lost. The two New Zealand forwards, Harrison and McDonald, were

103

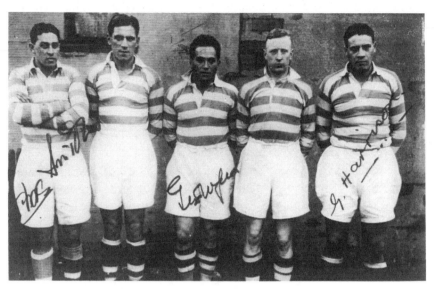

Streatham's New Zealanders. George Nepia is in the centre (Courtesy Les Hoole)

George Nepia and Jim Sullivan after the Streatham v Wigan match
(Courtesy Les Hoole)

Streatham's stars on a heavy pitch. However, the *South London Press* reported that Hitchen had made the difference, as winning the ball in the scrums would allow the team to get the ball to their "fast and clever" backs. The reporter outlined that Hitchen would do the side "more good than all the All Blacks in the world".

At the end of January, the *South London Press* reported that a London Baseball League was being set up, including Streatham & Mitcham, and that they were "banking on the experience of George Nepia, the famous full-back, who had a lengthy connection with the baseball game in America." This was another example of the "sports promoters" of the 1930s attempting to introduce new forms of entertainment.

William Fawcett was now appointed as trainer, but could not prevent a defeat at Lancashire Cup winners, Salford. Streatham hooker Harling had broken his shoulder, and had to go off after 10 minutes, leaving the team with 12 men against powerful opposition. However, things improved with a win against Bramley at the beginning of February, with Streatham's three-quarters' "brilliance" being responsible for the victory, although Nepia had a poor game.

Streatham & Mitcham team at Hull KR   (Courtesy Les Hoole)
Back row: Hitchen, Smith, Jones, Langford, Harrison, Whitworth, MacDonald.
Front row: Walsh, Banks, Nepia, Hunter, Holder & Berry

A good Challenge Cup win at Hull KR, with Nepia's kicking prominent, gave the season some sense of purpose. Streatham's main problem was that they had many brilliant individuals, but were beaten by better organised teams.

The most important game so far was the visit of Leeds in the second round of the Challenge Cup. The match again brought into opposition Nepia and Leeds' full-back, Great Britain international Jim Brough. They had played against each other in a Rugby Union international at Twickenham 11 years before. The *South London Press* reported that Streatham's supporters were in a "cup fever", and that the team "had been welded together into a fighting force" for the match.

However, Streatham lost, with Maori winger George Smith scoring their only try. The crowd was reported as 4,000 in some papers, and 6,000 in others, despite torrential rain. Nepia and Brough put on a "fine exhibition", and the game was dominated by "stern defence". Leeds went on to win the cup that season, beating Warrington in the final.

Meanwhile, Parkes was still trying to establish greyhound racing at Mitcham, but Surrey County Council again denied him a licence for the stadium. John Wilson, secretary of the Rugby League, spoke at a meeting of the supporters club in March, and praised Mr Parkes' "splendid courage, enterprise and business ability", and added that "everybody who was concerned with the welfare of Rugby League owed him their full support." The meeting also discussed the number of scrums in the game, with Mr Wilson agreeing with the criticism that there were too many, adding "I welcome any suggestions to introduce the ball in any other way".

Streatham's only win in a sea of defeats was at home to Leigh, with Hunter, Walsh and Smith scoring the tries. If Nepia was missing, the team seemed unable to cover for his absence. The club was now firmly encamped in the bottom quarter of the league.

A rare away win at mid-table Halifax raised the gloom a little, and the side went on to record a 3-point victory over Swinton at Mitcham Stadium. Liverpool Stanley won at Mitcham in a match played in very strong winds. Streatham failed to score at home for the first time. The Merseyside club were to finish the season as runners up in the league table and, included players who had previously played for London Highfield,

In the second London derby against Acton, Streatham were the victors, 21-12, with Hunter, Harrison, Holder, MacDonald and Walsh the try scorers.

The attendance of 4,000 was 6,000 less than the previous encounter.

The final league game of the season was at Warrington, and the home side won 20-12 with Walsh and Langford scoring the Hams tries. This was followed by the hospital charity challenge match against Acton, with Streatham winning 33-19 at the Wandsworth greyhound stadium.

The season ended on a sad note, when Acton and Streatham's joint close season tour of France was marred by the death of three-quarter Harry Berry, who died of lockjaw following an injury in a match. Berry had played 23 games and scored eight tries for Streatham.

The playing side of the season had been disappointing, with Streatham finishing three places behind Acton in 24th place, scoring 390 points, but conceding 520. Hunter was the top try scorer with 14, Nepia kicking 29 goals and Walsh 23. Their league record was:

Played	Won	Drawn	Lost	For	Against	Points
38	12	2	24	390	520	26

COMBINED LONDON TEAM

Successful by 26 Points to 12 in France

LYONS, Sunday

The ,combined Rugby League team, composed of players from the Streatham and Mitcham and Acton and Willesden clubs, defeated the Lyons-Villeurbanne team by 26 points to 12 here to-day.

G. Nepia, the Streatham and Mitcham full back, converted four of the six tries which were scored by the London side. The tries were scored by Cutbush, Holder, Langford, Banks, Smith and Jenkins. The outstanding London players were Nepia, Langford, Harrison, Smith and Holder.

The London team dominated the play almost throughout, and at half-time led by 18 points to 4. The Londoners were untiring in their efforts, and their play often surprised the Frenchmen.

While the Frenchmen had vigorously to defend their "25" they also often attacked, but only succeeded in scoring two converted tries and a goal.

Teams:—

COMBINED LONDON TEAM.—Nepia (Streatham and Mitcham), capt.; Veysey (Acton and Willesden), Smith (Streatham and Mitcham), Cutbush (Acton and Willesden), Holder (Streatham and Mitcham); Bibby (Acton and Willesden), Jenkins (Acton and Willesden); Banks (Streatham and Mitcham), Murphy (Acton and Willesden), Morgan (Acton and Willesden), Harrison (Streatham and Mitcham), McDonald, and Langford (Streatham and Mitcham).

LYONS-VILLEURBANNE. Marty; Lambert, Aquilla, Barbazanges, Barnoud, Bamatan, Mathou; Levraf, Anclades, Plant, Petit, Griffard, Barcella.—Press Association Foreign Special.

Report from one of the matches in France

107

1936-7: Streatham's last season

At the start of the season Parkes had posted signs at Mitcham Stadium announcing that it was for sale in a bid to provoke Surrey County Council into granting a greyhound licence. Although the club had the support of the local Mitcham Council, they had failed to gain the support of the Surrey County Council. Greyhound racing was still politically contentious, and presumably Surrey was more conservative than the London County Council. The posters were a ruse, and when people asked for the price of the property they were told it was not for sale.

Despite the lack of a greyhound licence, Ivor Halstead, the general manager of the stadium had stated to the supporters club that Streatham would see the season out, though, without greyhound racing, the company stood to lose £60,000 in revenue. In a bid to raise funds to cover the financial losses, the players entered two teams in the 1935 London Baseball League. However, the experimental league did not prove popular with the London public.

The closure of neighbours Acton at the end of the 1935-6 season quite clearly indicated the precarious future of Streatham. Although there had been the nominal merger of the two clubs, and its playing strength was boosted by signing 10 of Acton's players, it was off the field activities that sunk League in London in the thirties. The *South London Press* said that "The coming season is of vital importance to the club, as it will determine its future, and will also go to prove whether the popularity of professional rugby has increased in the south."

On the playing front, the paper was more optimistic, saying that "The team is composed of players of the top class only... the best teams in the north... are in for a shock."

A trial match before the season started was preceded by a short game of "Rugby Netball", claimed to be "the fastest field game in the world." It was an odd combination of the two games, originally invented around the turn of the century because the London County Council had forbidden balls to be kicked in its parks.

Streatham's playing season started on a positive note, a win at lowly Bramley, with Nepia kicking five goals. Bramley were also the first visitors, and Streatham's first ever double was duly completed by 37-4.

However, Broughton Rangers brought the Hams down to earth by winning at Mitcham. Apparently, without McDonald and Smith in the backs, the forwards' good work was wasted. It looked like the home side were to have another up and down season. When Streatham lost to Barrow at home in the Lancashire Cup, despite the return of the missing backs, Nepia was relieved of his duties as manager. His place was taken by Harold Ashton, a former Broughton player. A six man selection committee was appointed which consisted of: Halstead, Palmer and Grant of the supporters club and three people with Rugby League management experience.

This new system brought immediate rewards with a win at Hull KR, with Nepia in the three-quarters scoring a try and kicking three goals. In an attempt to boost crowds, buses were being laid on for home games bringing supporters from the defunct Acton club.

An easy home victory followed over fellow pioneers, a struggling Newcastle side, although the first half had been a "very hard-fought affair". Wingers Holder and Veysey both scored hat tricks, and a match report said they were "again full of dash". Newcastle had taken over Acton's fixtures, and were also based at a greyhound track, but the club only lasted two seasons.

A late Halifax score in the next game meant a narrow away defeat. Nepia had scored all 12 points, taking his tally to 60 in six games, including a very cheeky try. Ordered to retake a penalty kick, which had originally been aimed for goal, he tapped the ball forward and touched down. He also hit the posts with three kicks in this match.

A narrow home defeat to Warrington, who would finish as runners up in the league, followed. The *South London Press* reported that Warrington's second try was scored "following a long punt to Streatham's line, and a melee resulted. Suddenly the referee piped up and adjudged a try to have been scored." The report stressed that Streatham were "definitely unlucky" to be beaten by one of the League's top sides.

The team then embarked on a seven match unbeaten run which saw them climb the table. During this period, they scored 277 points in 14 games, a remarkable feat of scoring in the less adventurous, less expansive playing approach of those days. In October, Eddie Holder and Arthur Veysey were joint top try scorers in the Rugby League, with Eric Harris of Leeds. At the beginning of November, New Zealander Jack Cutbush signed, who had played for Acton the previous year. There were discussions taking place about a Southern League being formed, and Streatham's A team played for the first time, against the amateur Harlesden All Blacks.

In the home match with Rochdale, popular singer Gracie Fields kicked-off. She was a great fan of the Rochdale team, as she came from the town, and was pictured in the *South London Press* in Rochdale's kit, including rugby boots. Even with her support for Rochdale, Streatham still won.

However, despite this success, the beginning of the end was the selling of Maori Charlie Smith to Halifax for £1,250, a record for the Yorkshire club. This was very close to the record transfer fee at the time. It was a sign that Streatham had to sell - apparently - to survive. The local paper commented that "his departure is sad, for he is an extraordinarily attractive player, but the club is not doing well financially, and something had to be done."

A narrow defeat at Barrow followed, but still the team had scored 60 more points than any other club, and they were joint second in the league, behind Salford who would end the season as league leaders.

The *South London Press* said that "Streatham are playing grand football, and it seems a scandal that they should only draw a meagre 3,000 to home matches, when the kind of rugby they play would pull in seven times that... in the North of England."

Swinton now won at Mitcham Stadium, and another blow was struck when Ike Jones and George Banks were sold to Wigan. Home and away defeats against Liverpool Stanley showed how form had suffered. These matches were played on Christmas Day and Boxing Day, so it was a miserable festive season for the club.

But the real body blow was delivered when Nepia was sold to Halifax for only £300, followed by Con Murphy and Dai Jenkins leaving to join Leeds at the end of December. Nepia's first match for Halifax attracted a crowd of 17,000 in foul weather, and he played 13 games for Halifax before returning to New Zealand at the end of the season. The *South London Press* commented that the team "had done better, and... have served up the brightest rugby football in the league, and in the most comfortable surroundings. South Londoners, however, refused to look at the game, and so, gracefully and barely noticed, it is dying."

The inevitable news came the next week: Ivor Halstead announced that the club would withdraw from the Rugby League for 1937-8, because of poor support, but they hoped to play instead in the proposed Southern League, which was then being formulated, either as an amateur or professional side. In fact, a Southern League did not get off the ground at this time.

It was remarkable that the players continued to play with verve under these circumstances, and the team lost only narrowly at Leigh and Oldham. At a supporters club meeting on 13 January 1937, the chairman of the supporters club, Mr Palmer, claimed the failure of Streatham was due to gross mismanagement. Players had not been paid, and the supporters club had paid the wages of the trainer and reserve player for away games. Apparently, many of the players had also been employed by Mr Parkes, and had been sacked in November, after having their pay reduced.

It was also said that Holder and MacDonald had been told to go on the transfer list, but had refused to comply. Interestingly, when considering later developments in professional Rugby League's chequered history in London, Mr Palmer said that "Mr Parkes has a perfect right to transfer these men provided they are agreeable to go. But he has no right to force them in the way he has. These men are free agents. They are not slaves." He also raised the question of the supporters taking over running the club, believing that the losses of £300 a week were greatly exaggerated.

Streatham then notched up their first victory of 1937, against bottom of the table Featherstone. But immediately after the match, Barnes was sold to Swinton, and Holder to Wigan. The *South London Press* headed their report "Streatham relics beat Rovers", and said that "The attendance was very scanty, and was, perhaps, the smallest seen at the stadium this season." The next game saw defeat at high-flying Salford, but the player drain did not stop, as Langford was sold to Huddersfield and Hunter to Dewsbury.

The leak of players now became a flood. After a 33 point defeat at Wigan, Harrison joined Wigan, Cutbush went to Rochdale and Veysey and Morgan to Dewsbury. The visit of Leigh was quite poignant. Not only was the 13-11 victory Streatham's last but it was to be the last club league match in the capital for 43 years. The try scorers were I. Williams, C. Williams and James with James kicking two goals. The Streatham side was:
Pritchard, C. Williams, Roberts, I. Jones, Avery, I. Williams, James, E. M. Jones, Crabtree, Sutcliffe, Hitchen, Baverstock and McDonald.

The *South London Press* was now speculating whether east London football club Clapton (now Leyton) Orient would move to the Mitcham Stadium, following the "flop" of Rugby League.

A 39-0 defeat at Bradford in the Challenge Cup followed, and Streatham's last game was at Swinton on 20 February. Despite losing 35-5, the best try was scored by Streatham's winger C. Williams, who went the length of the field to score. The side that sad day was:
Pritchard, C. Williams, James, McDonald, Roberts, I. Williams, Egan,

Sutcliffe, Crabtree, Thompson, Hitchen, Baverstock and I. Jones.

The club then formerly announced that they could not fulfil the rest of their fixtures and withdrew from the league. Despite this, they finished 23rd, one place better than the previous season. They had scored 366 points and conceded 339. The league record was: *

Played	Won	Drawn	Lost	For	Against	Points
26	14	0	12	366	339	28

The failure to establish greyhound racing had sunk the club. The management clearly needed the dogs to make the Mitcham project succeed, because, although gates had dropped in the second season, they were still estimated at between 4,000 and 5,000. The constant changes of manager cannot have helped the players achieve consistency, and it was significant that only three players appeared in both the first and last Streatham fixtures: Crabtree, Egan and Ike Jones.

So, despite crowds of over 20,000 and Streatham's first season average of 11,000, League did not survive in 1930s London, although the gates were higher than for many clubs in the north. If the marriage of greyhounds and Rugby League had worked, League would have been established in London long before Fulham started in 1980.

Greyhound racing never was staged at Mitcham. But Rugby League was played again for one season, when the Mitcham amateur club played there in 1949-50. Until its demolition in 1956, the stadium was only filled when the Gaelic games were staged there.

* The final league table shows 24 defeats, as the 12 matches not played by Streatham were recorded as wins for their opponents. Had their form over matches played continued over the whole season, they would have finished with 41 points, in 13th place. However, many games were lost after the playing squad was being broken up, so even that estimate is not a fair reflection of their actual playing strength.

8 Interlude: 1938 to 1979

The next appearance of professional club Rugby League in London came in 1955, in the Independent Television Trophy. Independent Television had been recently launched, and was looking for ways to win audiences from the BBC. Part of this was using sport, and therefore Associated Rediffusion launched the Independent Television Trophy. It was only staged once

Eight clubs took part, with matches on midweek evenings, under floodlight at London football grounds. They were only on television in the south. Why they were played in London, when there must have been grounds available with floodlights nearer to the teams involved, is a mystery. Each club received £400 for taking part.

The tournament took place in October and November. Four first round games were played, with the two winners by the highest margin going into the final. The results were:

Huddersfield	33	Wigan	11
Leigh	46	Hunslet	20
Oldham	8	Featherstone R	7
Warrington	33	Wakefield T	9

So the final was between Leigh and Warrington, which was played on Wednesday 16 November at Queens Park Rangers football ground, ironically very close to the previous homes of Acton and London Highfield.

Leigh had played their first round match four weeks before, but Warrington had only played two days before this encounter.

Warrington had a full strength team, but Leigh were missing seven first team regulars. Leigh were soon 15-2 down, but recovered so that Warrington were only winning 15-10 at half-time. But Warrington dominated the second half, winning 43-15. The crowd was 3,500.

The scorers were :

Warrington: Tries: Bevan (2), Bath (2), W.McFarlane (2), Fraser, Naughton, Helme. Goals: Bath (8).

Leigh: Tries: Holden, Wilson, Dickens. Goals: Ledgard (3).

(A fuller account of this tournament, and the final, is given in *Leigh Rugby League Club: A Comprehensive Record*, by Michael Latham.)

In 1965, a Festival of Sport was held at the Crystal Palace National Sports Centre. On Thursday 12 August, a Seven-a-side Rugby League tournament was held. Wigan beat Workington 14-13 in the final. Six days later, a Commonwealth XIII played New Zealand. Although the attendance was very small, one benefit to come out of this game was the revival of amateur Rugby League in London. League enthusiasts attending the game set up the Southern Amateur League that became the basis for the relaunching of the amateur game in the south.

However, it is probably worth recording that neither of these events seems to have been linked to any particular promotion strategy.

Part 3: The second try

Fulham 1980-1991

London Crusaders 1991-1994

London Broncos 1994-1995

By Dave Farrar and Peter Lush

9   A chance to dream: Fulham 1980-81

Somerset Maughan once said that facts are poor story tellers, and if one looked at the trophy cabinet, or the league tables, they would show very little. However, this would be to miss the point entirely. This season was to be the start of a strange odyssey, which to date has travelled 15 years through the pages of Rugby League history.

It was always the intention of the Fulham Football Club Board which launched Rugby League at the Craven Cottage football ground in 1980, that it should be a money making venture, a similar view to that of the greyhound moguls of the 1930s. As Ernie Clay, the chairman said: "We want to make some brass." In November 1979 Malcolm MacDonald, the former Newcastle United and Arsenal footballer, and England international, had become Fulham FC's commercial manager. He was trying to raise more money for the club, and discussed with Ernie Clay the need to make more use of the Craven Cottage ground.

They considered staging pop concerts and boxing, before Ernie Clay suggested Rugby League. MacDonald says he investigated this, discovered the matches that had once been played at White City, (by London Highfield), and talked to Rugby League officials. He says that the introduction of Rugby League was the most important fund raising initiative in his time as commercial manager.

In May 1979, after attending the Challenge Cup Final in London, Harold Genders had realised there was potential for a Rugby League club in London. He investigated possible sites, and approached Fulham in the spring of 1980. He was still a Warrington director at this time, so had to approach Fulham and then the Rugby League very discreetly. He does not feel that Fulham had done any investigation into the possibility of launching a club, and at the initial meeting he had with them, were dubious about whether it was possible.

Now, after 15 -sometimes uncertain- years of professional Rugby League in London, and other initiatives to establish new teams, it is important to appreciate what an exciting and unexpected venture this was. For the underachieving Thames riverside football outfit the move was entirely speculative.

Not only did it take the Rugby League world by surprise, it also captured the imagination of the London sporting public, and the followers of Fulham FC. However, League had been played at Craven Cottage before, England having lost to Australia 11-6 many years ago in October 1911.

In football, Fulham are the eccentrics among the London teams. Craven Cottage itself is a unique ground, set in a beautiful location at the side of the Thames, with the old cottage, after which the ground is named, in the corner, as a viewing place for the privileged. The club has never been really successful, constantly fighting against relegation from the First Division (now the Premiership) in the 1960s. But it had entertained its supporters over the years, with former great players such as Johnny Haynes, Tosh Chamberlain, George Cohen, Rodney Marsh, George Best and Bobby Moore in the latter days of his career. Comedian Tommy Trinder was chairman for a long time. In 1968 Fulham sacked Bobby Robson from his first job as a team manager. Robson, of course, was later to manage England, and 14 years later, with his son, was part of a consortium that put in a bid for the London Crusaders.

At the time Rugby League was first mooted, the football club were in the third (now second) division. Malcolm MacDonald soon took over as team manager and started to build a team that won promotion to the Second Division, and which nearly won promotion to the First Division in 1982-3. Sadly for the club's supporters, that team broke up, with many of the young players being sold off, and, at the time of writing, the club is in the third division (formerly the fourth), for the first time.

The Rugby League setup was somewhat *ad hoc*, with the announcement of the rebirth of the sport in London coming on 27 June 1980, and the first game being scheduled for only 11 weeks later on Sunday 14 September. After discussions with Rugby League officials at the beginning of June, the new Club were accepted into the Rugby League on 27 June. There had already been some press coverage, which was generally very sceptical about whether Fulham could recruit a team for the new season.

Harold Genders was responsible at board level for team affairs. He had resigned as a Warrington director when Fulham were accepted into the league. He recruited the players. After the initial signing of forward Roy Lester, then the signing of scrum-half and coach Reg Bowden from Widnes, there was a gradual growth of the playing squad as that remarkable summer went by.

John Risman, the sixth player to sign, remembers that with every addition to the squad, the drinks round increased after training, with a final round of more than 15. The quality of the squad was, in some measure, down to the persuasiveness of Harold Genders, and the prospect of fat pay packets. Some of the players were coming towards the end of their careers, and the move offered a new challenge. The success of Fulham in the 1980-81 season has been described as the last triumph of the great Widnes team of the 1970s, and there certainly was a strong Widnes element in the squad.

There was considerable speculation about who would be signed by the new club. One journalist named a possible Fulham team, and out of thirteen players, the only three correct ones were players who had already joined. Some of the new recruits were near the end of their careers, and were free transfers, or relatively cheap. But at that time, the record transfer fee was only £40,000, so buying Reg Bowden for £25,000, and two other players for £20,000 each were high quality buys.

No one quite believed the fairy tale of Rugby League in London, and the surreal nature of the project intrigued not just the RFL, London and the national press but was also attracting international interest from as far away as Hong Kong.

The signing of Reg Bowden as player coach and scrum-half was a crucial one. He had forged a famous career at Widnes, winning medals for his exploits captaining the Cheshire club in the Lancashire Cup, BBC Floodlit Trophy, Championship and four Wembley Challenge Cup Final appearances, ending with a Premiership success against Bradford. Having won all the honours available, Bowden joined Fulham in an attempt to pioneer the game in the capital. However, had he stayed at Widnes, he would have been challenged for his place by an up and coming youngster called Andy Gregory.

Within weeks of the announcement, Bowden had brought a coterie of Widnes players with him. Among the signings were half-back David Eckersley, centre Mal Aspey, forwards David Allen, David Hull and utility man Tony Kinsey. Other recruits were hooker Tony Karalius, Roy Lester, the giant prop Ian Van Bellen, forwards Tony Gourley and John Wood, and backs Derek Noonan, John Risman and Iain MacCorquodale. From the Rugby Union ranks came winger Adrian Cambriani, an 18-year-old Welsh junior international.

There were some minor problems in relation to the pitch requirements. A whole section of the perimeter track and the terracing had to be taken up to enlarge the in-goal areas. The problem of erecting the goal posts was not so simple. Deeper holes were drilled for the posts but attempts to erect them via aluminium scaffolding were practically life threatening, as Malcolm

MacDonald recalls in his *Autobiography* (as told to Jason Tomas) "It got hairy when we were trying to put the third and last section of the post in. Just imagine it... I'm standing astride Fred at the top of this scaffolding, lifting the post in the air so he can manoeuvre it into the hole, and every time we move, the whole bloody scaffolding moves too." Before Fulham faced claims for an unusual industrial injury, they devised a scheme using a metal knuckle joint, so the posts could be erected by turning a handle. A similar device was used when Fulham later moved to Chiswick. The goal posts were a gem, with a miniature Craven Cottage on of top of each one.

In the background, the newly constructed Fulham Rugby League board was an amalgam of Fulham FC and League enthusiasts. It was chaired by Ernie Clay and the board consisted of Gregory Clay (Ernie's son), Harold Genders, Brian Dalton (Fulham FC financial director), Malcolm MacDonald, and Colin Welland (actor, playwright, scriptwriter and League supporter). George Noyce was club secretary of both the football and rugby clubs.

The team for the inaugural game on that historic Sunday in September had never played together, even in a trial match. However, the training had been intense, as Roy Lester commented later: "we had never trained so hard in our lives". But the Widnes connection, and the experience in the team that

The programme from
the first game

120

consisted of mainly seasoned campaigners, as well as fascinating characters, held them in good stead. Fulham had no idea what response they would get, but the game certainly stirred the public's imagination, with 9,552 turning up for this Second Division encounter, far higher than Fulham's football crowds at the time.

The crowd was boosted by the imaginative distribution of free tickets to all Fulham FC season ticket holders. Some would later become stalwarts of the Rugby League club, in preference to watching the football team.

It helped that the opponents, Wigan, who had just been relegated into the lower division, but were still a draw to the London sporting public. Not that the Wigan ranks that day were to be sniffed at. Any team with George Fairbairn, Green Vigo, John Pendlebury and Dennis Boyd deserved respect. To help the locals the rules were explained in the programme and a commentary was broadcast on a warm-up game by Keith Macklin, the well-known Rugby League commentator. There was also a large northern element in the crowd, including a sizeable Wigan contingent. With a full press box and TV coverage from BBC's famous *Match of the Day* soccer programme, never can a Second Division fixture have attracted such media interest.

Soon the crowd were roaring to the first score, a penalty from Fulham's Iain MacCorquodale. Playing with bravado and egged on by an increasingly committed Craven Cottage crowd, the black-shirted home team swept to a convincing 24-5 result, with the only Wigan try coming in the later stages. The crowd really took to Fulham prop Ian Van Bellen, the 6 foot 3 inch, 18-stone, Bobby Charlton hairstyle, forward, with his pot belly and his amazing ability to run straight into his opponents.

To mark this famous victory, the players did an impromptu lap of honour, almost as if they didn't believe what was happening any more than the fans or assembled journalists. Such was the enthusiasm that Bowden later remarked that the Craven Cottage crowd even cheered knock-ons. The merit of this victory became apparent at the end of the season as Wigan were promoted as runners-up.

One player who immediately got attention was 18 year old Adrian Cambriani. He was named as *The Observer's* "Sports Personality of the Week" after the victory over Wigan. The national press were swept up by the passion of the first game, as *The Sun* said: "a right old knees-up and under" and that Fulham's "norf and sarf stretched from 'earhole to 'earhole."

121

The local press gave the match star billing, with the *Fulham Chronicle* headlining its two page photo-spread "When the Kissing Stopped" (presumably a reference to soccer), and said "It was a novelty, it was different. It was an experience - and on last Sunday's showing it was certainly entertaining." Ernie Clay's comment was significant: "We're doing this to save Fulham, and it's a marvellous day."

The inaugural Fulham team:

1. John Risman:
Son of famous international League player Gus Risman, signed on a free transfer from Workington. Welsh international. His brother Bev later managed the club.

2. Adrian Cambriani:
Former Welsh youth Rugby Union international. For many years the youngest player ever to play for Fulham.

3. Mal Aspey:
Vastly experienced centre signed from Widnes, his only previous club. Played over 500 games and scored 200 tries for Widnes, including three Wembley final appearances.

4. Derek Noonan:
International centre, formerly with Warrington. Signed from St. Helens.

5. Iain MacCorquodale:
Goal-kicker, formerly with Salford and Workington. Broke the record for the number of points scored by a Workington player in a season in 1977-8, with 306.

6. David Eckersley:
International back, formerly with Leigh, St. Helens and Widnes.

7. Reg Bowden:
Signed from Widnes for £25,000, his only club. Played in 16 cup finals, including four Wembley appearances.

8. Ian Van Bellen:
18 stone prop, formerly with Huddersfield, Castleford and a Premiership winner with Bradford Northern.

9. Tony Karalius:
International hooker. Formerly with Wigan, St. Helens and Widnes. From a famous Rugby League family.

10. Roy Lester:	16-stone prop. Was in the Leigh squad at Wembley (as non playing substitute) with David Eckersley. Joined Fulham from Warrington on a free transfer.
11. Tony Gourley:	16 stones. Signed from Salford for £13,000. Had also played for Rochdale Hornets.
12. David Allen:	Former Union player, signed from Widnes for £2,000.
13. David Hull:	Formerly with St. Helens. Signed from Widnes for £16,000. Had played for both clubs at Wembley
14. John Wood:	17-stone forward. Formerly with Widnes, signed from Wigan for £18,000.
15. Neil Tuffs:	Back signed from Featherstone for £6,000.

The birth of the club was greeted at first with incredulity in the media, but later the capital-based papers were supportive if a little patronising. Some were cynical. After the good start and good gates what, they asked, would be the crowd for the match against Batley in midwinter? The answer a rousing 6,000, which was close to the average for the season, as one Fulham fan pointed out in the newspaper's letters page.

In their first away game, Fulham came unstuck at lowly Keighley, losing 13-24 after being ahead at half-time. Harry Beverley and Tony Kinsey made their debuts against a side which included Tony "cockney rebel" Banham, one of the few southerners then playing professional Rugby League. A bumper crowd of 3,000 saw the defeat and it proved to be a taste of things to come as lowly northern teams raised their match for a game against the "soft southerners from London."

This game also saw the debut of Fulham's famous "fifty stone front-row" consisting of Harry Beverley, who had been signed from Workington for £18,000, Tony Karalius and Ian Van Bellen. Only a handful of Fulham fans made the trip.

Two new players signed, full-back Chris Ganley from Warrington for £10,000, and Welsh Rugby Union forward Peter Souto.

One problem the club faced was being challenged over playing on Sundays. This was before professional soccer was played regularly on a Sunday, although the Sunday Cricket League for first-class counties had been established for over 10 years. Although Sunday matches in the north were accepted without question, in London it was something new. Fulham were

The first points:
Iain MacCorquodale
kicks a penalty
(Photo: Ken Coton)

The first try - Adrian Cambriani scores in the corner (Photo: Ken Coton)

The lap of honour after beating Wigan (Photo: Ken Coton)

The match ball - with Fulham players' signatures
(Courtesy Ron Snares, photo: Peter Lush)

always careful to comply with the law, giving "membership", or admitting fans by a single sheet "programme", which just happened to be on sale at the turnstiles. Club secretary George Noyce wrote in frustration: "our problems associated with the Sunday Law continue with members of the Lord's Day Observance Society...in attendance at today's match doing their best to disrupt the smooth running of our match day affairs." A local residents association had also tried to stop the club playing on Sundays.

The next seven matches were won, including a crucial victory against York, who were to finish the season as Second Division champions. Reg Bowden won the Second Division Coach of the Month award for October, and the team won the Team of the Month award.

Then came a real test: a John Player Trophy game against First Division Leeds in November. Leeds were to finish 10th that season, but were still powerful opponents. The crowd of 12,583 was the second highest in the John Player Trophy that season, and only 237 less than that for the final.

Programme from
the Fulham v Leeds match

This was the club's first giant-killing act, as Fulham won 9-3. Two penalties from Iain MacCorquodale and two drop goals from David Eckersley gave the Londoners a 6-0 half time lead. Leeds then replied with a try from Graham Eccles, before an Eckersley try five minutes from time clinched the match. The *Fulham Chronicle*'s headline said that "Battling Fulham ARE TREMENDOUS", and commented that "It is not surprising that this game is winning more and more supporters in the capital." The Leeds squad included

Gary Hetherington, later to launch another of the sport's new clubs at Sheffield.

However the winning run came unstuck, and the team lost in the league at Wigan, and also at mid-table First Division Leigh in the second round of the John Player Trophy by eight points. After easy wins against Hunslet and Batley at home, two defeats, at Whitehaven, and against Rochdale kept supporters nerves on edge. The latter match was the season's only league defeat at home, Rochdale being the only club to travel down the night before the game.

The programme for the this game included a letter from Mrs B.L.(Barbara) Close, saying how as Fulham (football) supporters, they had attended the first game more out of loyalty than real interest, but now "we are totally committed and enthusiastic and thoroughly enjoying every game." In less than four years, she was to become the first female chairman of a Rugby League club, when she and husband Roy took over the club in 1984.

Adrian Cambriani was the club's first player to win international honours when he was picked for Wales against France. After Christmas, the win at Bramley was notable for Iain MacCorquodale scoring the 2,000th point of his career. At Whitehaven forward Martin Herdman made his debut. This was particularly significant, as he was the first player signed from amateur Rugby League in London, joining Fulham from Peckham.

A further league setback at Swinton was not the best preparation for the biggest game yet, a Challenge Cup tie against mighty Wakefield Trinity, who were second in division one at the time. They brought more than 6,000 supporters to Fulham in a record gate of 15,013. David Hull scored a late try, and Fulham lost 5-9. However, Fulham were pressing near the end of the match, and the local paper speculated that "if the game had been played over 90 minutes instead of 80, the outcome might well have been very different."

Fulham now had games in hand, but had slipped out of the promotion frame in fifth place. Four wins followed, before defeat at promotion rivals York. A further slip at Batley delayed promotion, but victory at Rochdale by 19-5 ensured a promotion place in the club's first season, with four teams going up.

Promotion was celebrated in the final league game against Doncaster, when Fulham scored a record 37 points to finish third in the league. The game saw a "precise" towering kick knock the 'L' off the Fulham sign on the Eric Miller stand. The journalist Huw Richards recalls Fulham fan Dave Ballheimer observing: "possibly the first time, but certainly not the last, that somebody kicked L out of Fulham." But the season still had a sting in it...

Harold Genders arranged a challenge match on cup final eve with Bradford Northern. The game was built up in the press, as Bradford had just won the First Division championship. Supposedly, a Bradford Northern director made disparaging remarks about the club, and for the press, Fulham rose to the bait. This match really put the hat on the season. The game, played for a sizeable bounty, was on the eve of the Wembley Challenge Cup Final and attracted a crowd of 11,926.

The Fulham players, sufficiently motivated by the promise of a continental holiday following the game won easily, with forward David Allen scoring four tries in a 20-8 triumph.

The *Fulham Chronicle* said that "Fulham's emphatic demolition of champions Bradford Northern more than confirmed their First Division credentials for next season", and confirmed the seriousness of the match, saying that "Fulham were stoked up to rampage to an incredible victory... (there was) nothing friendly about uncompromising Bradford." Dave Allen's fourth try on the final hooter provided "an incredible climax to an incredible season."

The statistics for the season were impressive, despite the low-scoring games. The average home attendance was 7,059 (6,096 for the league) with a total of 112,937 passing through the Craven Cottage turnstiles. Only Humberside giants Hull and Hull KR, and Bradford Northern had a better average league attendance than Fulham. In the Second Division, the closest was Wigan, with an average of 4693.

Top try scorer was Mal Aspey with 16 and top goal scorer was Iain MacCorquodale, with 78 (including 3 drop-goals) for a total of 171 points. In *Open Rugby's* awards, Fulham were the "Team of the Year" and that Reg Bowden was the best scrum-half in Britain. Bowden also won the Coach of the Year award. On the surface, all seemed well, and the club could look forward to its first season in the top flight. The final league record for the season was:

Played	Won	Drawn	Lost	For	Against	Points
28	20	0	8	447	237	40

Looking at the attendances, it seemed that the Football Directors' wish to "make some brass" was coming true. Before the season, Fulham had said

128

Fulham RLFC 1980-1 (Photo: Ken Coton)
Back row: G. Noyce, T. Kinsey, D. Hull, T. Gourley, I. Van Bellen, J. Wood, D.
Allen, R.Lester, D.Eckersley. Front row: M.MacDonald, M.Aspey, R. Bowden, E.
Clay, T. Karalius, H. Genders, D.Noonan, A.Cambriani, C. Welland

Fulham v Bradford Northern - challenge match at Craven Cottage
(Photo: Ken Coton)

that the break even level was 3,000. This had easily been passed. However, Chairman Ernie Clay's Christmas message in the Batley programme makes interesting reading. He referred to the introduction of Rugby League as "a bold and imaginative step to secure the long term survival of this marvellous football club." He analysed the costs of running Craven Cottage, and said that "the money we take from Rugby League is a substantial boost to our income, but a relatively small increase in expenditure." His attitude to Rugby League is to see it as an adjunct of the football team, bringing in additional funds.

The accounts for 1980-81 show a loss of £307,446. However, £192,100 had been spent on transfer fees and signing-on fees, and the players' registrations were a tangible asset to the club. The income was £202,692, mainly from match receipts, while of the £510,138 expenditure, apart from transfer and signing on fees, the next biggest item was wages and salaries at £151,200. The accounts also showed £175,714 due to Fulham Football Club, repayment of an advance, presumably used to pay for the transfer and signing on fees. It is also not clear from the accounts how the administrative staff salaries were split between the rugby and football clubs. Certainly, some rugby supporters believed that the rugby team were subsidising the football club at this time.

Some players were clearly coming to the end of their careers, and younger replacements would be needed. The size of the playing squad was thin, with a couple of amateurs being drafted in during injury crises. There was also clearly no intention to base the playing squad in London in the near future.

There had also been very little done about development, although some responsibility for this must rest with the Rugby League. Schools matches were staged before the matches at Craven Cottage, and the programme had adverts for the amateur game in London. Future All Black and London League star John Gallagher was playing schoolboy Rugby Union at this time in London, and Wigan and Great Britain record-breaker Martin Offiah was living in east London, and developing his rugby skills at boarding school in Suffolk. Who knows what other gems a youth scheme could have found if any systematic development work had been done.

10   Up and Down: Fulham 1982-1984

1981-82: The challenge of the First Division

The start of the 1981-2 season saw a limited turnover in personnel, as Fulham faced the huge task of life in Division One. Out went Iain MacCorquodale, prop Ian Van Bellen and John Risman, who all joined Blackpool. Man-of-the-season for 1980-1, and former captain, Tony Karalius, planned to retire, but changed his mind and joined newcomers Cardiff.

On the plus side, new recruits included back Steve Diamond, the third top points scorer in Rugby League in 1980-81, from Wakefield for £8,500 John Crossley, a stand-off from York, who had just broken the Second Division's try scoring record with 34, and hooker John Dalgreen from Warrington, an under-24 international, who was bought for £15,000.

In September, they were joined by Shaun Hoare, a young second-rower from Rochdale, who was signed for £32,000, a very high fee considering his inexperience. Apparently Fulham had the choice of Hoare or winger Henderson Gill, who later starred for Wigan and Great Britain, but plumped for the forward, who had played a storming game when Rochdale had won at the Cottage in the previous season.

However, despite the signings, the club still operated on one squad of players, with no reserve team. Player coach Reg Bowden had said the previous season that "Should we get promotion, a reserve squad playing regular competitive rugby will be essential to maintain our position in the top flight." These words were borne out during this injury plagued season.

Two pre-season friendlies saw defeats at Widnes and at home to Carlisle, the latter being the very first game for the Cumbrians. A 32-15 Lancashire Cup victory over Second Division Swinton lightened the gloom. However, a pattern started to develop, as injuries led to a 35-4 crash at St. Helens. The injury crisis was so bad that centre Mal Aspey played in the second-row.

Apart from the casualty list, the first blows were transfer requests from John Wood and Derek Hull just before the Warrington game. They were immediately dropped, and a weakened team took the field. However, Warrington were conclusively beaten 28-9, Fulham's first top-flight victory.

The *Fulham Chronicle*'s report was headlined "Fulham surpass even themselves" and said that "Fulham's amazing victory had to be seen to be believed." After trailing early on by seven points, Fulham struck back with tries from Martin Herdman and Adrian Cambriani. Then: "Demoralised Warrington completely disintegrated under Fulham's relentless pressure." Roy Lester, playing against his old club, had his best match for Fulham. After being kicked in the head, he scored a try under the posts. He was so tired after the match he could not take his boots off. However, the match report noted that "The only disappointment was the depressingly small crowd of 5,057."

Derek Noonan had also asked for a transfer, and when major injuries to Harry Beverley and Tony Gourley were taken into account, the squad took on a threadbare appearance. A home defeat by Featherstone, who were to finish close to the relegation places, was followed by a first away victory in Division One at Barrow.

A new face at both these games was a Moroccan under the unassuming names of Smith and A. N. Other. He was still a Rugby Union player, and had not yet got a work permit. The mystery man was Hussein M'Barki, a Union player from the Cahors club in France, who had been born in Rabat, Morocco. When he arrived at Heathrow with a one way ticket, a passport and rugby kit, stating he was here to play professional Rugby League in London, it took him three hours to convince immigration control that he was not a terrorist or illegal immigrant. He received a reported £25,000 for turning professional, and became the first Moroccan player in British Rugby League.

A home win followed against struggling York. Injuries continued to dog the team. On top of this, the fixture list and the weather also combined to provide a run of no home games for four weeks, although later in the season there were home games on five consecutive Sundays.

A narrow defeat at home to Widnes was followed by a further setback at Warrington in the John Player Trophy in a televised match. However, one of the season's best results followed at Leeds where a 12-12 draw was achieved in the last minute, which saw Fulham comfortably mid-table with nine points from the same number of games.

With Joe Doherty, Martin Herdman, and Peter Souto playing well, and the return of John Wood who had settled his dispute with the club, in November, it looked like the team had turned the corner. However, home defeats by Wigan and Castleford, who were both in the lower half of the table, and at Warrington proved this not to be the case. A single point win against Wakefield at home was the only cheery light in a cold January, and this was followed by defeats at Widnes and Castleford.

But the club still had celebrity status, and it was not only Colin Welland who represented Fulham in the world of show business. On television in the north of England at this time there was an advert for grill steaks, showing two Rugby League forwards clashing in the mud, whilst discussing what was for tea after the match. The two players were Tony Gourley and Roy Lester, apparently chosen for the parts as they had fewer teeth than the other players in the commercial. All the players featured were from Fulham.

On the playing front, the biggest blow was an injury to Reg Bowden, and the team lost five of the six games from which he was absent, the exception being Second Division Hunslet at home in the Challenge Cup. Transfer requests from new signings John Crossley and Dalgreen hit the club hard, and although the departure of centre Mal Aspey to Wigan for £10,000 was considered "good business" given his age, he would have been an asset in the injury crisis that was to follow. In February, Harold Genders said that the club wanted Crossley and Dalgreen to stay, adding "heaven knows our resources are stretched at the moment."

The limited playing staff also made it more difficult to rest players who had lost form. At the end of February, a frustrated Reg Bowden wrote in the programme that "in many ways we were our own worst enemies...a lack of professionalism on our part cost us silly points...We have not yet mastered the art of not making mistakes."

The big game of the season was in the Challenge Cup at home against Hull. The two previous fixtures had been with Hull's Humberside neighbours Hull KR, both of which were lost. Unfortunately the cup game was lost 5-11, with a try from John Crossley and a goal from Steve Diamond being Fulham's only scores. The crowd, however, was the largest home gate of the season at 9,481. The dismal state of the squad was highlighted by Harold Genders' comment that Hull had more players on the transfer list than Fulham had fit to play in the game.

This slump was arrested with a home victory against Whitehaven, but the club was now firmly in the relegation dogfight. The losing run included a game against champions Bradford Northern. The Yorkshire team played a young hopeful named in the programme as Ellery Manley; it is unlikely that his name would be spelled incorrectly today.

One bright note was Colin Welland becoming the first director of a Rugby League Club to win an Oscar. This was for the "Best Screenplay" award for the film "*Chariots of Fire.*"

The strain clearly showed, despite the enduring efforts by the players on the park. Such was the player shortage that things came to a head when Fulham were fined £1,000, later reduced to £250 on appeal, for failing to raise a team away at Bradford, and having to postpone the match. For the away game at Featherstone, Fulham could not even name a forward substitute, and to add to the problems, Reg Bowden was sent off for the first time in his career. In this week at the end of March, out of 24 registered players, including an amateur and a player on loan, the club had 14 on the injury list.

The fixture backlog also took its toll, with the season ending with five home games crammed into a month, including wins, perversely, against champions elect Leigh and Hull, who finished second. The Leigh match was very tense, with even the ball boys being told off by the referee for wasting time, when Fulham were ahead by one point and only minutes to go.

Still, the team only just failed to beat the drop, losing the last two games narrowly to Leeds at home and at Bradford, taking the last relegation place behind Castleford, who finished only two points higher. Poor away form was a major contribution to Fulham being relegated, with only three wins and the draw at Leeds. The final league playing record showed:

Played	Won	Drawn	Lost	For	Against	Points
30	9	1	20	401	694	19

Overall, it was the small squad that proved the team's undoing coupled with the fact that, unlike the established clubs, there was no reserve team to call on in case of injury. Fulham were one of only six Rugby League clubs not to run a reserve team and, despite the lack of playing resources, Harold Genders argued at the end of the season that "it would not be financially viable. If we were forced to run an A team you could forget about Rugby League in London." But relegation to the Second Division was also a further blow to the long term development of Rugby League at Fulham.

All the problems might have been overcome, but for the disputes with transfer requesting players, and the horrendous fixture and injury situations. The club had also faced what London's listing magazine *Time Out* described as "the worst winter since Captain Scott's visit to the Antarctic."

The supporters also missed some of the heroes of the first season, although, in playing terms, releasing characters such as Tony Karalius and Ian

Colin Welland, with his Oscar, and the Fulham team (Photo: Ken Coton)

Relegated Fulham beating Champions elect Leigh. (Photo: Ken Coton)

Van Bellen made sense for the First Division campaign. We remember talking to a couple of pensioners at one match, who said that "it hadn't been the same since the Dutchman left." Somewhat mystified, we then realised they meant Ian Van Bellen.

Despite the visits of the more glamorous First Division clubs, it seemed that the London public wanted to see a winning team. John Crossley topped the try scorers with 15 and Steve Diamond kicked 92 goals scoring 203 points in total.

Net gate receipts fell from £187,837 in 1980-81 to £151,522. Although the wages and salaries bill was reduced, and other income increased, the season showed a loss of £155,017. Despite this, and maybe to restore confidence, Harold Genders had written in the club programme in February: "...there have been several rumours about the future of Rugby League at Craven Cottage. Let me say that as far as I am concerned the sport has a bright future here. Each week we are making money and very few clubs can match that either in Rugby League or soccer. So relegation or not we intend to be here next season."

The club clearly needed a new impetus. There had also been no visible progress on the development front, beyond publicising amateur and schools Rugby League in London in the club programme. The last programme of the season reported on plans to start a Rugby League team at Charlton FC in south-east London, but this did not materialise. A couple of months later, the Charlton club changed hands, and was to become enmeshed in a complicated battle over the future of their ground as a sports venue, similar in many ways to the one that was to develop at Craven Cottage in the mid 1980s.

1982-3: Second Division

Welcome news in the summer was forward John Wood being selected for England XIII versus France in a promotional match in Venice, an unlikely place for a Rugby League match.

The new season opened quietly with Fulham as 5/2 favourites to bounce back into the top ranks. The first game saw the previous season's bottom club Doncaster demolished 30-10 before a crowd of 2,715. A good run commenced with wins at Bramley and Hunslet both in the league, and at home against Swinton in the Lancashire Cup. A win at Rochdale was followed by another of those perennial giant-killing feats, with a second round Lancashire

Cup triumph at First Division Wigan by a magnificent 15-4. Wigan, fourth in the First Division at the time, were restricted to just two penalty goals. Tries from Bowden and Gourley gave Fulham a 12-4 half time lead, and a Crossley try in the second half sealed the victory. The report in the club programme said that this was a better victory than the famous win in the opening match at Craven Cottage.

More success continued in the league, seeing off title rivals Wakefield before 3,855 at home and then overwhelming a previously unbeaten Salford. Fulham's unbeaten run had stretched to eight when the club met Warrington in a Lancashire Cup semi-final at Wigan. Fulham had won their appeal to have the game played at a neutral venue as Warrington's lights were out of action. The game could not be played at the weekend due to league fixtures. Unfortunately, basic mistakes gave Warrington a 10-0 lead and, despite a fight back, Fulham went down 17-8. The team's displays were recognised when they won the Second Division "Team of the Month" award for September.

In the league, the winning run continued until a drop in form saw a home defeat by Blackpool Borough, the visitors racing into a 15-0 lead, and despite a try from debut winger, Londoner Frank Feighan, on trial from London amateur side Peckham, the club lost its unbeaten league record, going down 15-8. By early November, Fulham were second in the league, two points behind Salford with a game in hand.

A welcome development was the announcement of a coaching course to be held in London in December, with Colin Welland writing in the club programme that "It is ... pretty essential that if Rugby League is not to remain merely an appendage to London life, that we sprinkle the schools, youth clubs and other organisations with qualified Rugby League coaches."

The big event of the year was a visit from the touring Australians, who attracted 10,432 fans despite a torrential downpour. The team acquitted itself well with Moroccan star Hussein M'Barki notching one of only nine tries scored against the all conquering tourists during the whole tour. The score was 22-5 to the Australians, whose team included Wally Lewis and John Ribot, who was later to become involved in Rugby League in London as a director of the Brisbane Broncos's London takeover.

The *Fulham Chronicle* reported that Fulham "showed tremendous commitment and bridged the difference in class magnificently until running out of steam in the second half."

What the game showed was that the London public would turn up if the rugby was of sufficient quality. Unfortunately, for the next home game against Rochdale only 2,714 turned out, making this dilemma most apparent. Fulham narrowly squeaked home 14-13, with new winger Steve Bayliss on loan from St Helens, scoring a debut try.

Further recognition of Fulham's progress came when hooker John Dalgreen became the first Fulham player to be selected for Great Britain, when he appeared against the Australians in the second test.

In the John Player Trophy the club were drawn away to mighty St Helens. This caused a mild furore, as John Dalgreen was sensationally dropped from the test team, it was believed to allow him to play in this match. The St Helens match was to be covered by BBC's *Grandstand* programme, with the test match being played on the Sunday of the same weekend. Had Dalgreen been selected, which his performance in the second test undoubtedly justified, the St Helens match would have been postponed, causing problems for the TV coverage.

Unfortunately, the team with several injuries went down bravely by 5-17. The next game saw Fulham chalk up a record score with a 50-5 victory at lowly Huyton.

This was the start of a long winning run in the league, with six successive victories, despite serious injuries to Chris Ganley, Adrian Cambriani and winger Carl Radbone. Steve Bayliss had been signed from St. Helens, with the transfer being funded by Roy and Barbara Close, and had notched up nine tries in eight games. A home win over promotion seeking rivals Salford in the first week of February confirmed the club's position at the top of the Second Division. In Rugby League overall, Steve Diamond was top of the goal-kicking list with 93 goals and John Crossley second in the try chart with 20.

The biggest cup game of the season at Craven Cottage was the second round Challenge cup tie with struggling giants Bradford Northern, who were in the bottom four of the First Division at the time. Fulham had fond memories of the challenge match with Northern at the end of the first season but, with coach Bowden on the substitutes bench, went down 11-4 with a try apiece before 4,977 people.

A 25-25 draw at home to Hunslet seemed to be a hangover from the cup letdown, but the team did not falter with wins at promotion rivals Whitehaven and Wakefield, two of the best results of the season. Fulham now led the league by three points with a game in hand, and it seemed that the

The programme for Fulham v Australia (Photo: Peter Lush)

John Crossley (6) and Martin Herdman(11) pursue Don McKinnon
Fulham v Australia November 1982 (Photo: Open Rugby)

bookies had it right after all. The Whitehaven game saw Charlie Jones and Steve Mills making their debuts, both backs who had arrived from Widnes. Initially signed on loan, part of the money for their permanent transfers was provided by the Closes. The strengthening of the squad through these new recruits, both of whom were to become long-serving players for the club, was offset by the surprise announcement of retirement by John Dalgreen. Joe Doherty took over the hooking role.

Further victories, against Keighley at home, and at Batley, confirmed the championship title. However, trouble with the Craven Cottage pitch, and the prior claims of the football team forced two of a backlog of home games to be played at Widnes - Swinton and Huddersfield were easily beaten.

While the problems with the Craven Cottage pitch were genuine, and the Rugby League was refusing to extend the end of the season, the switching of the two games out of London did a lot of damage to the club's relationship with its supporters. Some drew the conclusion that Fulham RLFC were now seen as "second class citizens" compared to the football team. The final games of the season were somewhat of an anticlimax, a home win against York and the final game against Cardiff, which was played at Chelsea Football Club's Stamford Bridge ground, on Challenge Cup Final eve. Although Fulham were presented with the championship trophy at the start of the game, the game did not enhance the reputation of Rugby League. The Welshmen ended the team's unbeaten home league record in front of a 3,321 crowd, apparently only a quarter of that expected by Fulham officials.

The game became known as "the battle of Stamford Bridge." Former boxer Martin Herdman was sent off early in the second-half for punching a Cardiff player and, five minutes from the end, following a mass brawl involving both sets of forwards, Tony Gourley and Cardiff's Chris Seldon were also given their marching orders. Two tries from Hussein M'Barki could not stop Fulham losing 14-20.

On the pitch, the season had been a great success, with only four league defeats, which meant that the Second Division title was won by three points from Wakefield Trinity. Unfortunately, the gates again had dropped this time to an average of 2,688, a fall of 1,633. On the good news front Steve Diamond finished with 136 goals to top the charts and stand-off John Crossley scored 27 tries.

The main strength of the team was its defence, only conceding 52 tries in 32 games which was the second best record in the league. The team also

140

beat its own points record by finishing with 699 points from 124 goals and 149 tries.

The final league playing record was:

Played	Won	Drawn	Lost	For	Against	Points
32	27	1	4	699	294	55

Although Steve Bayliss had been an excellent signing, and some of the younger players had gained more experience, the squad did not look strong enough to tackle a First Division campaign. In those days of four teams being promoted and relegated, the gap between First and Second Division was substantial, and some quality players were needed if Fulham wanted to avoid the drop again. On the financial side, net gate receipts had fallen from £151,522 in 1981-2 to £126,073. The loss for the season was £121,247.

1983-4: Back to Division One

Some important changes were introduced to the Rugby League rules at the start of the season. A try became worth four points, and if a team was tackled in possession on the sixth tackle, the opposition would play the ball rather than form a scrum.

There was no new influx of players for the second attempt to secure a more permanent place in the upper flight. Centre Trevor Stockley joined from Salford, but this was in exchange for John Wood, who was a major loss. John Dalgreen had come out of retirement. With the drop in attendances and warnings in the programme from club officials of the less than healthy financial situation, it was a more chastened Fulham who re-entered the upper echelons. Harold Genders warned that "Fulham may cease to exist this time next year unless there is a rise in the number of people coming through the gate", and said that attendances of 5,000 were necessary for the club to break even.

It is clear, in retrospect, that a new injection of capital was needed if Fulham were to prosper in the First Division, both to strengthen the squad, and to market the club more effectively. But the football team at Craven Cottage had been promoted, and were now in the Second Division, and the question of the future of the ground was starting to become a major issue, with the proposed property deals on the horizon. The Closes had been negotiating for over a year to become majority shareholders in the Rugby Club, which would have given it the impetus it needed, and additional capital. But these negotiations did not succeed, and the club struggled on without extra resources.

An early defeat at fellow promotion club Wakefield was a warning of the team's problems to come. A further defeat at mid-table Leigh did not automatically spell disaster, and it seemed that with the first home win against Featherstone, before a crowd of only 2,401, First Division safety could be achieved. In the Lancashire Cup, the team lost narrowly at Salford, despite still leading three minutes from the end. We attended this game, at times cheering for different teams, with Dave's Salford origins at that time overcoming his new support for Fulham! He's 100% for the Broncos now.

After a comfortable home win against Whitehaven, it looked like another roller-coaster season was on the cards. Former Widnes forward Alan Dearden was signed, after recovering from a knee injury that had forced him to retire two years earlier. Fulham went down at Oldham in the first ever fixture with the Roughyeds, and then, amazingly, beat the reigning champions Hull 29-24 at home before 3,838. The backs really cashed in with tries from Allen(2), M'Barki, Bayliss and Crossley, against a side packed with internationals such as James Leulei, Dane O'Hara, and David Topliss.

Unfortunately, October it was announced that Harold Genders, one of the club's founding fathers had left, with the club merely saying that his departure was "for his own reasons." This was a major loss, as he had consisderable Rugby League expertise.

This was the start of a bad period. Fulham suffered their heaviest home defeat against Leeds, 10-44, the only bright news being David Eckersley's return after injury. Reg Bowden described this as "the worst game we have ever played since the formation of the club... It was as though we'd all forgotten the basics of rugby." A week earlier, he had described the performance at Warrington as playing "like a bunch of idiots." But the small squad gave little scope for changes, and there was clearly no money available for acquiring new players.

An experimental Saturday home match brought a win against Wakefield, but a record low crowd of 1,570. Three away games produced defeats at Bradford, Hull KR, when John Dalgreen was sent off, and a two-point John Player Trophy defeat at Featherstone, with Tony Kinsey scoring four drop goals, a new club "record."

Dalgreen was banned "*sine die*" after this sending off. This was later reduced on appeal to a three month ban after Fulham provided a lawyer to put forward his case.

A home win against Oldham, followed by a home draw against Castleford appeared to show that the ship was steadying, but Fulham seemed incapable of pulling away from the relegation zone following a home defeat by Bradford, and a heavy defeat at Leeds. However, Hussein M'Barki was clearly in his element in the top flight, with 11 tries from the first half of the season. The programme for the Bradford game had a full page feature on the Southern Amateur Rugby League, some welcome publicity from Fulham for the amateur game.

A fine win at Salford, who were to be relegated, gave the club hope and marked the debut of Fulham's first of many Australians , Bob Jackson, a forward from Penrith. As was the way with this yo-yo season, a home defeat by 20 points followed against leaders Hull KR , the club having three wingers injured at the time. A further heavy home defeat by St. Helens meant that relegation was now threatening, though it was not yet a certainty. The crowd dipped again below 2,000. St. Helens were in a mid-table position, and Fulham desperately needed to win this match, making a 30-0 home defeat in the rain and cold even more depressing.

A preliminary round Challenge Cup tie against Second Division Swinton brought relief with a 16-4 home win. By now, Chris Ganley had gone on loan to St. Helens, in exchange for Saints' John Butler. However, defeat at Castleford meant that Fulham were now in the bottom three.

A win at struggling Whitehaven in the Challenge Cup first round, and a meritorious home win against Wigan with Steve Diamond scoring 12 points meant that safety looked possible. However, John Dalgreen announced his retirement -again- and was put on the transfer list.

A narrow home loss in the Challenge Cup, by cup kings Widnes, seemed to sum up the season, a missed conversion being the only difference between the teams.

After that, the wheels really began to fall off. Defeats at Whitehaven, who were to finish bottom of the table, and mid-table Wigan dropped the club into the mire. The squad situation was shown with Bowden drafting in two amateurs, Mark Hodson and Jimmy Ward from Widnes St. Maries, for the Whitehaven game. And the injury problems were further illustrated by playing five different hookers during the season, at a time when hooker was a far more

143

specialist position than it is now. Loan signing Ray Tabern was number five, having joined from First Division Leigh, Londoner Martin Herdman moving on loan in the opposite direction.

Nonetheless, the best result of the season was achieved at Widnes with a 16-14 win. M'Barki scored a try after a 75 yard run, with Stockley and Allen adding the others. This was described by Fulham's fans as the best ever away performance. With salvation only a dim hope, the team lost at home to already relegated Salford, and were booed off the pitch. The gates were now down to the 1,500 mark. A 32-58 home defeat to Warrington confirmed relegation. This was Fulham's record defeat and at the time, a record score for a Division One losing side. The team managed to win its last home game in the division against Widnes, thus doing the double over the Merseyside club. However, the crowd, at 1,146, was an all-time low. If the final four home games had been won, relegation could have been averted as the club finished with 19 points (the same as the first season in the top flight), five points behind Featherstone.

Reg Bowden recognised the problems, writing in the programme for the Warrington match that "Some of the lads have just not come up to standard, or aren't showing enough interest in playing for Fulham, and we are going to have to wave them goodbye." The season was clearly ending on an unhappy note. Phil Shaw's report of the Warrington game in *The Guardian* outlined that Fulham were "beset by rumours of closure, or a wholesale transplant to Runcorn, Mansfield and all points north." Reg Bowden denied this, saying "I've heard the rumours, but there will be no problem. I've had talks with the Board and Rugby League is staying at Fulham." Harold Genders had never been replaced, and only Colin Welland was now a board member from a Rugby League background. Brief hopes of a First Division future were knocked back when the Rugby League confirmed that four teams would be relegated. Fulham had hoped that the admission of new clubs Sheffield and Mansfield could mean that only two clubs would go down.

Hussein M'Barki finished as the season's top try scorer, with 17. Steve Diamond kicked 77 goals. The team's final league record was:

Played	Won	Drawn	Lost	For	Against	Points
30	9	1	20	401	694	19.

But worse was to come when in July, the fans' worst fears were confirmed. Fulham announced they were withdrawing from the League.

11   Out of Craven Cottage and into Court

In June Fulham had sent out a letter to season ticket holders about arrangements for the next season. However, the club then suffered a major blow with Reg Bowden's decision to leave and become coach at Warrington. Immediately following Bowden's departure, seventeen of the club's twenty-five players asked for a transfer. On top of this, David Eckersley had retired and emigrated to Australia.

It cannot have been much of a surprise to anyone when the Fulham Directors pulled the plug on the Rugby League Club, and on 18 July 1984 announced their intention to put the Rugby League Club into liquidation. The club had, after all, been set up to "make some brass" as Ernie Clay put it With gates down from the heady 6,000 average to 1,500, the writing was on the wall for all to see. As well as the financial situation, there was also the problem that the northern-based players were more and more reluctant to make the 400-mile round trip every fortnight for Second Division walkovers or First Division hidings. The lack of any reserve strength was another reason for the club's downfall, as its limited playing strength meant it was practically playing with one hand tied behind its back compared with the northern outfits.

Until the second season the club was reasonably secure financially, but the fact that no major signings were made for the final season spoke volumes about the financial position. Indeed, the board had obtained financial support from Roy and Barbara Close to fund the transfers of Steve Bayliss, Charlie Jones and Steve Mills.

It seemed that some members of the Fulham FC Board were more concerned with getting a good price for Craven Cottage for building development than with saving Fulham RLFC. Indeed, some people believed that the Rugby League club was seen as a potential obstruction to the property development plans.

Fulham's resignation statement said that they had "decided to allocate a sum of money for four years to test the market. That money was spent perhaps unwisely without achieving the success or financial viability we hoped for. We were not able to recruit sufficient local talent to identify with the locality and the players we had were not willing to travel and be away for two days each home match without their wives. When our director responsible for forming and running the team (Harold Genders) left we bit the bullet for a while but unfortunately could not arrest the slide."

However, Phil Shaw, writing in *The Guardian*, said that "Fulham's failure to put down roots in the South.... is an indictment of the board's lack of vision and resilience." The *Fulham Chronicle* reported that "Dark rumours about Fulham's future existence were rife in the dressing room for most of the season and the inevitable end came with relegation from the First Division and the shock departure of player coach Reg Bowden to Warrington... The decision to play two home games at Widnes' Naughton Park in April 1983 was seen by many as obvious proof that Rugby League had become the poor relation of soccer at Craven Cottage."

There were soon reports in the press that Maidenhead-based businessman Roy Close was attempting to buy the club, and there were indications that the team could continue to play at Craven Cottage. In fact, Roy and Barbara Close had been engaged in negotiations with the Fulham RLFC directors since 1982 over taking control of the rugby club, although these talks had been finished by the Fulham Directors, without agreement being reached, in February of 1984.

On 22 July, the Closes met the players, and outlined their plans if they could take-over the club. Many of the players accepted their proposals, but Steve Diamond and John Crossley said that they believed they should be free agents if the old company was wound up, and this influenced some players.

The decision to put the Rugby League club into liquidation, so it ceased trading immediately, rather than administration, which would have meant it could have been sold as a going concern was a very important one for any future Rugby League under the Fulham name. Roy Close had raised this point at the liquidation meeting on 1 August, but had been told to "mind his own business", and a liquidator was appointed.

The Closes then proceeded to buy the assets of the club from the liquidator, which were mainly the club name, "associated goodwill", the registration with the Rugby League, some kit, goalposts and training equipment and, so the letter from the liquidator outlined, the players' registrations.

The Closes were already aware of a possible legal problem regarding the players' registrations automatically being transferred to their new company, Fulham RLFC (1984). They went ahead with the purchase on the basis of the registrations being offered for sale by the liquidator, who was selling the assets of the old company.

Roy Lester was appointed as Manager and, by 17 August had arranged to play at the Crystal Palace National Sports Centre, assurances of being able to continue to play at Craven Cottage having been withdrawn.

The players had been offered new terms and conditions, as was normal for a club that had just been relegated. The quality of the players on the books at the time, meant that, had they stayed with Fulham in the Second Division, they undoubtedly would have had a successful season, and probably earned more from the game than in the losing team in the last season at Craven Cottage. The Closes also made it clear that any players who wanted a transfer, at an appropriate fee, would be allowed to leave. Income from the transfer fees would then have allowed them to sign quality players committed to playing for the Club. They had also made it clear to the players that they believed they could not be given new signing-on fees, even though a new company now owned their registrations, as this was not allowed under the Rugby League's rules.

However, the cause of the players who wished to leave was backed by the Rugby League Professional Players Association, who saw the case as "our struggle to establish freedom of contract." Despite this, the Rugby League had written to all the players involved, and to all the Rugby League clubs, saying that as far as they were concerned, the players registrations did transfer to the new club.

So the Closes were faced with a situation of trying to establish the Club at a new ground, cope with all the tasks of setting up an administrative apparatus, while having a number of key players staying away from training. Some players had offered to play on weekly contracts, but the club rejected this, as it could have allowed them to leave and join another club at any time.

At the beginning of October, the Rugby League received a letter from a solicitor claiming to represent several of the players, and challenging the club's right to hold the players' registrations. The Rugby League replied, saying that Fulham had been a member of the League for several years, had never ceased to be a member, and had submitted its retain and transfer list of players on 15 June 1984. Soon afterwards, Roy Close received a letter from a different solicitor, acting for John Crossley, Steve Diamond and Martin Herdman, raising the issues of whether the players' registrations lapsed when the "old" Fulham club went into liquidation, and whether the Rugby League's rules regarding the retain and transfer system were a "restraint of trade."

On 18 October, a High Court writ was issued by Crossley, Diamond and Herdman against two members of the Rugby League Council, Reg Parker and Jack Seddon, (who were being sued on behalf of themselves and all other members of the Council of the Rugby Football League), Roy Close, and Fulham RLFC (1984) Ltd. Although only three players were taking legal action, it was clearly a test case which could affect the position of all the players from the 1983-4 squad.

The case was clearly crucial for the future of professional Rugby League in London, but also challenged the whole "retain and transfer" system of players' registrations and contracts, and therefore had wider implications for the sport overall.

In football, the "retain and transfer" system had already been subject to legal challenge by the players, with the George Eastham court case in the early 1960s winning more freedom for the players and then, in 1977 and 1978, when the Football League finally accepted that "The Clubs accept totally the

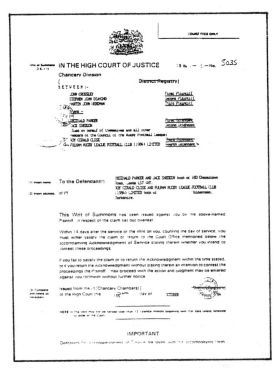

The writ that started the court case

148

player's right to move freely at the end of a contract and with every possible safeguard to ensure that right." The key point was that when a player's contract was over and the club wanted to retain him, or receive a transfer fee for his registration, the club must offer him the opportunity of another contract on at least as favourable terms as before. If the contract offered was less favourable, the player was automatically entitled to a free transfer. Rugby League players had not yet established these rights, and the Football League regulations were raised by the players in evidence in the court case.

The case was heard in the High Court, evidence having been submitted by the three players, the defendants and David Oxley, the general secretary of the Rugby League. The "note of judgement" of Judge Peter Gibson's decision is nine pages long. The judgement was made on the issue of the players' registrations, as this was the most urgent matter, although the Judge also commented on the retain and transfer system.

After examining the arguments of both sides, he decided that Fulham Rugby League Football Club ceased to exist as a member of the Rugby Football League and of the Rugby League when the company Fulham Rugby League Football Club Ltd ceased to carry on the undertaking (i.e. went out of business) on or after 16 August 1984, and that the respective registrations of the players with the club thereupon lapsed.

The effect of this judgement was potentially devastating. Not only had the players who had been registered with the old club been declared "free agents", but the club's membership of the Rugby League was in doubt, as Fulham RLFC (1984) had not gone through the procedures for a new club to join the League. In fact, the Rugby League avoided throwing the Second Division into chaos, and accepted the "new" club as taking over the fixtures and membership of the "old" one, and Fulham continued to participate in the League.

In the close season in 1987, the Rugby League changed its retain and transfer system for players, and came into line with that used by the Football League. Players were no longer tied to a club indefinitely, but arranged contracts to cover a specific period. If a player moved to a new club, and a transfer fee could not be agreed, an independent tribunal would fix the price.

Note on Liquidation and Administration

When a company goes into liquidation, it ceases trading immediately. The company's assets become the property of the liquidator, who has a duty in law to get the best possible price for the assets, and therefore maximise the payments to outstanding creditors.

Liquidation of a company may be initiated by the shareholders, directors, its creditors, or by a court order if the company is insolvent.

In certain circumstances, the best price sale price can be obtained if the business is still functioning, and then the company is put into administration. The administrator continues to run the company, and owns the assets. The administrator will try to sell the business as a going concern.

If this is successful, having sold the business as a going concern, the company is then liquidated. The business and assets have been transferred to the new company.

12   Off to the Palace - are they still playing?

1984-5: Second Division

Despite the turmoil, Fulham were still the bookmakers' second favourites at 3/1 to win the Second Division; one case of them being out of touch with reality. It was not even clear who was going to be playing for the club. Roy Lester was negotiating to borrow players or recruit amateur trialists to ensure a team could be put out for the opening fixtures.

The Crystal Palace National Sports Centre, in the south London suburbs, was obtained as a new home. It was somewhat remote from Fulham, but was a 16,000 all-seated stadium, with facilities on a par with the Cottage. The electric scoreboard was the largest in the League at the time. The stadium had one major disadvantage after Craven Cottage - it lacked atmosphere, and the home support struggled to create the spirit of Craven Cottage.

The Closes were the directors of Fulham RLFC (1984). With Roy taking the position of managing director, Barbara became the first female chairman of a Rugby League club. This was to bring the Club some publicity, including the chairman of Swinton being interviewed for Radio 4's *Women's Hour* about her appointment. Interviewed in *The Guardian*, she said that the players had got used to her, adding "I don't know whether they're stunned or just too polite, but they've been very nice", and assured writer Phil Shaw that "It's not a cosmetic thing. Roy's got the business expertise but I chair meetings of our management team and do a lot of administration. I even threatened to fire him a couple of weeks back...."

A feature in the *Daily Express* described her as a "petite 45 year-old mother of three", and quoted husband Roy: "She'll make a first-class chairman... I've seen her in action with the Conservative ladies. She is no gimmick." While the article cheekily suggested that Barbara could bring her dressmaking skills to use in repairing the players' kit, the interview showed she had a good understanding of, and feeling for Rugby League, and a clear commitment to the game and Fulham. Eighteen months later, a women's magazine had a three-page interview with her, an unusual area for Rugby League to get publicity.

The Closes formed a new management committee, which included Ron Snares, the chairman of the supporters club, to represent the supporters' views.

The rest of the management committee was based around people who had been involved in the supporters club, or had professional expertise to offer.

Barbara Close outlined the club's aims in the first home programme. In an article headed "Dawn of a new era", she said that they were aiming for a team playing fast, attractive rugby, and, in the longer term, a club with all the players living in the south. They were also aiming to build close links with the Southern Amateur Rugby League.

The team made a good start with a win at new league club Sheffield Eagles. The first team of the new era was:

Mills*, A.N. Other, Jones*, Parkes, Driver, Wilkinson, Green, Hoare*, Doherty*, Gourley*, Dearden*, Garside, Garner. (* Craven Cottage squad).

Crystal Palace was not available until 6 October, so Fulham's Lancashire Cup match with Swinton was switched to Station Road. Fulham lost, and went down in the next two away games, after being in contention at half-time in both.

The main problem was that, with only a third of the old squad participating, the club was awash with trialists and players on loan. However, Roy Lester could spot potential, making a valuable signing in Chris Wilkinson from the Boars Head pub team in the seventh division of the North West Counties League. David Driver, joined on loan from Salford, and scored six tries in seven games. Experienced scrum-half Ken Green was another important signing. The programme for the first match still optimistically featured all the players in the "free agents" dispute as Fulham players.

The first game at the Palace was on a Saturday, against Carlisle, as near neighbours Crystal Palace Football Club were playing at home on the Sunday. Despite a 14-7 first half lead, Fulham slumped to a 47-18 defeat. The consequences of the summer's traumas were there for all to see. The published attendance was, however, reasonably healthy at 2,300, though it was believed that this figure was inflated, and anyway, the fans were lost in the cavernous ground. The difficulties of travelling to Crystal Palace on public transport, the loss of many of the well-known players, and uncertainty over the club's future had all had their effect.

The club was now in the lower echelons of the Second Division and looked set for a struggle. The next home game against Huddersfield saw a much needed win, 26-8. Glen Townsend made his debut, the first New Zealander to play for the club. The player situation also began to pick up. David Eckersley, now in Australia, helped the club to sign forward Don Duffy

Chris Wilkinson's registration form - one of the best players to be signed in this period

from Paramatta, half-back Michael Davis from Penrith and Paul Rochford from Brisbane Souths.

A defeat at table-topping Whitehaven followed, with two Fulham players sent off. And shortly afterwards four-point home defeat by Blackpool saw the Stockley brothers, John and Trevor, playing on opposing sides and both scoring a try. The matches showed the disjointed nature of the squad, and the need for the new Australians to blend in. Fortunes rose slightly with a home win against well-placed York, Paul Rochford scoring a club record 18 points, his best ever game for the club despite only arriving in Britain the day before.

The "free agents" dispute was still hanging over the club, with press reports that Warrington were claiming to have signed Hussein M'Barki, and Reg Bowden, now of course Warrington's coach, saying "We consider that M'Barki is a free agent with no contractual obligations to Fulham."

The club got a plum draw in the John Player Trophy, at home to First Division giants Hull. What a game it was. Fulham rocked the Humbersiders and went 14-0 up. A freak try, scored when the half-time hooter had gone, got Hull back into the match. In the second-half, they took command, winning 36-14. One of the features of the game was the performance of Michael Davis

153

against Hull's Australian international scrum-half Peter Sterling. Davis had been Sterling's understudy at the Australian club, Paramatta.

The same weekend, Steve Diamond and Hussein M'Barki made their debuts for Reg Bowden's Warrington side, having now won the court case. Bowden commented that "Justice has been done, but I don't want Fulham to fold, and won't be making a move for any more of their players." However, an angry Roy Lester said that the players may be legally right, "but morally they are wrong. They have been superbly treated by Fulham and the fans in the past [and] have now deserted us for other clubs." He said that Bowden was being hypocritical, and had sucked "the lifeblood out of the club." However, this spurred the team on, with wins against Wakefield and Bramley.

By now, the club had signed second-rower Harold Henney from Salford, a Cumbria County player, who had been on loan. He became a key figure for the next eighteen months. Other new signings included a winger from Northern Queensland, George Bryan, and two New Zealanders, prop Ivan Kete, who had been released by Leigh, and Maori back Takura Tawera. This was part of the policy to use Australasians to strengthen the team, and increase the number of London-based players.

At the beginning of December, another four players who had been part of the Craven Cottage set up left, taking advantage of the "free agents" ruling. However, two of these, Tony Kinsey and Shaun Hoare soon rejoined, as later did Martin Herdman and Adrian Cambriani. Roy Lester commented : "We've got rid of people who don't want to play for us and now we've got a squad made up of people who want to play rugby for Fulham." Huw Richards wrote that the main loss was Joe Doherty, who "had played superbly this season." A home defeat by high flying Salford was followed by a southern "derby" triumph at strugglers Southend Invicta by two points. Southend were coached by Bill Goodwin, later to play a major role at Fulham as coach and team manager. New signing from the Widnes Rugby Union club, Frank Matthews, had a double disaster on his professional debut - he fractured his collarbone, and arriving back in Widnes, found that his car had been stolen. The two matches against Southend are the only league games against other teams from the south east that Fulham ever played, never having met Kent Invicta.

Press coverage of the "free agents" dispute continued , with Londoner Martin Herdman claiming in the *Rugby Leaguer* that he and other players involved in the dispute had been "frozen out" of the game, as they had not yet found new clubs. This was denied by Rugby League chairman Reg Parker. One

Roy Lester: player, manager - fondly remembered by Fulham fans
(Photo: Peter Lush)

of the players mentioned, John Crossley, had just signed for Bradford Northern. Steve Diamond was released by Warrington.

The antipodean base of the side, which was to become a feature of professional Rugby League in London, continued to grow with Duncan Webster being the latest Australian recruit. Forward Steve Garner joined from Keighley, and "free agent" Shaun Hoare made his peace with the club and returned. A win at Huddersfield at the beginning of February meant that the team had won half its league games, quite an achievement considering the turmoil of the previous six months.

A home draw against First Division Halifax in the Challenge Cup was a test for Roy Lester's team. Despite heavy snow, with local trains cancelled, the fans and the referee cleared the pitch. A radio appeal had got the supporters' help. Despite a heroic effort, Fulham lost 14-17. It was so cold that Australian George Bryan got frostbite, made worse when he rang home to Mackay in tropical Queensland, and was told that it was 102 degrees.

A poor defeat at mid-table Blackpool, with "tackling machine" Don Duffy breaking his arm, was followed by a home win against bottom club Bridgend. Tony Gourley was injured in the Bridgend game, and missed the rest of the season, the neck and head injury he received leading to his retirement from professional Rugby League. At the beginning of March, Tony Kinsey returned to the Fulham set up, having failed to secure a new club in the north.

At the beginning of April, another "free agent" came home, with Adrian Cambriani magnanimously welcomed back to the club.

However, financial problems were never far away, and in March, Roy Close outlined in the club programme that "the club is still losing money all the time", and that efforts were being made to move back to west London.

Attendances continued to be low, dipping beneath the 1,000 mark. The need for a change was recognised when the club played an experimental home match against Runcorn at the Polytechnic Stadium, Chiswick. The stadium facilities were semi-derelict, and Roy Lester brought his welding skills to the assistance of the club, repairing the tannoy system, as supporters helped prepare the pitch and set up the posts. The attendance was only 650, but this was higher than the last two matches at Crystal Palace. Fulham won by one point. Chiswick was nearer the original west London base of the club, and, despite the low crowd the atmosphere was better. The attendance was not helped by a downpour, and a football cup final at Wembley the same afternoon. Despite the variety of home venues, Fulham began to climb the table. In the return against Southend, a further victory was marred by three sendings off: Shaun Hoare, and Southend's giant ex-Australian test prop John Donnelly, and Frank Feighan, the latter soon to be in Fulham's colours. At this match, filming was done for a BBC TV series, "Hold the Back Page", with Harold Henney playing a prominent role. It was shown later in the year.

Wealdstone Football Club in north west London was used for three home games, with the best attendance being 1,047 against table-topping Swinton on Challenge Cup Final eve. To prompt Fulham's supporters' dreams, Wembley was visible from the train on the journey to Wealdstone.

Four further victories followed, and a draw with Whitehaven, before a final defeat at home against Swinton ended an unbeaten run of six games. The club finished eighth, 10 points behind Dewsbury, who were promoted in fourth place. After the win at Southend on New Year's Day, the team had won 11 and drawn one out of 16 league games. By this time, Roy Lester had started to get a more settled side, and the players in dispute with the club had left. Had this form been shown throughout the whole season, Fulham could have been promoted. Steve Mills and Mike Davis both ended the season with 17 tries, with Chris Wilkinson kicking 60 goals. The final league record was:

Played	Won	Drawn	Lost	For	Against	Points
28	16	1	11	521	526	33

13   Chiswick 1985-1989: Rugby League's lost tribe

1985-6 Second Division

In June 1985, Fulham negotiated a move to Chiswick's Polytechnic Stadium. It was certainly an unusual site for Rugby League. Across the road was a yachting marina, and a miniature railway ran behind the grandstand.

It was also quite a comedown after Craven Cottage and Crystal Palace, and was more like a non-league football ground, or much of Rugby League's Second Division. But the club now had a stadium that was to be its home for five years. Volunteers, under the supervision of Ron Snares, supporters club chairman and management committee member, who was a builder, worked all summer to renovate the ground. This included rescuing the original posts from Craven Cottage. The group who repaired the ground were called the "Fulham Maintenance Crew", showing that the pioneering spirit of Fulham was still alive.

However, the job was not finished, and there was an appeal for building materials and more voluntary help in the first match programme. An announcement at half-time that the club needed to borrow a lorry, was met with one fan's reply that it should bring a "lorry load of players from Wigan", which was a little unkind as Fulham managed to beat Blackpool 6-2.

By starting the new season, the club had survived longer than any of the others that had been formed in the past outside Rugby League's traditional areas. There was a hint of things to come when an article in *The Guardian* reporting that the club had decided to change its name. It was somewhat premature, as the Fulham name still had six years to run.

However, the financial position was still shaky. The Closes revealed that they had lost £120,000 (or £6,000 each home game) in their first year in control - a staggering figure. It was also announced that the break-even attendance figure was 3,000, but only 1,000 turned up for the Blackpool game. It had been hoped that a competition to find a club sponsor would make a £50,000 profit, but in fact it only raised £3,000. However, the winner and new sponsor Richard Lawton was to prove a valuable asset to the club.

One new player was Australian Glen Nissen from Penrith, who achieved little at Fulham, but later starred in the finals of the Australian

Winfield Cup. Don Duffy, Mike Davis and 5ft 6in prop Andy Key all returned.

Fulham started with high hopes, after the good run of results in the second half of the previous season. An early test was an away Lancashire Cup encounter at Challenge Cup holders Wigan. A crowd of 8,943 saw the Riversiders shocked when Fulham led 13-12 well into the second half, with tries from Cambriani and Garner, but a late rally saw Wigan home 24-13.

Goal-kicking forward Alan Platt, described by Roy Lester as a player of "proven class" was signed from Oldham, but failed to prevent a defeat at Wakefield. Poor form continued as mid-table Batley won at Fulham, helped by a Carl Gibson hat-trick. Veteran Billy Platt came on loan, but was released after a couple of games. Apparently, he was keen to join Fulham, and after the club released him, he responded to his release with brilliant games against the Londoners for years to come.

However, wins followed at Bramley and at home to high-flying Whitehaven, who were unbeaten until this game. Fulham won in injury time with a suspicious looking forward pass to put Mike Davis over in the corner. The team was now mid-table.

A debate now appeared in the programme concerning the club's name. As the team was no longer based in Fulham, a change of identity was being considered to help attract new support. One suggestion was London Crusaders.

The team had failed to continue the promotion-winning form of the second half of the previous season, although their cause was hindered by facing the top five clubs in consecutive matches. One welcome initiative was the establishment of an A team, which played its first friendly against Bramley, before the league fixture, although the first team blighted the day by throwing away an 18-6 lead to lose by two points in the main match.

The club's luck with cup draws continued, with First Division Warrington coming to Chiswick in the John Player Trophy. This was Roy Lester's old club, and something of a needle match, as they were managed by former player-coach Reg Bowden. He did not improve matters by criticising the Chiswick setup, leading Roy Lester to respond "Having seen the way our fans battled through the summer to get this ground ready, I'm disgusted that he should criticise their achievement in this way."

Warrington included Andy Gregory, Paul Bishop, Kevin Tamati and Les Boyd. Despite this, Fulham led 7-6 at half-time, and an upset looked possible, but First Division class told, and Fulham lost 13-20. One Fulham supporter, seeing a flock of geese fly over during the game, shouted "Sign' em

A poster publicising the clubs' return to its west London roots

Fulham worked with a local Brownie group to help raise money for Save the Children (Photo: Barbara Close)

up Bowden, they're free agents." The bitterness of the previous autumn was not forgotten, although fortunately it did not spill onto the pitch.

The Warrington match clearly inspired the team, as three consecutive wins put Fulham into eighth place. Unfortunately for Rugby League expansion in the south, Fulham's only local rivals, Southend had folded at the start of the season. This allowed the club to sign Bob Mordell, a former England Rugby Union international, and former Fulham trialist Frank Feighan. From Wigan, winger Gary Henley-Smith was signed. Martin Herdman also returned to the club, having had trials with American football team Kansas City Chiefs. So another of the "free agents" had reappeared.

Nonetheless, two defeats followed, at home to table-topping Leigh, and at Keighley, who were to finish one place from the bottom. But the club was still keen to strengthen the squad, and the transfer fee for forward Dave Bullough was partly paid for by bucket collections at the gate. The fans raised £2,000 of the £3,000 fee. He had initially been signed on loan in November. The fund raising campaign included a "Wanted" poster, which, given Bullough's disciplinary record of three sending-offs in 17 games, was appropriate.

A sign of the future was a report on a Southern Amateur Rugby League representative match in the programme, with the SARL team including four future Fulham first team players. Also, Bev Risman had been appointed as Regional Coach for development areas, and outlined his plans to build the game in the south.

The poster that helped raise money to sign Dave Bullough

Long-term development plans for the stadium were outlined by club architect Stuart Barlow. Apart from extra paving, additional lighting for training and better toilets, the club was also looking at providing covered terracing. However, major developments rested on getting a long term lease, or purchasing the ground, which never proved to be possible.

Due to continuous bad weather, the home Challenge Cup tie against Barrow was played at Wigan's Central Park, which had undersoil heating. Fulham lost by 12 points to the eventual Division Two runners up. A home tie with First Division Castleford had been the prize for the winners. A couple of weeks before this game was finally played, Harold Henney joined Runcorn, having played a key role in Fulham's pack during his eighteen months with the club, and bearing out Roy Lester's decision to sign him.

Two home wins kept the club in eighth place. But then a bombshell was dropped by the Closes, who made public on 11 March that they could not continue funding the club, and were proposing to put it into liquidation on 1 April, unless a buyer could be found. A pessimistic Roy Close was quoted as saying that "we have to bow to the inevitable", and "I cannot see anybody rescuing the club this time." Roy Lester said that he was "devastated", but sympathised with the Closes' situation, adding "it would have been financial suicide to carry on." *The Guardian's* report was headed "Expansionists' bitter end", although the Rugby League's David Howes said they were looking for the club to be rescued. Kent Invicta had only lasted a year, before a disastrous one season transfer to Southend. Cardiff had moved to Bridgend with equally lamentable results, also closing down. This time, it really looked as though Rugby League's attempts to establish itself outside the Lancashire, Yorkshire and Cumbria areas had come to a halt. Coincidentally, discussion about a "Super League" was starting to appear in the Rugby League press. And, ironically, the day Fulham's closure was announced, Reg Bowden was sacked by Warrington.

However, the players' response was very different to the end at Craven Cottage. Meeting for training on 12 March, they offered to play at Huddersfield for nothing, while frantic efforts were made to save the club. Two players refused to play: Mike Davis, who never played for the club again and was transferred to Leigh, and on loan Trevor Worgan. However, Warrington prop Mal Yates did play. This was his only game for the club. Roy Lester welcomed the players' "magnificent gesture", adding "what a tragedy it would be if a rescue cannot be launched." Roy Close added that he was "overwhelmed" by the players' decision.

Following this marvellous gesture, the players made their way to Huddersfield by various forms of transport. Frank Feighan showed the Fulham spirit by announcing that if necessary he would walk up the motorway to play. The *Rugby Leaguer* headlined Huw Richards's front page report of the players' decision: "For the Love of Fulham."

The team had a makeshift appearance, with Duffy at full-back and Cambriani in the second-row. Some supporters wondered if Adrian Cambriani would have the unusual distinction of scoring the club's first ever try, and then its last. With 150 travelling Fulham fans almost turning it into a home game, the team went down narrowly on a glue pot pitch, 14-8. Fittingly it was Feighan who scored the first try. Such was the enthusiasm of the Fulham supporters that one crusty Huddersfield steward commented: " What the 'eck are you closing for? We could do with some of this."

It was hoped to play the next match, at home to Hunslet the following Sunday. Leaflets were given out about the game on the supporters' coach, but it could not be played, because of the financial uncertainty. The Hunslet fixture was also announced in the local paper, which said that "The Club is hoping that at least 2,000 fans will turn up - otherwise it may be Fulham's final game."

Team sponsor Richard Lawton came to the fore, issuing a letter to try to find people interested in keeping the club running. Some offers came in, but not enough to prevent closure. Fighting to the end, he commented: " While it is difficult to hold out a great deal of hope, we will not give up the attempt to save this club until we have to."

A saviour was found at the 11th hour in Paul Faires, who had previously been involved with the Kent Invicta club. Faires agreed to buy the Closes' shares for a peppercorn figure, and hoped to use his contacts to bring in new sponsors to put the club on a firm financial footing. The liquidation meeting planned for 1 April was therefore cancelled.

Former Kent Invicta and Southend coach Bill Goodwin took over as manager from Roy Lester, who for various reasons did not want to be part of the new set up. Roy left with the best wishes of all connected with Fulham. At Huddersfield, he had received a tumultuous standing ovation from the Fulham fans. After the bitter taste left by Reg Bowden's departure, he had rebuilt the playing squad, and shown great management skills in welding the team together into an effective unit. He had also established a tremendous rapport with the supporters, and as Huw Richards wrote in a moving tribute in the club

RUGBY LEAGUE IN
LONDON

FULHAM
V

HUNSLET
SUN 23 MARCH '86

KICK OFF«» 3-00p.m.

POLYTECHNIC·STADIUM·CHISWICK·W4

The programme for what many supporters believed would be the last game

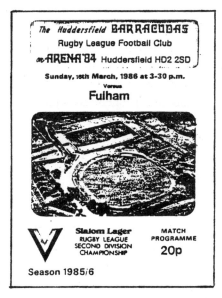

Leaflet issued for the Fulham v Hunslet match. Because of the financial crisis, the match had to be postponed.

programme: "the amount of time, miles travelled and emotional commitment he invested in the club was staggering." He was given an inscribed rose crystal bowl, as "Personality of the Year", by the supporters club at their Player of the Year award night at the end of the season. After a couple of months break, he became manager at Carlisle.

The team had not played after the Huddersfield match, so now faced a major fixture backlog. The priority was to finish the season, which concluded on 18 May in bright sunshine. Bill Goodwin used the opportunity to give some southern amateurs trials and, not surprisingly, form slumped. The best results were a win at Hunslet, and a draw at home to Huddersfield. The season finished with home wins against Hunslet, in which Gary Henley-Smith scored Fulham's only hat-trick that season, and Keighley.

Some of the innovations that Paul Faires brought in were female cheerleaders and a new nickname, "the Bears", although the club were close to parody, playing the theme tune "Teddy Bear's picnic." When a try was scored the disco truck blared out "Another One Bites The Dust." One wonders whether visitors Keighley subliminally took these ideas on for the later invention of Cougarmania. Another entertainment in one match at half-time was a fire-eater, who attempted to swallow 100 fire sticks in the interval, but had only reached 10 when play restarted.

Another idea was giving the referee a microphone, linked to the PA system, to explain decisions to the crowd. Referee Cliff Hodgson had this dubious pleasure for the game against Doncaster, which Fulham lost.

On a more serious note, Paul Faires proposed to run three junior teams for the next season, at under-13, under-16 and under-19 level. Bill Goodwin declared that he was aiming for a southern based squad, with a small number of specialist players based in the north. The team finished ninth, with Steve Mills being the top try scorer with 11. Chris Wilkinson kicked 72 goals, and Alan Platt 27. The final league record was:

Played	Won	Drawn	Lost	For	Against	Points
34	16	1	17	679	709	33

The financial position at the end of the season was a loss of £56,599, with a further £75,213 owed to creditors. The average league attendance had fallen by 132 to 817, but was still higher than ten other Second Division clubs.

The flame still flickered.

1986-7: Second Division

The season started very much as the previous season had finished - in crisis. Paul Faires's plans for sponsorship had not developed, and the financial problems were still there. Indeed, Paul Faires announced the club's withdrawal from the League with the opening of the season less than a fortnight away. The Rugby League had then awarded points to the teams Fulham were meant to play, and this brought protests from the three teams in the Second Division the club were not due to play that season, due to the strange fixture list. The club then applied for reinstatement, and was accepted back into the League.

Saviours had come forward, in the shape of 1985-6 team sponsor Richard Lawton, and match day manager Tim Lamb. These two purchased Paul Faires' shares for a nominal amount, and became the new directors. By 4 September, the Rugby League had approved the new set up, and, as the *Fulham Chronicle* headlined their report, "Resurrection for Fulham" had happened again. In the *Rugby Leaguer*, Huw Richards wrote that "Lazarus was a mere novice compared to Fulham. The Biblical character who defied contemporary medical opinion by coming back from the dead only did it once. Fulham have now done it three times."

The day-to-day running of the club was by volunteers. The Closes took a supportive role, with Barbara remaining as club chairman, and Roy representing the club on the Rugby League Council. In practice, the supporters had taken over running the club. The outstanding debts were gradually to be paid off with help from the Closes, and the club for the first time ran on a break-even basis. Launching the Friends of Fulham Fortune Society was an important initiative, which still provides funding for the development of Rugby League in London today. The Society involved members making a weekly payment, with a weekly prize draw.

The problems had taken their toll on the playing staff, and it was a makeshift team that finally appeared at promotion favourites Whitehaven in the Lancashire Cup. Fulham were bolstered by picking up two Wigan reserves on the way, made available by Maurice Lindsay, the Wigan Chairman and a great friend of London Rugby League. Also making debuts were London based amateurs Colin Fenn and Dominic Cooper. The coach to Whitehaven contained 16 players and the team was picked on the way, with the unfortunate Andrew Render missing out. Fulham briefly took the lead with a try from Wayne Millington, but unfortunately, although not surprisingly, the club registered

165

its record defeat, 72-6.

Bill Goodwin recognised the task ahead, writing "We can... start our league programme afresh and get down to the work that we really ought to have started during the summer - strengthening the squad, developing our own resources in the south, and building a strong club... it may well be a slow process, but I'm certain it can be done." Many of the previous season's squad had left, including Alan Platt to Hunslet, Tony Kinsey to Huddersfield and Don Duffy had joined Roy Lester's Carlisle. Gary Henley-Smith had returned to Australia, and Norman Barrow was playing amateur Rugby League in Lancashire.

The first home match brought a record home defeat by Sheffield, 14-68, although Frank Feighan scored a fondly remembered length of the pitch try. Despite the result, the team were cheered off the pitch, for, as long-standing supporter and committee member Sandra Barlow said: "They were an odd mix of strangers and amateurs we'd never seen before, but they were heroes just for going out and playing that day."

With skilful Australian forwards Glen Haggath and Pat O'Doherty arriving, it was only a matter of time before fortunes improved. Defeat at Mansfield was a precursor to the first win of the season, 44-12 at home to Keighley. Four further defeats followed, and Fulham were now in joint last place in the Second Division. How the mighty had fallen. The caution about the club's prospects was reflected in the programme, which promised a refund to season ticket holders "should the club be unable to complete the season."

The inspirational Bill Goodwin started to turn things round, with a home win against Dewsbury. But defeat at Bramley was no preparation for a home John Player Trophy tie with mighty First Division Castleford. On a positive note, Huw Rees, a Welsh B Rugby Union international, and Kieron Murphy were recruited. The team lists for the first eight games reflect the instability of this period, including "A. Northerner", "A. Stranger", "A. N. Other", "S. O. Else", "A Trialist" and "B Trialist." Also, 14 other players had made debuts in these matches. Some would go on to give the club valuable service, including Russ Bridge, Colin Fenn and Dave Gillan.

An unplanned but significant signing was Australian hooker Craig Taylor, another "tackling machine" who regularly topped the tackle count. Peter White, a huge Australian forward, was another Fulham recruit. Like Taylor, he just turned up and asked for a trial, and soon became team captain and a stalwart of the pack. At the end of the season, Taylor won the "Away

Player of the Year", and White became the "Players' Player of the Year", showing the impact they had made.

The Castleford game was one of titanic proportions, the visitors being both the Challenge and Yorkshire Cup holders. At half-time the score was 10-10, but Fulham finally lost 24-34 before 1,374 fans, with two tries from Mills, and one from Glen Haggath. One Castleford international player was moved to say "I don't know what you lot are doing in the bottom four, you should piss the division." Fulham had played most of the game with 12 men, after having prop Bob Knight sent off after 17 minutes. The *Paddington Mercury* reported that Fulham's "brave, sometimes skilful performance must surely have won them a whole crowd of new fans."

Before the home match with York, supporters were treated to a 15 minutes each way clash between the Fulham supporters club ladies team, and a Metropolitan Police Select. The Police included Sergeant Neil Robinson, later to become honorary club secretary, and play a key role in keeping the club alive.

Three defeats in the next five games meant that Fulham went to Whitehaven to play amateurs Kells in the Challenge Cup preliminary round with some trepidation. The game took place on a Thursday night, much to Fulham's annoyance, in front of 2,310 (the largest crowd Fulham played before that season). An early Fulham sending-off meant that the team were happy to grab a 4-4 draw, although Kells never looked like scoring a try, their points coming from two penalties. The replay was just as tense with Fulham edging home 22-14 on a Tuesday afternoon. A late switch of fixtures saw Fulham playing at Huddersfield on the Sunday after the Kells game, instead of the replay at home. Evidently there were communication problems, scrum-half Kieron Murphy and some supporters (including us) arriving at a deserted Chiswick when the team were playing a league fixture at Huddersfield.

Bill Goodwin's comments on the Kells matches outlined Fulham's problems. Contrasting the situation facing the amateurs of Kells and professionals of Fulham, he pointed out that Kells "are a very well run outfit - they have more players than we have, they have more supporters than we have, they certainly have more money than we have, so just who are the professionals here?... they are reaping the benefits of years of community caring and involvement, which we can only dream of."

The reward for beating Kells was a home match against First Division champions Halifax. At half-time the Londoners led 10-8 with tries from Rees

167

and O'Doherty. Unfortunately, and not surprisingly, Halifax exerted themselves in the second half and won 38-10 before a Chiswick record crowd of 1,562.

In the middle of February, the club said goodbye to three Australians: Haggath, O'Doherty and full-back Greg Pratt. All gave good service, although Haggath's more defensive Australian style had sometimes clashed with the more open game favoured by coach Bill Goodwin.

A marvellous home draw against second-placed Swinton included Steve Mills scoring a club record 50th try for Fulham. And plans were being made for the future, with the announcement of the formation of a colts team.

By March, the situation had stabilised. Writing in the club programme, Tim Lamb and Richard Lawton outlined how the playing strength had improved, and that "We have been able to obtain the cooperation of our major creditors and our debts are gradually being repaid, and whilst we still have a long way to go, we have every reason to believe that the critical period is behind us."

The season finished with two wins, a heroic draw with Whitehaven, and five defeats. It was an achievement to survive the season, let alone finish in 12th place. A supply of players was coming through from the rejuvenated Southern Amateur League, and the colts side played their first match before the league fixture with Mansfield. Included in the team listed in the programme were four players who would later play for the first team. Dave Bullough, whose transfer fee was raised largely from the supporters, left to join Salford, not having played for the club this season.

The financial position was also healthier. "Football and commercial operations" on the balance sheet showed a profit of £6,970, compared to a £48,510 loss the previous season. Although gate receipts had fallen, the wages and salaries bill had been cut by nearly 50%. Overall, there was a £20,262 loss for the year because of expenditure on transfer and signing on fees, and amounts due to external creditors fell to £55,388. The average league attendance had fallen to 684, a further drop of 133.

Steve Mills was the only player to get into double figures for tries scored, with 12. Colin Fenn scored 65 goals. The league record for the season was:

Played	Won	Drawn	Lost	For	Against	Points
28	8	2	18	461	632	18

1987-8: Second Division

It was reassuring that the season started without the uncertainty of the previous year. A new appointment saw Bev Risman installed as team manager. His brother John had played for the club in the first season. Risman had the distinction of being a dual international (Union and League) and had been the club's amateur liaison officer for the previous two years. Bill Goodwin remained as coach. One of the changes introduced by Bev Risman was to make Colin Fenn the first Londoner to captain Fulham.

The three mysterious trialists of the previous season were signed up from Rugby Union: Full-back and goal-kicker Steve Guyett, and forwards Nick Grimoldby and Mike Hutchinson. The club now had a squad with a southern base with a growing sprinkling of antipodeans. Australian recruits included loose-forward Paul O'Riley, and scrum-half Santi Masa. The problem for the supporters was that the rapid turnover meant that as soon as they had got to know the players, they were largely replaced by a new set.

However, the preseason optimism soon drained away, with three defeats in succession, including a heavy Lancashire Cup thumping at First Division Salford.

The changes in playing personnel were reflected in the programme for the Doncaster game, at the beginning of October. Of the team that had played against the Yorkshire side in April 1986, only Adrian Cambriani and Frank Feighan were still involved. In fact Cambriani's Fulham career only had a few weeks to run.

In September, Steve Mills had joined Carlisle, finally tiring of the travelling to London. Signed with Charlie Jones from Widnes, to strengthen the squad in 1983, he had been one of the most consistent players ever to play for Fulham. His loyalty during the "free agents" period, and other times of uncertainty was never forgotten by Fulham's supporters. He was also the first player to score fifty tries for the club.

The next match programme plotted the whereabouts of the 41 first team players of the 1986-7 season. Eleven had returned to Australia, others were playing amateur Rugby League, one decided to stick to Rugby Union, as he could earn more that way, and Martin Herdman was working as a nightclub bouncer, which, he claimed, did not allow him time for Rugby League.

Two wins and two defeats followed, before a superb win at home to promotion certainties Featherstone. Featherstone included two Great Britain

Bev Risman, Fulham's
manager from
August 1987
to October 1988
(Photo: Peter Lush)

internationals, and John Crossley, "free agent" from the Craven Cottage days.
Tries from Adrian Cambriani and Dave Gillan put Fulham ahead and, when
Masa chipped through and scored from his own kick, Fulham were 13 points
ahead. Featherstone came back strongly, but Fulham hung on to win by three
points. Unfortunately, this triumph was not to be typical of the season.

A milestone was reached at Dewsbury, when the club played its 250th
competitive game. Alas, Fulham lost 10-32, and gave a poor performance. Of
the 250 games, 117 were won, eight drawn, and 125 lost.

The confidence of the Rugby League in the new set-up came when
Fulham were rewarded with a tour match, which was the highlight of the
season, attracting the highest home attendance of 1,216. The visitors were
Papua New Guinea, who were making their first tour of Britain. Fulham
performed with credit but only had goals from Huw Rees and Colin Fenn to
show in a 4-12 defeat. The *Shepherds Bush and Hammersmith Gazette*
reported that "Fulham's showpiece game against the tourists...was better than
the final low score suggests, but it did not live up to expectations of a free-
flowing game of rugby... The Kumuls' sound defence ensured Fulham rarely
got within scoring range of the line."

Labour Party Leader Neil Kinnock attended the game. This was also
the final game for Adrian Cambriani, who had scored the club's first try back
in the distant days of 1980. He retired from professional Rugby League.
The team that day was:
Lawrie Feighan, Rees, Gillan, Cambriani, Guyett, Murphy; Hutchinson,

Taylor, Miller, Grimoldby, Manning, O'Riley with substitutes Fenn and Kelly.

The team came down to earth in the next game, an 8-36 hiding at Division Two leaders Oldham in the John Player Trophy, Dave Gillan getting the only try.

A home win against Bramley was followed by four consecutive defeats. Dark days indeed, and the club found itself second bottom of the league. On the positive side, the colts team were playing in the colts league. Although most matches against stronger and more experienced northern opponents were resulting in defeat, the initiative showed the club were serious about developing a southern base.

The depressing losing sequence was broken with a 24-0 win over Dewsbury, with tries from Rees, Grimoldby, Murphy and Paul O'Riley.

Australian loose-forward Paul O'Riley returned unexpectedly to Australia, for trials with Paramatta. The club then lost seven consecutive games, including at home to Mansfield in the Challenge Cup first round. This run was a club record. At one stage the team went 186 minutes away from home without a score and played 333 minutes without kicking a goal. Things could only improve from here.

In March, Fulham were given special dispensation to exceed the import quota for the 1988-9 season, although there was a general tightening of the rules regarding overseas players. This meant that Fulham could play more Australian players who had played less than 20 first grade games in either the Sydney or Brisbane competitions. David Howes said for the Rugby League: "This is an important step forward in helping Fulham. It is the first time this sort of ruling has been made with the specific intention of helping the club", although Huw Richards pointed out that in reality the League had previously operated a "blind eye" policy about the number of Australians appearing for the club.

An improvement began in a bottom-of-the- table clash at Batley, with a 34-6 win. The appearance of colts player Justin Herbert, at the age of 18 years and six months, meant that he was the youngest player ever to play for the club, a record previously held by Adrian Cambriani from Fulham's very first game. The return match against Batley saw a 40-16 win and the club safely off the bottom of the table, and the team augmented this with a final home win against fourth-placed Springfield 9-8 in a nail-biter, with a try and drop goal from Nick Grimoldby and two goals from Colin Fenn. Despite this late rally the club finished in its worst ever position, 17th out of 20 clubs in

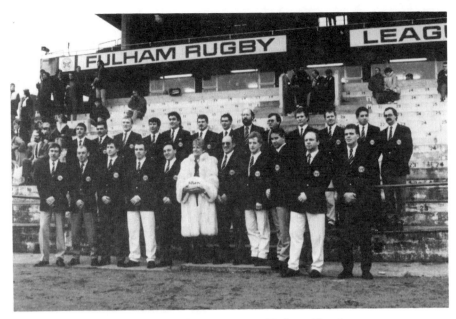

Fulham 1987-8 (Photo courtesy Barbara Close)

Fulham v Featherstone: New tackles old. Nick Grimoldby about to ground former
Fulham player and "free agent" John Crossley (Photo: Open Rugby)

Fulham v Papua New Guinea: Kieron Murphy being tackled (Photo: Open Rugby)

```
13.00  Teams arrive at the ground.  PNG players
       to sign match ball.
13.30/ Official guests arrive.
14.00
14.15  Both teams to be presented to official
       guests in front of main stand.
       Fulham team will present PNG team with
       souvenir pennants.
14.30  Kick-off.
15.10/ Half time: refreshments for players/staff
15.25  in changing rooms.
16.10  Full time: light refreshment/drinks for
       players in changing rooms.
16.40/ Drinks in the club bar with the fans.
17.45/
18.00  Cross over to pavilion for Reception.
18.15  Sit down for Reception meal.
19.00  Guest speakers.
19.30  Retire to the bar for drinks,raffle, RL
       videos.
21.30  Bar closes.
```

The plan of the day's events for the visit of Papua New Guinea

Division Two. Dave Gillan finished as top try-scorer with nine, and top goal scorer was Londoner Colin Fenn with 40. Kieron Murphy played in 31 of the club's 32 games. The league record for the season was:

Played	Won	Drawn	Lost	For	Against	Points
28	10	0	18	382	559	20

Off the pitch, the financial stability remained. Income from gate receipts was virtually the same as for the previous season, and the overall loss for the year was £20,943. The amount due to external creditors had also fallen, to £52,007. The average attendance remained amazingly stable at 615, a drop of only 69. But now, only three Second Division sides had a lower average home gate than Fulham.

1988-9: Second Division

The pre-season messages from the club were positive, a summer bulletin saying that "all of us at Chiswick are sure that this will be a much better season for the club." However, the limitations of the Chiswick ground were recognised by director Tim Lamb, although no clear alternative was available and "our players and supporters see it as home."

Ten new players joined: Australians Earnie Garland, Jeff Coutts, Bob Boyce, Gary Lane, and Brian Brown, Londoners Andrew Mighty and Roy Leslie, Hugh Francis from Student Rugby League, and Tongans Albert Helg and Lawrence Johansson. Attempts to recruit former captain Glen Haggath had not been successful. One historic link was finally broken as there were now no players who had played at Craven Cottage.

An unusual sponsorship had been attracted, with Dave Gillan's kit being sponsored by the "Communist Party of Great Britain." Apparently, this was not in line with Dave's political views, and the actual sponsor was believed to be a longstanding Fulham supporter, although as Huw Richards' report in the *Rugby Leaguer* pointed out, it was not Labour supporter Colin Welland.

If Fulham did not have the best team in Rugby League, they probably had one of the best educated. Huw Richards outlined in the *Rugby Leaguer* that the club had a Cambridge University PhD Philosophy student training with them, and that the first team squad included at least five graduates.

174

A first game defeat at much-improved Doncaster was followed with a home win against promotion candidates Sheffield Eagles, and a win at Huddersfield. However, the club's management felt there was a need for a change in the coaching staff. After a 22-2 home defeat against the previous season's bottom club Batley, Bev Risman's period as Manager came to an end, and Bill Goodwin again took control. The club advertised for a player-coach. Risman's departure also saw Earnie Garland and Brian Brown leave.

Huddersfield came to London going through an even worse patch and were beaten 61-22, Fulham's record score. This was something of a mirage as four consecutive defeats followed, including at Bramley in the John Player Trophy. The A team were now playing friendly matches, and were surprised to find Great Britain internationals Steve Norton and David Topliss playing for Wakefield Trinity's A team against the Londoners.

The only good news during this period was the return of Hussein M'Barki. So yet another "free agent" had returned. Originally joining Warrington, he had also played for Oldham and Hull during his period in the north. He soon completed his 100th game, scored his 50th try and overtook Steve Mills as the highest try scorer in the club's short history.

An injury hit side brought off a great victory at Workington and was complimented by the legendary international and Workington player Gus Risman who said "you ought to be proud of such a side." Nevertheless, the inconsistent form continued.

In the second week of December, the club announced that Mike Stephenson had been appointed as Team Manager for the rest of the season. Although now well known to British Rugby League followers through his work for *Sky* Television, at that time he was a playing name from the past, having been resident in Australia for 15 years. The announcement was, in fact, premature. Stephenson had a last minute change of heart following a telephone call from someone vaguely linked with the club, which claimed to outline problems the club faced, and never caught the plane to London. The club programme later criticised his lack of commitment, (they were unaware of the telephone call which had raised major doubts in his mind), but club officials also realised that recruiting a coach without meeting him was difficult. They thus invited the next contender, Australian Phil Sullivan, to come to London for discussions about the post, and a trial period, which he started in mid January.

The club then faced Bradford Northern in the Challenge Cup, a game that was unfortunately played in a torrential downpour. Fulham managed tries by Aussie Glen Mansfield and M'Barki, and were only 8 points down at half-time, but the final score was 10-28. The attendance of 1,487 was the best of the season.

The Bradford chairman made some unkind comments to the effect that: " It's easier playing Warrington or Widnes than Fulham, because with Fulham you never know who you're playing against, they put a different side out every week. Down there they've got all these Australians and New Zealanders that they just bring in for the bigger games." Considering the dire straits the club had gone through, the comments were risible. He was clearly unaware of the difficulties of running a club outside the League heartlands.

Phil Sullivan's trial period seemed to be going well, with three victories, and a good contest with Bradford Northern in the cup. But surprisingly, his trial period was terminated, and he was replaced, on an acting basis, with Bill Goodwin. The club's management committee was split down the middle over the dismissal, with Tim Lamb justifying the sacking by saying that he originally thought Sullivan was Canberra's assistant coach rather than an assistant to the coaches.

There was a furore, with petitions supporting Sullivan from the fans and the players. A report in the club programme issued after Sullivan had already left, publicly outlined the split, saying that "the Committee Members who took the original decision, notably Tim Lamb and Paul Spencer-Thompson, are prepared to admit their decision was perhaps a hasty one... they are both in absolutely no doubt it was a correct one... whereas Roy and Barbara Close, and most other Committee Members, wish to disassociate themselves from that decision." Despite the petitions, it was clear that Sullivan's position was not viable, and the result was that the team manager post was still not filled on a permanent basis. Sullivan himself felt that "I don't feel that I've been judged on my coaching ability - I've been the victim of friction between two camps within the club with different views on how to run it."

The immediate aftermath of Sullivan's departure was a 60-0 defeat on a muddy swamp at Whitehaven. A weakened Fulham team could not stem the tide, and one player left the pitch in tears of despair. The Fulham club programme commented: "When we die, some of us will go to heaven, while the rest of us will probably go to Whitehaven." The only positive point to come out of this match was Dave Rotheram's first team debut. After this debacle, only three out of the last eight games were won.

176

Fulham v Bradford Northern, Challenge Cup January 1989
(Photo: Sporting Pictures (UK))

One note of controversy was the comments of former programme editor Paul-Spencer-Thompson, who circulated 400 copies of an unofficial letter on the club's notepaper to the fans attending the final home match of the season. A banner was also displayed attacking the club owners. His criticisms were directed at the management committee, and he alleged that the club seemed to be "a private plaything that could be thrown away at any time." Further criticism came from "long suffering" fan Keith Gorman.

These comments were met stoutly by director Tim Lamb, who pointed out that the present owners had put their money where their mouth was. He poignantly asked where these critics were in the dark days of March 1986, when the club nearly fell into the hands of the receivers. One other question posed by the supporters was whether the club would actually appear for the new season. But while much was uncertain, the club was actually set to experience better days.

The club finished well outside the top eight spot that had been an early season target, and in fifteenth place had exactly the same number of wins as last season, ten from 28 games. One improvement was the team's disciplinary record, as for the second season running, no first team players were sent off. Top try scorer was Kiwi centre Dave Gillan with 14, and Steve Guyett was top goal scorer with 65. The final league playing record was:

Played	Won	Drawn	Lost	For	Against	Points
28	10	0	18	464	650	20

Attendances were down by a marginal 27 to an average of 588.This showed there was still a loyal hard core of supporters, but on the other hand, only Chorley, Mansfield and Runcorn had less support. There had been no great upturn in the club's finances or its play on the field. There was more stability than before, but a new impetus was needed.

At the end of the season, discussions were concluded with Australian Ross Strudwick, the former Halifax coach, and he signed an agreement to become team manager from 1 July 1989. This gave the club the higher profile manager many people felt was necessary. Huw Richards wrote that "The dynamic Queenslander represents their best, and quite possibly their last chance of success. The boost to morale at the Poly grounds... will be massive." The club had initially contacted Strudwick by accident. While trying to track down prop Andy Zillman, a committee member found himself talking to Strudwick, who was related to Zillman. Negotiations went from there. Strudwick had experienced an unhappy time at Halifax, inheriting a successful but aging team, based on Australians recruited by former coach Chris Anderson. He was there only six months before being sacked and, as Dave Hadfield outlined: "He was just the wrong man in the wrong place at the wrong time." However, he did have a successful record in Australia. A new era would start in August.

14   Strudwick takes over

1989-1990: Second Division

This was the start of a new era and a new direction for the game in London. Apart from the appointment of Ross Strudwick, the other change was that the Closes again became directors.

Strudwick recruited better Australian players, such as stand-off Brett Daunt, the best half-back seen in London since Reg Bowden or Mike Davis. Daunt later played First Division rugby at Featherstone. Forward Eric Kennedy was also a great asset to a club now determined to climb out of the lower reaches of the Second Division. One loss on the playing front was winger Andrew Mighty who went to First Division Hull, with Fulham missing out on a transfer fee as he had been playing as an amateur.

Strudwick began commentating on the game for BBC TV, which also helped raise the profile of the sport in London, fortunately restraining his often robust language. During Fulham home games, he often watched from the bank behind the goal at Chiswick, while barking out orders from his walkie-talkie to the bench.

The team got off to a great start with a home win against Ryedale-York, whose chairman had threatened to resign should his team lose (he didn't). Further wins followed, and when Fulham faced Wigan in the quarter final of the Lancashire Cup, the team were fourth in the league.

The game was played at Hendon FC in north-west London, whose ground could better cater for a large crowd for this midweek game under floodlights. Although star-studded Wigan strolled home eventually, the 4-34 scoreline showed there was promise in the London lineup. The club benefited from a crowd of 3,200, the best home gate since Craven Cottage, and exposure on television and in the national and London press. The improvement in the team was shown by Fulham winning the September Team of the Month award.

Chiswick then attracted 1,014 fans who saw a 50-6 win over Carlisle; Dave Gillan and Hussein M'Barki both scoring two tries. A couple of defeats followed, but the target of a top eight place seemed realistic. The A team were also putting in some good performances in the Alliance Second Division, including an appearance by R. Strudwick. Another new Australian player signed was Darryl Pitt, who had previously played for Carlisle, and was to become one of the club's longest serving players.

The gap in class with the top teams in the division was shown with a 44-0 defeat at Hull KR. But both Whitehaven and Bramley were unable to score against Fulham, so Strudwick had tightened up the defence; after all he was the inventor of the sliding defence.

Mick Taylor, a summer recruit from Oldham was becoming a firm favourite with the crowd, and with half-back Wayne Sanchez linking well with Daunt, the fans had a good standard of play to watch, compared to the mix and match of previous seasons.

A heavy home defeat by table-topping Oldham set a pattern to be repeated over the next three seasons: the team could live with their peers, but struggled against teams with First Division pretensions. 1,440 attended the Oldham game, a record league gate for Chiswick.

Strudwick's former team Halifax then came to Chiswick in the Regal Trophy. Fulham put up a sterling performance before going down 18-32 to a side that had lost only once in the league and actually went on to the Regal Trophy final, only losing to Wigan. Unfortunately, Hussein M'Barki's sending off finished a club run of 80 games without a dismissal. A new ground record was set at the Halifax game when 1,542 attended.

Tim Lamb reported in the club programme that the Rugby League had set up a task force to help develop the game in London, and that Harry Jepson, a director of the League, and Geoff Keith, an administration officer, had spent three days in London on behalf of the League. Their view was that Chiswick was not suitable for long term development, although Tim also denied rumours that the club had decided to move to Hendon FC.

In the next programme, Harry Jepson explained what the League were trying to do in London. He said that he had been impressed by the level of commitment, and that "Nowhere else in the nation has the development potential that exists in London. Fulham RLFC is a very special case and must be so regarded by the rest of the League." He also said that Ross Strudwick was "the key factor for London and Fulham RLFC and must be given practical and visible support by everyone." Clearly, the Rugby League finally had a commitment to try to develop the professional game in London. By January, having failed to secure a long term agreement to use Chiswick, which could have justified investment in the ground, the club announced they were "actively searching" for a new ground.

Fulham team 1989-0. Bill Goodwin is on the left in the back row. Ross Strudwick
is next to Barbara Close in the centre.

On the pitch, the next test was Hull KR at home in the league. Fulham
were outplayed in every department, and went down to a record home defeat
6-60. Unfortunately, the game was marred by a pitch invasion from visiting
Hull KR "supporters." This event was one of the reasons the club were later to
move to Crystal Palace, as crowd control at Chiswick was next to impossible.

With Fulham safely in mid-table, Ryedale-York's visit in the
Challenge Cup brought the prospect of progress on the Wembley trail. A tense
game resulted in a 14-14 draw with two tries from Taylor. Incredibly, the team
won the replay 16-12, with tries from Taylor and Greg Pearce. Allegations that
the club were "stretching" the overseas player quota regulations surfaced again
when a black player played in one game, and a white one in the replay, both
using the same name. The second round of the cup gave the club a home draw
against top side Bradford Northern. The team lost 2-20, and again the
Chiswick attendance record was nudged forward to 1,665.

A win at struggling Nottingham meant that a top eight place was
entirely feasible. An end to the season that saw seven wins in the last 10 games
meant that Fulham finished eighth, and were rewarded with entry into the
Second Division Premiership for the first time.

This brought a match at Second Division Champions Hull KR. Played before the biggest crowd for a Fulham match that season, 4,308, the team could not bring off a miracle and went down 6-40 with a try from Redvers McCabe and a goal from Greg Pearce. One end of season departure on the playing front was hooker Russ Bridge, who was moving back up north.

Eighth place was a vast improvement on the previous season, and combined with a little cup success, the fans had seen a season to cheer.

The 1989-90 top try scorers were Brett Daunt and Mick Taylor on 12 with Greg Pearce kicking 47 goals and Steve Guyett 33. The final league record was:

Played	Won	Drawn	Lost	For	Against	Points
28	16	2	10	496	488	34

There had also been changes at the top in the club. At the end of February, Tim Lamb and Richard Lawton had resigned as directors. Tim Lamb had not been happy with the decision earlier in the year to make Ross Strudwick general manager, feeling that too much power would be held by one person, and that Strudwick should concentrate on the coaching side. However,

Exiles on the grass bank. From the left, Huw Richards (former programme editor), Tim Lamb, (former director), Paul Spencer-Thompson (former programme editor), and Harold Nass (former commercial manager). (Photo: Richard Lawton - former director)

the Rugby League clearly felt that Strudwick could build the club, and this change was actually at the RFL's prompting.

Huw Richards had reported in March that "The Rugby League has made an improvement in club management a condition of their proposed £150,000 cash injection over the next three years, and made it clear that they regard Ross as an essential part of any acceptable Fulham package." Tim Lamb had stayed on as club secretary until the end of the season.

For the new season, the directors were to be David Price, a Manchester based businessman, and Roy and Barbara Close. Huw Rees, Ron Snares, David Oakes, Bill Goodwin, Alex Fotheringham and Ray Stoner were to make up the new executive committee. The internal disagreements of the past few years had taken their toll, and several volunteers had dropped out of involvement in the club.

For supporters, there was further concern when the news came that the club planned to move back to the Crystal Palace National Sports Centre the next season, having rejected the possibility of moving to Brentford, Hendon or Hounslow Football Clubs. The supporters had bitter memories of the 1984-5 season there, which had ended with matches being moved to Chiswick and Wealdstone. Doubts over the future of Craven Cottage, and opposition from some leading Fulham FC officials prevented the hankered-after return to Craven Cottage. However, Fulham had little choice, as one of the preconditions of the money from the Rugby League was a move to a better stadium.

Back to Crystal Palace: 1990-91 Second Division

Pre-season financial problems had led to reports of the club "being in danger of collapse", but the difficulties seemed to have been overcome by the time the first match was played.

The move to Crystal Palace went ahead, but with much foreboding. Because the owners of Chiswick Polytechnic Stadium had refused a long lease or to sell the stadium to the club, there really was no alternative but to move. In the first programme, Ross Strudwick outlined that: "The move to Crystal Palace has been one of adversity and has not met with approval from all our supporters. As coach, I cannot express strongly enough how imperative... the move was, as the player environment and spectator facilities are by far the best in the league." He also outlined that the club had launched a vice-presidents lounge, and had sold two private viewing boxes.

The club also developed links with Charlton Athletic, and announced that Fulham's merchandise would be on sale at Charlton's shop. Maybe it was an appropriate link, as Charlton were playing at Crystal Palace FC's Selhurst Park ground, miles away from their real home, and much to the dissatisfaction of their supporters.

The old problems resurfaced, as the atmosphere at matches was almost nonexistent, with the large stadium rarely filled to more than 5 per cent of capacity. There is a pets corner overlooking the ground and it was suggested that the club should sign up the donkey, so its braying could gee up the players.

The new season brought a new board of directors: Ross Strudwick, David Oakes, and Ray Stoner. David Price had resigned in June, and the Closes too had stood down as directors. There was also the executive committee to help with day to day management. Reports appeared stating that the Rugby League was paying the £24,000 annual ground rental and Strudwick's salary in a three-year deal worth a reputed £180,000.

Brett Daunt was replaced by half-back David Cruickshank, who was joined by forward Mark Lee and fellow half-back Craig Grauf in the first Australian contingent of the season.

Although the club was still called Fulham, on the front of the programme the team was titled the Londoners, a distinct down-play of the Fulham name and a clear portent of things to come. Eric Kennedy, Andy Zillman, Russ Bridge and Brett Williams had all left, a substantial part of the club's forward strength.

A 50-0 home win against lowly Runcorn was in fact not a good indicator of future form, as the side struggled to find its feet. Two defeats, at Leigh in the Lancashire Cup, and at Workington, were a better measure of the side. A home win against Barrow, which marked the tenth anniversary of the famous debut match against Wigan in 1980, was a temporary reprieve. It had started with a moment of administrative confusion, when no match balls were available at kick off. Then successive defeats against Whitehaven and Dewsbury left the club struggling again. Crowds were lower than at Chiswick, as a sizeable section of the supporters had voted with their feet at the move to south London.

However, a run of four consecutive victories followed, including one against Batley, before the largest home crowd of the season - 804. Ross Strudwick noted in one of the November programmes that 20,000 people could turn up at the Palace for a firework display, but Fulham was unable to raise

1,000 for Second Division Rugby League. It was an indicator of the task facing the sport in the capital. In October, Bill Goodwin had resigned, ending 22 years continuous service to Rugby League in London, and a long association with the club, during which he had seen it through some difficult times.

With Tim Dwyer kicking goals, and a smattering of tries shared around the team Fulham were well inside the top eight, and few clubs now relished coming down to London. The A team was also settling down to some sound performances in the Alliance, and the club was benefiting from a large squad structure. The A team also made history by playing the touring Moscow Spartak team. Fulham lost 20-23, but the international clash was another landmark for London Rugby League.

The biggest test of the season was against First Division giants Castleford, at home in the Regal Trophy. The match kicked off at 1.00 p.m. because of a cable TV deal. The Londoners caught the Tigers dozing, led 2-0 at half-time, and only the fact that M'Barki had a try disallowed in the last minute saved Castleford from a shock. M'Barki had scored the only London try, leaving the final score at 14-8 to the Yorkshire visitors.

A hard fought win at Doncaster kept the club in the hunt for Strudwick's aim of a top five place. This was followed by a home win against Trafford, but the team were unable to stop Leigh who won 23-20 at the Palace.

Early in January 1991, the latest financial crisis was outlined in the programme. Fans were implored to bring a friend to help lift the gates to the 800 break-even level. A pessimistic Huw Richards wrote that the Rugby League's change of ground had lost a layer of Fulham's support, but that the inadequate facilities of Chiswick were "way behind longstanding administrative, commercial and playing development inadequacies", and that the League had failed to address these problems.

A further blow to the club's administrative structure was director and club secretary David Oakes' resignation. Despite the financial adversity, the team hit good form with a win against table-topping Swinton, and two wins and a draw in the next four league fixtures.

The Challenge Cup brought a match at highflying second division Halifax, but Fulham went down 46-6 on a snowbound pitch. Still the crowd of 4,624 brought the club some much needed cash. However, Ross Strudwick wrote in the programme that "unless we secure backers who want to sponsor the club into the First Division, we may have to suffer Runcorn and Nottingham type results." He also outlined that **"It is important to note that**

185

the name of Fulham shall remain with this club to infinity" (his emphasis). In fact, it only had a few months left.

The fine league form kept the club in the hunt for a top eight place. The goal-kicking duties had been taken over by Greg Pearce and he was averaging three per game. However, this was not enough to avoid a home defeat against top-eight chasing Doncaster. But it was only a blip as Fulham Londoners (as Strudwick now was referring to them) finished the season by beating Keighley and Runcorn at home.

This meant the club finished in seventh position and so qualified for a Premiership match at second-placed Halifax. Despite a spirited performance the team went down 42-24, with Darryl Pitt (2), Mark Lee and Tim Look scoring the tries.

Top scorers for the season were Darryl Pitt with 10 tries and Greg Pearce with 74 goals.

The final league record for the season was:

Played	Won	Drawn	Lost	For	Against	Points
28	17	2	9	448	338	36

Progress on the pitch was not matched by the gates. The crowd for the last two games of the season were a pitiful 252 and 354. The club was clearly wondering where to go next. The fans that were lost in the move from Chiswick had not been replaced, and the cash-strapped club was in no position to splash out on expensive advertising. One problem was an identity, and the name of Fulham, although dear to the original fans, meant less to the new fans and potential new supporters from south London. The club had not played in Fulham for seven years.

15   The summer 1991 tour of Russia

Over the summer of 1991, the Londoners took part in a Rugby League history-making event when they travelled to Russia and other states of the former Soviet Union alongside-Ryedale-York. The club was included when Leigh dropped out, and it was to be their last major engagement under the Fulham label.

Players who could get time off, or were unemployed, took part but had to go unpaid which was a real commitment, but worth it to become part of the first official visit to this fledgling League country.

The first game was in Alma Ata, capital of Kazakhstan near the Chinese border in central Asia. Fulham scraped home 6-4 against a local side, the Allstars of Asia before a crowd estimated enigmatically at between 6,000 and 15,000, very different from the few hundred who watched the club in London.

At the famous Lenin Stadium, in front of 1,000 spectators against the Leningrad club, Fulham won 18-12, with Greg Pearce playing a key role. After the possible 15,000 at Alma Ata it must have seemed like playing at the Palace.

York and Fulham then combined to play as a Great Britain Select side to play against the Soviet Union in Moscow with the tourists winning 42-10. Mick Taylor, Darryl Pitt, Russell Browning, Dave Rotheram, Mark Lee and Greg Pearce were the Londoners selected with Tim Dwyer and Glen Workman as substitutes. Greg Pearce scored a try and four goals to show that Fulham were an integral part of the squad. The crowd was a disappointing 3,200 for the Russian organisers.

One benefit of this successful tour was that three of the Russian players in this "test match", Mikhail Piscunov (Tiraspol) - a player timed as being faster than Martin Offiah - Andrei Olar (Tiraspol) and Andrei Sokolov (Moscow Magicians) later signed for the Londoners along with Sergei Bolonkin (Red Arrows). However, only Sokolov went on to play for the Londoners in the second-row away at Swinton and as substitute at home to Huddersfield in March 1992. The Russian players stayed for free at one of the houses in the Palace complex, but later all left when it became apparent that they would not be recompensed for their efforts.

Barry and Gwen Warren were two of the Fulham supporters who went on the trip. This is their recollection of it:

"5 supporters went on the trip. It was a joint trip with York, and was arranged through a travel agents up north. The first match was in Alma Ata which we couldn't get to.

We flew to Moscow, and stayed in a hotel with a couple from York. When we flew to Leningrad on Aeroflot, a pilot staggered onto the plane, very drunk. We were relived when he sat down and fell asleep, as we thought he was going to fly the plane. Our courier was from Halifax, and knew Ross Strudwick and Glen Workman.

In Leningrad, there was a reception for our party. At the reception there were jugglers and dancing bears. The second game of the tour was played at the Lenin Stadium. It is a big concrete bowl that can hold 100,000 people. The match was Fulham v York, and we won.

There were about 1,000 there. We didn't have any change for a programme, as it was very cheap, so we offered a Fulham badge in exchange, and were given about 300. It was 1 rouble to get into the match -about 2 pence at that time.

Before the trip, three of the players had been to the hairdressers, and had their heads shaved. One had USSR on the back of his head, another had a hammer and sickle.

After Leningrad we went back to Moscow by train. There were people selling souvenirs and contraband goods all the time, and we thought on the train we would get a break from this. When we got on the train, we found the sellers had a whole carriage. We got quite friendly with them by the end of the journey.

In Moscow, we stayed in the Cosmos hotel, which has 4,000 rooms. The players stayed there, and Maurice Lindsay, Bob Ashby and David Oxley from the Rugby League. They were very friendly. We were invited to the reception for the "Great Britain" party.

The two teams combined to play a Russian side, in the Dynamo stadium. Again, the stadium held 100,000, and there we around 2,000 there. It was not very successful from a promotion point of view, but it was a great trip."

An advert for the Soviet Union v Great Britain Select match

The programme from the Fulham v Ryedale York match

189

USSR 10 - Great Britain 42 (Photo: Gwen Warren)

The Fulham team (Photo: Gwen Warren)

Haircut for the tour. (Photo: Gwen Warren)

On tour - Barry Warren in the Fulham shirt, Dennis Samuels and Roy Close

Fulham and Ryedale York players leave the pitch (Photo: Gwen Warren)

Relaxing after the game - supporters club Secretary Barry Warren (left)
with Ross Strudwick (Photo: Gwen Warren)

16   A London Crusade

London Crusaders 1991-2: Second Division

The Fulham RLFC name surfaced only briefly in a preseason friendly at Nottingham in August, but that was the last game the club would ever play. Ross Strudwick had been canvassing for a new name, and the club now became the London Crusaders. This was fitting both geographically, and in keeping with the task the club had before them to capture the hearts of the capital's sports fans. Of course, diehard supporters still shouted "Fulham", a sentimental attachment rather than a slip of the memory, and it can still be heard today.

The club had secured the sponsorship of the national tabloid newspaper *Today*, and produced a rather dazzling red, white and black new shirt. Nonetheless, it was an improvement on the strip offered under the previous SHG Alarm sponsorship. Also sponsoring the club were the Australian Forwarding Agency (AFA), who had Kiwi Graeme Pickering as a Director. He was soon to be heavily involved with the club.

On the field Ross Strudwick rang the changes, and brought in a whole host of new players to the club. Among these were antipodeans winger Shane Buckley, half-backs Lachlan Churchill, and Ray Ovens, and forwards Steve Rosolen and Ben Olsen.

An unusual signing was Jason Wing, not surprisingly a winger. He had been a British Olympic bobsleigh and sprint champion and had played one game as a trialist at Chiswick. He was not however the only bobsleigher to play for the club, Dennis Trembath being the first.

This was the first season that the Rugby League had been split into three divisions. The Crusaders were in an eight team Division Two, all clubs playing each other four times.

The season started with a defeat at Workington, with Shane Buckley getting the newly-named club's first try and Chris Smith kicking two goals. That first Crusaders side was:
Buckley, Atkinson, Taylor, Pitt, Wing, Churchill, Ovens, Browning, Tuson, Rotheram, Olsen, Smith and Wilkinson, subs: Roberts and Winborns.

The second game was at Rochdale, and the Crusaders recorded their first victory.

The biggest game of the season came early on. The Crusaders were drawn at home to Wigan in the Lancashire Cup. There is some dispute about the size of the crowd, some sources saying 1,893, and the programme claiming 2,700. Even so, it was a large improvement on the 354 for the previous home game. A spirited performance by the Crusaders saw tries by Buckley and Wing, and Wigan only ran away late in the game to win 38-10.

The club were brought down to earth with the first home league game against Sheffield Eagles, who had just been relegated from the First Division, as they went down 22-44 with London's Bernie Wilkinson sent-off. The afternoon also brought news of the club's first attempt to sign Mal Meninga, Australian captain and League legend.

The Crusaders soon bounced back with a home win against Leigh, and as the first two league gates were over 1,000, things were looking up. However, the club had hit bad luck with injuries. Ray Ovens received a serious knock on the head and newcomer Frank Rolls sustained a double fracture of the leg in his first game. Ovens was soon replaced by John Plath, who covered the scrum-half place until the end of February.

The wide open spaces of Crystal Palace: London Crusaders v Sheffield
(Photo: Peter Lush)

Rochdale then came to the Palace and won 22-14. The game was memorable because the team roared into an early 14 point lead, only to blow it with some inept defence. Ross Strudwick was so angry that he soaked all the players' clothes with a bucket of water after the game. This was followed by further defeats at home to Sheffield and at Oldham in the Regal Trophy. To fill the obvious gaps in the line up, Tim Wilby and Nick Halafihi joined from Sheffield and full-back Matt Dray from Batley.

Following an improvement in the team's form, including a 10-0 win at third placed Oldham, much to the delight of the 30 London fans in a crowd of 3,200, the team only just managed a draw at Third Division Highfield in the Challenge Cup, and struggled to win the replay 24-12, before the club's lowest ever crowd of 250. The cup run ended with defeat at Workington, in the second week of February.

The club was desperate for publicity and found some via the pages of sponsors *Today* and with the help of football playing supporter Vinnie Jones, (who shared a flat with Tim Wilby) and from famous heavyweight boxer Gary Mason having trials with the A team. TV cameras even covered Mason's Alliance debut at Sheffield.

Boxer Gary Mason, whose appearances for the A team got the club some publicity
(Photo: Sporting Pictures (UK))

The Crusaders were never really consistent enough to challenge for promotion, but the top four teams were to enter the end of season Premiership, so there was an incentive to finish as high as possible.

The reward for finishing fourth was a draw at home to Alex Murphy's Third Division championship-winning Huddersfield in the play-offs. A stormy game saw the Crusaders home 14-4, although Huddersfield appealed to the Rugby League claiming London fielded ineligible players.

The Rugby League, while recognising Huddersfield's claim, found it "not proven", and allowed the club to play Oldham in the Premiership Semi-Final. Oldham were too strong, and the Crusaders lost 22-14, Halafihi and Buckley scoring tries.

Shane Buckley finished as top try scorer with 17 and Chris Smith kicked 78 goals. A large squad of 38 players was used. The second season at the Palace had partially proved the doubters wrong with league gates up by 167 to 724. The final league record was:

Played	Won	Drawn	Lost	For	Against	Points
28	14	0	14	428	483	28

Fulham RLFC (1984) had finally been wound up in April 1992, and its former subsidiary company, Vintagefile Ltd, now traded as London Crusaders RLFC. Ray Stoner had left the board, and Chris Blanchard had joined, but the club was now even more under the direction of Ross Strudwick.

1992-3: Second Division

A Rugby League ruling allowed the Crusaders to field five overseas players instead of the standard three; although the club had asked for an unlimited number. In a further move which showed the League was more serious about its London initiative, Roger Draper was appointed as a new London development officer.

Ross Strudwick and Chris Blanchard were now the club's directors, with Roy Close continuing to offer financial support to the club. A new category of life members was instituted to aid finances, and the club still relied on volunteers for many administrative tasks, particularly on match days. Ross Strudwick continued to supplement his income with broadcasting on big games for the BBC.

On a more troublesome note, the Rugby League insisted that the money owed to Wigan for their part of the receipts for the previous season's Lancashire Cup tie should be paid, and as this had not been done, the club was unable to enter the Lancashire Cup.

Despite new Australian signings were forwards Darryl Duncan and David King, and backs Scott Roskell, and Paul Fisher, the Crusaders suffered a first day defeat at Oldham by 27-12, with tries from Halafihi and Atkinson. This was followed by a rich vein of form, with three straight wins. Scott Roskell scored five tries in three games with Chris Smith kicking 18 goals. The club only needed to win at newly-promoted Bramley to go top, but lost 30-8, again showing a frustrating inconsistency.

Defeats followed at Swinton and Featherstone, when former Welsh Union international David Bishop played his only game on loan from Hull KR. He then played for Wales while still registered with the club, allowing the Crusaders to claim an international honour.

The club, still searching for a stable set up, was being courted by Australian company Playmaker, but the most significant development was the introduction of Richard Bartram and his Britannic Touchdown Promotions Company who took over the role of looking for sponsors and marketing for the club. The club also had a new shirt sponsor, Bass, and Carling appeared on the shirts. In November, the existing directors were joined by Bartram and Graeme Pickering.

A home draw with struggling Carlisle did not dispense the gloom, as the Crusaders were now in the lower half of the eight-team league. On the development front the club had helped set up a local amateur club Crystal Palace. It had a short-lived, but successful life, although in practice became the club's third team, rather than a purely amateur set up.

Once when the side was short of players, one of the squad suggested playing a friend of his who was over on holiday. He brought along Julian O'Neill, who had represented Australia, Winfield Cup clubs and Widnes. Of course he played a blinder.

The visit of Wakefield Trinity in the Regal Trophy provided first division cup opposition. This game saw the debut of the diminutive Kiwi scrum-half Mark Riley, a player announced as being from Peckham, but in reality brought over from New Zealand by Playmaker . He was to become one of the club's best overseas signings.

Amazingly, the First Division Yorkshire Cup-holders were sent packing 30-0. Throughout the match, Crusaders fans held their breath expecting the usual First Division comeback, but the score mounted with tries from Pitt (2), Fisher, Buckley, King, Roskell (a big occasion man) and five goals from Chris Smith. The crowd was 900, the best of the season. The team that day was:

Fisher, Blackman, Roskell, Pitt, Buckley, Halafihi, Riley, Rotheram, Workman, King, Gilbert and Smith, subs: Holderness and Mulkerin.

Unfortunately, the team's league form plummeted, with four defeats in the next five games. The club was now in danger of dropping into one of the two relegation slots.

Two home wins steadied the ship, but further heavy defeats followed, at home to Featherstone and at Oldham in the Challenge Cup, where new recruit from a famous Rugby League family, Warren Mann scored the club's only try. A Mark Riley hat-trick brought a rare away win at Carlisle, but this was followed with another thumping at Featherstone. Some sad news received by the club was the death from cancer of Ray Ovens, who had played for the Crusaders in the previous season.

Then a bombshell was dropped. Darryl Duncan was appointed as player-coach, although Strudwick remained as team manager. The move was a surprise, but a vacancy had arisen with the loss of assistant coach Tim Wilby to Hemel Hempstead. However, Duncan's appointment was short-lived, and suddenly the end was in sight for Ross Strudwick.

From the outside, it seemed a coup had taken place, and Strudwick left very rapidly, in the second week of February. He had been in a position of complete control over the club on a day-to-day basis since 1990, and it is questionable if so much power should have been concentrated in one person.

It appeared there were concerns over the management of the club's finances, but on the other hand, Strudwick had attracted some talented Australasian and British players to the club, and more high-profile sponsors. However, he was a big advocate of the move to Crystal Palace, which was probably a mistake, as it held bad memories for some fans who stopped coming, and the expected local support did not materialise.

He left the playing side of the club in a far stronger position than when he arrived, with the team being better organised, and the A team developing well. However, it could also be argued that he had failed to recognise the potential of some of the English players in the A team, preferring to recruit further overseas players. In one away match, the two English players in the

198

team were rather taken aback when Strudwick appealed to the players' "Aussie pride and spirit" to motivate them for the second half.

He had been employed by the Rugby League in his last season, as a London development officer. This was never a satisfactory arrangement, although it was in practice another way of subsidising the League's London outpost. The main development work was done by Roger Draper. With Strudwick's departure, the club announced that Graeme Pickering would become general manager.

Meanwhile a home win against lowly Bramley brought some relief on the playing front. With three-quarters of the season gone, the club appointed New Zealander Tony Gordon as the new coach, a big signing indeed, which had been set up by Rugby League chief executive Maurice Lindsay. He had previously played as a winger and full-back, coached the New Zealand national team, and was known as "The Tank". Gordon had received a call and had travelled from New Zealand to take over, clearly impressed with London's potential. It was interesting to see how his more expansive style compared to the defensive organisation of Ross Strudwick.

The first game under his management was a narrow defeat at Swinton. Things soon picked up and the team won at home to Huddersfield, and at already promoted Oldham. Defeat at Huddersfield did not dampen the team's mood, and they finished with two wins and a draw, to take fifth place in the league table.

Gordon had immediately brought in Kiwi Neville Ramsey from Bradford Northern, and South African winger, Mark "Magic" Johnson, who scored four tries in five games. Cambridge University amateur Ady Spencer played three end of season games. These matches, and two appearances in 1993-4 were to make news in the 1994-5 season. Spencer was banned by the Rugby Union for 12 months. When he turned out for his University Union team at Twickenham in the Varsity match, it was pointed out that he had played Rugby League for a professional club, which prompted the Rugby Union's ban. Still, he did achieve the unusual double "blue" for Cambridge in both rugby codes.

The season had been a traumatic one. Ross Strudwick, a seemingly permanent fixture, had gone, and it seemed that the Bartrams were now to be the driving force in the club's fortunes.

Top try scorer was again Shane Buckley with 16 and Chris Smith kicked 61 goals. The club had scored 534 points, the best for seven seasons, although gates had dropped back to an average of 554, the worst in Division Two. The final playing league record was:

Played	Won	Drawn	Lost	For	Against	Points
28	12	2	14	534	562	26

With yet another new management in charge, supporters again finished the season wondering what was next on the horizon for the club. No one could have predicted the drama to follow.

17   Tankie Gordon's Barmy Army

1993-4: Second Division

In June 1993, Vintagefile Ltd, which had been trading under the name London Crusaders, was put into liquidation and Britannic Touchdown Promotions purchased the business of the club from the liquidator. Richard Bartram and Graeme Pickering were directors, with Samantha Bartram as company secretary.

Preseason was full of rumours in the league press, including some that the club would not survive. A month before the season's opening game, nobody even knew where the club would play. This might have been shocking for fans at Headingley or Central Park but London supporters coped with this in their usual way. "We'll turn up wherever they play" has always been the norm.

A message from Maurice Lindsay that "The Club and all associated with it seem set for exciting times" was to come true, but not in the way the Rugby League's chief executive anticipated. In the *Daily Telegraph*, John Whalley wrote that "How London perform this season at a new venue with a high profile performer like John Gallagher will be a litmus test for expansion hopes, and should answer the perennial question of whether the capital can support Rugby League." Incredibly, expansion outside the game's traditional areas was still contentious, Dave Woods writing in the *Rugby Leaguer* that "we should all be giving our energies to promoting the prosperity of the game in the north and forget the rest of the country for the time being."

But the decision to play at Barnet's Copthall Stadium, could not have been anticipated. The ground, near the borders of Hertfordshire, had a capacity of 9,999 with 800 seats. The cynics said that the ground was picked more for the travelling northerners than the Londoners, as it was well placed for the A1, M1 and M25. It was also clear that the stadium would be fine for the Second Division, but clearly would struggle with crowds of over 2,000 as it only has four turnstiles and few toilet facilities. It also has a poor view from behind the goals. The lease had only been signed in August, a couple of weeks before the first game.

More exciting was the news that the club had made three major signings in the summer break. Londoner John Gallagher signed from First Division Leeds. He had played Rugby Union for New Zealand. He had been a record signing for Leeds, but was released on a free transfer after failing to fit in with coach Doug Laughton's plans. He was the biggest name to sign for the club since the Craven Cottage days. In September he was appointed as a development officer for London. After traumatic times at Leeds, Gallagher was looking forward to the new season, outlining that "It's a fresh start and my confidence and enthusiasm are high." National press coverage of the relaunch of Gallagher's career did bring the club some publicity.

Sam Stewart, a former New Zealand League forward, was signed from Australian club Newcastle Knights. Finally, winger Abi Ekoku, an international standard discus thrower, who had had trials for Wigan, was recruited. He had represented Great Britain at the European and Commonwealth games. Abi's brother is Wimbledon football striker, Efan Ekoku. He had a 100 metres sprint time of only 10.6 seconds, and had once even beaten Olympic champion Linford Christie.

Other arrivals were hooker Scott Carter, forward Darren Michalski, both from Newcastle Knights and centre Jason Walker from New Zealand. And in October, Australian stand- off Troy Rugless was signed. A major loss was prop David King to Huddersfield, which would be felt before the season was out. Paul Fisher and Shane Buckley had stayed in Australia, and Nick Halafihi had returned north, joining Hull KR.

There was a new fanzine, *London Calling* which was soon to be popular with the news-starved supporters, giving an alternative view of the club's activities.

The Rugby League had reorganised again, with three clubs being demoted to the newly-formed Conference League, and the Second and Third Divisions being merged, with clubs once again playing two matches against all the other teams in the division.

The season started with three straights wins, and London were suddenly favourites to win the title. Coincidentally, the first two home games were against Batley and Doncaster, who were to be unexpected promotion rivals. The first Copthall fixture attracted an encouraging 1,010 on a Friday night. Mark Johnson scored the first try at the club's new home, and John Gallagher converted for the first of his many goals. A win at promotion favourites Keighley followed, a photo of this game even made the *Daily Telegraph* sports page. As Tony Gordon pointed out, Keighley's programme had inspired the team, as the Yorkshire club had headed the page about the London players "Today's victims." One report of this match said that the

Crusaders were now "genuine championship material."

The victory against Doncaster was unusual, as the team's mascot for the game, Leon Blackman, younger brother of winger Richard, was not allowed to come to the game as his mother felt he had been naughty, and therefore could not lead the team out after all.

The atmosphere at Copthall was certainly an improvement on the Palace. However, it was difficult for the supporters to get to, although the club ran special buses from the nearest underground station to help alleviate the problem.

Unfortunately, after the optimistic start, three straight defeats followed, a heavy loss at Huddersfield, despite an early lead; an even bigger shock at home to Dewsbury, with the visitors scoring 25 points in the final quarter before 1,124 fans; and then at lowly Barrow, despite a Mark Johnson hat trick. Captain Sam Stewart was sent off, John Gallagher carried off and spirits were sinking really low. Unknown to the fans, a financial crisis had partly caused the sudden and unexpected loss of form. Prior to the Barrow game, the players and Tony Gordon hadn't been paid, and this situation so early in the season cast doubts on the club's new set up.

Abi Ekoku, one of the new Crusaders stars (Photo: David Stevens)

Tony Gordon gradually brought the team around, but the management was already in crisis. Richard Bartram chided the fans for lack of support and revealed that he had budgeted for a break-even crowd of 2,000, which long standing supporters felt to be "crowd cuckoo land." The players were forced to take a pay cut, and the supporters wondered what could possibly happen next.

In fact, five wins followed, which included Mark Riley setting a new club record with four tries against Highfield, French champions St. Esteve being beaten at Copthall in the Regal Trophy, and a fine win at promotion favourites Workington.

The biggest game at Copthall so far saw First Division Featherstone arrive in the Regal Trophy. They clearly hadn't done their homework, and were stunned as they were seen off 26-12 before 1,336 fans. The Londoners were never behind, and defended heroically against their illustrious opponents. Tries came from Ekoku, Johnson, Rosolen and Ramsey with three goals from Gallagher. The team that day was:

Gallagher, Ekoku, Roskell, Walker, Johnson, Rugless, Riley, Mulkerin, Carter, Stewart, Rosolen, Michalski and Ramsey, Subs: Rotheram and Whitely

The Regal Trophy then bought a trip to York. The game was played in a blizzard, with all the other games cancelled, except one at Hull. Even Leeds's game was called off, the underfloor heating saving the pitch but the crowd unable to reach the ground. The referee for the game only got to Leeds, so a local referee took the game with *London Calling* editorial board member Paul Taylor running the line. London adapted much better to the terrible conditions, and in an eight try rout won 42-10, despite the impartial reserve linesman ruling out an Ekoku try. It was a creditable win, particularly as some of the Australian players had never seen snow before. London were now in the quarter finals, their best run ever in the competition. This victory coincided with the Rugby League taking over the financial running of the club. A worried Maurice Lindsay arrived in York just before kick off, and asked to be directed to the visitors' dressing room, to tell the team that the future was hopefully more secure.

The quarter-final opponents were First Division Bradford Northern at Copthall, who were to finish the season as runners-up in the First Division on points difference, and included seven players with international honours. And what a shock the Crusaders gave them. Two Scott Roskell tries saw the Londoners lead 10-0. The 1,818 crowd were stunned, especially the 800 travelling Bradford fans. If the game had not been six days before Christmas, on a cold and wet day, the crowd would have been much bigger. Unfortunately, the heavy conditions did not help the fast-flowing London style, and Great Britain International Paul Newlove scored for Bradford just before half-time. The Londoners were still leading 10-6 at the break. However, in the second half, two long range tries by Cordle saw Bradford home 22-10, despite London being camped in Northern's territory for much of the second half. Bradford's coach Peter Fox recognised that the Crusaders were " a very good side."

This defeat had bought the club's longest ever unbeaten run to an end, as the team had not lost for ten games. Off the pitch, a first sign of the change in management was the Bartrams' names not appearing in the programme as directors.

To end an eventful year, Swinton were beaten at Copthall. Just when Scott Roskell was predicting a championship on the *Club Call*, the Crusaders' telephone information service, the wheels came off again.

The club had entered a state of limbo as the Bartrams departed. The Crusaders were now being run by volunteers, ably led by honorary secretary Neil Robinson, and became financially controlled by the Rugby League. Rumours abounded about new buyers. Jason Walker had to return to New Zealand as the transfer fee had not been paid by the previous administration. The situation was so desperate that the supporters paid for a new strip, to allow the players to change at half-time when playing in heavy conditions.

Abi Ekoku was injured in a defeat at Rochdale, which put him out for the rest of the season. Logan Campbell was brought over from New Zealand to replace Walker. In the Challenge Cup, a patched up side struggled to beat amateurs Shaw Cross. Defeat at highflying Doncaster seemed to finish the promotion hopes, although Troy Rugless scored the club's 100th try of the season.

The Crusaders again welcomed Featherstone, this time in the Challenge Cup, before 1,553 fans. The Yorkshire side were ready this time, but the makeshift Crusaders managed to sneak in front in the second-half, 14-12. A surprise was not in the making though, as the Yorkshiremen shifted up a gear but were flattered by the 28-14 scoreline. Once again, Scott Roskell scored two tries.

Astounding news followed the Featherstone defeat overshadowing events on the field. The famous Australian club, the Brisbane Broncos were to become the new owners. They had fought off a rival bid from a consortium including former England football manager Bobby Robson, whose son was assisting the Crusaders with fund raising. The immediate playing benefit of the new owners was the arrival of forward Victor "Turbo" Timms and stand-off Leo Dynevor from the Brisbane Broncos. Off the field, the Broncos announced they were going to bring an accountant over, as well as a fitness conditioner.

The Brisbane Broncos had entered the Winfield Cup in 1988, and were one of the major successes of the expansion of Rugby League in Australia. They had established a wide base of support, and lucrative sponsorship deals. They had won the Winfield Cup in 1992 and 1993, and had beaten Wigan to win the World Club Championship in 1992. Among their 19 players to have won international honours were Wally Lewis and Allan Langer.

At the end of January, Ernie Clay had died, at the age of 76. The tribute in the Crusaders' programme noted that despite "his sudden withdrawal of support after the end of the 1984 season", it had been his initiative that had bought Rugby League to the capital.

Huddersfield won handsomely at Copthall, the squad injury situation being so bad that forward Darren Michalski played on the wing, as Mark Johnson was on South African international duties in the Sydney World Sevens. A further defeat at promotion chasing Batley, meant that it would take a herculean effort to get something out of the season.

A narrow win at home to promotion aspirants Keighley, with Namibian Andre Stoop, on loan from Wigan, making his debut for London, kick started the remnants of the season. Stoop had made 16 appearances for the Wigan first team, including in the World Club Challenge against Brisbane Broncos, but had become homesick and returned to Namibia, where he had been playing Rugby Union. Maurice Lindsay had contacted him about joining the Crusaders.

Off the pitch, the Broncos "skills and development officer", Robbie Moore, was making a three week visit, and in the summer would become the new club's chief executive.

Four further wins set up a crucial clash against table-topping Workington, in front of the Sky television cameras and 1,500 fans at Copthall. It was the first Second Division match shown in full on Sky's Rugby League coverage.

The Crusaders stormed into a first-half, 18-4 lead, with another try disallowed. A disallowed penalty try early in the second half seemed to take the wind out of the home side, and Workington stormed back to pinch a 20-20

206

draw with John Gallagher's last minute drop-goal attempt clipping the post.

Bramley were pushed aside by a record breaking 64-0 in the next home game, with John Gallagher scoring two tries and eight goals to break the match points scoring record with 24. Next, the away points scoring record was broken at hapless Highfield, who were beaten 58-6 with Mark Johnson scoring a record-equalling four tries. Four further victories followed to keep Crusaders in the promotion hunt.

The long running problem of finding a suitable stadium, seemed to have been solved, when the *Rugby Leaguer* announced that the Broncos would play at Twickenham, home of Rugby Union, the following season. Hopeful fans then checked the date of the paper, which was 1 April!

On the final day of the league season at Carlisle, the situation was such that should Doncaster and Batley draw, and London win, the Crusaders would be promoted. Alas, it was not to be. London won easily 26-12, but Doncaster pipped Batley to go up for the first time. However, the Premiership still remained.

Unfortunately, bad news shocked the supporters when they learned that Tony Gordon could not agree terms with the new owners, and would leave at the end of the season. Gordon had steered the club through one of the most difficult periods off the pitch in its history, and his team had played breathtaking rugby. In the club programme, Neil Robinson wrote that "Tony Gordon will be sorely missed by everyone connected with the club...[he] will always be welcome by all connected with London Crusaders, and I personally will be saying farewell to a great friend." When he returned to watch a match the following season, he was given a great reception.

The badly timed withdrawal of Timms and Dynevor back to Brisbane by the Broncos annoyed the supporters, as it endangered the club's Premiership aspirations. Still, the team produced miracles for Tony Gordon's last home game, the Premiership quarter-final. The club now had only 16 players with Second Division experience, but Keighley were imperiously brushed aside 66-12. 50 points were scored in the second-half with a Mark Johnson hat-trick. He was now in the hunt for the season's overall top try scorer place.

The semi final at Doncaster saw a historic victory by 16-6 in quagmire conditions. Johnson scored the winning try after the home side had been in front early on, and the club now faced the biggest game in its history, a Second Division Premiership Final at Old Trafford, a far cry from Copthall or Chiswick. The crowd was 35,644 and the 600 Crusaders supporters who had

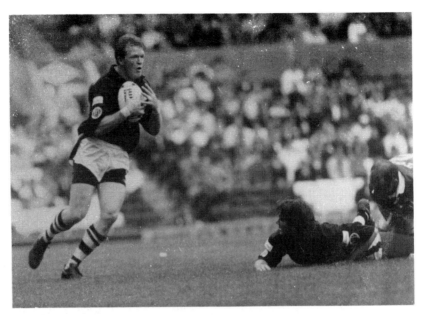

John Gallagher in action at Old Trafford in the Premiership Final
(Photo: David Stevens)

Tony Gordon at Old Trafford (Photo: David Stevens)

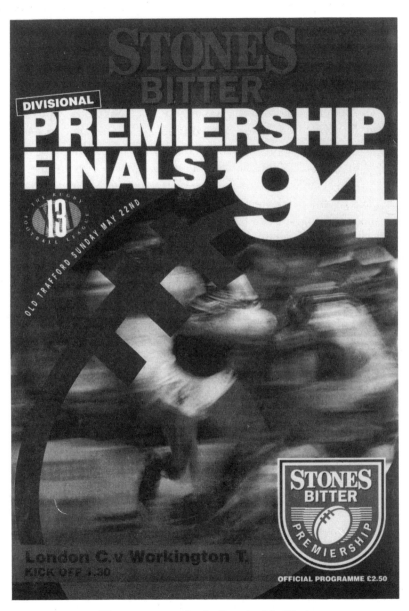

The programme for the Premiership Final

209

made the trip were a tiny but enthusiastic handful. But this figure itself was incredible, as it was only 130 short of the average home gate, and the club had only six days to sell the tickets. A 1.30 pm kick off also meant a very early start from London.

The team for this historic game against champions Workington Town was the side that had won in the previous rounds:
Stoop, Gallagher, Roskell, Campbell, Johnson, McIvor, Riley, Whitely, Carter, Rotheram, Stewart, Rosolen and Ramsey, Subs: Smith and Luxon.

An early Workington try was a shock, but the response was swift with a try in the corner by Johnson. Then disaster struck as both Riley and Carter went off with serious injuries and London's luck ran out. Workington made the most of the Crusaders' difficulties and were clear away by half-time.

Tony Gordon fired up the team for the second-half and with a Logan Campbell try and Mark Johnson completing his hat-trick, there seemed hope of a shock comeback, but a late try sealed the match for the Cumbrians. The final score was a presentable 30-22. It was to be the Crusaders last game, and the swansong for Tony Gordon, who would be missed.

Mark Johnson finished with a club record 43 tries for the season and he also finished top of the Rugby League try scorers. So a South African playing for the only professional club in the capital in his first full season, finishing as the League's top try scorer. John Gallagher also broke the club goal and points record with 159 goals and the Crusaders had also broken their points record with 842 for the year, with an incredible 212 tries scored in the season, but more importantly, they still missed out on promotion by just one point. The final league record was:

Played	Won	Drawn	Lost	For	Against	Points
30	21	2	7	842	522	44

One of the club's most traumatic seasons in its history off the pitch had combined with one of the most dramatic on it. The Crusaders' free-flowing rugby had enthralled the fans, compared to the forward based game of the early days, and Ross Strudwick's well organised and methodical sides.

And the takeover by the Brisbane Broncos seemed to offer a more stable future, as the Broncos would have the resources to invest that professional Rugby League in London had needed for so long.

18   The Broncos takeover

London Broncos 1994-5: Second Division

The new season started very quietly. As before, not only were the fans not certain where the club was going to play, there were even the perennial rumours that the club might not even re-surface. Having failed to find a more suitable home, the club stayed at Copthall. However, the first home game had to be re-scheduled to Carlisle as the Copthall pitch was not yet ready for use.

The new chief executive was Robbie Moore, a former Brisbane Valleys player who had worked with Ross Strudwick at Halifax. The new coach was Gary Greinke who had been a successful coach of Brisbane Wests, and briefly played with St Helens. Neil Robinson remained as Honorary Secretary. Former coach Tony Gordon had returned to Britain, and taken charge at First Division Hull.

So London Rugby League was once again a part of a unique experiment, with Brisbane Broncos being the parent club and London their offspring. Director John Ribot outlined that Castlemaine XXXX and Puma were backing the new venture, and said that "The directors of the company have invested heavily in the club and are committed to seeing it succeed to the highest possible level."

However, little marketing was done, the club saying that their priority was to win promotion, then find a new ground suitable for the First Division, and then put resources into marketing First Division rugby.

On the development front, Roger Draper had moved on to a job with the Lawn Tennis Association, and John Gallagher had taken a teaching job, so both the development officer posts were vacant. However, the Broncos had agreed to fund a further two posts.

On the playing side, Andre Stoop had joined Keighley, who had snapped up the player who had been on loan from Wigan. Fans' favourite Neville Ramsey had been declared surplus to requirements, and gone on a free transfer to York. New signings were experienced Australian prop Cavill Heugh from Rochdale, backs Peter Liddell and Craig Green, and forwards Luke Massey and Darren Shaw. The supporters also had the promise from the Broncos that they would attempt to sign the Aussie Legend Mal Meninga when he completed the Australian 1994 Tour. However, the nucleus of the previous season's team was gone, with hooker Scott Carter injured and not returning, full-back Andre Stoop at Keighley, and John Gallagher due to retire after three games because of work commitments.

The bookies made the Broncos red-hot favourites for the championship, but Maurice Lindsay, Rugby Football League chief executive, somewhat prophetically, observed that the Broncos had "underestimated the Second Division." The players appeared in a new strip with the sponsors Castlemaine XXXX very prominent in shirt resplendent in Navy blue and gold stripes, an abrupt departure from the black of Fulham and the Crusaders.

The first league game at Carlisle was a comfortable victory despite the Cumbrian side being fired up and audibly shouting "lets get those ****ing Aussies" as the match commenced. Logan Campbell scoring a hat trick as the Broncos eased home.

The second game at lowly Hunslet saw an inspired home team shock London by 25-14. *London Calling* described this as a "humiliation", and so bad was the performance that long-time London fan Harry Stammers ran to the dug out in the second-half to remonstrate with the coach. Even more surprised were the Hunslet directors who thought they would lose by 50 points. The London pattern of play was extremely stereotyped. This was followed by a poor performance at Barrow, although the Broncos managed their second win.

The first home game was on Sunday 11 September at Hendon FC, as the Copthall pitch was still unplayable. The visitors were Keighley who had been hammered 66-12 on their last visit to London in Premiership Play-offs in May. The crowd was boosted by hundreds of visiting fans and the attendance was a healthy 1,302. Abi Ekoku celebrated his first game since his injury at Rochdale in January, but his efforts were wasted as the visitors romped to 30-10 victory, much to the disquiet of the London supporters. The next game was at bottom club Highfield and although the Broncos were soon in a comfortable lead, the team had the embarrassment of the Lancashire side out-scoring the Broncos in the second half.

Form improved in the next two home games with relatively easy wins against Swinton, with Australian teenager and under 19 international Sid Domic making his debut, and Batley. One of the reasons for the improved form was the appearance of forward Justin Bryant.

Justin had come to England from Toowoomba in Queensland, the birth place of the legendary Brian Bevan, to play League and after being rebuffed by Hemel Hempstead, contacted the Broncos after missing the train

212

for a trial with Hull Kingston Rovers. He added some penetration to the pack, and his Australian nickname "Pig Dog" was to mystify away fans all season. He followed in the tradition of players such as Peter White and Craig Taylor who had turned up unannounced, and asked for a trial.

Defeat at promotion rivals Dewsbury underlined the problems facing the club. Their rivals always raised their game to beat the "Australians" and the new forward orientated game plan left potential match winners Riley and Johnson often marginalised.

A mysterious South African Rugby Union full back played three games on trial. He kicked three goals, but broke his nose, and decided not to join the Broncos.

An emerging star was Sid Domic, who had come on loan from the Brisbane parent club. As the season developed so did Domic, although he returned to Australia before the end of the season to try for a first team place in the Winfield Cup. This showed one of the problems of the link with the Broncos, as two players had done the same the previous season.

Poster for the home match with Batley, played at Hendon FC because the Copthall pitch was unfit

213

The home game against Rochdale was played the night before the First Test between Great Britain and Australia. Despite hopes of a record crowd, as tickets had been given to the Australian supporters in London for the test match, the attendance was 1,202 for a very lacklustre affair. Then Ryedale York won at Copthall, inspired by ex Crusader Neville Ramsey, who scored a try and was sent off.

Wins followed over Carlisle, with debutant English full-back John Scourfield scoring a hat-trick, and a poor Hunslet side. The fans were now split, some wishing to give the new regime the balance of the doubt and others who remembering the Gordon era, wanted a more attacking style.

The news that the club had failed to sign Mal Meninga prompted them to announce that at the end of the 1994 Australian tour two Brisbane Broncos tourists, half-back Kevin Walters and wing Michael Hancock, would come for a short stay with the club. This was greeted with caution by experienced London fans.

Incredibly, the team even struggled to beat Hemel Hempstead in the first round of the Regal Trophy at Copthall. The plucky Hertfordshire amateurs only going down in the latter stages, having led 16-12 at half-time. The scoreline of 34-16 flattered the Londoners. One player in form was forward Dave Rotheram, who was scoring a try every other game after only scoring two in his previous six seasons.

The programme for the Hemel Hempstead match, on 27 November, featured a report from the Courier-Mail in Brisbane that a Super League was to be set up, as the brainchild of Rupert Murdoch's multi-media organisation. It said that the Broncos would be in the league, starting in the summer of 1996, and that there would be club mergers to form big city teams. This was dismissed by Maurice Lindsay, who was quoted as saying: "The only people not consulted are myself and the 10 teams... If the Australians want to form their own super league that's fine by me."

Paradoxically, one of the best performances followed away at First Division Salford in the second round of the Regal Trophy, which saw scrum-half Kevin Langer's debut. His younger brother is Australian Test Legend Allan Langer, and when the Broncos rang him, he thought they wanted his brother. Salford led 14-0 at half time, but a gem of a try by Mark Riley and a crashing try from Dave Rotheram saw the home side worried in the final stages. Only goal misses by stand-in kicker Cavill Heugh allowed Salford to

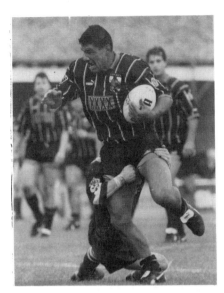
Club captain Sam Stewart in action (Photo: David Stevens)

sneak home 16-14. One landmark was Darryl Pitt's 100th game for the club.

Kevin Walters and Michael Hancock had been injured on the Australian tour, and did not come to the club. Instead, Australian hooker Tony Rea was signed on a two year contract.

It seemed that this defeat and the form of scrum-half Kevin Langer had revived the season as Barrow were disposed of by 30-6. But at Leigh on Boxing Day, with Tony Rea making his debut, the Londoners lost in freezing mud, conditions not familiar to many of the Australian players. The gloom continued at Hull KR, with a heavy defeat.

The next game at leaders Keighley saw the Broncos totally dominate the game with Roskell and Langer in form, and deserved their 25-14 triumph. But four days later, defeat at Huddersfield also saw Mark Riley break a kneecap, which would keep him out for the rest of the season.

Sam Stewart, Steve Rosolen and Tony Rea were appointed as development officers, with a further appointment to cover south London. So the vital promotion work in the schools could start again after a six month break.

Cumbrian amateurs Ellenborough Rangers were beaten at Copthall, before only 363 fans. A magnificent win at Batley kept promotion hopes alive. In the Challenge Cup Hull KR were to be the visitors. Due to an athletics meeting at Copthall, the game was scheduled for Hendon FC. Unfortunately, on the Saturday, the pitch was declared unfit but due to a magnificent effort by the club's staff the game was transferred to Copthall, with the game to be played directly after the athletics with a 4.30 kick-off. The team did not match the administrative success, losing by 6 points.

The Broncos had still not found a new home for the 1995-6 season, and various options were being considered, including sharing with a Rugby Union club. Another possibility was for the Broncos to take over the Copthall Stadium, and develop it. However, the club wanted a home ground nearer the centre of London. On the playing front, a third team was started, playing friendlies against amateur sides, and an under 16 team was being set up.

The team's form improved, with four league wins, including a thrilling last minute triumph at home to second placed Whitehaven. Justin Bryant scoring the winning try with 15 seconds to go. At Bramley, Scott Roskell scored a record equalling four tries in the win. This was to be John Gallagher's last game.

An off the cuff comment by John Ribot about the losses the club was sustaining was blown up by the press, with stories that the Brisbane Broncos were to pull out at the end of the season. While this was denied in the club programme, which said that new players were being signed, and a new development officer for south London had just been appointed, the incident did show once again, that the future of the club could be changed by decisions made thousands of miles away.

The team now knew they had to win all the games to have chance of a promotion place, but defeat at York, inspired by Neville Ramsey, deflated such hopes. But the Broncos bounced back with a cracking home win over Hull KR, the first time the club had defeated the Humbersiders. On the Super League front, there had been debate in Australian Rugby League about whether the Winfield Cup was sustainable in its present form, and whether a Super League should be formed.

The next home game against third placed Huddersfield looked to have all the importance of the previous season's home game against Workington. The game was overshadowed by the announcement of the Super League in Britain. This threw Rugby League into turmoil, and took away any real interest in the Second Division campaign. To London supporters' delight, the Broncos

216

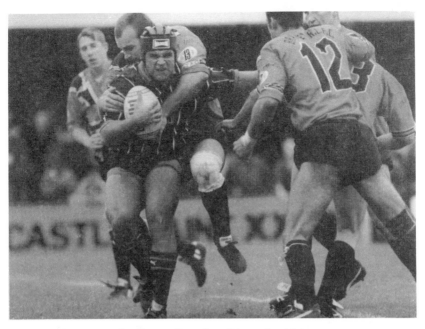

Sid Domic takes on Bramley (Photo: David Stevens)

London Broncos 1994-5 (Photo: London Broncos)

were included in the Super League. The "moral" side of winning promotion through a reorganisation of the game, rather than on the pitch, is another matter.

The Huddersfield game was a thriller, ending 24-24. But it had lost its meaning. The club had some success in recruiting three young English players on loan, Jason Roach from St. Helens, goal kicker Craig Booth from Oldham and Paul Stevens from Wigan. On the Super League front, Robbie Moore wrote that "the Broncos have been given a huge role to play in the new set up", and said that finding a new ground, and strengthening the playing squad were both very important for the new challenges ahead.

Following a Good Friday slaughter of a poor Leigh side, the Broncos arrived late at Rochdale on Easter Tuesday, having been held up in a three hour traffic jam. The match was being covered by Channel Four News for a report on the Super League, but the Broncos failed to score a try in a poor defeat. The league season ended on a high note, with a win at Whitehaven.

So the Broncos had finished fourth, one place below the previous season. This gave them a home match with Whitehaven in the Premiership. Played on VE Day, a minute's silence was held before the game, and the Broncos then won easily, restricting their Cumbrian opponents to one point. This led to a semi-final at champions Keighley. The Yorkshire side saw this as a grudge match as they had been omitted from the Super League, despite finishing as Second Division Champions. They cruised home 38-4 with Scott Roskell scoring a late consolation try.

One of the final acts of the season was the permanent signing of stand-off Paul Stevens from Wigan. He had been on loan.

Top try scorer was Scott Roskell with 24, who also finished as top points scorer. Despite only playing 12 games, John Gallagher topped the goal kickers with 39. Seven players had kicked goals. The final league record was:

Played	Won	Drawn	Lost	For	Against	Points
30	20	1	9	732	480	41

Postscript: Into the Super League

The proposals to establish a Super League, playing in the summer, and involving mergers of long established clubs shook Rugby League from top to bottom. Apart from the plans, which were announced at the beginning of April, defusing any interest in the 1994-5 promotion battle in the Second Division, they also seemed to wipe out the game's rich heritage at a stroke.

Nothing had been learnt from the few attempts in Football to merge clubs in the early and mid 1980s. Not surprisingly, faced with a rebellion from supporters, the League backed down, and the new Super League proposals, albeit introduced in a ham-fisted way, are more based on playing performance in the 1994-5 season.

Except, of course, for London Broncos "promotion" to the Super League, despite having finished fourth in the Second Division. Possibly because of all the greater controversy over mergers, London's place in the Super League has not been one of the key points of debate in the restructuring. However, Keighley, Batley and Huddersfield, and the teams now put into the "first" division are rightly indignant

Maybe there is now more of a recognition that if the sport is ever to truly establish itself as a national game, a high profile operation in London is essential, and the Brisbane Broncos have the resources and experience to do this. There has never been a better opportunity for the sport to really develop. Supporters may be critical of News Corporation's role in the sudden development of the Super League, and the apparent spilling over into Britain of a battle for television coverage rights in Australia. But, there can be no doubt that *Sky's* coverage of Rugby League has given the sport more viewing time then ever before.

Indeed, Paul Wilson, writing in *The Observer*, saw London's role as crucial, saying that if there is "a convincing showing from the London Broncos, the game will have taken a significant step forward." The article was headed: "Super idea rides on the Broncos."

Undoubtedly, some supporters in the Rugby League heartlands would be content to see the game remain in the M62 corridor. One commented "I don't care whether Rugby League is a success in the South of England or in France. It has been and still is part of the life-blood of Northerners, the competition between towns is great..." (*Merging on the Ridiculous*). But with the increased marketing of other sports, including Rugby Union, the higher profile of football with the Premiership, and American Football's continued attempts to establish a European base, Rugby League cannot afford to stand still.

Change has also become inevitable because of full-time professionalism coming into the game. The debate years ago that led to the foundation of the Northern Union, was not about full-time professionalism, but about players working full-time, and being paid compensation for missing work when they played Rugby. But Wigan's adoption of full-time professionalism, followed by Leeds, has put them ahead of the other clubs. There must be a more level playing field. Otherwise, despite the sometimes marvellous spectacle provided, if the game loses genuine competition at the highest level, which it is in danger of doing, it can also lose support. "What's the point...Wigan always win", is as much a danger to Rugby League as the parochialism of some of those who believe it should only be played in the north.

Pumping money into a sport does not guarantee success. Unless the Rugby League finally manage to develop a strategy for growth, the Murdoch millions may be wasted. It still seems that it is necessary for clubs or local groups of businessmen to approach the League, such as Newcastle United, rather than a strategy existing to build in the Midlands, and then to reach areas such as Bristol, Birmingham and Milton Keynes. The Australian Rugby League did have a strategy, and it is now paying dividends, despite the game's current disputes.

Rugby League is at a crossroads. There is the opportunity to become a national sport, taking advantage of the increased television coverage the game has had, and the marvellous product on offer. If this does not happen, the game may never develop beyond the traditional heartlands.

The next five years will be crucial, and the establishment of a high quality operation in London is a key element. Not only will the ever present problems of marketing, a stadium and building a profile need to be tackled, but a successful team is vital. People may come and watch the northern giants once, but a team losing regularly will not attract support. Harold Genders, who set up the first Fulham club, believes that a winning team in London could attract 25,000 people, and with the resources crowds like that could bring, could come to dominate Rugby League.

The Broncos have been enormously successful in Brisbane. they have the marketing knowledge and experience to attract major sponsors. This must surely be the best opportunity ever for Rugby League to really establish itself at club level in London. Finding a suitable ground is crucial, and a team that plays attractive, winning rugby. For once, London's supporters can look to the future with confidence.

19 Interviews

The interviews we did were with people who had been involved on the management side of the club. Most were conducted before the Super League was announced.

Roy and Barbara Close

Roy and Barbara Close took control of Fulham when the original club was liquidated. From then, until the end of the 1992-3 season, except for a short period in 1986, they were majority shareholders. They were directors from 1984 to 1986, and again from 1989 to 1990. Barbara was the first female chairman of a Rugby League club, and Roy represented the club on the Rugby League Council for many years.

(N.B. The interview was done with Roy and Barbara together. Where one person answered a question, or was responsible for something, that is shown, but for most questions, they both answered together.)

How did you get involved?

We were Fulham FC season ticket holders. We always felt that Fulham didn't sufficiently promote any big games they got, and therefore didn't get a big crowd. We thought the match against Wigan might be the same - just a damp squib. So we thought we'd go along to give our support, and see what it was all about. We got complimentary tickets for the first game, as Fulham FC season ticket holders. Every soccer season ticket holder got a complimentary ticket.

R: It was only in the second game we went to that we were told we weren't watching "rugby", but "Rugby League."

B: I was aware that they were different games.

The matches being on Sunday changed our whole Sunday routine. Before we started going to the rugby games, we had a roast lunch at home. Instead, we started having lunch at the club restaurant, which we had regularly used for football game days for years. Not many people did that, and the people involved with the club noticed us, and talked to us. At first, we sponsored the kit of a couple of players.

Then they asked us to sponsor a player, and pay the transfer fee for Steve Bayliss. Harold Genders told us that Ernie Clay had run out of money to put into the Rugby club, so we undertook to pay the £28,000 transfer fee from St Helens. He had not been playing for them, and it took us 5 hours, with him making many telephone calls to his mother in Wales, to convince him to join Fulham. We also paid half the transfer fees for Steve Mills and Charlie Jones.

R: We had not been involved with the Football Club, beyond sponsoring kit, etc. I had the ambition of owning Fulham FC, and the Bayliss transfer started our moves to buy the Rugby club. We were negotiating to buy the Rugby club for two years. I saw this as a first step towards buying the football club. At one time, we were supposed to be owners of the Rugby club by the Australia game in November 1992.

B: I was very keen for us to buy the Rugby club.

R: Ernie Clay used to talk of our two families working together, but we couldn't agree anything - he had no idea of the finances of the Rugby club. We met his sons and Harold Genders in Huddersfield. At that meeting, someone said "Why do the Closes know more of the finances of the Rugby club than we do?"

Now, I believe that the reason they didn't sell the Rugby club to us was that they were intending to wind it up, as they didn't want the Rugby club confusing the freehold of the ground.

For some time, Ernie Clay had been trying to buy the freehold of Craven Cottage, which was owned by the Church Commissioners, as the Fulham Football Club lease had a restrictive covenant that meant it could only be used as a football club. He owned Fulham Football Club, and the football club had a 115 year lease, at a rental of £2,500 per annum. In my view, the rent review clause was not enforceable. Ernie Clay had suggested the figure of £2,000,000 for the purchase. I said this was nonsense, and offered to talk to the Church Commissioners for him in early 1983. In my discussions with them , I said that I thought the real value of the freehold was about £50,000, but as they would not accept this, I offered £125,000 on behalf of Ernie Clay . Cluttons (who were acting for the Church Commissioners) considered this to be very reasonable, and I reported back to Ernie Clay.

Subsequently, I believe he bought the freehold for about £2,000,000, but without the covenant restricting its use. This meant it was a potential building site from that day, and still is. The Church Commissioners, in removing the covenant, made Craven Cottage a potential building development. Subsequently, he sold the Football Club, which now included the freehold, at a profit, to a property company.

Eventually, we were told by the Clays that they were not going to sell the Rugby club, but build it up. The next thing we heard was that it had been put into liquidation.

R: Someone phoned, and told us that the club was to be put into liquidation, and asked if we would buy it. We went to the liquidation meeting, and Stoy Hayward were advising that the club must go into liquidation. Although I was only an observer, I was aware that there could be a problem with players contracts and registrations, and I suggested in the meeting that they should consider putting it into administration before liquidation.

I was told to mind my own business, and it was put into liquidation. The consequence of this was the court case, which confirmed my original fears.

Later, there were reports in the press that the club "may be saved by a Maidenhead businessman."

Immediately after the liquidation meeting, we entered negotiations to buy the club from the liquidators. The first question we asked was "have you got the players' contracts to sell?" We were, on several occasions, told "Yes", and got this in writing. It was on the basis of these assurances that we signed the contract.

During the negotiations, we were told that we could continue playing at Craven Cottage. The agreement we signed had a 31 day "cooling off" period. Two days before the end of the "cooling off" period, we were told that Craven Cottage would not be available for the Rugby club.

So, we held a board meeting (i.e the two of us), and we decided to go ahead. We thought if we held the registrations of the players we had, and strengthened the team, and got the Supporters Club involved, we could get the Club into the top half of the first division. So we let the "cooling off" period lapse, and bought the club.

We thought we had purchased the registrations of all the players, posts, kit and some jockstraps! We had also bought the name of the club, associated goodwill, and the membership of the Rugby League (i.e. the fixture list). All this happened two weeks before the start of the season.

By the way, we were then declared "persona non grata" at Craven

Cottage. I didn't go to a match there for a year, and Barbara never went regularly again.

We appointed Roy Lester as manager. We needed someone with a Rugby League background to run the team, and he was the most senior person available. Harold Genders and Reg Bowden had already left. At this time, we met the players to discuss us taking over. I feel that Reg Bowden became disillusioned.

Roy Lester taught us a lot about Rugby League. We taught him about management and business. He signed players such as Chris Wilkinson, from a small amateur team, who was one of the best touch kickers in Rugby League. He originally signed for £1,000. We unilaterally increased it to £5,000. He didn't ask for it, we gave it to him.

Our only criticism of Roy Lester was that he didn't like staying in London. We would have liked him to have spent more time in London, to develop a London based team.

The infamous contract court case........

The court case about the registrations was in November 1984. I believe the players got outside support in taking the case to court. The case was against both the Rugby Football League and Fulham RLFC (1984) Ltd.

We had to oppose the players becoming free agents, as we wouldn't have a team otherwise! We could have held off on the court case, but the players involved were staying away anyway. We decided, on the suggestion of the Rugby League, to have one solicitor, and one barrister to act for both parties.

There were two issues at stake, the question of the players becoming free agents, and in the background, the whole contract system used in Rugby League at the time.

The issue for us was around the difference between a "contract of service" and a "service contract." The case was adjourned four times, as the players' counsel was not available. The day before it was finally heard, we learnt that our barrister was not available. In my view, the barrister who took over had not been briefed adequately on the case. In the end, the Rugby League won the point they were concerned about, and we lost. So we had paid out to buy the club, based on a valuation of the players we expected to "inherit", and then lost players worth around £250,000. A few of the players stayed loyal, but most of the key ones left, and the case was a huge setback.

Soon after this, the Rugby League changed their contract system. The essence of the change was that it went from a player being signed for a club "for life" to contracts being issued for a fixed period and at a stated remuneration.

The first female chairman of a Rugby League club...

B: As the two directors, one of us had to become chairman. Roy is not very keen on socialising, and chatting with people, so we agreed that I would become chairman. I was not trying to prove anything, although it did gain us some publicity. My intention was to run the club, as with other things we'd run together. We could run a business, a family, etc. Roy would run the administrative side as managing director, and so I became chairman.

The boardrooms were usually a male preserve. Men run rugby clubs, so the boardrooms were for men. My first away game as a director was at Swinton, which was a "male" boardroom, with another room for guests, ladies, etc. Some one spoke to John Rathbone (our club secretary) that they weren't really sure what to do with Barbara! He said that if she didn't go in the boardroom, no one from Fulham would. In fact, Ian Clift, the Swinton chairman at that time, came out and made me very welcome, so there were no problems.

I very rarely had any problems, but I didn't make a great fuss. I wasn't in fact the first lady director - one of the committee run clubs had a woman on their committee. But I never had to say I must be let in.

One Yorkshire club were very inhospitable, and didn't invite me into the boardroom. And no one even spoke to me. So after Roy made a brief foray into the boardroom, neither of us went in.

The most hospitable club were always Huyton, or Highfield as they became.

Starting afresh - the summer of 1984....

During the summer, we had a meeting with the players at a hotel up north, and invited Ron and Mo Snares from the supporters club. It was the first time the supporters club had been involved properly with the Rugby club.

Someone suggested we try the Crystal Palace National Sports Centre as a home ground. We had spent two weeks trying different football clubs, but without success. We agreed to lease-hire the ground on a match by match basis, and pay for each game.

I believe we stopped the club from dying at that time. It was "reprieved", not saved. We went to the Rugby League headquarters, and met David Howes and Reg Parker. We asked what they were doing about expansion, and David Howes said that if someone phones, we talk to them. There didn't seem to be any plan to develop the game.

We felt they should have a "starter pack" for new clubs, or for people who were considering taking over an existing club. This could explain the rules and regulations, etc. As far as we are aware, nothing ever happened about this.

Gary and Kathy Hetherington were starting Sheffield at about this time, and Kathy and I were elected to the Rugby League Council on the same day.

We were keen to get things going, but we had to ring the Rugby League for advice all the time.

So, we had moved to Crystal Palace, having lost most of our assets, (the players' registrations) and around 3,000 fans, who did not follow the club to Crystal Palace from Craven Cottage. We thought that if we could involve the Supporters Club, and get a few good Australians, we could improve things.

This was a difficult time. One player said that if we paid him the money he was owed on his original contract, he would stay with us. We gave him that payment, around £4,000, but he still joined another club.

Moving on....

By the end of the 1984-5 season, it was obvious that we couldn't continue at Crystal Palace. It had a good pitch, and good floodlights (onto the track), and 16,000 seats. But it was difficult to get to, was desolate in winter, and it was clear that we had to move.

Two options at the time were Wealdstone F.C., and Chiswick. Wealdstone's ground was possibly going to be sold for redevelopment, so we went to Chiswick. Someone suggested Chiswick, with a view to us buying the ground, and developing it.

The ground actually belongs to trustees, not to the Polytechnic of Central London (now University of Westminster) directly. The Chief executive of PCL (who was secretary of the trustees) said that a purchase could not be arranged in time for the 1985-6 season, so we came to a lease-hire agreement for a year, with the aim of sorting out a purchase or a long lease, which would have allowed investment in the ground. In the end, this went on for 4 or 5 years, and we gave up.

Martin Offiah...

We were told there were a couple of good black Rugby Union players playing for Rosslyn Park. So we went to see them, wearing our Fulham RLFC sweaters. That caused a stir! Both the players looked good, but we were not able to judge, and had no money in the club and no coach, so we didn't follow it up. A couple of years later he signed for Widnes, and I'm sure, on reflection, we could have matched what Widnes initially offered him.

We had the idea that if a London based Rugby Union player joined us and turned professional, and would sign for a reasonable fee, if he made the grade, and joined a club up north, we would split part of the transfer fee with him. If Martin Offiah had signed for us, and we'd sold him to Wigan for £450,000, he would have got around £300,000!

Mind you, we had Rugby Union players coming for trials, and when we told them how much the wages were, they said they could earn more from Rugby Union.

I believe the original club never saw the potential of players based in London, beyond a couple of players.

Liquidation...

In the meantime, problems were developing. In August 1984, we had set up a management committee, which we hoped would run the club on a day to day basis. We would set down guidelines and polices, but they would run the club. In practice, we were involved in day to day management most of the time.

By the spring of 1986, we got fed up with things; had lost a lot of money, and announced that we were going to put the club into liquidation on 1st April 1986, because there was no one around with the money to buy it.

Then at the eleventh hour, Paul Faires approached us, the liquidation meeting was adjourned, and we sold him our shares for £10. We knew that he had been involved at Kent Invicta, and although we had some doubts, the club was going into liquidation anyway. This meant that the club continued. So he took over for the last 6 weeks of that season. He was the only director, which was rather unsatisfactory.

When Paul Faires took over, Roy Lester left, and Bill Goodwin took over as the manager.

At the end of that season, Paul Faires pulled out, and over the summer, Tim Lamb and Richard Lawton became directors. We soon again became the biggest shareholders, and we continued to back the club financially, but not to be directors. I continued as the Rugby League Council member.

Tim Lamb set up a new company (Hadenford Investments) for the 1986-7 season, and the Rugby League accepted this. Occasionally, we were directors after this, but we let other people run the club.

Coaches and managers...

In the summer of 1987, Bev Risman became manager. He had been an international in Rugby Union and Rugby League, and we got on well with him. But in the autumn of 1988, results had not been good, and there was a management committee meeting which we attended. Everyone was dissatisfied with the results, and felt the team had not made as much progress as it should. We felt that Bev should be given a warning that if results did not improve, he would be sacked. But everyone else voted to sack him without any warning.

R: I met him with Tim Lamb and Richard Lawton. We all looked at each other, and no one said anything. So I had to say that the management committee has decided to sack you, even though I had voted against it.

So Bill Goodwin again took over temporarily, and it was suggested to us that we contact Mike Stephenson in Australia, and he agreed to come over for a trial period. I was going to meet him at the airport, and rang his home to check that the plane had left on time.

His wife said that he had not caught the plane, but had gone out for a walk. It turned out that someone loosely connected with the club had phoned him, and discouraged him from coming, and he changed his mind.

So then Phil Sullivan was recommended to us. After our experience with not actually meeting Mike Stephenson, we said come over, we'll pay your fare, and have a trial period of a few weeks.

He was a rough diamond, and came to see us once a week for a discussion about the club. The team seemed to improve, won four games, and gave Bradford a fright in the cup. He asked what his future was, and we said that the management committee had to decide. But to us, it seemed obvious that he should be given a longer term contract.

The following Sunday, we were clearing up in the Boardroom, and two of the players came in, saying they were representatives for the team, wanting to protest about the sacking of Phil Sullivan. We had both been unaware of the"decision" of the management committee and were certainly not involved in it nor did we agree with it. There was a petition from the players and supporters, but in the end he did leave - he would have been in an impossible position if we had over-ruled the management committee. I have a suspicion that he had made it clear that only he would pick the team, and maybe that was behind it.

B: By this time, we were rather worn down with all the wrangles. All we wanted was to help run a rugby club. And don't think this was for the "glory" - I cleared litter from the ground at Chiswick on the Mondays after a match. One Monday it rained so hard I was wet through four layers of clothing when I got home.

The appointment of Ross Strudwick...

R: Ross Strudwick had been coach at Halifax, and had had problems there. He was introduced to us, and Barbara interviewed him (she is a better judge of character). Barbara felt that he could work for Fulham, although he wouldn't necessarily be an easier person to deal with than Phil Sullivan. He was appointed, using a contract based on his Halifax one, although ours gave him sole control over team management.

Ross was very keen on the move to Crystal Palace. Chiswick could not be developed without a long term lease, or by purchasing the ground. We could have got Sports Council grants, but needed a minimum 28 year lease. Crystal Palace had good training facilities, and 6 houses we could use. But I don't think Ross realised how depressing it was with a small crowd.

Ross Strudwick should be given credit for keeping the club alive in that period.

Tim Lamb's departure....

Ross Strudwick felt that Tim had too much on, and that the Club would run better if he became general manager, and let Tim concentrate on financial matters as finance director. Ross Strudwick has a chain of shops in Australia, and had some commercial knowledge.

I met the directors of the Rugby League in London, as we needed advice, as I could either lose our club secretary, or not have a general manager. The Rugby League were in favour of Ross Strudwick becoming general manager, and that was what we did. We wanted Tim to stay involved, but the new arrangement was not acceptable to him, and he left the club's management.

The change of name from Fulham to London Crusaders....

After the club left Craven Cottage in 1984, there was an ongoing discussion about a change of name. Barbara and I resisted this not because we didn't want a change, but we wanted a permanent future and venue first. We didn't like "West London", which had no particular meaning. It was Ross Strudwick who suggested London Crusaders. Crusaders had a certain ring to it, as it was a "Crusade" we were involved in, and we willingly agreed.

Canberra....

R: In the summer of 1990, I went to Canberra with Ross Strudwick. We went to a match, and Ross said that Roy Close from London was with him, so we were invited into the Boardroom, and went onto the pitch, and met the players.

As a result of that, we had discussions with their chairman about them taking on the London club as a sister club. He was interested, but then Canberra hit financial problems, and the idea was dropped. We were still anxious that the club continued and succeed, but there were still tremendous problems.

I had lunch with Maurice Lindsay in Wigan, during which I re-iterated that all the stops should be pulled out by the Rugby League for the club in London to succeed. I believe that a team in London would only succeed if it is in the top half of the first division.

I said that if necessary, the quota should be abandoned for London. I felt that it had to succeed quickly, as we couldn't bring on London based players quickly enough. At that stage, Maurice Lindsay hinted at someone with huge assets who wanted to get involved in London, and wanted an all Australian team in the city. I believe it was linked with an Australian TV deal.

Rebuilding....

We said to Ross Strudwick that we had had enough - the club had to get a new board, sponsors, and a finance director. There had been a lot of disputes, and we didn't want to be involved on a day to day basis any more. We gave a financial guarantee to the club up to a limit, but if new sponsors were found, they would not need the guarantee. It was around this time that the Bartrams first appeared on the scene, through Britannic Shipping Services as a potential sponsor. Until February 1993, the directors were the Bartrams, Graeme Pickering and Ross Strudwick. The Bartrams then sacked Strudwick

Barbara Close presenting Michelle Snares with a Player of the Match award
(Photo: The Snares family)

Roy Close at Chiswick (Photo: Barbara Close)

with my concurrence. Once he had left, the Bartrams were in control, although I was still the majority shareholder.

Towards the end of that season (1992-3) Richard Bartram told me that it had become clear that the club would be around £25,000 in deficit. We offered to cover 50% of the deficit, if the directors covered the other 50%, or planned to recover their half in the following season's budget. This was largely explainable by an expected sponsor not coming forward with their contribution.

But the anticipated deficit grew, and by the time it was over £50,000, it was more than we or the Bartrams could cope with. The deficit could not be covered, and the directors, with our concurrence, put the club into administration. The business of the club was then sold to a new company, controlled by the Bartrams. This company purchased the business and assets from the administrators, and took over the Rugby League registration.

Subsequent to this, the old company was put into liquidation, and we weren't shareholders after that. However, we did pay Tony Gordon his outstanding wages at the end of the 1992-3 season, to make sure he came back, otherwise he wasn't going to.

The Broncos...

After the Bartrams took over, we were no longer involved with the club. But we were delighted when the Broncos took it over, as it means it will stay alive. I believe the Broncos have the money, expertise and ambition. They need a good team and a good stadium. A good stadium is essential. A return to Craven Cottage is always a "possibility", but I think there are some people at the football club who fear that the a successful Rugby League club could overshadow the football club.

Over the years, what has all this cost you....

In direct financial terms, not including time, secretarial and office expenses, players staying with us, etc, around £300,000.

Roy still attends virtually every London Broncos match, home and away. Barbara attends most of the home games, but cannot travel to away games because of a bad back. In recognition of their contribution to Rugby League in London, the Broncos have given them Board room facilities as honoured guests.

The Australians arrived....

One of the most important parts of rebuilding after leaving Craven Cottage was finding Australian players to strengthen the team. Many clubs used Australian players, but most did not stay with the club owners.

When we took over in 1984, we decided to bring a couple of Australians over to strengthen the existing team. We thought that with a stronger team, we could rebuild the gates to 6,000, and get promoted to Division One.

Don Duffy and Mike Davis were the first two we signed. Mike had been Peter Sterling's understudy at Paramatta, and gave him a hard game when we played Hull in the Cup. The Australians were the only players we could get. At that time, the quota applied to work permit players only, who were earning over £15,000 per annum. Players on a "working holiday" were not included in the quota.

Initially we were restricted to 3 quota players. We had an argument with the Rugby League, who accepted that "working holiday" players were not included, and that we could have more quota players. We agreed a quota of 5, that would fall to 4 and then 3. We couldn't afford first class players so we went for younger players. At first, Mike Davis and Don Duffy lived here. Mike's wife came as well, and she was very vocal at rugby matches! They moved on, and lived at Crystal Palace.

Then Paul Rochford and George Bryan came. Paul had his best game ever in his first match, when he was only just off the plane, and then got worse. George arrived a few days later, and was terrible in his first game, and got better. He got frostbite in one game. Paul knew that we needed players, and a friend of his was playing in France, and was not happy. So he contacted Duncan Webster, and he came over as well, and he stayed with us as well.

B: His girlfriend came as well, and the house was starting to get a bit full, as one of our daughters was still living at home, so we had the family, and three Rugby League players. Duncan and his girlfriend moved on, to my sister's house, and I believe they later got married. They all helped clear the ground at Chiswick before the first game there. They had to borrow the car so they could get to training at Chiswick. And there was all the kit to wash after training. I used to go to a launderette in the evening, as I was worried I wouldn't be allowed to put such muddy shirts in the machines.

The next season, we had a break, and no players stayed. But then in

1986-7, four more players arrived. Glen Haggath and Pat O'Doherty were more experienced than the Australians we had had before, and it saved some money by them staying with us. Greg Pratt and Darren Rampling stayed as well. I think Pat thought he was coming to a mansion, as it was the club owners' house. He was mad on martial arts videos, but wasn't so enthusiastic about training. He used to have tomato sauce with everything.

We got a huge phone bill one quarter, and realised that Australians and BT don't mix. One player was mainly responsible, and he did (eventually) pay off the bill. Bob Knight also stayed for a time. He was the tidiest rugby player I ever met - his room was like another world compared to the others.

Darren Rampling came to play for Fulham, but the Club released him, so he went to play for Runcorn. He didn't do very well there, and they let him go the week before Christmas. We felt we couldn't leave him on his own in the north at that time of year, so we invited him back for Christmas, and he stayed until April. He played a few more games for Fulham. His nickname was "Ramp", and one day, he bought a "Ramp" roadsign back with him.

When Greg Pratt came, he told us he had a friend in London, and wanted to visit him, on his first night in the UK. He had never been here before, and came from a small country town in Australia. I was quite worried about this, but he went off, and then didn't come back that night. He hadn't phoned, and in the end I rang the police. They said someone has to be missing for 24 hours before they do anything. He did find his own way back, and as we were out, climbed up the front of the house to get in through a window. A woman passing by asked what he was doing, and he said he lived here. She believed him!

Douglas McClelland, the Australian High Commissioner got involved at this time. Neil Robinson used to accompany him to the matches. I didn't realise till then that Neil was a policeman. One night, we had seven Australians staying. The house isn't that big, but they said that "a bit of floor" was alright. "She'll be right" they used to say.

R: And it was always "Barb", not "madame chairman."

We used to give the players complimentary tickets to give out in the Australian clubs, and a commission on ticket sales. But we never attracted a great following amongst Australians in London. One of our best Australians ever was Peter White. He came here on holiday. I remember a tall bloke coming into the boardroom at Chiswick, and saying "duck", as he is 6ft 6." He said "I play rugby" - so we gave him a trial.

Harold Genders

Harold Genders was managing director of Fulham from 1980 to October 1983. It was his initiative to set up a club in London.

What was your background in Rugby League before you became involved with Fulham?

I signed for Rochdale Hornets as a nineteen year old in 1949. At the time, I was an apprentice joiner and studying three nights and one day at Warrington Technical College. My subject was construction and I was taking Higher National Certificate and the City & Guilds.

Due to my studies, I was deferred from National Service, which was compulsory at that time but, at twenty one years of age, I was conscripted and joined the R.A.F. for two years.

At weekends I was playing for Rochdale but on sports afternoons, on a Wednesday, I played for Rugby Union for R.A.F. Stoke Heath where I was the captain and coach. I also played for Maintenance Command and the Combined Services.

Other clubs that I played for were Widnes, and, finally, Blackpool Borough. I retired from playing at the end of the 1957-8 season as I realised that I needed to concentrate on my job as is to be appreciated that Rugby League did not pay the satisfactory wages they do today.

I was employed by a small builder as a general foreman before finally working for Leonard Fairclough Limited (now known as AMEC plc) in September, 1959 at the commencement of the Thelwall Viaduct as a Chargehand/Joiner.

I was promoted eighteen times and became managing director of Fairclough Civil Engineering and I now hold the position of special advisor to the chairman, Sir Alan Cockshaw, in a semi-retired position.

Sir Oswald Davies, the chairman of AMEC plc took over Warrington RLFC and reduced the number of Directors, having made the retiring Directors life members, down to two - Mr Brian Pitchford, Managing Director of Lockers, and himself.

Sir Oswald sent for me and requested my help, due to my intimate knowledge of Rugby League as, although he had watched rugby all his life, he had never participated on the inside, as it were, of the sport. I initially founded the Primrose Club and shortly after, was made a director of the club.

The secretary, appointed by Sir Oswald, was Phillip Worthington, who was very knowledgeable with regard to Rugby League and he too was promoted to a directorship.

As a Director, I was involved in the scouting, recruiting, signing and negotiating the terms and conditions of players with the club. John Fieldhouse, Ken Kelly, John Dalgreen and Billy Benyon, who replaced Alex Murphy as the coach, were, amongst others, some of the signings I helped to recruit along with Philip and Alex.

The dream of a London team

Ironically, it was at Wembley the dream began. Two years before Fulham's big night in 1981 against Bradford Northern, I sat in my hotel room searching through the southern editions of the national and local newspapers, desperately looking for a reference to the match the following day.

None was to be found. On the Sunday after the game, watched by 96,000 people, all that could be found was the result. The miserly result. Rugby League's biggest day and all it merited - in southern eyes - was a single line score.

Something, I thought, must be done to spread the gospel, but how? The only possibility could be the creation of a Rugby League club in the south. A southern outpost. But where?

On the Monday, I obtained a map of England and searched for the right venue. After much deliberation, I decided there were two alternatives, Hereford United or Fulham.

Hereford, newly voted into the Football League, after an encouraging start to their league career, hard returned swiftly to the Fourth Division. Hereford itself was in an ideal position. Close to the Welsh borders, close to the mass of population in the Midlands, yet linked with the old established areas of Rugby League by the M5 and M6 motorways.

Relegation for any soccer club is a costly matter. Gates tumble, advertising revenue drops and players leave. Rugby League could be the medicine the bank balances desperately needed.

Fulham, once proud cup finalists and First Division material were also faltering. After disastrous season, they had been relegated to the Third Division. Their chairman, Ernie Clay, a man who was prepared to take risks, fascinated me.

Ernie Clay is not frightened to venture into the unknown. His signing of the controversial George Best and also Rodney Marsh, had shown the risks he was prepared to take.

London, in my opinion, is the greatest city in the world and to have a Rugby League side there would be the greatest boost the sport ever had. The site at Craven Cottage was also ideal.

Setting up the club

After a lot of deliberation, I decided... Fulham was my target. The problem was - how the target could be achieved.

All the negotiations had to be carried out in secret because I was still a Director at Warrington at the time. It was not a case of being a traitor to the Warrington cause - the club were, and still are, very close to my heart - but this was a chance to further the cause of Rugby League. In a choice between club and sport, the sport came first.

I contacted the late Ernie Clay by various means and the following meeting took place on the 6 May 1980. Brian Dalton, Fulham's financial director, brought Gregory Clay, Ernie's son, with him and I shocked them both by suggesting that Fulham should sell their soccer team and take up Rugby League full time.

" I thought you told us that you weren't mad," said Dalton. The other alternative, I told him, was to play Rugby League at Craven Cottage every other week.

In hindsight, my first suggestion was correct. Had they sold the soccer team, Fulham RLFC by now, would have been in Wigan's position, the only difference being, there would be 25,000 regular gates against 14,000 average.

That caught their interest and after I outlined the advantages of playing Rugby, as a back-up to soccer, they left to put the scheme to Ernie Clay.

A further meeting was arranged with Ernie Clay and his only question was - "What are our prospects?"

" We will be promoted in the first year," I replied. The man never questioned me. "Get on and do it" was his instruction.

We shook hands on the deal and that was that. There were no long drawn out board meetings. Ernie had decided that he wanted Rugby League at Craven Cottage and he was determined to get it. Later, in the birth of the club, he was to prove a vigorous and determined fighter to keep the scheme alive and, later still, instigated by one other, he made the wrong decision and sacrificed the Rugby League club.

237

Your record

I have still to put all my memories to paper but perhaps the following facts are of interest to the reader.

I bought a team in eight weeks that on the 14 September 1980 played Wigan at Craven Cottage, never having played together before, and beat them 24-5.

We lost only one game at home in the season, and seven away. I fulfilled my promise to Ernie Clay by obtaining promotion in the first season, relegated by two points in the second season and won the Second Division championship outright in the third season.

Our average gates at home were 6,096 for league matches and 7,152 including cup ties. Our gates were well in excess of Fulham FC. We were top of the Second Division and Wigan were second with 4,693. We were fourth of all the clubs in the First and Second Division, Hull with 11,711, Hull KR 8,904 and Bradford Northern - 6,105, just above our 6,096.

In the first round of the John Player Trophy (which is now called the Regal Trophy), before a crowd of 12,583 at Craven Cottage, we knocked out Leeds. I understand that this is still a match record for the first round to this day. The birth of Fulham RLFC was considerably responsible for the increase of the Second Division total gates by 39%.

Ernie Clay once made a statement that he was selling Richard Money to Liverpool (and did so, I believe, for £300,000) and buying a Rugby League club.

From July 1980 to September 1983 I bought 32 players. I sold four players in July 1981 and gave free transfers to Tony Karalius and Neil Tuffs in September 1981. I sold John Wood in 1983. From November 1981 to January 1983 no new players were purchased.

Never, at any one time, did I have more than 24 players but most of the time less than 22. The total expenditure on players was approximately £275,000 only, thus fulfilling Ernie Clay's boast. In fact, he had £25,000 change from Richard Money's fee.

Highlight of one era - David Hull scores against Wakefield Trinity in the Challenge
Cup at Craven Cottage, in front of Fulham's record crowd (photo: Ken Coton)

Another era ends - the last match at Chiswick, with the grass bank on the right
(Photo: Richard Lawton)

Tim Lamb

Tim Lamb was match day manager in 1985-6, and then became a director, with Richard Lawton, in August 1986. He remained a director until February 1990.

How did you get involved?

I went to the first game at Craven Cottage. I have only missed four home games since then, when I was out of the country. I was involved in the club for 6 years, and during that time only missed 2 games.

I was involved in the business side, using my professional knowledge, as I am a qualified accountant. I wasn't involved in the club after the Chiswick period, although I remained a supporter.

In the summer of 1984, the Closes were buying the club, and held a meeting for supporters, which I attended. They wanted more involvement, and wanted to create a management committee to run the club on a day to day basis. All the management committee members were required to put £1,000 into the club by way of financial commitment.

They got about 6 people involved initially at that time. However, as the Closes were using their own accountant, I did not offer my services at that point.

They invested around £120,000 that season. They were losing money all the time, and it seemed that every game at Crystal Palace could be the last game.

John Rathbone had become the club secretary, and he got me involved. Towards the end of that season, Harold Nass and myself offered to put in £1,000 each. I had enjoyed watching the club for five years, and wasn't worried if the donation only helped the club last another week. At first, Roy wouldn't accept our money, as the position was so precarious.

We were playing Whitehaven, at Wealdstone F.C. We said that we would put our money in to ensure that game went ahead. But the club carried on, finding ways of getting out of trouble.

The first game at Chiswick was at the end of the 1984-5 season. I live very close to the ground, so I got more involved and became a member of the management committee.

In 1985-6, I became match day manager, looking after the turnstiles, the St John's Ambulance, the pitch, goalposts etc.

In March, the Closes had decided they had had enough, and announced the club's liquidation. They said they were "bowing to the inevitable", and the club was on ice for three weeks. Paul Faires came in at the twenty third hour. He offered to buy Roy's shares for a nominal amount, and ran the club for the rest of that season. The club had players worth around £100,000 at that time on the open transfer market.

Paul had been involved with Kent Invicta, and indirectly with Southend. He was a sports fanatic, who had been to matches at Fulham, and played amateur Rugby League for Peckham. that was how he knew Bill Goodwin.

I believe that Paul had Rugby League's interests at heart. He had some commercial contacts, and was trying to arrange a sponsorship deal. He became sole director, and appointed Bill Goodwin as coach.

He asked the management committee if we would carry on to finish the season. John Rathbone left at that time, as he was due to move up north. So I became club secretary.

Richard Lawton was the club sponsor that season. There had been a draw where a number of companies had put in £100, and the "winner" was the sponsor for that season. Richard had won the draw, and that was how he became involved.

Then Paul Faires dropped out, having written to the Rugby League to withdraw the club from the Second Division. Roy was still the Council member, and he proposed to the Council that they accept the Club's new structure. I attended a Council meeting, and they agreed to a deferred start, with our first match being at Whitehaven.

Bill Goodwin had kept the players together over the summer, so there had been some pre-season training. We borrowed John Mayo and Andy Collier from Wigan, and had 16 players on the coach to Whitehaven. Andrew Render was the unlucky one who was not in the team. We got smashed, and then lost to Sheffield at home very heavily, although Frank Feighan scored a wonderful interception try from his own line. But everyone could see that the players were trying.

Restructuring.....

The original company formed by the Closes was still trading, so it was agreed that Richard Lawton and I would become directors, with the Closes as backers, and that the debts would be paid off gradually. We contacted all the creditors, who agreed to take deferred payments. We agreed with Roy to run the club at "break even."

So at the beginning of the 1986-7 season, we restructured the management of the club. Richard Lawton and myself became directors, with the Closes as major shareholders. I continued as club secretary, and became company secretary. There was a new management committee of seven or eight people. And that is how things ran for the next four years.

When I was chief executive, I was working full time at my daytime occupation, so I was putting in around 20 hours a week as a volunteer.

I had overall responsibility for the club, although certain matters were done by other people. I wasn't involved in the commercial side, which Harold Nass did.

Only the players and the coach were paid. On reflection, we should have had a paid administrator as well. Everything else was done by volunteers.

I wasn't involved in coaching. Bill Goodwin picked the team. He did consult me, although the team invariably picked itself.

I dealt with players negotiations, contracts, match fees, etc. I was responsible for match day organisation. Roy Close kept the books, but I prepared the accounts, VAT etc.

I was chair of the management committee, and co-ordinated with MC members in their different roles.

The most time was spent on dealing with players' problems and contracts. But we couldn't offer things we couldn't afford.

Moving forward....

The debts went down, and we ran the club on a "break even basis." We did invest some money in better players, but the problem we had was how to go forward. We felt that Rugby League players would not move down from the north, and decided that players must live in London to play for the club. In the 1986-7 season, we still had a group coming from the north, Steve Mills, Charlie Jones and Chris Wilkinson, as they still had outstanding contracts.

Bill Goodwin had become coach, and then Bev Risman started to get more involved. He introduced some players to the club from student Rugby League, such as Kieron Murphy and Russ Bridge. We also got some better Australian players, and could have signed a young Allan Langer.

The players at that time felt that we needed a change of coach. I was in favour of Bev Risman becoming team manager, with Bill Goodwin as coach. At that time, I dealt with matters such as contracts, match terms, accommodation etc, which could have been handled by a manager. However,

Bev Risman was not keen on this idea. He wanted overall control of all coaching matters.

We had a directors meeting with the Closes, and went ahead with this arrangement, with Bev Risman picking the team. We sent Bev Risman to Australia at the end of the 1986-7 season, but he didn't find any potential players for us, due mainly to the limited budget that we enforced. Things didn't really work out with him as manager, and he left after a year, and Bill Goodwin took over again. Many of the players we recruited at that time were ones who "turned up" at the club.

What about Phil Sullivan...

I realised from the beginning that he was not right for the club. We had agreed a 3 week trial period for him, but I had not read his CV properly, and realised that he was assistant to the coaches at Canberra, and not assistant coach. I took the view that he did not have the profile or experience to match our requirements, and did not extend his trial period, against the consensus of opinion at that time. I accept that my actions made me unpopular. The games we won were home to Mansfield, and home and away to Dewsbury, all of which we could have expected to win anyway. Soon afterwards, we lost 60-0 at Whitehaven.

Ross Strudwick and your departure...

I introduced Ross Strudwick into the club. In the past, we had not spent much on coaches, but had concentrated on players. We realised we needed a good quality coach.

Ross said that things had not worked out for him at Halifax, and he seemed very positive. He had good Australian contacts, and could bring players over for us as well. He was also a terrific talker, and we thought he would be good for media work. He became a BBC and Sky commentator.

The deal was that he was signed for one season initially, and the Closes underwrote the costs. We went to the top of division two, but the Australians we signed weren't as good as we hoped and our form was not maintained.

Then the Rugby League finally took an interest in the club. They were prepared to put some money into the club, if the Closes did as well. I wasn't prepared to take the financial risks, as the arrangements did not appear to be too clear cut. Ross wanted to become general manager, which would give him more power. I was concerned that this could be financially dangerous for the club.

In January 1990, there was a meeting with the Rugby League board members (except Maurice Lindsay). I felt that it would be best for the club if Ross concentrated on coaching, and winning promotion for us. He had told the Rugby League that there was a fundamental difference of opinion between myself and Roy Close, and that he felt I was holding the club back by being over cautious.

They wanted a set up where Ross became general manager, and I became finance director. I didn't feel this would work, so I walked out.

Part of the deal where the Rugby League invested in the club was to move away from Chiswick, where we couldn't get a long term lease. Crystal Palace wanted us back, and could offer good facilities. The Rugby League had doubts, as the club had failed there once. We tried football clubs, but they wanted too much money.

I wasn't involved in the move to Crystal Palace, although it was my original suggestion, as I had left the club's management by then.

Richard Lawton

Richard Lawton was the club sponsor in 1985-6, and then became a director from August 1986 to February 1990.

How did you get involved and start watching Fulham?

I have a family background in Rugby League. My father, who used to support the team at Chiswick, had watched Huddersfield before World War One. He had met people like Harold Wagstaff and Albert Rosenfield. A relation of his was president of the Rugby Football League in 1921.

I had watched Rugby League occasionally over the years, mainly at Warrington. In 1980, I was a Fulham FC supporter, but I was getting bored with football. I was astounded when they decided to start a Rugby League team. I was a Fulham FC season ticket holder, so I got a complimentary ticket for the first match. I thought it was very well set up, and the first season went very well, but this didn't continue into the second season.

Your role prior to the March 1986 financial crisis

I had won the team sponsorship prize for 1985-6. There had been a competition, and they managed to pick the right person, as it drew me into involvement with the club. I am a manufacturing silversmith, and make sporting trophies. At that time I was based in Hatton Garden.

I was asked to go to the management committee meetings, and it was clear that the club had problems.

Roy Lester asked me to buy a set of shirts for the team, which had my company name on them, as there was no money available for them otherwise. Throughout the season, it was clear that the Closes were becoming less interested. It was costing them a great deal to keep the club going at that time, as the financial structure was largely what had been inherited from the Craven Cottage days.

It became clear that something was going to happen. then it was suddenly announced that they would pull out, and unless someone else could be found to take over by April 1st 1986.

Your role in the March 1986 crisis

I distributed a letter to the press, with my telephone number on it, saying that there were people who wanted the club to continue, and offering to try and set up a consortium to try to keep the club going. The period leading up to the Huddersfield game was chaos, trying to keep the belief that the club could survive. There were a couple of other vague possibilities apart from Paul Faires, but they didn't come to anything. Certainly I hadn't envisaged all this when I became the club sponsor.

At the Huddersfield away game, there were lots of Fulham supporters there - for what most of us then believed would be the club's last game. Because I was in the forefront of trying to keep things together, I remember being cheered as I walked into the bar!

The Paul Faires period

Paul phoned. I knew of him through his involvement in Kent Invicta, but I had never met him before. There is no question that but for him, there would not be Rugby League in London now. Paul wanted to take over, and asked if I would go in with him. I was doubtful about it, and said "you take over" and I'll decide. That was also Tim Lamb's position.

He did succeed in buying the shares. He called a meeting with the management committee, and announced his plans. One or two of the committee felt unable to go along with his ideas, and so resigned, but the majority of us felt that at least we should try and battle through to the end of the season, and then see what happened.

There was a enormous backlog of games, and we even played on FA Cup Final Saturday. However, we did manage to survive the season. At the end of that season I was still the team sponsor, and a member of the management committee, but much more heavily involved. I even wrote and produced an emergency programme for one match!

Your role from the summer of 1986

So we got to the end of the season. But by the start of the next season, Paul Faires had ceased any involvement. There had been a number of committee meetings during the summer to try to sort things out. The club was on the verge of bankruptcy, with huge debts. Tim Lamb and I had met regularly through the summer, and decided that if we could get the shares from

Paul Faires, we would see what we could do about resuscitating the club, and running it along proper financial lines. We met Paul Faires and persuaded him to sell us his shares, so on August 1st, Tim and I became the club owners.

We then had a meeting with Roy Close. He was not prepared to be a director, but said that he would provide certain financial guarantees in order for us to be able to keep the club going. I was never totally happy with this arrangement, which often proved very difficult to work.

It was an extraordinary period. It was the first time a Rugby League club had been taken over and run by its supporters. We were directors, but we were still supporters. Tim and I get on well, and the management committee all played their parts to the full. I remember at a secret meeting with the Rugby League, David Oxley saying we were probably the best run club in the League.

We had taken over with £85,000 worth of debts. It was our responsibility to try to get the debts down, and we did that, to the extent that when we both resigned in February 1990, the debts had come down to approximately £17,500 or so.

We had a meeting at Liam Bushell's wine bar, to tell the supporters that the club was carrying on. Bill Goodwin and Frank Feighan came, amongst others. We had a subsequent meeting at the ground with whatever players were still there, to see who would be willing to play for £25 a week. Nearly all were willing! We had only three weeks to get a team together, and I remember on the trip to Whitehaven for our first match, we picked up two Wigan players on the way, on loan just to fill up the team.

The "Friends of Fulham"

We started the "Friends of Fulham", which was mainly my initiative,. I designed the leaflet, and got it going. An incredible percentage of the crowd joined, and we got members from all over the country, and amongst others, Ray French joined. There was a great rush - a lot joined on the first day. A few visiting fans joined, but the real problem was that there was so much to do, and for a while I did little else but run it. But it was a great success. Sandra Barlow was very helpful in the early days, she coped very well with the queries and new memberships at the ground.

Running the club

Tim dealt with the administrative and financial side. I dealt with representing the club on match days, meeting people, and all the social side of the club, including meeting the opposing directors on match days. My father helped a lot with this, he could talk to anybody! I remember the Papua New Guinea game very well, which I think was the high point of my involvement. I particularly remember sitting at the dinner afterwards, listening to the Papuans singing their South Sea songs. It was a magic evening, but I felt after that, the club started top go down hill a bit, and certainly there was more tensions and problems after that.

The changes in coaches

Bill Goodwin had worked wonders to get a team together. He had been involved in southern Rugby League for years, and knew everyone. He did a good job, and I was not in favour of the change to Bev Risman. I have the greatest respect for Bev, and I like to think we are friends, but I didn't think he was the right person for the job. He was too technical, and it didn't really work.

The team were playing badly, and the supporters were saying there was the need for a change. We lost to Batley at home, and had a board meeting, followed by a management meeting. Some of the committee would have preferred him to stay on, but the club was really hanging on, even at that point, and we could not risk losing any of our supporters.

So Bill Goodwin took over again. He was brilliant at unearthing new players. I wasn't that much involved in the attempts to get Mike Stephenson. Phil Sullivan came as a temporary measure and had three league games as coach, all against weak opposition. We won all three, which gave a rather false impression of his abilities.

The decision not to offer him a contract caused a huge amount of uproar. The management committee was totally split, and we had a whole string of meetings to try to sort out the mess. My own feeling was that it would have been best to keep him on till the end of the season, which was, I believe, the original intention.

Why did you resign

For personal reasons, I hadn't been involved all that much in the 1989-90 season, and was looking for an opportunity to end my involvement. I did keep a "watching brief" on the club in that period, and didn't like what I saw. Tim and I resigned on the same day at the end of February 1990.

I was not in favour of Ross Strudwick being given such a major role, he was a good coach, but the problems arose when his role was enlarged to general manager. The Rugby League got more involved, and started laying down unacceptable terms.

We had run the club successfully since 1986, without much help from them, and it was no coincidence that once Tim's very firm hand and my involvement went that the debts soared again.

I was opposed to the move to Crystal Palace, and liked Chiswick, and saw no reason to move. I thought the move to Crystal Palace was lunacy. We had been so relieved to get out before. Hendon FC were very keen for us to move there, and if we were going to move at all, we should have gone there.

I have good memories of Chiswick and liked the atmosphere there. I made many good friends there, many of whom I still see regularly.

Since then

I vowed never to go to Crystal Palace, so I started watching football again, when a neighbour started taking me to Orient. I'm also involved in junior football, which my son plays, and have become a director of the Newham Community Leisure Trust, which is in the forefront of developing sports facilities in North Newham for the use of the community and schools. I have found the Chiswick years most useful for this task.

I watch the Broncos occasionally. I enjoyed the 1993-4 season, and went to quite a lot of matches then, but have not been that much in 1994-5. Hopefully they will move to somewhere a bit easier to get to, although I now feel less and less part of it.

I am glad I was involved in Fulham during the Chiswick period, and am very grateful that I happened to be in the right place at the right time. It was a fascinating time. The clubs' debts were substantially reduced in that period, and it was in a stable position when I resigned.

Had I not had personal problems, and had there not been such a substantial clash of personalities at the club, I think both Tim and I would still be there at the helm. However, we just could not paper over the cracks any longer! What I do know is that we performed miracles with no money at all to keep the club going, and had we had even half the money that has been frittered away in the last five years, we would have made a far better job of it.

Roy Lester

Roy Lester was the first player to sign for Fulham. In August 1984, he became team manager, which he was until March 1986.

Why did you sign for Fulham originally?

I signed before anyone else, including Reg Bowden. Harold Genders was very convincing - he had his dream of establishing a team in London. He was a director at Warrington, and asked to see me. I'd been at Warrington for five years. I was a Warrington fanatic - I'd been a supporter, and then played for them. I'd joined Leigh originally, as they had made me the best offer to turn professional. I was at Warrington with Alex Murphy.

I took some convincing, but I got on well with Harold Genders, and he told me his plans, and who he had spoken to. He was determined to make it successful. I discussed it with my wife, and she agreed I should give it a go.

Reg Bowden signed a couple of days later. It took five or six weeks to set it all up, as new players joined. In the first week, there were five players, gradually the group got larger. As more players joined, the drinks round got bigger. Tony Karalius was one of the key signings. It was really hard training, there was so much enthusiasm. We trained at Golborne sports ground. They were pleased, with local Rugby League stars using their ground, and people coming to watch.

The first game at Craven Cottage

The first match was against Wigan, who were a big club. They weren't as good as they are now, but we knew they would draw a good crowd.

The result was tremendous. It was a real boost for us, and a really good atmosphere.

We had a real team of characters - Ian Van Bellen, Harry Beverley, Reg, Mal Aspey. The younger players were often very nervous, but after talking to players like Tony Karalius, they were enjoying it.

Martin Herdman signed, and we decided we had to bring him down to earth. So we decided he should room with Tony Karalius. Tony couldn't play if he hadn't had a drink the night before a game. He always had a four pack with him. Martin had a liquidiser to make "Tiger's Milk." When he got the liquidiser out, Tony asked what he was doing, and what he was going to drink.

Tony asked how he had played in the last match, and Martin admitted he hadn't done very well, and hadn't been able to get into the game. Tony asked how he had played, and Martin said he had won the "Man of the Match." So Tony threw the liquidiser out of the room, and gave Martin a can of brown ale.

A few of that team could only play if they'd had a drink the night before. But Ian Van Bellen used to have a full Sunday dinner before a game. Reg Bowden found out, and asked him to try playing without it. Ian's mother heard about this, and came down to the ground to confront Reg: "What's all this, why can't Ian have his Sunday dinner before the games?"

There was excellent team spirit, and it was a real education playing with all those characters.

The problems of being a team based in the north, and playing in London, from a player's point of view

Originally, it was not a problem. We travelled together, and would stay in a hotel. But towards the end, people got fed up with it, and wanted to leave. I remember going to watch a football match on the Saturday before one of the home games. It took us eight hours to get there.

Some of the players couldn't adapt to it, being away from their families. But the first 12 months were OK. When we were travelling, we used to meet at the Greyhound hotel in Leigh. We got adopted" by them as well.

How you first got involved in coaching

I injured my knee ligaments. But I still went training every week. I found myself in a position where I couldn't play, so I helped other people. Harold Genders and Reg asked me to become assistant coach. This was half way through the second season at Craven Cottage. I really enjoyed it, although I didn't think I would at first. It took my mind off my injury. I had played under some good coaches, such as Alex Murphy and Bill Benyon, and tried to learn from them. Mind you, I played under some bad ones as well.

The purchase of the club by the Closes, and the move to Crystal Palace

I knew of the Closes' interest in buying the club, but I was on holiday. Roy had no contacts in the north, so I said to him that if you want to make a go of this, I would liaise with players for him.

I spent most of that holiday on the phone, ringing the Rugby League, Roy Close, the players and so on.

We arranged a meeting at Haydock Park with the Closes for the players. Some of the newer players wanted to get something out of the situation for themselves.

I think there as interference from other clubs with the players - that they would sign them if they became free agents. Some were just fed up with the travelling, but others didn't care about Rugby League in London, just looked after themselves.

A couple of the better known players were promised things by other clubs if they were free agents, and they influenced the others.

They would come to training, but not join in, just stand around having little meetings. I said to them, either have meetings, or support the club and get involved with training. So some of the players stopped coming to training.

Some players had given their all for Fulham, but the issue of freedom of contract was not just about Fulham.

I got ten years experience in two years as manager of Fulham. I was a solicitor, priest, accountant, hole digger and joiner. It was good business experience as well - I certainly learnt a lot.

Your role in the "free agents" dispute

I didn't know where Lincoln's Inn was. An inn is a pub to me. I ended up in the middle of the place, swearing affidavits about the case, although I didn't actually have to give evidence.

It wasn't just Fulham, but the case was also against the Rugby League. Ronnie Teeman, who was chairman of Bramley, was the legal representative for the Rugby League, and he got barristers and so on. There were meetings with him, going to London, swearing affidavits.

It was decided that the Rugby League's laws couldn't be upheld legally, so the case was won by the players, and they became free agents.

Rebuilding the team...

I didn't want players who didn't want to play for the club. I got a couple of amateurs, and signed a couple of players on loan. I knew of Chris Wilkinson, who was playing for a pub team. He was pleased to sign for us. He had a good kicking game, and could kick goals.

Harold Henney came on loan. I knew that you had to get on with him to make him play for you. We were going to play Salford, and he couldn't play unless he had signed for us. I was advised not to sign him, but I sat down with him, and said I'm worried about signing you, what about it? He said I won't let you down, so we signed him, and he played well for us.

For the first game at Crystal Palace, I was on the phone at one o'clock in the morning to David Oxley, asking if the players were covered for insurance, as we weren't clear what the position of the club was, and if we were part of the Rugby League.

Some of the players were still not happy. A few played some games, and then left. Some weren't happy with the travelling.

I decided we had to make a fresh start. I needed 13 players who were committed to Fulham.

We had signed two Australians, Mike Davis and Don Duffy. Don Duffy was known as Jack Gibson's tackling machine. Jack Gibson is a coach I respect, so I thought - fine. In the first match, he went to tackle Hugh Waddell, who was playing for Blackpool, and was carried off unconscious. "What have we got here?" I wondered. But we got him back on the field, and he did live up to his reputation as a tackling machine.

Mike Davis had had a bad neck injury in Australia. He came over and was a superb player. Very exciting, not a team player, more of an individual. He could win games for you. George Bryan was brilliant, and he had no reputation when he came here. Paul Rochford could play well on occasions.

By the end of the season, we had got a good team together, and finished eighth.

One game that stands out, may be not for the right reasons, is the away game at Rochdale. I was waiting for the Australians to arrive, and they only made it 20 minutes before kick off. I was ready to tell them off, but realised this wouldn't be good for the game, so I calmed down, and we went on to win 25-0, with Mike Davis scoring three tries.

Charlie Birdsall was playing for them, and we didn't get on very well. I believed that he had elbowed Chris Wilkinson in the first half, and should have been sent off. Then I thought he went for him again.

For this game, I was wearing a new black mac, and an "Eddie Waring" hat. I said to the players before the game "have a laugh now."

Towards the end of the game, Mike Davis intercepted a pass from Charlie Birdsall, and scored. I was shouting "waste of time" at Charlie Birdsall. As the game finished I took my false teeth out, and handed them to Billy Kindon in our dug out. He was a bit surprised. I was very angry with Charlie Birdsall, but thought the players would cover me. He came towards me, but our players all went off the other way. I hit him, and then ended up under all these players. My mac was ripped, and my hat went flying.

The referee said he would report me, and when I got into our dressing room, all our players burst out laughing, as I looked like I had been in an explosion.

A few weeks later, David Oxley was sitting next to me at a Lancashire Dinner, and said, Roy, I've got to do this, and smacked my hand. "That's for what you did to Charlie Birdsall." I never got called before a disciplinary committee.

Becoming a manager - how did you adjust to the change in role

With all the work involved, I decided I couldn't play as well. It was a conscious decision not to carry on playing. Also, I had had an accident at work, and had a neck injury, which was another reason to retire from playing.

I thought, "how do you go about telling other people not to do things you've done?." If they say that, I would say that I know, as I've made mistakes, and you learn from my mistakes. In the manager's role, I think I'm a good learner, and have had good teachers in managers I've played for.

I also learnt a lot on the business side. But with the people I was working with, I couldn't fail to learn.

Some times, Roy Close and I would discuss things until 4 on the morning, and not agree. But then I'd go away and think - maybe he's right. Roy would write letters to me, and sometimes even dictate them over the phone to my wife Jacqueline, as she can do shorthand.

I got on very well with Roy and Barbara and their family. He said that if I hadn't spent the time on holiday phoning , he wouldn't have bothered trying to buy the club. There were a series of obstacles. I went to see Brain Dalton to see if we could continue playing at Craven Cottage.

I drove 25,000 miles in one season. I would take training in Lancashire on a Tuesday, drive to London on Wednesday to run a session for the London based players, and then come back to Lancashire to run a session here.

Huw Richards used to ring me late on a Sunday night, to do the column for the programme, and his piece for the *Rugby Leaguer*. These phone calls could be at 11.30 p.m., or later. Once I was so tired I fell asleep in the middle of the conversation.

The move to Chiswick - rebuilding the ground etc

It was clear from the beginning that Crystal Palace was no go. You almost had to get a bus from the changing rooms to the pitch.

At the beginning there was not separate dressing room for the team, so I couldn't do team talks properly. I don't swear much, but sometimes to emphasise a point in a team talk... Anyway, then they sectioned off part of the dressing rooms, and although other people could still hear, that didn't worry me.

Chiswick had potential. It was built up from nothing by Ron Snares and others, who put a lot of time in. Really, it was their place, but we couldn't get the crowds there. If we'd been able to spend a bit more, it would have been more comfortable. We were surrounded by football and Rugby Union clubs there.

I did some of the work, and Roy Close helped as well. I got there once, and Roy, who was usually well dressed, had his sleeve rolled up, and his hand down a drain, trying to clear some leaves that were blocking it.

Roy wanted other people to get involved, and do things for the club. He wanted the club to survive on its own, and for other people to be committed as well. Fortunately, Roy didn't need to spend a lot of time on his business, so he could spend a lot of time on Rugby League.

He and Barbara were both trying their best, but felt that they were getting nowhere.

The financial crisis at Chiswick, and the "play for free" game at Huddersfield

Roy phoned me, and said that he had decided to pull out. They had put a lot of money into the club, but felt it was getting nowhere. This had been coming for a few weeks - it was a matter of whether this week's game would be played.

There was no money to pay the players. But because the supporters and the Closes had done so much, I got the players together and said that as a gesture, we should give it a go and play at Huddersfield.

We knew the players would not be paid, but would get expenses. But we would play for nothing for the supporters. A couple weren't happy, and Mike Davis didn't play. We had Mal Yates on loan, and he had been training with us. I persuaded him to play - it was the only game he played for the club. I met him recently, and he still can't believe I persuaded him to play. The players went in cars, and made our own way there.

It was a very emotional day. We were sorting out the team before the match, as we had to have some organisation. I asked Don Duffy to play at full back, which he'd never done before. In the end, Huddersfield won narrowly.

Your departure from the club, and involvement in Rugby League since then.

I got a telephone call, that someone had decided to buy the club for a pound, which included over £70,000 in debts. But I decided I didn't want to get involved with Paul Faires, as I didn't think I'd be able to work with him.

I went down to one match, before the Wembley Cup Final, and there were loudspeakers in each corner, and music played after each try. There was a fire eater at half time, and he was still putting fires out when the second half started. I'd never seen anything like it at a Rugby League game.

I then had a break for a few months, but three or four weeks before the new season, Carlisle asked me to become their manager. They were convincing people, and one was originally from Warrington, so I though I'd give it a go.

They were playing at the football ground then. At the first training session, I found things were even worse then when I'd taken over at Fulham. There was one player who ran one lap, and then said he was tired. There was a group of Yorkshire based players who weren't really committed to the club.

I had a meeting with them, and one said he was due a set of boots for last season, and one for this season! I asked - do you really want to play for us? So it was a matter of starting again, a few of them came to training.

We played a couple of games, and then were drawn away to St Helens in the Lancashire Cup. I had some players who were very inexperienced, and some who were half committed. The two centres were about 5 ft tall. And we lost 112-0. I locked the players in the dressing room after the match, and had it out with the players. I got rid of some of the Yorkshire based players after that. I have a sign on the wall at home: "A winner never quits, a quitter never wins" Is this true, I thought, as it would be easy to quit now. At least things could only get better. We were playing Doncaster the next week, and I knew we must put up a good performance. I bought in some amateur players, and played a motivational video I have. We ended up beating them.

Then we were thrown out of the football club. So we had to build another ground in Carlisle, and again I was photographed with a hammer on the roof of the stand.

I stayed there for nearly 3 years. By this time, I had gone into business with two of the Carlisle Directors, and was doing a lot of travelling. I nearly had a car crash on the motorway, and decided then to leave.

Then I had a break from the game. Warrington rang me, and asked if I would manage the Alliance side. Because it was Warrington, I agreed, and have done that ever since. I also do some work with the Academy team, and I enjoy working with youngsters. I haven't got the time to became a club manager again, but I still love the game, and enjoy still being involved.

Entrance to the Polytecnic Stadium - Fulham's home during Roy Lester's second season as manager (Photo: Richard Lawton)

257

Robbie Moore

Robbie Moore became chief executive of the London Broncos in June 1994.

(N.B. This interview was done in two parts, the first one in October 1994, and the second in May 1995).

How did the Brisbane Broncos become involved?

We were here for the World Club Challenge against Wigan, and the World Cup Final in 1992, and it was suggested to our directors that we should buy an English Rugby League team. A throwaway comment became a good idea. Then the media got hold of it, and things went from there.

Maurice Lindsay instigated the purchase. The club in London would have been non-existent if the Rugby League had not taken it over, but in the long term, there was no reason why the Rugby League should continue to run the club. If the Brisbane Broncos had not got involved, and we had taken over, then the club would have disappeared, and the Rugby League could not afford for that to happen.

Why become involved, from the Brisbane Broncos view?

Our directors have a background of involvement in different sports, but they see Rugby League as having the potential to be a world game, and this was an opportunity for us to establish ourselves in London. From this base, we hope to expand further. The opportunity to buy the club was too good to pass up. The Broncos' directors have a vision of Rugby League that could be watched by masses of people, and become a truly world game. It is easy to understand, unlike American Football, and does not have the problems baseball has being shown on television.

Also, it is played out of doors, so there are not the restrictions on crowd sizes with sports such as ice hockey or basketball. It can be a very watchable sport for a new audience.

How much did the Broncos pay for the club? Is the figure of £200,000 correct?

How much it actually cost to buy the club is hard to pin down. We bought the players contracts, and there were minimal assets otherwise - some pieces of equipment such as an ice machine, altogether worth about £3,000.

We had to be careful not to inherit all the debts the former club had run up. The key issue was the players contracts. The issue of the players being "free agents" did not arise. (Unlike the Closes' takeover in 1984).

Why did Tony Gordon leave?

There were reasons on both sides - we parted on amiable terms. We wish him well in the future.

Why did Neville Ramsey leave?

Neville is a decent bloke, but he's an individual player, and can be hard to coach. We felt we were better served with another player, who would not be so individual a player, and not so hard to control. The player we wanted to replace him with was Sid Domic, who fitted into the team, and developed well. Whenever he finished a game, we won.

And what about Andre Stoop?

We phoned Andre in Namibia, to ask him to wait until the new contracts were sorted out. We wanted to make them more incentive based. Now there is no "losing pay", and the players get a percentage of the winning money in cup games.

I had spoken to Andre, but when I tried to contact him again, he had already left for Namibia. When I rang him there, he had already signed for Keighley. He didn't want to go, but he makes better money up there. We believe that we could offer him a better lifestyle and future.

We spoke to Jack Robinson at Wigan to check who's player he actually was. At that time, Keighley hadn't paid for him, and we said we were prepared to offer £25,000, if Keighley hadn't paid. But when we offered the money, Keighley then paid the transfer fee, so he was their player. Wigan had already lodged his contract with the Rugby League. We believe he would have come to us if he hadn't signed the Keighley contract. On the other hand, they offered more than we would have done. We tried very hard, but there was nothing we could do, as Wigan had been paid.

How much are the Broncos prepared to invest?

The figure of £1 million has been mentioned, and that still holds true. It was the same in Brisbane - we had to invest a lot before getting a return.

When will a youth team be set up?

We need to develop a youth team, and that is linked to having four development officers in London. We are hoping, with the Rugby league, to establish four centres of excellence in London, and players from them would feed into an Academy side. We will have an Academy team from March 1996, and have some players now who could play for it.

The changes in Rugby Union towards professionalism can also work to our benefit. At the moment, a London RU player cannot come to train with us, and have a few games without risking burning their Rugby Union bridges. It will become easier for 17 or 18 year old RU players to have trials with us, and for us to recruit from there as well. Together with the Rugby League, we are funding the four development officers, who work in the M25 area.

We have three years to work on this, before we lose the quota for overseas players we have at present. We need to work in three areas: the schools; the 15, 16 and 17 year old players, who could join an academy team; and the amateur clubs in London. We hope the development officers will work with the amateur clubs in their areas. These could be natural feeder clubs for us, but this hasn't been developed yet. We also have a good relationship with Hemel Hempstead.

Are there any plans to play at a new ground next season?

There are plans being made at the moment, and negotiations are still going on. We could continue to use Copthall for offices and training. We would prefer a ground in the West of London, with good access to the underground. Some football grounds were interested for the 1994-5 season, but it was too short notice.

How much contact and help have you had from the Rugby League?

Help from the Rugby League has been good initially. They are attempting to help us, but we cannot be a special case within the help they give to all clubs. The development plans they have for London will be a boost .

One of the problems we have is that we are isolated down here, and don't know when other players are becoming available. There was a young reserve player at a first division club recently, who we believe would have been an asset for us, and capable of playing first grade, but by the time we heard he was available, another club had signed him. We are developing our contacts as well. There are some people up north who help us. We have given a player to Barrow, and helped with the transfer of Chris Whiteley to Doncaster. We will also look out for players coming to London for college courses.

The directors are based in Brisbane - how will this work?

The directors will visit at least once a year. The general manager will come four times. Two have already visited this season (1994-5). At the Brisbane Broncos the board meets every two weeks. The general manager runs the club. On the coaching side, all the decisions lie with the coach.

At the Brisbane Broncos, Wayne Bennett chooses the coaches and players he wants. The pressure is on the coach for results, therefore he has all the say in who plays. In Australia the coaches are not sacked during the season, unless they are incompetent, in which case they wouldn't have got the job in the first place.

What is your relationship with the press?

Relations with the press are as good as we can get. The problem is building the profile for the London press. Look at the test much coverage - when Britain won it was on the front pages, but when Australia won, it was only a smaller report on the inside.

We give information to the papers, but how can we get them to print it? There has been some TV and newspaper coverage, but most of the material we issue is not used. The Rugby League press give us as much coverage as anyone else, but they are not widely read in London. In Brisbane, we have the Courier\Mail as a sponsor, so they cover stories for the club.

Robbie Moore (Photo: Peter Lush)

How important are the fans in your future plans?

The fans are really important to us. The people who do regular unpaid work for the club is a feature of sport in England that you don't see at this level in Australia. We offered to pay two of the volunteers who do work on match days, but they refused the money.

What about the supporters club?

There are not similar organisations in Australia, although some teams have social clubs for the fans. So an independent supporters club is something new for us. We are happy to listen to the supporters club, and ideas they have. They are a committed group with consensus views on issues they have discussed as a group. An organised club which comes up with ideas will always to worth talking to. There will always be a role for a club like that.

Looking back at the 1994-5 season - was the standard of the Second Division higher than you expected?

Not higher than we expected, but higher than last year. It was hard for the players to adjust initially, particularly in the first half of the season. Some of our players had not played in England before, and had to get used to the conditions.

Our involvement made the standard higher, as people assumed there would only be one other place available for promotion. There is also the north v south thing, plus the Australian dimension. Every team wanted to beat us.

What will the Super League mean for the London Broncos?

It is what Rugby League has needed, as we have a situation where only two clubs have their heads above water financially. But the game will need to develop as well, and aim for crowds of 10,000. The Murdoch money won't solve problems on its own.

From a London point of view, it is a saviour, and after 15 years in the capital, will finally have the input, backing and money it needs. The game needs a higher profile. It needs to be on television, and in the newspapers regularly.

What impact do you think summer rugby will make?

Summer rugby and the Super League go together. I think the switch to the summer would have happened anyway. Since the impact the Australian team made in 1982, the game has changed. Wigan have done it, with a different style of play, and being faster and fitter. All teams must look at it as an opportunity to play in better conditions, and then the whole game will get stronger. I think we will get better media coverage in the summer. Kick off times could vary during the season. One possibility would be a 6.00 p.m. start, with the Alliance game played at 4.00 p.m. Changes in the licensing laws will also help, so we can serve drinks. This is an opportunity to really develop the game, in London, Paris, Cardiff and Newcastle. Birmingham would be another possibility. In the future, there may only be four or five teams from the north in the Super League. This is the pattern that has happened in Australia, where some of the inner city teams in Sydney can't survive now.

What would have happened to the Broncos if the Super League had not been formed?

It's hard to tell. The owners couldn't continue to lose money year in, year out. A switch to summer rugby may have been enough, with better matches. A decision would have had to be taken at some time. We would have needed to know what was happening in 2 or 3 years time.

How does the club intend to strengthen the team for next season?

We will sign players from anywhere. We don't know what is going to happen with the quota. Some players from the north are asking for very high sums. We are aiming for players from London. There are thousands of Rugby Union players in London. How will people identify with the team? Does it matter where the players come from? It's easier and cheaper to get players from London. We won't be railroaded into taking players from the north, who may not fit in with our style. There will be good players from Australia, who won't regard it as down-grading themselves to come to England, as they will be playing in the Super League. They will be particularly attracted by the idea of playing in London. We're aiming for a squad of 25 who could play in the first team. We want the majority of A team players to be ready for the first team within a year. We may not get all the players we want for the short season that is going to start in August, but we will be ready for the Super League.

Neil Robinson

Neil Robinson was match day manager for the 1993-4 season, and became honorary secretary when the Bartrams left the club

(N.B. This interview took place prior to the announcement of the Super League)

How did you become involved and what is your background?

I went to the first game at Craven Cottage. I also went to the second game - the away game at Keighley, which we lost. I believe there were 6 Fulham supporters there, although around 75 claim to have been there.

I work as a Sergeant in the Metropolitan Police. I was in Cumbria for 7 years, then got a transfer to London. When I was in Cumbria, I was a village policeman in Great Broughton, and was involved in helping run the Broughton Red Rose Rugby League club. I had played Rugby League in my younger days.

I missed Rugby League when I came to London, so I went to watch the first game. I only missed two games in the first season, and one of those was at Huyton, where I didn't fancy taking my new car. I went regularly at Craven Cottage, but didn't like Crystal Palace, and only went occasionally during the first season there. By the time we played there again, I was more involved.

When we played at Workington, as I knew the Workington directors, I would be invited into the Boardroom. Ross Strudwick noticed this, and asked me to welcome the visiting directors. I did that at Crystal Palace during the second period there.

After the game, it is traditional for a director from both clubs to make a speech. I did this for Fulham, and developed the best losing speech in Rugby League!

Ross Strudwick was a good coach, and was very committed. He couldn't speak to people if the team had lost, so I dealt with the people from the other team.

How did you become honorary secretary and what did it involve?

The Bartrams came on the scene - initially as sponsors at Crystal Palace, then came onto the board, with the aim of moving the club to North London. At the start of the 1993-4 season, with the move to Copthall, they didn't know how to run a club, so they asked me to form a committee of volunteers, who then became the matchday committee. I was the chair of that committee, and ran the match days.

Then the Bartrams disappeared! The first indications there were problems were at the away match at Barrow, when it transpired that the players hadn't been paid. When the Bartrams left, I became honorary club secretary. There was no one else! The Rugby League took over the financial side of the club, and paid the back wages to the players.

How much did you have to do with the Bartrams and Richard Pickering and why did they leave?

The Bartrams took over towards the end of the 1992-3 season. They got rid of Ross Strudwick. They had started as a sponsor, and hadn't been involved in Rugby League before. As far as I know, they haven't been involved since.

How much day to day control did the Rugby League have when the Bartrams left ?

The Rugby League ran the club's finances. Tony Gordon and I had to ring David Peacock to get authority for any expenditure. They didn't have any involvement in day to day management.

Maurice Lindsay was very supportive, if it wasn't for him, we wouldn't be here now! Also, the Bartrams did play a role with the move to Copthall, and starting the 1993-4 season. The Rugby League's control of the club started at the York away match in the Regal Trophy. The Broncos came to Copthall in January, and sent a couple of players over. They took over on March 23rd.

Was a budget done before the 1993-4 season started at Copthall?

The Bartrams had a plan based on crowds of 2,000. In my opinion, we were never going to get that at that time. The gates at Crystal Palace were as low as 250 to 300 towards the end of our time there. At Copthall, they were starting to move towards 1,000. The publicity has improved, including sending out posters. The coverage in the local press is very good. But it takes time to build a base of supporters in an area.

Was the collapse just down to inexperience ?

Inexperience, combined with a lack of capital. There was a £75,000 loan from the Rugby League at the start of the 1993-4 season.

How much did the Rugby League put in to keep the club going ?

I don't know the amount, but they paid all the wages and running costs.

Do you see yourself having any role in the immediate future of the club?

I didn't ask to do this job, and I have put a lot of work in. The Broncos needed someone with a working knowledge of English Rugby League, and I was available. They are still happy for me to run the match day organisation.

We have more full-time staff than any other second division club. But we must get into the first division for the club to develop. If we were playing Wigan at Copthall, there would be a lot of local interest. The second division teams are not a draw.

What does the role of secretary involve?

I am responsible for all the players registrations. Only the secretary can sign them. I also deal with loans, transfers, etc. I may be involved with the negotiations, but only the secretary can sign the forms.

I do all the match day organisation. I also arrange all the travel and hotels for the away matches. I do the liaison with the opposing teams. I greet the away team's directors, and my partner (who isn't interested in Rugby League!) does the food in the boardroom. We are the only club that provide a hot meal for the away team's directors.

I organise the A team's matches. I do the videos of the matches, although that isn't really part of the secretary's role. I do the referee's reports.

I organised moving the Hull KR cup match from Hendon FC back to Copthall, with a later kick off a couple of weeks ago, when the Hendon FC pitch was declared unfit on the Saturday at 1.00 p.m. By 4.00, we had rearranged the game for Copthall with a 4.30 kick off the next day, after the athletics meeting would be finished. I even managed to get this announced on Grandstand that afternoon.

If I'm not working, I can be at the club for eight hours a day. Most weeks, I spend around 30 hours on club business. But my employers are supportive of my involvement.

What about the future?

I think the role of the development officers is very important. Already, they have more schools to cover than they can cope with, and the other players are helping out. I feel the posts should have been covered from the day John Gallagher left.

For example, Sam Stewart organised an under 16 team a couple of weeks ago. Only two of them (his sons) had played before, but they only lost 28-24 to Hemel Hempstead, and had four tries disallowed!

There is a Rugby Union club in Bristol who want to switch to Rugby League, as they think it is a better game. The Broncos have offered to pay for a coach to bring them to one of our matches, and arrange a game for them in London, if they can fill a coach. that is the sort of initiative we need to support.

I am the link between the last three club managements, so I have quite a wide view, and I am sure the game can continue to develop in London.

The Snares family - Ron, Mo, Kevin and Michelle.

Ron and Mo Snares were chairman and secretary of the supporters club until 1990. Ron was on the club management committee. Kevin was involved in the early years, but then concentrated on playing amateur Rugby League. Michelle was also heavily invovled, and played for the Fulham womens Rugby League team.

How did you get involved ?

Kevin: I supported two football teams - Manchester City and Fulham. I heard about the Rugby League starting at Craven Cottage, and went to the first match. Michelle went to the second game. I started travelling to away games after the third away game.

Ron: I had no great interest in sport, but Kevin persuaded me to go, after four or five games. My first away game was at Wakefield. Mo's first away game was the Mick George testimonial at Widnes. By the end of the first season, everyone was involved.

Michelle: My first away game was at Bramley. I remember that Kevin got a £20 note out to pay for some drinks, and someone said "Bloody Southerner."

Who were your favourite players ?

Michelle: Steve Mills

Kevin: John Dalgreen and Joe Doherty.

Mo: Joe Doherty, Tony Kinsey, Dave Allen and Reg Bowden.

Ron: We got to know a lot of the players very well. It was completely different from football, where the players are a different race from the supporters.

Reg Bowden used to give us complimentary tickets, and we could go to the Riverside Bar after the game, and have a drink with the players. It was a completely different atmosphere from football. We went to Shaun Hoare's wedding, and stayed with Reg Bowden afterwards. We had never been to a wedding up north, and didn't realise we had to buy our drinks from the bar!

How did the Travelling Supporters Club get started ?

Kevin: The same group of people tended to travel to away matches. the coaches were run by the club. At the end of the first season, we approached someone we knew who owned his own coach, and realised we could offer cheaper travel than the club. We canvassed the supporters we knew, and found a lot who were interested in coming with us.

The first game was at St Helens. We parked outside some houses, and when one of the women living there found out we had come from London, she made tea for everyone on the coaches - 104 people.

There had been another supporters club, but we didn't think it was run very well. Fulham FC didn't recognise a supporters club, and Ernie Clay did the same with the rugby. So we started our club as a travelling supporters club.

We filled coaches for every away game. Then we formed the Fulham Travellers RLFC, and our first coach was Bill Goodwin. There are still five of the original Travellers team playing. In the summer of 1982 we joined the Southern Amateur League.

It was about that time that I dropped out of activity in the supporters club to concentrate on playing. But the league arranged our fixtures so our home games coincided with matches at Craven Cottage, so we could play in the morning, and go and watch the match.

There was a film being made about the first Kangaroos tour, with Dennis Waterman, that was filmed at Craven Cottage. I was an extra - we were meant to be the Bradford players, on a cold afternoon, and they filmed us coming out of the tunnel. To finish it, we went to Richmond RUFC at 5.30 in the morning, and filmed a sequence when the great Australian player, Dally Messenger ran through the opponents handing us off.

Ron: There was a big meeting at the Golden Lion, and I was elected as chairman. From being a travelling supporters club, it developed into home supporters as well.

We organised end of season parties at the Clarendon Hotel in Hammersmith. Up to 500 people attended them. I remember John Risman and Tony Karalius being guest speakers.

We had joined the Lancashire Federation of Supporters Clubs, and I was elected chair for 3 years.

John Risman at the Travelling Supporters Club end of season party. Ron Snares is on the left
(Photo: The Snares family)

What contact did you have with the club management ?

Ron: By then (1983), the Rugby club still wouldn't officially recognise us, but we were tolerated. We were allowed to use one of the bars, and had some pieces in the programme. By then, we were the only people running coaches to away games. The other supporters club had collapsed.

How much did you know about the soccer club pull-out ?

Ron: We got a phone call from Roy Close, saying that he was thinking of buying the Rugby club, and could we come to a meeting at Haydock Park. He said he wanted to work with the supporters club. The meeting was at 10.00, so we left at 6.00 in the morning. We met everyone, and Roy said to us to tell him if we didn't want to go along with this, as he valued the supporters' views.

Kevin: When the Rugby club started, the football club were in the third division. But then they got some better players, got promoted, and had nearly got into the first division. Initially, the Rugby Club had been a valuable source of income for them , but then I think they started to feel that the football club didn't need the Rugby club.

Ron: We got on well with the Closes. I remember a party at their house, which included races in the swimming pool. Dave Bullough got sent off for splashing.

How were you and the supporters club involved during the set up of the first Crystal Palace era ?

At Crystal Palace, a new management team was formed which was mainly people who'd been involved with the supporters club. There had been "50 days of madness" when the football club had pulled out, and the Closes had bought the club. They hired buses to take people from Fulham to Crystal Palace. Roy had tried to get a ground everywhere, and in the end Crystal Palace was the only option.

For the cup match with Halifax, we asked on the radio for people to come and clear snow off the pitch. We had to leave snow on the centre circle, where there was thick ice which we couldn't clear.

Michelle: I sat next to Paul Langmark, one of our Australian players, for the whole game, and he didn't stop shivering.

What role did you have in the move to Chiswick ?

Ron: I did the organising for us to move grounds. I put in the posts at Chiswick and Wealdstone. There was a sponsored walk to get the original posts from Fulham FC to Chiswick. One of the supporters had made sockets to put in the ground for the posts, and you put the post into them, and then pushed it upright.

We bought two caravans for Chiswick, to be the club shop and a smaller one to be the burger bar. It took two weeks to make the caravans into a club shop. Glen Townsend helped. The supporters did everything to make Chiswick ready for Rugby League. We cut the grass, and with Roy Lester, repaired the turnstiles. The wiring in the stand was so old, it was the "cloth covered" type. The owners had to have it completely rewired so we could use it. The track and the changing rooms were in use before the rugby was played there. The stand was derelict, and the building we made into a bar was a shed.

We had to repaint the stand, and I got some scaffolding boards for us. The groundsman than used them for the banking for the model railway that ran behind the stand. We hired a small bulldozer to make the path to get to the grass bank on the far side. Bob Evans was driving it, and it toppled over.

Were you involved with the Faires salvation scheme ?

We had met Paul Faires at Fulham, at the time he was setting up Kent

Invicta. He asked if we would run their supporters club as well, but we weren't interested.

What are your memories of the Chiswick period ?

Ron: Tim and Sheila Lamb were key people at that time. Richard Lawton as the other director, with the Closes in the background. Harold Nass and Paul Spencer Thompson were also involved. I was on the management committee, and was the first supporters club member on a Rugby League club management committee. Except for financial issues, which Tim and Roy Close dealt with, everything was decided by votes.

But once Ross Strudwick took over, although I felt he was a good coach, I felt there were young English players in the "A" team that were not being given a chance because he preferred to play Australians. The "A" team had Noel Keating, Justin Herbert, Roy Leslie and Andrew Mighty.

Michelle: I played for the Fulham womens' team at that time, on and off for about five years. We played a full season in the womens league in 1989-90. I broke my nose, and went to hospital at Leigh. I remember they said I should have taken my muddy boots off before going into casualty. All they did was X-ray it , confirm it was broken, and send me home! We trained at Chiswick.

The Lancashire Federation of Supporters Clubs

Mo: 6 people from Fulham went to the first meeting . We were made very welcome. At most clubs up north we got a good reception. I think we bought some new ideas into the Lancashire Federation. Most of the people involved had been there for years. We got very involved, went to social events, the Wigan Sevens, and the quiz.

Michelle: At one of the quizzes, we were winning halfway through, then there were a lot of questions about amateur clubs which we couldn't answer.

Kevin: At Widnes, I was wearing a Fulham shirt, and so many people wanted to buy it from me that in the end I sold it to someone, and had to go home without a shirt.

Why did you cease involvement ?

Ron: I resigned in 1990. I wasn't happy about the way the club was being run financially. Also, my health was not very good at that time.

How did you get involved in the amateur East London RLFC?

Kevin: I had moved back to East London, and went to watch the Travellers in a BARLA cup game. I met Gordon Anderton there, and he told me about this team starting in east London, and that I should go and play for them. I hadn't played for 2 years. I got a phone call, and was told that East London were playing at Hemel. I was one of the substitutes, and came on after 20 minutes, as someone broke his leg. I enjoyed playing again. East London joined the league last season. We were struggling to get players, and at one time only had 10 players. But we gave out leaflets, and got some publicity to get more players. Ron has come onto the committee, and Michelle is the physiotherapist. We play at East London RUFC, and have a good relationship with them.

Barry and Gwen Warren

Barry and Gwen Warren have been supporters of the club since 1980. Gwen became treasurer of the supporters club in 1984, and Barry became secretary in 1992.

How did you get involved ?

W,e went to the first game at Craven Cottage - we were Fulham Football Club supporters. We were worried about what would happen to the pitch! We don't go to football now.

We got involved in the supporters club in the fourth season. We went to a meeting at the Golden Lion pub in Fulham. The travelling supporters club had been going since the first season. It had started as a travelling club. We got membership cards number 66 and 67. For the first few years, there were probably only about 60 members. The Fulham RLFC also ran coaches to away matches.

The Fulham Travellers also started playing Rugby League, and there is still an amateur club going today. At that time, Ron Snares' son Kevin started playing Rugby League, and Ron then got involved. He became chairman, and his wife Mo was the secretary. Their children, Michelle and Kevin also went to all the games.

John Marshall was the treasurer then. He dropped out when we moved from Fulham, which happened with other people as well.

Gwen became supporters club treasurer in 1984. Barry became a committee member in the last season at Chiswick, and secretary in 1992.

How independent was it originally ?

The travelling supporters club was independent of the main club. It was not recognised, and not given any authority by the club, until the Autumn of 1983. We were not allowed into the Riverside Bar! People joined through word of mouth. Bob Evans and Mike Geen produced the Rugby League Diary for the supporters club.

The main revenue was from the coach travel. We took two or three coaches to each away game. We used the income to fund the player of the year awards at the end of each season. In the early days we had big end of season parties at the Clarendon in Hammersmith. We usually had 500 people there. Mal Meninga came to one of them.

During the first four years, the supporters club used to organise food at the Golden Lion for the away supporters. The aims of the supporters club (in the constitution) are to ensure there are travel facilities to away games, and to fund the player of the year award. No money was given to the Rugby League club at that time. In the Craven Cottage period, the supporters club produced a tee shirt: "10,000 miles a season and still going strong." In the early years, we took London based players with us on our coaches. Bob Jackson travelled with us.

The Crystal Palace period

Things changed at the start of the 1984-5 season, when the Closes bought the club. They had no administrative backup, so the supporters club got far more involved with helping run the club. Roy and Barbara had a meeting with the supporters club in the summer of 1984 to explain what was happening to the Rugby club. The Closes did open things up. Ron Snares went onto the management committee, so the supporters club had representation in the running of the club. Many of the players walked out. We admire Roy Lester, as he stayed, and managed of the team. Many people who got involved were already active supporters. At Crystal Palace, the supporters club took over running the shop, selling programmes, and any job that would save money.

And on to Chiswick

We went to see the Polytechnic Stadium at Chiswick, and it was falling apart. A working party as set up to renovate the ground. Roy Lester was an engineer, so he repaired the turnstiles. Ron Snares is a builder, so he got the building materials. We got a caravan to become the club shop, and another to make a burger bar. An old storage area became a bar, and we had to rebuild it so it met the fire regulations. Probably about 50 supporters gave up their summer to assist with getting the ground ready.

The summer we moved to Chiswick, a group of us went to collect the original posts from Craven Cottage, which belonged to the club. They had little Cottages on the top of each post. We carried them along the tow path from Craven Cottage to Chiswick on a Sunday, past people in the pubs on the river. A lot of families were involved. The Bandey family sold drinks at the games, and their son Steve marked the pitch. Chris and Sue Blanchard got involved at this time. They would go along on training nights to make food for the players. The supporters club would buy food on the Saturday to sell at matches on the Sunday. We would arrive between 9.00 and 10.00 on Sundays to help get everything ready. Stuart Barlow was matchday manager then, and his wife Sandra was also involved. Helping included cleaning the toilets! The bar takings at this time helped keep the club going.

We even helped fund a player's transfer for the club when we were at Chiswick. Collections from supporters raised £2,000 of the £4,000 to bring Dave Bullough into the team. He later joined Salford.

The supporters club continued to run away travel. We had joined the Lancashire Federation of Supporters clubs in 1982, and we had good relations with the other supporters clubs. During the Chiswick period, for a time we shared a coach to away games with the players. At one time, we used a double decker, with the supporters on top, and the players downstairs. At Chiswick, everyone worked together to keep the club running. The team didn't do very well, but the players gave everything in the matches.

Crystal Palace - again

When we moved back to Crystal Palace , under Ross Strudwick, there was still some liaison with the club, but not the same as at Chiswick.

Were the supporters club consulted on the move back to Crystal Palace?

Ross Strudwick had big plans for the club at Crystal Palace. We said don't go there - we remembered it from before. We were told that the club could get grants at Crystal Palace that we couldn't get at Chiswick. We were impressed by him - he was always working on a shoestring. At Crystal Palace, supporters were still involved in helping run match days. Initially, we did the merchandising, but then Ross Strudwick took over.

The move to Copthall

The Bartrams asked us what we thought of the move to Copthall. They said it would be easier for supporters to get to, and felt the club could do better in North London. I suppose anywhere was better than Crystal Palace.

The Broncos take over

Robbie Moore came to a supporters club meeting early in the season. He asked for people to help out in the first year. Next year, the administration will develop. We've been disappointed with the lack of publicity despite the links with News International.

Any honours for the supporters club?

We have nominated our players for the Lancashire Federation Player of the Year. We have won the second division award twice - Darryl Pitt in 1991-2, and Mark Riley in 1993-4. Bob Evans was "fan of the year" in a national competition. Ron Snares was runner up another year. Harry Stammers won a talent contest at the Lancashire Federation. Harry entertains supporters in the bar after away games by singing cockney songs.

What about unusual events on away trips?

In the early days, there were a lot of prison warders from Wandsworth who supported the team. We were playing at Bramley, so they arranged for the supporters coach to go into a local prison where everyone was given a meal.

We were playing Workington away one year, and broke down on the top of Shap Fell. We were stuck there all night, and got home at 9.00 a.m. the next morning. At Doncaster two years ago, Oliver Reed was filming in the area, so he was at the match, and was in the bar afterwards. We presented him with a Crusaders scarf. Last year at York, in the Regal Trophy, one of the linesmen couldn't get to the ground, so one of our supporters, Paul Taylor, ran the line. He is a qualified referee. And he disallowed a try by Abi Ekoku.

This season, at Bramley, it was snowing. For some reason, one of their supporters called us "soft southerners." So, one of our supporters took his jacket and shirt off, and watched the match stripped to the waist!

And the high spot in the last 15 years?

The trip to Old Trafford, for the 1993-4 Premiership final. It was the first time the club had ever got to a major final, but we only had 6 days to organise things. And the 1.00 p.m. kick off meant an even earlier start than usual. We took 3 coaches, and believe that over 500 London supporters attended the match. Even though we lost, it was still a great day.

20   The Key Players

This was the most difficult section of the book to edit. There were players who made a major contribution, but only over a short period, or others who were not so outstanding, but were important because of their role in the development of the club, such as some of the "Chiswick generation."

In the end, it came down to our choice.

Reg Bowden
Russ Bridge
Shane Buckley
Adrian Cambriani
John Crossley
Michael Davis
Steve Diamond
Don Duffy
Colin Fenn
John Gallagher
Dave Gillan
Tony Gourley
Steve Guyett
Martin Herdman
Mark Johnson
Charlie Jones
Tony Kinsey
Roy Lester
Hussein M'Barki
Steve Mills
Kieron Murphy

George Nepia
Greg Pearce
Darryl Pitt
Neville Ramsey
Huw Rees
Mark Riley
Scott Roskell
Steve Rosolen
Dave Rotheram
Chris Smith
Sam Stewart
Mick Taylor
Chris Wilkinson
John Wood

And:

The first Australian:
Bob Jackson

Reg Bowden

First player-coach, and a key figure in the formation of the Club. Scrum-half, and mainstay of the team until 1984, when he left to become coach at Warrington. As coach at Warrington, signed a number of the players who had left Fulham as "free agents." Went from being a hero to villain very quickly in the eyes of many Fulham supporters, but his achievements in the first four years of the club should not be forgotten. Played 119 games in his four seasons with the club, scoring 14 tries.

Joined Widnes in 1968, and played in 16 major cup finals, including four Wembley appearances, and 4 John Player Trophy Finals. Key figure at Widnes in 1970s. Unlucky never to have been capped.

Reg Bowden (Photo: Sporting Pictures (UK))

Russ Bridge

Won Great Britain Student honours in Rugby League, and joined Fulham in September 1986 from West London Institute. Made his debut in a 68-14 defeat, and initially played as a centre or winger. In 1988, moved into the pack as a hooker, and established a reputation as a very hard working player, with a high tackle count. Scored 12 tries in 109 first team appearances. Became the first London based Fulham player to reach 50 and 100 appearances for the club. At the end of the 1989-90 season, he moved back to Lancashire for work reasons, and joined Leigh, having had a trial period with Wigan. Later joined Highfield.

Shane Buckley

Australian winger or centre. Very quick consistent try scorer, joined Fulham in August 1991. Previously played for Valleys in Brisbane and for Queensland. Returned to Australia at the end of the 1992-3 season. Top try scorer in both his seasons with the club, with 17 in 1991-2, and 16 in 1992-3. Averaged over a try every other game.

Adrian Cambriani

Scored Fulham's first try in his first game of Rugby League in the opening match against Wigan. Also scored the club's first hat trick of tries, and was the first Fulham player to win an international cap, playing for Wales against France in the 1981-2 season.

Joined Fulham at age of 18 at start of the first season. Just under 6ft, and 13.5 stone, well built for a winger. From Swansea, where he won schoolboy and youth honours for Wales in Rugby Union. Joined Penlan RUFC at 16, subsequently played for Swansea RUFC before joining Fulham. Second highest try scorer in the first season, with 13. Scored 10 in the 1985-6 season, and averaged over a try every 3 games, with 42 in 119 appearances over eight seasons. Briefly left the club in the "free agents" dispute, then returned. The latter part of his career was blighted by injuries.

Capped by Wales in Rugby League, and one of the key players in the first four seasons, although never fulfilled his potential. Hit by injuries after 1984, and retired in 1987. His final game was against Papua New Guinea.

John Crossley

Signed from York in August 1981, had been leading try scorer in Division Two in 1980-1 with 35 tries. Previously played for Wakefield and Castleford.

Very fast stand off, consistent try scorer with Fulham, including being top scorer in 1981-2. His 27 tries that season was a club record for the number of tries in one season until overtaken by Mark Riley and Mark Johnson in 1993-4. Top scorer in 1981-2 and 1982-3. Left in 1984 as one of the "free agents." In November 1988, rejoined York from Featherstone Rovers. Ended his career at Batley.

John Dalgreen

Signed by Fulham in August 1981, to replace Tony Karalius as hooker. Prior to joining Fulham, had played for Halifax from 1974 to 1977, and joined Warrington in October 1977. Had been selected for Great Britain under 24 team, but then broke his ankle. Played for Warrington in the 1978 JPT final against Widnes.

Fulham's first Great Britain international, playing one test match against Australia in 1982. Competitive player, with occasionally explosive temper, who added quality to the Fulham pack from 1981 to 1984. Retired and came back into action at least twice. Left as one of the "free agents" in 1984.

Mike Davis

Dynamic Australian scrum-half signed in October 1984. Played for Paramatta and Penrith in Australia.

Regular try scorer, and was very quick. Top try scorer in 1984-5. Won the Player of the Year award for 1984-5. Played until March 1986, when he refused to play in the "play for free" game at Huddersfield, and subsequently joined Leigh.

Steve Diamond

Signed from Wakefield in August 1981. Had joined Wakefield in 1978 from Newbridge RUFC. Capped for Wales in Rugby League. Excellent goalkicker, who in 1982-3 set the club season points record, 308, and the most goals in a season, 136, until both records were beaten by John Gallagher's prodigious 1993-4 season. Scored 305 goals, and 3 drop goals, in 109 appearances. Consistent player who usually played full-back for Fulham, also appeared in the centre or as a winger. Left in 1984 as one of the "free agents."

Don Duffy

Hard working Australian loose-forward or second-row who regularly topped the match tackle counts. Joined Fulham with Michael Davis in October 1984. In his early days, played for John Monie at Woy Woy in New South Wales, and then followed Monie to Paramatta. Played in a Grand Final against Manly.

Left Fulham at the end of the 1985-6 season, and subsequently played at Carlisle, with Roy Lester, and Warrington.

Frank Feighan

Made his debut against Blackpool in 1982, as a trialist, when he was playing as an amateur for Peckham. Was not signed up by Fulham, and turned professional with Kent Invicta in 1983-4, at the age of 27. Won the Try of the Year award for a spectacular run to score against Castleford in the John Player Trophy. Then moved to Southend Invicta, and joined Fulham when Southend dropped out of the league.

An enthusiastic Londoner, whose commitment to the Fulham cause won him great respect. Moved into the pack in the later stages of his career, retiring in 1988.

Colin Fenn

Londoner who joined Fulham from South London ARLFC in August 1986. 6ft forward, whose commitment was always respected by the supporters. Also was team goal kicker for a time, with an unusual action.

Became the first Londoner to captain the club in 1987-8, but retired at the end of the 1988-9 season.

John Gallagher

Born in London, before emigrating to New Zealand, and becoming a regular player for the All Blacks in Rugby Union. Voted "The World's Greatest Player" before switching codes and signing for Leeds in the summer of 1990. His previous reputation and reputed signing on fee made him a target in every match, and a spear tackle in his first season undermined his confidence. Could not win a regular place at Leeds after Doug Laughton became coach.

Joined London Crusaders on a free transfer in the summer of 1993. Played at full-back, then on the right-wing. Broke numerous club records, including most goals in a season, and most points. Valued member of the 1993-4 squad, he also worked as a development officer in London for the Rugby League.

Retired in September 1994 to take up a teaching post. Had become a very popular player amongst London's supporters, if only for the torrents of abuse he attracted from northern fans, particularly those in Yorkshire. Made a surprise comeback for the Broncos at Huddersfield in January 1995, but retired again in March, although he still ended the season as top goal scorer for the Broncos.

Dave Gillan

Born in Auckland, joined Southend Invicta in 1984, and also played for London Colonials and Papkura in New Zealand before joining Fulham in 1986. Initially played as a centre, then moved to loose-forward. Became club captain, and was a mainstay of the team in the latter part of the 1980s. Top scorer in 1987-8 with 9 tries, and in 1988-9 with 14. Altogether scored 38 tries in 97 games. Retired at the end of the 1988-9 season.

Tony Gourley

Signed by Fulham from Salford in August 1980. Previously had played for Rochdale for 8 years. 6ft 3 inches, nearly 16 stone, with Harry Beverley formed a formidable pair of props in early Fulham teams, appearing more fierce because of their beards. Became club captain in 1928-3, and stayed with the club at the time of the "free agents" exodus in 1984. Retired in 1985 following a head injury. A key player for the club in the first five years, whose efforts were always appreciated by the supporters. After retiring, coached in amateur and youth Rugby League in the Rochdale area.

Steve Guyett

Londoner, joined Fulham in 1987.Played Rugby Union for Feltham and Middlesex under 21s. Had trials for Oldham before joining Fulham. Usually played at full-back or on the wing. Also accurate goal-kicker, who was top goal-kicker in the 1988-9 season. Retired at the end of the 1989-90 season.

Martin Herdman

Signed by Fulham at the beginning of 1981 from Peckham amateur Rugby League club. Second-row forward, and one of the few Londoners to make an impact in professional Rugby League. Played on loan for Leigh in the 1983-4 season. Became one of the "free agents", but returned to Fulham for occasional games in 1985-6 and 1986-7. Another player who never fulfilled his potential. Played for Wales RL. When he signed for Fulham, had been South west London ABA champion for 3 years, and boxed for England as heavyweight. Also had brown belt in karate, and had trials in American football. Made 86 appearances in 6 seasons, scoring 14 tries.

Mark Johnson

Joined London Crusaders in March 1993, initially on trial, then given a contract. Started his rugby career playing Ruby Union in South Africa, for the Johannesburg Pirates. Won representative honours for Transvaal "B." His brother is a South African RU international, and was on the Springboks tour in the Autumn of 1994.

Very fast winger, and prolific try scorer. His hat trick at the 1994 Premiership Final against Workington ensured he finished top try scorer in Rugby League in 1993-4. During that season, broke John Crossley's club record for the number of tries in a season, and broke the record for the number of tries in a match.

Represented South Africa in the Rugby League World Sevens in Sydney in 1994, and has won international honours for South Africa.

Charlie Jones

Joined from Widnes in March 1983, with Steve Mills. Played in any position, and gave marvellous value to the club, and won the supporters' respect, both for his loyalty, and energy and commitment to the Fulham cause. Played 116 games, and was the last northern based player with Fulham in the Chiswick period. After only playing three games in the 1987-8 season, joined Runcorn Highfield in August 1988.

Tony Kinsey

Signed at the start of the 1980-1 season. Had previously played for Widnes colts and Lancashire under 18s. Utility player, who covered most forward positions, and scrum-half during his time with the club. Briefly left the club in the "free agents" dispute, but returned, and left at the end of the 1985-6 season, having scored 18 tries in 156 games. Subsequently played for Swinton and Huddersfield.

Mark Johnson - London's speedy South African winger (Photo: David Stevens)

Roy Lester

First player to sign for Fulham. Became Assistant Coach in 1982, and stayed loyal to the club after the "free agent" defections, and was a key figure as coach in holding the club together from August 1984 to February 1986. Left when it was decided to base the team in London, but had won the respect and admiration of Fulham's supporters. Was given awards by the supporters when he left the club in recognition of his work.

Had played for Leigh from 1968 to 1977, including being non-playing substitute in the 1971 Cup Final when they beat Leeds. Also played for Warrington before signing for Fulham, winning Lancashire representative honours. He played for Warrington when they beat Australia in 1978, currently the last club team to beat the Kangaroos.

Hard-working forward, whose efforts as a player were not always recognised. On leaving Fulham became manager at Carlisle. Later joined Warrington's coaching staff.

Hussein M'Barki

With Adrian Cambriani, a player regarded as "ours" by the Fulham supporters, as he made his name with Fulham, and had not played in British Rugby League before. Joined in October 1981, making his first appearances under the name of "Smith" while work permit problems were resolved. Had won 20 caps at Rugby Union for Morocco, and had been playing for Cahors in French Ruby Union.

Aged 24 when he signed for Fulham. Skilful speedy winger, and regular try scorer. One of the few players to score a try against the 1982 Australian tourists.

Left as a "free agent" in 1984, subsequently playing for Warrington, Oldham and Hull. Never established himself as a leading player in the first division, and rejoined Fulham in September 1988. It is an indication of his popularity that he was welcomed back at the club, Played regularly until 1991, usually as a winger, with occasional appearances at full back. Had the unusual distinction of playing for both the "A" team and the first team on the same day.

He was top try scorer in 1983-4, with 17. Also reached double figures in 1982-3 with 23, and 1989-90 with 11. At the end of 1994-5, was still the Club's top ever try scorer.

On retiring as a player, became Rugby League development officer in Morocco. Always given a warm welcome on occasional visits to Fulham or London matches.

Steve Mills

Signed from Widnes in March 1983, initially on loan, then purchased for £10,000. Signed with Charlie Jones as part of moves to increase the playing strength. Only started playing rugby at the age of 17, and played for

West Park RU until joining Widnes. Had a short period on loan at Leigh before joining Fulham.

Regular try scorer, playing full-back, on the wing or in the centre. Established a regular place from 1984, and was one of the mainstays of the team from 1984 to 1987. One of the few Fulham players to have scored 50 tries and played over 100 games. Joint top try scorer in 1984-5 with 17, and was top scorer in 1985-6 with 11, and 1986-7 with 12. Subsequently joined Carlisle before retiring from playing.

Hussein M'Barki - one of London Rugby League's greatest players
(Photo: Sporting Pictures (UK))

Kieron Murphy

Played for Richmond and Nottingham at Rugby Union. Then capped by Great Britain students in Rugby League, playing in the same team as Russ Bridge. Joined Fulham, in October 1986, establishing himself as scrum half. Another key player in the latter half of the 1980s, during the period the team became to be based in London, although for much of this period, he was based in the Midlands. Lost his regular place at the end of the 1989-90 season, having played some games on the wing. Retired during the 1990-91 season.

George Nepia

Caused a sensation when he joined Streatham & Mitcham from New Zealand Rugby Union in 1935. A Maori, he played 9 test matches for New Zealand, and would have won more caps, but for injuries and dubious selection policies. He was also excluded from the 1928 tour of South Africa.

Regarded as New Zealand's greatest ever Rugby Union player, he played at full back, and was also a highly skilled kicker. Turned professional with Streatham & Mitcham in December 1935. Within four weeks, despite his lack of experience of Rugby League, was made acting manager of the club. In December 1936, he was sold to Halifax for £300, and returned to New Zealand at the end of that season. One of the group of All Blacks who joined Streatham, who started a tradition of Australasian players in London Rugby League.

With a rare flexibility in their rules, he was allowed to play Rugby Union again, when he returned home.

When he visited Swansea RUFC with the touring Maori team in 1983, he was walking along the front of the stand, unannounced. When the crowd realised who it was, he was given a standing ovation.

Greg Pearce

Born in New South Wales, and played his early Rugby League for Central Coast and Wyong. Came to England in October 1988, playing initially for Hemel Hempstead, and was then signed by Fulham in March 1989. Played at full-back or loose-forward, as well as being a consistent goal kicker. Joined Huddersfield at the end of the 1990-91 season. Kicked 11 goals in a game against Runcorn in August 1990, a club record.

Darryl Pitt

Australian who joined Fulham from Carlisle in 1989. Had played for Valley Diehards in Australia. Played as a centre or second-row forward. Took on the goal kicking duties. Top try scorer in 1990-91 with 10, and second highest try scorer in 1991-2 with 12. Missed most of the 1993-4 season following an injury, but returned to the first team in 1994-5. Regular try scorer. Passed 100 tries and 100 games for the club in the 1994-5 season. Always easy to spot on the field because of his enormous knee bandage.

Neville Ramsey

Signed by Tony Gordon in March 1993 for the London Crusaders. Had won representative honours for the New Zealand Maoris. Strong tackling stand-off or loose-forward. Also played occasionally at hooker and scrum-half. Had previously played for Bradford Northern, Halifax, Trafford Borough, and had trials with Widnes. Released by the London Broncos at the start of the 1994-5 season, he then joined York. Known by the fans as "Sir Alf", he had been a major contributor to the 1993-4 team.

Huw Rees

Joined Fulham in October 1986. Played Rugby Union for Wales "B", Swansea and Penarth. Had overcome knee surgery in 1978 when he had not played for three and a half years. Played in the centre, and had occasional games at stand off or in the pack. Added experience to the Fulham teams of the late 1980s, but never reached his full potential in Rugby League. Also had periods out through injuries. Also played for Western Suburbs in Australia. Known as "Sumo" by the crowd, he played amateur Rugby League after leaving Fulham.

Mark Riley

Scrum-half, from New Zealand. Made his debut against Wakefield in November 1992, when Crusaders beat the Yorkshire First Division club 30-0. Had played in Auckland for Otahuhu, and Mangere Easts. Also played in Perth, winning two Perth Grand Finals. Had previously come to England in 1987, but could not get clearance to play for Rochdale. Very fast, consistent try scorer, with excellent sidestep and acceleration. Broke the club record for the number of tries scored in one match in the 1993-4 season. Broke a kneecap at Huddersfield in January 1995, and missed the rest of the season.

Scott Roskell

Australian who joined London Crusaders at the start of the 1992-3 season. Powerful centre, capable of breaking through the best defences. Regular try scorer. Had previously played for the Gold Coast Seagulls and Runaway bay in Australia. Won representative honours for New South Wales Country XIII. His distinctive long hair made him an easily identifiable target for northern opponents. Top try scorer in 1994-5.

Steve Rosolen

Australian second-row or loose-forward. Started playing Rugby League in Brisbane, for the Wide Bay Bulls. Then joined North Sydney, playing in the 1991 reserve grade final. Joined Fulham in the autumn of 1991. Had previously played for Salford for 50 minutes before breaking his arm. Strong running, reliable player.

Dave Rotheram

Played for Fulham under 19s in 1986. Also played in student Rugby League. Capped by England in student Rugby League, and played against Australia in student world cup final. Originally from St Helens. Made his first team debut in 1988-9, in a 60-0 defeat at Whitehaven, and went on to become one of the most consistent members of the Fulham and London set up. Played at hooker or front-row forward. During his career, up to the end of the 1994-5 season had played for six managers, on three home grounds, and under three different team names. After averaging less than a try a season, suddenly scored 10 tries in 1994-5.

Chris Smith

Played for Richmond Rugby Union as a full-back, then for St Marys in amateur Rugby League. Joined Fulham in 1990. Consistent second-row forward, also goal-kicker. Top goal scorer in 1991-2 with 78. Couldn't win a regular place in 1993-4 or 1994-5, partly due to injuries, but was still an important squad member.

Sam Stewart

Joined London Crusaders in July 1993, linking up again with Tony Gordon. Many of his New Zealand test honours were won with Gordon as coach, including as captain in the historical 1987 win against Australia.

Had played for Wellington from 1980 to 1987, then joined the Newcastle Knights. Became club captain for the Crusaders, playing at second-row or loose-forward. His leadership, and strong running were crucial for the 1993-4 team. Still a regular team member and inspirational figure in 1994-5. Became one of the new development officers for Rugby League in London.

Mick Taylor

Joined in August 1989, for £7,000 from Halifax, where he had played for new Fulham coach Ross Strudwick. Had previously played amateur Rugby League, then joined Oldham. Joined Halifax in 1987 for £20,000. Skilful centre and winger, who in the latter part of his Fulham and London career also played in the pack. Added experience and determination to the teams of that period. Joint top try scorer in 1989-90 with 12. Returned "up north" at the end of the 1991-2 season, joining Bradford Northern, playing mainly for their "A" team. Subsequently played for Huddersfield.

Chris Wilkinson

Played for Oldham's colts and reserves, but was playing in the lower reaches of the North West Counties League when Fulham signed him in September 1984. Goal kicking stand off, and played regularly until 1987. Another key member of the team in the 1984 to 1987 period, scoring 17 tries, 141 goals and 13 drop goals. Second highest try scorer in 1985-6 with 10. Joined Chorley on loan in September 1988, and then left Fulham permanently to join Dewsbury. Later played for Leigh

John Wood

Signed from Wigan in 1980. Had played for Wigan since 1977, and prior to that had five seasons with Widnes, including a cup final appearance in 1978, when they were beaten by St. Helens.

Played for England schools at Rugby Union. Won Great Britain under

24 honours in Rugby League. Played for an England XIII in 1982 against France. A well built second-row forward, with good ball playing skills. Quickly became a hero for the Craven Cottage crowds, and was elected player of the year in 1980-81. Stayed away from the club for 3 months at the start of the 1981-2 season, in dispute over the Club's playing potential. This reduced his popularity, and in August 1983 he joined Salford in part exchange for Trevor Stockley. Later played for Widnes and Swinton. Retired early because of back problems. Had been a mainstay of the Fulham forwards in the first three seasons. Scored 11 tries in 66 appearances.

The new generation: Chris Wilkinson (right), and Steve Mills (passing the ball) playing at Chiswick. (Photo: Open Rugby)

The first Australian: Bob Jackson

By Garry Clarke

Just before Christmas 1994 Warrington forward Bob Jackson announced his retirement as a player after 220 first team games for the Wilderspool club. Halfway through his testimonial season, Jacko, who has become a firm favourite of the Wire fans with his all action style, finally succumbed to the injuries which have blighted his career.

Born in 1960 on the outskirts of Sydney, on 2 January 1984, Robert Jackson became the first Australian to play Rugby League for Fulham.

How did he become a history maker paving the way for so many of his countrymen to hop on a plane and come to England and play for Fulham, London Crusaders or London Broncos?

After playing three seasons in the Sydney League with Penrith, he packed his bags in 1983 and headed for London as the starting point of a European sightseeing tour.

"Home became the Royal Oak Pub in Islington where I was employed as a cellarman/barman and it was from there that I rang Reg Bowden at Fulham and asked for a trial. We met up after the game against Bradford, which Fulham won. I told Reg that if I couldn't get into the Fulham pack I'd eat my boots. Reg gave me a 'heard it all before' look, and the phone number of a bloke called Bill Goodwin, who was to arrange the trial.

"I, of course, was quite naïve about the English game. First of all I thought it was a 'national' game, and that all pro teams would have at least three sides like the Sydney league. I didn't know that Fulham had only one team, and that most of the players were based in the North 200 miles away.

"Bill Goodwin was coaching Peckham Pumas, and so it was that Robert Jackson caught the tube to Brixton, met up with Bill, and made his British debut on a desolate field in North London in front of five spectators and a dog as Peckham Pumas defeated Hemel Hempstead 70 odd to something, after another game for Peckham (v London Colonials), I decided if I didn't hear anything from Fulham, I would call it quits"

At this point, we will bring in the then Fulham coach Reg Bowden, "Bob asked for a trial, at the time I got about ten requests a week from overseas players, so it was no big deal until he introduced himself after a game and said he was as good, if not better than I already had on the field. I thought nine out of ten for guts, as my front-row at the time was Harry Beverley and

Bob Jackson in the bar on his first visit to Fulham (Photo: Ron Snares)

Tony Gourley.

"A friend of mine was Bill Goodwin, who was running Peckham, so I asked him to give Bob a trial. This I had done with a few Aussies, and not one had come good! So I forgot about Bob and pushed him to the back of my mind, I had enough problems with the players I already had.

"Two weeks later at 7 am. Bill rang me, 'Reg, you better get this guy signed on quick'. I replied "which guy?"

"Bob the Aussie. He's the best thing I've seen in years. He's had two games. p****d the man of the match, topped the tackle count, and the bugger even kicks goals'. "Every now and again a gem drops into a coaches lap. Bob Jackson was my gem." Back to Bob, who continues his story:

"Then I got a call from Reg Bowden. They had serious injury problems. Could I catch a train to a place called Runcorn as they might use me on the bench for an away match at Salford. I met up with Hussein M'Barki and Martin Herdman at Euston, and we headed north for Runcorn. After listening to the two of them for two and a half hours, I was quite excited that I was going to be playing with two of the games greatest players!

"Reg picked us up at Runcorn, and booked us into the Hill Crest at

295

Widnes. I signed a registration form and a three match trial contract, which was the period he'd give me to see how I fared. By kick off time, Fulham's injury crisis had worsened and now I was to start the match! Since coming over from Australia, I'd done little serious training, and had played in two amateur matches in London, yet now I was to play a first division match with players I'd never met before. "We beat Salford 6-4 at the Willows (Fulham's first away win that season) and I'd arrived. More good results followed, until I broke my arm in an excellent win against Wigan. For me then the season was over, and I promptly packed my bags, to join my friends who had already started their tour of Europe." By the time Bob returned from the continent, Fulham were in disarray, and Bowden had gone north to Warrington. Bob was one of five Fulham players who became "Wires" the following season. So Bob Jackson's Fulham career came to and end after just eight games, but he had started a trend. Of eight games he played, four were won, including two cup ties.

Jackson went on to play for Warrington for 10 years, being given a testimonial by the club in 1994-5.

21   No place like home

Fulham, London Crusaders and London Broncos have played matches at various grounds. Grounds covered in detail in this section are those used regularly. The stadiums used by the clubs in the 1930s are described in the chapters on those clubs.

Craven Cottage: 1980-1984

Craven Cottage is the home of Fulham Football Club, and an unlikely venue for Rugby League. Situated in a middle class residential area of South west london, the ground backs onto the river Thames, and football fans have been able to watch the University Boat Race before a match. Next to the ground is Bishop's Park, with tennis courts and a pleasant walk from Putney Bridge station to the ground.

The ground has two stands. The original one is on Stevenage Road, and seats around 2,400 people. It was designed by the famous architect, Archibald Leitch. In the corner, next to the open terrace known as the Putney End, is the Cottage. Built at the same time as the stand, it has the Club's reception area, and dressing rooms. It is probably a unique feature on any British sports ground.

On the river side is the Eric Miller stand. Named after a former Fulham FC Director, it seats around 4,000 people with an unobstructed view.

The west end of the ground is a covered terrace, known as the Hammersmith End.

The capacity of Craven Cottage is now 9,147, having been drastically reduced under the sports grounds safety legislation.

The best crowd at Craven Cottage for a Fulham match was the 15,103 against Wakefield Trinity in the Challenge Cup on 15th February 1991.

Crystal Palace National Sports Centre: 1984-5 and 1990 - 1993

Following the break with the Football Club in 1984, the only ground that could be found at short notice was the Crystal Palace National Sports Centre. The move was intended to be for a one season trial, and it quickly became apparent that the venue was not suitable. Apart from its layout, it was difficult to get to by public transport from west London, and the team did not seem to pick up much local support.

Although the club had access to useful training facilities, and houses for some of the players, the stadium was depressing for the matches, especially compared to Craven Cottage, where even a relatively small crowd could generate some atmosphere.

The matches were played in the main stadium at Crystal Palace, which has an athletics track, and 16,500 seats. Even the average crowds at Craven Cottage would have been lost in this bowl, let alone the crowds that did attend the matches.

During the second spell at the stadium, supporters were allowed to stand by the advertising hoardings by the pitch. This might have offered some vocal encouragement to the players, but did little to improve the atmosphere.

Even floodlit matches were not very successful, as the lights were more angled at the track than the pitch, and seemed to be played in a gloom at times, even when the team were winning.

Rugby League had some strange companions at Crystal Palace. Included in the grounds are a small zoo, and model car racing.

The best crowd at Crystal Palace was 2,324 against Hull in the John Player Trophy on 18th November 1984.

The Polytechnic Stadium - Chiswick: 1985 - 1990

Believing that a move back to West London could rebuild some of the support that had been lost in the move to Crystal Palace, the team played one match at Chiswick in March 1985, and then moved there permanently that summer.

The Stadium belongs to what was then the Polytechnic of Central London (now the University of Westminster), and was managed by trustees for the Polytechnic.

When Fulham moved in, initially on a lease-hire agreement for one season, the stand was not in use, except for the changing rooms. The stand was renovated, turnstiles rebuilt and a PA system fitted by supporters over the summer of 1985, to bring the ground up to an acceptable standard. Team manager Roy Lester also helped. The original posts were retrieved from Craven Cottage.

The supporters got caravans for a club shop and burger bar, and renovated a store to become a bar. The main stand has two tiers, and can seat around 600 people under cover. There are a couple of other small areas of terracing on that side, but the rest of the ground was a grass bank. This offered little protection from the weather.

The stadium is surrounded by playing fields , and is near to a yachting marina on the nearby Thames. It also has a model railway running down the back of the stand. There were no floodlights, and matches in the winter kicked off at 2.15 p.m. or 2.30 p.m. One cup replay was held on a mid week afternoon. The ground was fairly inaccessible by public transport, with Chiswick station being fifteen minutes walk away, or a bus from Hammersmith being the alternative. The stadium did have potential, but the club were unable to negotiate a long term lease or purchase the ground from the Polytechnic, and therefore could not secure Sports Council grants to improve the facilities. The best crowd at Chiswick was 1665 against Bradford Northern in the Challenge Cup on 11 February 1990.

Barnet Copthall Stadium: 1993 to present

With attendances declining at Crystal Palace, the club's new owners decided to try their luck in North London. Barnet Copthall Stadium is owned by Barnet Council, and is in a predominantly middle class north London suburb of Mill Hill.

The main stand seats around 800 people, and includes the dressing rooms, office facilities and two bars. On the far side, there is some terracing, and open seats, which are not used for the rugby matches. Although Copthall has all the disadvantages of staging rugby in an athletics stadium, because supporters are more concentrated together than at Crystal Palace, the atmosphere is more lively.

The stadium could theoretically hold up to 9,500. However, what view they would get of the pitch is another matter. The public transport problems were improved by the initiative of running a bus from Mill Hill East station to the ground, and the car parking facilities are good. One of Copthall's main attractions is that it is five minutes drive from the M1 motorway, allowing easy access for travelling supporters from away teams. The biggest crowd at Copthall was 1,878 against Bradford Northern in the Regal Trophy on 19 December 1993.

The entrance to Craven Cottage (Photo: Sporting Pictures (UK)

The main stand at Craven Cottage, with the Cottage on the right, during the record crowd - Fulham v Wakefield 1981 (Photo: Ken Coton)

Moving home - taking the posts from Craven Cottage to Chiswick in 1985
(Photo: Barbara Close)

Rebuilding Chiswick - the Fulham Maintenance Crew in action
(photo: Barbara Close)

The stand at Chiswick during the summer of 1985 (Photo: Barbara Close)

The main stand, now in use- the view from the grass bank (Photo: Peter Lush)

Medford station - part of the model railway behind the stand at Chiswick
(photo: Peter Lush)

The move to north London - the main stand at Copthall (Photo: Peter Lush)

The scoreboard at Copthall (Photo: Peter Lush)

Other grounds:

1982-3: Two matches staged at Widnes, against Swinton and Huddersfield, because of fixture congestion at the end of the season. The final match of the season was staged at Chelsea Football Club.

1984-5: Three matches staged at Wealdstone FC at the end of the season. These were quite well supported, including some Wealdstone FC supporters. The ground's future was uncertain,and it was subsequently sold for a supermarket development.

1985-6: The Challenge Cup match against Barrow was played at Wigan on a Wednesday night, after being postponed numerous times at Chiswick.

1989-90: The Lancashire Cup match against Wigan was played at Hendon Football Club in north west London. The match attracted 3,200 people, the best since the departure from Craven Cottage.

1993-4 and 1994-5: A small number of matches were played at Hendon Football Club when the pitch at Copthall was unfit, in particular at the start of 1994-5, when the pitch was being reseeded.

22   The Companies

Fulham Rugby League Football Club Ltd was set up in 1980. The Board was based on the Fulham FC Board, with Ernie Clay as chairman, who was also chairman, and effectively owner of Fulham FC.

The club secretary was George Noyce, who held the same position for Fulham FC. Other board members linked to the football club included former England football star Malcolm MacDonald, commercial manager for Fulham FC, Brian Dalton, Fulham FC's finance director, and Gregory Clay, Ernie Clay's eldest son.

Former Warrington director Harold Genders was managing director. With Reg Bowden, he was responsible for team affairs. Colin Welland, the actor and playwright also came from a Rugby League background. He was the only person who continued involvement after the original club was wound up.

In November 1980, Malcolm MacDonald became manager of Fulham FC, and resigned from the board of the Rugby League club.

In the summer of 1981, George Noyce left the club to work in Australia, and Yvonne Haines was appointed as his replacement. Again, she combined the posts of Secretary of Fulham FC with that of the Rugby club, and was the first woman to be secretary of both a Rugby League club and a Football Club. At the start of the 1982-3 season, Godfrey Clay, another of Ernie Clay's sons, also joined the Board. In September 1983, Harold Genders left the club. Reg Bowden described him as "The driving force behind Fulham's founding."

In June 1984, Fulham announced that the Rugby League Club was to be put into liquidation, claiming debts of £600,000. Roy and Barbara Close set up Fulham RLFC (1984) Ltd, and took over the registration of the Club with the Rugby League.

The Closes were the major shareholders in Fulham RLFC, and set up a management committee, mainly based around supporters club officers and members, to run the club on a day to day basis. Barbara Close became chairman of the club. The new club secretary was John Rathbone.

In March 1986, the Closes announced that the club was to cease operations, because of ongoing concerns over its financial viability.

Paul Faires than took over control from the Closes, purchasing their shares in Fulham RLFC (1984) for a nominal amount. He had started Kent Invicta RLFC in 1984. He ran the club until the end of the 1985-6 season. Tim Lamb became club secretary at this time.

In the summer of 1986, Paul Faires withdrew from the club, having failed to develop the sponsorship he hoped would make the club financially viable. Tim Lamb and Richard Lawton then became directors, having made an agreement with the Closes that they would provide financial support. They purchased Paul Faires' shares in Fulham RLFC (1984) Ltd for a nominal sum.

Hadenford Investments was formed to act as an investment holding company for Fulham RLFC. In December 1986, Tim Lamb and Richard Lawton were appointed as directors of this company. This was done to facilitate a restructuring of the club's shareholdings to enable further capital to be introduced. When Tim Lamb and Richard Lawton became directors of Fulham RLFC (1984) Ltd, the Friends of Fulham Rugby League was set up, to raise money for the club. This was done under the umbrella of Vintagefile Ltd, which was a sponsorship and season ticket marketing agency for its parent company, Fulham RLFC (1984) Ltd.

In July 1989, Roy and Barbara Close again became directors of Hadenford Investments Ltd and Fulham RLFC (1984) Ltd. In February 1990, Tim Lamb and Richard Lawton resigned as directors of both companies.

The summer of 1990 saw further changes, with the Closes resigning as directors, and a new board of David Oakes, Ross Strudwick and Ray Stoner being set up, with David Oakes as Club Secretary. David Price, who instigated the new club sponsorship with SHG Alarms joined the Board in April 1990, and resigned in June 1990. In February 1991, David Oakes resigned as a director and club secretary. Ross Strudwick became general manager \ secretary.

For 1991-2, the club name became "London Crusaders. During the second half of the season, Chris Blanchard joined the board, but soon afterwards, Ray Stoner left. In April 1992, a winding up order was made against Fulham RLFC (1984) Ltd, with liabilities of £161,071, including the shareholders' investments.

At the start of the 1992-3 season, Ross Strudwick and Chris Blanchard were the club's directors. Just before the winding up of Fulham RLFC (1984) Ltd, Vintagefile Ltd started trading as London Crusaders RLFC. In November 1992, Richard Bartram and Graeme Pickering were appointed as

I, Paul Edward Faires, hereby agree to transfer, after 31st August 1986, on demand, 100,000 ordinary shares of £1 each in Fulham Rugby League Football Club (1984) Limited to Richard Lawton and Timothy Alan Lamb for the consideration of the sum of £10 (ten pounds only).

I hereby acknowledge receipt of the sum of £1 (one pound only) in full consideration of the grant of the above option.

I further agree to make available to Richard Lawton and Timothy Alan Lamb, no later than 31st August 1986, such information relating to the financial and other affairs and liabilities of the company as they may require in order to decide whether to exercise their option to acquire the shares in the ccmpany.

Additionally, I will endeavour that by 31st August 1986 the Club's books will be brought as much up-to-date as possible.

Signed : .... Date 1.8.86

Letter from Paul Faires agreeing to transfer his shares to Tim Lamb & Richard Lawton

Share certificate in Hadenford Investments

directors. By this time, the "Friends of London Rugby League" was operating as a separate enterprise.

In February 1993, Ross Strudwick left the club. In June 1993, Vintagefile Ltd was put into administration. The Closes had resigned as directors of Vintagefile in October 1992. Roy Close was still the major shareholder, with 18,250 £1 shares, and with Britannic Touchdown promotions also holding 6,600 £1 shares. The report by the insolvency practitioners shows debts of over £88,000.

Britannic Touchdown Promotions then purchased the business of London Crusaders RLFC from the administrator of Vintagefile Ltd in June 1993 for £6,500. This company had been set up in December 1992, with Richard Bartram and Graeme Pickering as directors, and Samantha Bartram as company secretary. Chris Blanchard resigned as a director of London Crusaders.

Graeme Pickering resigned as a director in November 1993, and the Bartrams resigned in January 1994. Roy Waudby and Maurice Lindsay were then appointed as directors in March 1994, with the shares in the company being purchased by Rugby League Enterprises Ltd. Neil Robinson had become honorary club secretary following the departure of the Bartrams.

On 25th March 1994, the business of the club was sold to London Broncos Ltd for £120,000. Britannic Touchdown Promotions was then put into liquidation, with debts of around £250,000 and assets of £118,000. For the start of the 1994-5 season, there were six directors. Robbie Moore came over from Brisbane as chief executive, with Neil Robinson continuing as honorary club secretary.

23   London's loyal supporters

Rugby League in London has always been intertwined with fans as committed to the cause as any in the Rugby League world. Being a fan in the capital city is like being a follower of a minority cult, some people know you exist but hardly anyone shows any interest.

There has always been a northern element amongst fans in London. Then there are some football converts, and a layer of the current London supporters came from being (or still are) Fulham F.C. supporters.

As with Rugby League in the north, League in London is a family game. This was particularly noticeable in the Chiswick period, when the supporters were doing a vast amount of voluntary work to keep the club functioning. This could be anything from making sandwiches for match days and training nights to setting up the posts and marking the pitch on match days.

Various proprietors of London Rugby League, from Fulham F.C. to Ross Strudwick have hoped that the Australian hoards would leave their Earls Court pubs and bedsits, and come and support the team. Although a few Australian supporters have got involved, including the High Commissioner, Douglas McClelland, who was president for a time, the mass influx has never happened. Many of the Australians in London are young people "doing Europe", and probably not followers of the game at home.

The first experiments in the capital in the 1930s also brought a development of supporters clubs at both Acton and Streatham, each having membership of over 1,000. The club failures of this period were not for a lack of committed support, who raised funds and travelled long distances just as London fans today. The Rugby League's secretary, John Wilson, spoke at a meeting of Streatham's supporters club. In January 1937, the club held a special meeting to discuss the crisis facing the Streatham & Mitcham club, and were very critical of the club's management.

Unlike in the north, where many supporters can walk to their home ground, the supporter base of the current club is spread well beyond the home counties with fans travelling regularly from as far away as Dorset. Even for those in London, a round trip of over twenty miles for home games is not unusual.

The Fulham management initially frowned on an organised supporters club. This was similar to their relations with the Fulham F.C. supporters, who were kept at arms length by the Fulham board. This was a major mistake, as it went against the traditions of Rugby League. It took a long time to break down the barriers, and for the first couple of seasons fans were prevented from having a drink with the players at Craven Cottage, although they could at way games. However, the fans organised independently. Two supporters clubs were set up, but the one that was lasted was based on travel to away fixtures.

In the first season the club organised travel to away games. But at the start of the second season, the Fulham Rugby League Travelling Supporters Club (FRLTSC) was set up, as they found they could undercut the club's prices. The Snares family were the driving force behind the new club. The new organisation also gave a boost to amateur Rugby League in London, setting up a new amateur club based on Fulham supporters.

By the fourth season, relations with the club had mellowed, and the supporters club was given a page in the club programme, and were the only organisation running away travel.

When Roy and Barbara Close took control in the summer of 1984, one of their aims was to involve the supporters club. They invited Ron Snares, as chairman of the supporters club, to a meeting they held with the players in July, when they outlined their plans, and he was given a place on the new management committee to represent supporters views.

The supporters club provided many of the volunteers who were to help run the club for the next nine years. Even today, selling programmes, running the club shop and many other match day tasks are done by supporters club activists.

And in the summer of 1985, a group of supporters worked every weekend to make the Chiswick Stadium fit to stage professional Rugby League on a regular basis. The move to Chiswick would not have been possible without this enormous voluntary input.

In 1990, for health reasons, Ron Snares had to drop out of activity with the supporters club, although he is now secretary of the amateur East London RLFC. Barry and Gwen Warren also were supporters from the first season, and with Liam Bushell have been London stalwarts since the early days. It was now these three who became the backbone of the supporters club, with Barry becoming secretary, and Gwen continuing the treasurer's role she had done for some years. In 1994-5, the supporters club had 170 members, around 20% of the average gate at Copthall.

Celebration - Fulham fans salute promotion at Rochdale in 1981(Photo: Ken Coton)

14 years on - London Broncos fans at Rochdale April 1995 (Photo: Peter Lush)

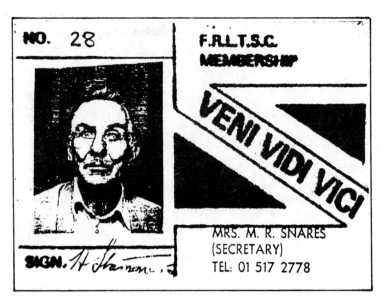

Harry Stammers' membership card for the original Travelling Supporters Club

Still in action - Harry Stammers (on right) with supporters club secretary Barry
Warren selling programmes at a home game (Photo: Dave Farrar)

Michelle, Ron and Mo Snares. Michelle and Mo are wearing the "10,000 miles a season" tee shirt. (Photo: courtesy the Snares family)

London Calling - the first issue

One of the features that has lasted from the first season is the end of the season dinner, which now includes presentations to the players who have won the "Player of the Season" awards.

In August 1983, the supporters club had joined the Lancashire Federation of Supporters Clubs, as their meeting had decided that Fulham was "west of the Pennines." Since then the club have played an active role in the Federation, with Ron Snares being chairman for a period. At the start of the 1994-5 season, the club also affiliated to the Yorkshire Federation.

At one time, the supporters were winning more awards than the team. Bob Evans won the Traveleads Fan of the year in 1988. Despite being born in York, Bob had never seen a game until he visited Craven Cottage in 1980 . He was immediately hooked and became a regular visitor up north at away games. Ron Snares was runner up in 1985.

One of the fans from the first day was cockney legend Harry Stammers. He had first watched league whilst working at the Tetley brewery in Leeds and when the game started at Craven Cottage, Harry was a permanent fixture. Harry now 76, proudly holds supporters club card number 28 and attends every game, home and away. He is best recognised by his Fulham hat and scarf which are festooned in Rugby League badges from all over the world, including five from Russia. The effect of all these badges mean that he looks like a version of the Pearly King, a title he was referred to in a Highfield programme. Harry also sells programmes before the games at Copthall, but also leading the cheering during the game. At the match against Huddersfield in April 1995, he was photographed with a 92 year old Huddersfield supporter.

The achievement of running transport to virtually every away game should not be under-estimated. The teeshirts of the early seasons, proudly proclaiming "10,000 miles a season and still going strong", were an accurate estimate of the mileage done. Only twice have coaches broken down, coming back from a match in Cumbria, resulting in a night spent on Shap Fell, and from Hunslet in April 1994. However, on that occasion, the team coach saw the supporters at the side of the road, and gave them a lift back to London. Further afield, Barry and Gwen Warren went on the club's trip to Russia in 1991, to see the games in Moscow and Leningrad.

Perhaps the greatest day for the travelling supporters was the premiership final at Old Trafford in May 1994. Despite having only 6 days to organise the trip, and a 1.30 p.m. kick off meaning an even earlier start then usual, three coaches made the trip, and probably over 500 London fans were

Fulham still there - Sue and Alex with their banner at Rochdale in April 1995
(Photo: Peter Lush)

Al Ferrier selling London Calling at Copthall (Photo: Dave Farrar)

315

there. Not much by Wigan's standards, but still around two thirds of the average home gate.

Although not strictly a supporters organisation, the Friends of London Rugby League lottery has played a vital role in fund raising. Set up when Tim Lamb and Richard Lawton became Directors in 1986, to provide regular funds to sustain the club, it now concentrates on raising funds for the amateur game and the Broncos alliance side.

Various publications have been published by supporters. In the early days at Craven Cottage, Bob Evans issued the Rugby League Diary. In 1984, Paul Spencer-Thompson, who was later to become the club's programme editor, issued a journal appeared called the 'Fulham File' which catalogued the club's statistics and records for the first four seasons in meticulous detail. In 1991, Phil Babbs published "Not an Official Programme." Although very rudimentary, it attempted to fill a gap for the Rugby League news starved capital's fans. Six issues were produced, until he felt the club programme had improved enough not to justify further ones.

At the final game at Crystal Palace, a small group of fans put out a questionnaire. From it came the "London Calling" fanzine. Instrumental in this publication were Al and Lol Ferrier, Steve Woodland and Paul Taylor. This was a new younger generation of fans who had not been around during the Fulham period and so added a new dimension to the ranks of the London supporters. This lively publication has so far lasted two seasons, and has included interviews with people connected with the Fulham period.

In general, the supporters have built up good relationships with supporters from the north. Usually, after the match the Supporters have a drink in the bar with the other team's fans, Harry sings some Cockney songs, and then another long trip down the motorway starts.

Fulham, London Crusaders & London Broncos Supporters Club Membership:

1983-4: 100	1987-8: 86	1991-2: 60
1984-5: 91	1988-9: 69	1992-3: 86
1985-6: 77	1989-0: 95	1993-4: 153
1986-7: 86	1990-1: 125	1994-5: 170

Part 4

Statistics and Club Records

International matches in London:

London Highfield, Acton & Willesden, Streatham & Mitcham:

Fulham, London Crusaders and London Broncos

Notes:

In all results, the score of the London team is given first

Where a player's appearances are in bold print, he played for more than one season.

Accurate attendance figures are always difficult to establish. The ones in the 1930s are mainly from press reports. Later ones, where possible, are from official club publications.

International matches in London:

i   Teams, scorers and attendances

Note: in many of the early matches, numbers do not necessarily indicate a specific playing position.

Great Britain 6 New Zealand 18   8 February 1908, Stamford Bridge

Great Britain:	H. Taylor (capt), J. Leytham, T. Llewellyn, B. Jenkins, A. P. Eccles, J. Jolley, G. Baxter, G. Ruddick, D. Jones, G. Thomas, A. Smith, H. Wilson, S. Warwick.
New Zealand:	H. S. Turtill, E. Wrigley, G. W. Smith (capt), H. H. Messenger, W.T.Tyler, L. B. Todd, R. J. Wynyard, D. Gilchrist, W. Johnston, T. W. Cross, C. J. Pearce, C. Dunning, W. M. Trevarthen.
Great Britain:	Tries: Leytham, Eccles
New Zealand:	Tries: Johnston 2, Smith, Todd. Goals: Messenger 3
Half time:	3-5 Referee: J. H. Smith (Great Britain)
Attendance:	14,000

Great Britain 22 Australia 22   12 December 1908, Park Royal

Great Britain:	H. Gifford, G. Tyson, G. Dickenson, T. B. Jenkins (capt), W. Batten, E. Brooks, J. Thomas A. Robinson, A. Smith , W. H. Longworth, W. Jukes, J. W. Higson , A. Mann
Australia:	M. Bolewski, W, G. Heidke, S. P. Deane, J. Devereaux, H. H. Messenger (capt) , A. Halloway, A. Butler, P. Walsh, E. J. Courtney, S. C. Pearce, A. Burdon, J. Abercrombie , L. O'Malley
Great Britain:	Tries: Batten 2, Tyson, Brooks, Thomas, Jukes. Goals: Brooks 2
Australia:	Tries: Devereaux 3, Butler. Goals: Messenger 5
Half time:	14-5 Referee: J. H. Smith (Great Britain)
Attendance:	2,000

England 6 Australia 11   18 October 1911, Craven Cottage

England: J. Sharrock, W. Batten, J. Lomas (capt), H. Wagstaff, W. F. Kitchen, F. Smith, T. White, W. Jukes, A. E. Avery, J. L. Clampitt, W. Ward, H. Kershaw, R. Ramsdale

Australia: 1. C. Fraser, A. Broomham, H. Gilbert, V. Farnsworth, C. J. Russell, W. Farnsworth, C. H. McKivat (capt), R. R. Craig, E. J. Courtney, W. S. Noble, P. A. McCue, A. R. H. Francis, G. Gillett.

England: Tries: Wagstaff, Kitchen
Australia: Tries: V. Farnsworth, W. Farnsworth, Craig. Goal: Francis

Half time: 3-8   Referee: T. H. Smirk (Great Britain)
Attendance: 6,000

England 5 Australia 4   10 October 1921, Highbury

England: T. Clarkson, W. J. Stone, F. Todd, W. Hall, J. Owen, J. Parkin (capt), J. Brittain, W. Cunliffe, J. Cartwright, G. A. Skelhorne, H. Hilton, R. Taylor, R. Taylor

Australia: R. Norman, J. Craig, C. Fraser, L. Cubitt (capt), C. Blinkhorn, D. Thompson, H. Caples, S. Pearce, W. Schultz, B. Gray, F. Burge, F. Ryan, J. Price, J. Watkins.

England: Try: Todd. Goal: Clarkson
Australia: Goals: Thompson, Gray

Half time: 3-2   Referee: Rev F. Chambers (Great Britain)
Attendance: 12,000

England 12 Wales 7   11 December 1922, Herne Hill

England: T. Clarkson, W. J. Stone, W. Batten, J. Trante, W. Bentham, J. Parkin (capt) J. Brittain, W. Cunliffe, G. A. Skelhorne, G. A. Skelhorne, J. Cartwright, R. Taylor, J. Darwell, J. Price

Wales: J. Sullivan, J. A. Bacon, J. Shea, C. W. Emery, B. Williams, E. Caswell, J. H. Rogers, B. Gronow (capt), B. Gould, G. Oliver,

T. Woods, W. Hodder, E. Morgan.

England: Tries: Stone 2, Taylor, Parkin
Wales: Try: Morgan. Goals: Sullivan 2

Half time: 6-7   Referee: R. Jones (Great Britain)
Attendance: 3,000

Wales 10 Australia 26   **18 January 1930, Wembley**

Wales: J. Sullivan, S. Ray, M. A. Rosser, T . Parker, J. Ring, W. Rees,
            D. M. Davies, W. A. Williams, L. L. White, J. F. Thompson (capt),
            F. Stephens, A. Evans, J. O. Meredith.

Australia: F. McMillan, W. Spencer, J. Upton, T. Gorman (capt), W.
            Shankland, F. Laws, J. Busch, W. Brogan, A. Justice, H. Steinohrt,
            G. Treweeke, W. Prigg, J. Kingston

Wales: Tries: Ray, Rosser. Goals: Sullivan 2
Australia: Tries: Spencer 3, Justice, Treweeke, Prigg. Goals: Shankland 4

Half time: 5-5   Referee: A. E. Harding (Great Britain)
Attendance: 16,000

Wales 19 Australia 51   30 December 1933, Wembley

Wales: J. Sullivan (capt), J. C. Morley, A. J. Risman, M. A. Rosser, F. G.
            Smart, A. R. Ralph, D. M. Davies, W. A. Williams, L. L. White,
            R. Green, A. C. Evans, N. Fender, I. Isaac

Australia: W. Smith, J. Why, C. Pearce, D. Brown, F. Gardner, V. Hey, V.
            Thicknesse, R. Stehr, A. Folwell, M. Madsen (capt), S. Pearce, J.
            Doyle, W. Prigg,

Wales: Tries: Morley, Fender, Isaac. Goals: Sullivan 5
Australia: Tries: Why 3, S. Pearce 3, Smith, Brown, Gardner, Hey, Doyle.
            Goals: Brown 9

Half time: 4-23   Referee: A. E. Harding (Great Britain)
Attendance: 10,000

321

England 5 France 12   12 March 1949, Wembley

England: J. A. Ledgard, G. W. Ratcliffe, E. J. Ashcroft, E. Ward (capt) , S. McCormick, J. Fleming, G. J. Helme, K. Gee, J. Egan, G. Curran, R. Nicholson, J. J. Featherstone, W. Hudson.

France: Puig-Aubert (capt), O. Lespes, R. Caillou, V. Cantoni, C. Galaup, J. Crespo, A. Ulma, M. Martin, P. Bartoletti, H. Berthomieu, E. Ponsinet, G. Calixte.

England: Try: Ratcliffe Goal: Ward
France: Tries: Lespes, Calixte. Goal: Puig-Aubert.
                Drop goals: Puig-Aubert 2

Half time: 3-7   Referee: A. S. Dobson (Great Britain)
Attendance: 12,382

British Empire XIII 26   New Zealand 22 3 January 1952, Stamford Bridge

British Empire: J. Cunliffe, B. Bevan, T. Allan, E. Ward, L. W. Cooper (capt), J. Broome, A. J. Pepperell, F. Barton, T. McKinney, A. G. Prescott, H. Bath, A. E. Clues, D. D. Valentine.

New Zealand: D. White, J. R. Edwards, W. B. K. Hough, C. A. Eastlake, W. Sorenson, D. A. Barchard, J. S. Haig (capt), C. R. Johnson, W. J. Davidson, D. L. Blanchard, C. McBride, D. Richards-Jolley, A. J. Atkinson.

British Empire: Tries: Cooper 3, Bevan, Allan, Valentine. Goals: Ward 4
New Zealand: Goal: White

Half time: 6-2   Referee: C. F. Appleton (Great Britain)
Attendance: 6,800

Great Britain 2 Australia 28   16 October 1963, Wembley

Great Britain: K. Gowers, W. Burgess, E. Ashton (capt), N. Fox, N. Field, D. R. Bolton, A. J. Murphy, J. Tembey, W. Sayer, B. Tyson, K. D. Bowman, J. Measures, V. P. P. Karalius.

322

Australia: K. Thornett, K. J. Irvine, G. F. Langlands, R. W. Gasnier, P. Dimond, E. Harrison, B. A. Muir, P. M. Gallagher, I. J. Walsh (capt), N. R. Kelly, R. N. Thornett, B. C. Hambly, J. W. Raper.

Great Britain: Goal: Fox
Australia: Tries: Gasnier 3, K. Thornett, Langlands, Irvine.
Goals: Langlands 5

Half time: 2-10   Referee: D. T. H. Davies (Great Britain)
Attendance: 13,946

Commonwealth XIII 7 New Zealand 15   18 August 1965, Crystal Palace

Commonwealth: R. James, T. B. Jones, R. J. Hagan, D. Wood, T. Lake, A. Broach, K. Hepworth, N. F. Dolton, V. Drui, J. Ravitale, T. H. Fogerty, M. J. Hicks (capt), C. W. Renilson. Subs: G. Coetzer, W. Ramsey.

New Zealand: J. E. Fagan, B. T. Reidy, R. W. Bailey, G. M. Kennedy, P. M. White, J. M. D. Walshe, W. L. Snowden (capt), S. K. Edwards, C. O'Neill, H. R. Emery, R. D. Hammond, E. Moore, G. Mattson. Subs: P. Schultz, R. I. Orchard

Commonwealth: Try: Ravitale. Goals: James 2
New Zealand: Tries: Reidy, Emery, Mattson. Goals: Fagan 3

Half time: 5-3   Referee: J. Manly (Great Britain)
Attendance: 1,200

Great Britain 11 Australia 17   3 November 1967, White City

Great Britain: A. Keegan, C. C. Young, I. Brooke, N. Fox, W. L. Francis, R. Millward, T. Bishop, W. Holliday (capt), P. J. Flanagan, C. H. Watson, R. A. Irving, C. H. Watson, J. Mantle, F. Foster. Subs: M. J. Price, D. Robinson.

Australia: L. H. Johns, J. W. Greaves, G. F. Langlands, J. N. MacDonald, J. C. King, A. R. Branson, J. W. Gleeson, P. M. Gallagher (capt), N. R. Kelly, N. J. Gallagher, R. J. Lynch, E. W. Rasmussen, R. J. Coote. Subs: K. J. Irvine, D. P. Manteit

| Great Britain: | Try: Bishop. Goals: Fox 3.Drop Goal: Bishop |
| Australia: | Tries: Langlands, King, Coote. Goals: Langlands 4 |

| Half time: | 2-2 | Referee: G. F. Lindop (Great Britain) |
| Attendance: | 17,445 | |

Great Britain 21 Australia 12   3 November 1973, Wembley

Great Britain: H. P. Charlton, C. A. Sullivan (c), S. Hynes, C. Hesketh, J. B. Atkinson, D. Topliss, S. Nash, T. Clawson, C. Clarke, B. Lockwood, P. Lowe, G. Nicholls, R. Batten.
Subs: D. Eckersley, J. Mantle

Australia: G. F. Langlands (capt), R. Branighan, R. Fulton, G. Starling, E. Goodwin, T. Pickup, T. Raudonikis, R. O'Reilly, E. Walters, A. H. Beetson, R. McCarthy, K. Maddison, P. Sait.
Subs: M. W. Cronin, T. Randall.

Great Britain:	Tries: Lowe 2, Clarke, Lockwood. Goals: Clawson 4.
	Drop goal: Nash
Australia:	Tries: Branighan, Fulton. Goals: Langlands 3

| Half time: | 4-2 | Referee: W. H. Thompson (Great Britain) |
| Attendance: | 9,874 | |

Great Britain 19 Australia 12   27 October 1990, Wembley

Great Britain: Steve Hampson, Paul Eastwood, Daryl Powell, Carl Gibson, Martin Offiah, Garry Schofield, Andy Gregory, Karl Harrison, Lee Jackson, Paul Dixon, Denis Betts, Roy Powell, Ellery Hanley (capt).   Subs: Shaun Edwards, Kevin Ward (Powell, 45 min), David Hulme, Karl Fairbank (Harrison, 72 min).

Australia: Gary Belcher, Andrew Ettingshausen, Mal Meninga (capt), Mark McGaw, Michael Hancock, Ricky Stuart, Allan Langer, Steve Roach, Kerrod Walters, Martin Bella, Paul Sironen, John Cartwright, Bob Lindner.
Subs: Greg Alexander (Langer, 79 min), Des Hasler (Cartwright, 72 min), Dale Shearer (Hancock, 79 min), Glenn Lazarus (Bella, 72 min).

Great Britain: Tries: Eastwood 2, Offiah. Goals: Eastwood 3. Drop goal: Schofield

Australia: Tries: Meninga, McGaw. Goals: Meninga 2

Half time: 2-2 Referee: Alain Sablayrolles (France)

Attendance: 54,569

Great Britain 6 Australia 10 24 October 1992, Wembley (World Cup Final)

Great Britain: Joe Lydon, Alan Hunte, Gary Connolly, Garry Schofield (c), MartinOffiah, Shaun Edwards, Deryck Fox, Kevin Ward, Martin Dermott, Andy Platt, Denis Betts, Phil Clarke, Ellery Hanley.
Subs: John Devereux (Connolly, 45 min), Kelvin Skerrett (Ward, 52 min), Alan Tait (Lydon, 48 min, Richie Eyres (Hanley, 75 min)

Australia: Tim Brasher, Willie Carne, Steve Renouf, Mal Meninga (capt), Michael Hancock, Brad Fittler, Allan Langer, Glenn Lazarus, Steve Walters, Mark Sargent, Paul Sironen, Bob Lindner, Bradley Clyde
Subs: John Cartwright (Sargent, 63 min), David Gillespie (Sironen, 40 min), Chris Johns, Kevin Walters (Clyde, 44 min)

Great Britain: Goals: Fox 3

Australia: Try: Renouf. Goals: Meninga 3

Half time: 6-4 Referee: Dennis Hale (New Zealand)

Attendance: 73,631

Great Britain 17 New Zealand 0 16 October 1993, Wembley

Great Britain: Jonathan Davies, Jason Robinson, Paul Newlove, Gary Connolly, John Devereux, Garry Schofield (capt), Shaun Edwards, Karl Harrison, Martin Dermott, Karl Fairbank, Denis Betts, Chris Joynt, Phil Clarke
Subs: Daryl Powell (Newlove, 68 min), Sonny Nickle (Fairbank, 53 min), Alan Tait (Devereux, 76 min), Richie Eyres (Joynt, 63 min)

New Zealand: Morvin Edwards, Daryl Halligan, Kevin Iro, Dave Watson, Sean Hoppe, Gene Ngamu, Gary Freeman (capt), John Lomax, Duane Mann, Brent Stuart, Stephen Kearney, Quentin Pongia, Tawera Nikau.
Subs: Jason Williams (Edwards, 60 min), Jason Mackie (Nikau, 70 min), Whetu Taewa (Halligan, 75 min), Jason Lowrie (Lomax, 58 min).

Great Britain: Tries: Robinson 2, Devereux. Goals: Davies 2.
Drop goal: Davies

Half time: 10-0   Referee: Greg McCallum (Australia)
Attendance: 36,131

Great Britain 8 Australia 4   **22 October 1994, Wembley**

Great Britain: Jonathan Davies, Jason Robinson, Gary Connolly, Alan Hunte, Martin Offiah, Daryl Powell, Shaun Edwards (capt), Karl Harrison, Lee Jackson, Chris Joynt, Denis Betts, Andy Farrell, Phil Clarke.
Subs: Bobby Goulding (Farrell, 32 min), Barrie McDermott (Powell, 23 min), Allan Bateman (Davies, 59 min), Mick Cassidy (Harrison, 61 min).

Australia: Brett Mullins, Andrew Ettingshausen, Mal Meninga (capt), Steve Renouf, Wendell Sailor, Laurie Daley, Allan Langer, Ian Roberts, Steve Walters, Paul Harragon, Paul Sironen, Bradley Clyde, Brad Fittler
Subs: Ricky Stuart (Daley, 57 min), Tim Brasher, Dean Pay (Sironen, 54 min), David Furner (Clyde, 40 min)

Great Britain: Try: Davies. Goals: Davies, Goulding
Australia: Try: Renouf

Half time: 6-0   Referee: Graham Annesley (Australia)
Attendance: 57,034

London Highfield, Acton & Willesden, Streatham & Mitcham:

ii   Club records and top scorers

London Highfield:

Biggest victory:	59-11 versus Bramley (h)	4 May 1934
Biggest defeat:	11-43 versus Wigan (a)	2 September 1933
Highest attendance:	14,500 versus Australia	22 November 1933

Top try scorers:	Jack Maloney	21	Jimmy Walker	15
Top goal scorers:	Sam Oakley	85	Robert Fraser	8
Top points scorers:	Sam Oakley	173	Jack Maloney	63

Acton & Willesden:

Biggest victory:	30-11 versus Bramley(h)	2 May 1936
Biggest defeat:	5-54 versus Leeds (h)	20 April 1936
Highest attendance:	17,841 versus Batley	28 September 1935

Top try scorers:	Jack Cutbush	17	Arthur Veysey	12
Top goal scorers:	Jim Addison	46		
Top points scorers:	Jim Addison	95	Jack Cutbush	51

Streatham & Mitcham:

Biggest victory:	44-8 versus Featherstone(h)	19 October 1935
Biggest defeat:	12-45 versus Wigan (a)	27 January 1937
Highest attendance:	24,000 versus Oldham	7 September 1935

Top try scorers:	Ernest Holder	28	Charles Smith	16
Top goal scorers:	George Nepia	73	Tom Walsh	20
Top points scorers:	George Nepia	170	Tom Walsh	85

iii   Fixtures and results

London Highfield 1933-34

Opponent	Competition	Date	Home or away		Result
Wigan	League	2.9.33	A	7,000	11-43
Dewsbury	League	12.9.33	A	1,000	18-6
Halifax	League	16.9.33	A	9,000	6-21
Wakefield	League	20.9.33	H	6,000	8-9
Wakefield	League	27.9.33	A		16-22
Rochdale	Lancashire Cup	30.9.33	A	5,637	10-19
Halifax	League	4.10.33	H	8,000	18-9
Rochdale	League	11.10.33	H	6,000	9-7
Broughton	League	18.10.33	H	8,000	15-11
Featherstone	League	21.10.33	A		18-3
St Helens R	League	25.10.33	H	9,000	20-12
Leeds	League	4.11.33	A	7,000	7-23
Leeds	League	8.11.33	H	8,000	3-5
Dewsbury	League	15.11.33	H		15-7
Australia	Tour	22.11.33	H	14,500	5-20
Swinton	League	2.12.33	A		8-16
Warrington	League	6.12.33	H		3-15
Warrington	League	9.12.33	A		5-8
Salford	League	13.12.33	H	2,000	15-10
Oldham	League	20.12.33	H		7-8
Broughton	League	25.12.33	A		8-23
Rochdale	League	30.12.33	A		0-16
Swinton	League	3.1.34	H		2-17
Barrow	League	13.1.34	A	5,945	11-2
Widnes	League	17.1.34	H		12-10
Oldham	League	27.1.34	A		4-5
Wigan	League	31.1.34	H	7,000	30-12
Hull St M.	Challenge Cup	10.2.34	H	1,000	32-2
Widnes	League	17.2.34	A		5-7
Warrington	Challenge Cup	24.2.34	H	5,000	19-5
Featherstone	League	28.2.34	H		22-8
Salford	League	3.3.34	A		5-26
Huddersfield	Challenge Cup	10.3.34	A		2-21

St.Helens	League	14.3.34	H		16-8
Batley	League	19.3.34	A		7-5
France	Tour	21.3.34	H		19-17
Bramley	League	30.3.34	A		31-9
Barrow	League	4.4.34	H		18-13
Leigh	League	7.4.34	A		16-15
Leigh	League	11.4.34	H	2,000	25-8
St Helens	League	14.4.34	A		12-34
Batley	League	18.4.34	H		7-9
St Helens R	League	2.5.34	A	3,000	17-16
Bramley	League	4.5.34	H		59-11

Acton & Willesden 1935-36

Opponent	Competition	Date	Home or away	Result
York	League	31.8.35	H 7,000	17 -17
Featherstone	League	5.9.35	H	29-14
Featherstone	League	7.9.35	A 2,000	15-13
Hunslet	Yorkshire Cup	14.9.35	A 6,000	5-18
St Helens	League	21.9.35	A	5-2
Batley	League	28.9.35	H 17,841	21-14
York	League	5.10.35	A 8,000	7-14
Barrow	League	12.10.35	H 15,621	7 -7
Hull KR	League	19.10.35	A	2-4
Castleford	League	26.10.35	H 12,000	9-13
Batley	League	2.11.35	A 4,000	5-19
Keighley	League	9.11.35	H 9,305	10-3
Castleford	League	16.11.35	A	5-28
Wakefield	League	23.11.35	H	19-7
Hull	League	30.11.35	A	4-16
Bradford	League	7.12.35	H 2,000	3-5
Bramley	League	14.12.35	A	3-22
Leigh	League	21.12.35	H 2,000	22-14
Streatham	League	25.12.35	A 10,000	15-7
Hull KR	League	26.12.35	H	8-10
Leeds	League	28.12.35	A	10-29
Rochdale	League	4.1.36	H	23-0
Keighley	League	11.1.36	A	0-9

St Helens	League	25.1.36	H 3,000	5-0
Wakefield	League	1.2.36	A 3,600	8-11
Liverpool	Challenge Cup	8.2.36	H	0-0
Huddersfield	League	15.2.36	H 1,000	5-9
Liverpool	Challenge Cup	17.2.36	A 2,000	3-29
Hull	League	29.2.36	H	3-19
Barrow	League	7.3.36	A 4,394	0-25
Huddersfield	League	11.3.36	A 1,000	5-30
Hunslet	League	14.3.36	A	3-10
Dewsbury	League	28.3.36	H	12-2
Streatham	League	10.4.36	H 4,000	12-21
Leigh	League	11.4.36	A	11-11
Dewsbury	League	13.4.36	A	13-15
Hunslet	League	14.4.36	H	16-6
Leeds	League	20.4.36	H	5-54
Rochdale	League	25.4.36	A 1,000	7-20
Bradford	League	27.4.36	A	18-18
Streatham	Friendly	1.5.36	Wandsworth	19-33
Bramley	League	2.5.36	H	20-11

Streatham and Mitcham 1935 -1937

Opponents	Competition	Date	Home or away	Result
1935-6				
Broughton R	League	31.8.35	A	4-24
Oldham	League	7.9.35	H 24,000	5-10
St Helens	Lancashire Cup	11.9.35	A 4,000	7-10
Widnes	League	19.9.35	H 2,000	2-8
Bradford N	League	21.9.35	H 20,174	14-9
Bramley	League	28.9.35	A	7-14
Warrington	League	5.10.35	H 16,000	7-17
St Helens Rec	League	12.10.35	A	5-16
Featherstone	League	19.10.35	H 15,278	44-8
Wigan	League	26.10.35	A 8,000	5-28
St Helens Rec	League	2.11.35	H 13,487	14-2
Barrow	League	9.11.35	A 6,034	9-9
Rochdale H	League	16.11.35	H 10,162	18-2
Rochdale H	League	23.11.35	A 4,097	5-31
Salford	League	30.11.35	H 10,000	3-9

Featherstone	League	7.12.35	A		11-21
Wigan	League	14.12.35	H	15,000	3-11
Acton & W	League	25.12.35	H	10,000	7-15
Liverpool	League	26.12.35	A		11-6
St Helens	League	28.12.35	H	8,000	3-3
Leigh	League	1.1.36	A	6,000	4-7
Batley	League	4.1.36	A	6,000	6-7
Swinton	League	8.1.36	A		6-21
Batley	League	11.1.36	H	6,000	16-6
Salford	League	25.1.36	A		11-35
Bramley	League	1.2.36	H	5,000	22-13
Hull K R	Challenge Cup	8.2.36	A	5,000	18-5
Widnes	League	15.2.36	A	4,000	9-20
Leeds	Challenge Cup	22.2.36	H	6,000	3-13
Bradford N	League	7.3.36	A	8,000	3-13
Leigh	League	14.3.36	H		15-2
Oldham	League	21.3.36	A		7-20
Halifax	League	25.3.36	H		8-21
St Helens	League	28.3.36	A		11-22
Halifax	League	30.3.36	A	2,500	18-10
Swinton	League	1.4.36	H		13-10
Liverpool	League	4.4.36	H	5,000	0-14
Acton & W	League	10.4.36	A	4,000	21-12
Broughton R	League	11.4.36	H	4,000	10-17
Barrow	League	13.4.36	H	5,000	21-7
Warrington	League	25.4.36	A		12-20
Acton & W	Friendly	1.5.36		Wandsworth	33-19

1936-7

Bramley	League	29.8.36	A		25-16
Bramley	League	2.9.36	H		37-4
Broughton R	League	5.9.36	H		7-18
Barrow	Lancashire Cup	12.9.36	H		8-23
Hull K R	League	19.9.36	A		18-13
Newcastle	League	26.9.36	H		39-3
Halifax	League	3.10.36	A	10,000	12-19
Warrington	League	10.10.36	H		5-8
St Helens	League	17.10.36	A		15-5
Hull K R	League	24.10.36	H		33-3

St Helens Rec	League	31.10.36	H		24-3
Broughton R	League	7.11.36	A		12-6
Rochdale H	League	14.11.36	H		15-0
Featherstone	League	21.11.36	A		32-9
St Helens	League	28.11.36	H	3,000	3-2
Barrow	League	5.12.36	A		0-3
Swinton	League	12.12.36	H		0-15
Dewsbury	League	19.12.36	A		15-8
Liverpool	League	25.12.36	A		9-21
Liverpool	League	26.12.36	H		3-17
Leigh	League	2.1.37	A		6-10
Oldham	League	9.1.37	A	4,000	15-28
Featherstone	League	16.1.37	H		11-4
Salford	League	23.1.37	A		0-33
Wigan	League	27.1.37	A		12-45
Leigh	League	6.2.37	H		13-11
Bradford	Challenge Cup	13.2.37	A		0-39
Swinton	League	20.2.37	A		5-35

After this match, Streatham & Mitcham withdrew from the league. The rest of their matches were awarded to their opponents.

iv   Players appearances

London Highfield 1933-4

Player	App	Tries	Goals	Pts
Belshaw, William	41	9	3	33
Collier, Chris	3			
Cuncliffe, William	1			
Davies, George	21			
Dysart, William	3			
Fairhurst, Joe	18	1		3
Fraser, Robert	16		8	24
Gordon, Joseph	20	4		12
Gray, Herbert	15	1		3
Griffin, Mick	38	11		33
Haigh, Herbert	34	11		33
Hill, E.C.	2			
Hitchen, C.	4			
Hunter, H.	31	11	1	35
Ilsley, Robert	8			
Maddocks B.	11			
Maloney, Jack	40	21		63
Merritt, W.F.	1			
Oakley, Sam	39	1	97	197
Oster, Jack	18	3	2	13
Richards, Eddie	18	8		24
Salmon, H.	25	7		21
Sherrington, John	8	1		3
Stock, R.	20	6		18
Sullivan, John	1			
Unwin, B.	32	1		3
Walker, Jimmy	38	15	1	47
Welsh, W.B.	21	10		30
Winnard, T.	2			
Winstanley, Tom	1			
Woods, Harry	42	3		9

Acton & Willesden 1935-6

Player	App	Tries	Goals	Pts
Addison, Jim	26	1	46	95
Allen, J.	3			
Atherton, G.	33			
Avery, Jack	24	1	1	5
Brown	1			
Cayzer, Jack	35	7		21
Cutbush, Jack	36	17		51
Edwards	1			
James, William	23	1	10	23
Jenkins, Dai	33	3		9
Johnson, Abe	12	3	10	29
Jones, E.M.	1			
Jones, Glyn	2			
Lawton, Jim	1			
Madden, Dennis	13	6		18
Morgan, Gill	36	4		12
Murphy, Con	38	4		12
Phillips, J.	8			
Pritchard, J.	2			
Roberts, Stanley	35	8	2	28
Sutcliffe, P.	31	1	1	5
Thomas, Elfred	7	1		3
Turton, J.	9	5		
Veysey, Arthur	36	12		36
Walton, Richard	38	2		6
Williams, Illtwyd	20	1	5	13

Streatham & Mitcham 1935-7

Player	App	Tries	Goals	Pts
Avery, Jack	7	3	1	11
Banks, George William	**51**	**1**		**3**
Barnes, Peter	**38**	**2**	**8**	**22**
Baverstock, E.J	**9**	**1**		**3**
Berry, Harry	28	8		24
Bibby, Fred	17	3		9
Birtwell	1			

Player	App	Tries	Goals	Pts
Briers, H.	1			
Brown	1			
Bullock, A.E.	1			
Crabtree, Shirley	**26**	**1**		**3**
Davies	1			
Egan,T.	**5**			
Harling, Clifford	**16**			
Harrison, George	**37**	**3**	**1**	**11**
Hitchen, C.	**15**			
Holder, Ernest	**50**	**28**	**8**	**100**
Horsman, Stanley	1			
Hunter, H.	**44**	**15**	**2**	**49**
Johnson, A.	**4**		**7**	**14**
Jones, E.M.	**16**			
Jones, Ike	**49**	**7**		**21**
Jones, Ken	**2**			
Langford, Brian	**62**	**3**		**9**
Lemon, Arthur	12			
MacDonald, Jack	**45**	**13**		**39**
McTiffin, J.	2			
Murphy, Con	19	3		9
Nepia, George	**38**	**8**	**73**	**170**
Nicholson, K.	**19**	**9**		**27**
Peebles, J.	3			
Pritchard, J.	7			
Roberts, Stanley	3			
Sayers, T.	**1**			
Shaw, William	**17**	**2**		**6**
Smith, Charles	**43**	**16**		**48**
Sutcliffe, P.	5			
Thompson	1			
Turton, J.	15	2		
Twose, A.V.	5		1	2
Veysey, Arthur	24	17		51
Walsh, Tom	39	13	23	85
Whitworth, Wilfred	33	4		12
Williams, C.	14			
Williams, Illtwyd	10	1	2	7
Williams, L.	**8**	**1**		

Fulham, London Crusaders and London Broncos

v   Club records and international appearances

Second Division Champions 1982-3
Promoted (third) from Second Division 1980-1
Second Division Premiership Runners Up 1993-4

Biggest victory: 64-0   versus Bramley (h)   27 March 1994
Highest score: 66-12 versus Keighley (h)   8 May 1994
Biggest defeat: 6-72   versus Whitehaven (a) 14 September 1986
Highest attendance: 15,013 versus Wakefield Trinity 15 February 1981
League record 1980-1 to 1994-5: Won 227 Drawn 15 Lost 196

International appearances:
Great Britain: John Dalgreen v Australia 1982.
England: John Wood   v France 1982 (not recognised as international match)
Wales: David Bishop v. England and France 1992
    Adrian Cambriani v. France and England twice in 1981
    Martin Herdman v. England twice in 1981, v Australia in 1982.
South Africa   Mark Johnson   Sydney Sevens in 1994.

Most tries in a match: 4
Mark Riley versus Highfield (h)   17 October 1993
Mark Johnson versus Highfield (a)   1 April 1994
Scott Roskell versus Bramley (a)   19 March 1995

Most goals in a match: 11
Steve Guyett versus Huddersfield (h)   23 October 1988
Greg Pearce versus Runcorn (h)   26 August 1990

Most points in a match: 24
John Gallagher versus Bramley   27 March 1994

Most tries in a season: Mark Johnson 1993-4: 43
Most goals in a season: John Gallagher 1993-4: 159
Most appearances: Hussein M'Barki (1981-4, and 1988-91): 148 + 15(sub)
Most tries: Hussein M'Barki (1981-4 and 1988-91): 74
Most goals: Steve Diamond (1981-4): 305 + 4 drop goals
Most points: Steve Diamond (1981-4): 691

Top ten appearances:

Hussein M'Barki	148 + 15 (sub)	163	Reg Bowden	116 + 4 (sub)	120
Tony Kinsey	131 + 25 (sub)	156	Kieron Murphy	105 + 14 (sub)	119
Dave Rotheram	114 + 36 (sub)	150	Charlie Jones	94 + 22 (sub)	116
Tony Gourley	125 + 6 (sub)	131	Darryl Pitt	95 + 20 (sub)	115
Adrian Cambriani	119 + 2 (sub)	121	Steve Rosolen	110 + 1 (sub)	111

Top Ten try scorers:

Hussein M'Barki	74
Mark Johnson	66
Scott Roskell	55
Mark Riley	54
Steve Mills	50
John Crossley	48
Adrian Cambriani	42
Darryl Pitt	47
Dave Gillan	38
Dave Allen	34

Top five goal scorers:

Steve Diamond	305 + 4 dg
John Gallagher	196 + 2 dg
Chris Smith	146
Chris Wilkinson	141 + 13 dg
Greg Pearce	121

Top five point scorers:

Steve Diamond	691
John Gallagher	470
Chris Wilkinson	363
Chris Smith	320
Steve Guyett	289

Top three drop goal scorers:

David Eckersley	17
Chris Wilkinson	13
Tony Kinsey	10

vi   Managers

Reg Bowden:	July 1980 to June 1984
Roy Lester:	August 1984 to April 1986
Bill Goodwin:	April 1986 to July 1987
Bev Risman:	July 1987 to October 1988
Bill Goodwin:	October 1988 to January 1989
Phil Sullivan:	January 1989 to February 1989
Bill Goodwin:	February 1989 to May 1989
Ross Strudwick:	July 1989 to February 1993
Tony Gordon:	March 1993 to May 1994
Gary Greinke:	July 1994 to present

Notes:	Reg Bowden was player-coach

vii   Top appearances, try and goal scorers season by season

Tries		Goals		Drop Goals	
1980-1					
Mal Aspey	16	Iain MacCorquodale	75	David Eckersley	10
Adrian Cambriani	13	David Eckersley	5		
1981-2					
John Crossley	15	Steve Diamond	92	John Dalgreen	2
				David Eckersley	2
1982-3					
John Crossley	27	Steve Diamond	136	David Eckersley	4
Hussein M'Barki	23				
1983-4					
Hussein M'Barki	17	Steve Diamond	77	Tony Kinsey	9
				Steve Diamond	3
1984-5					
Mike Davis	17	Chris Wilkinson	63	Chris Wilkinson	7
Steve Mills	17	Paul Rochford	14		
1985-6					
Steve Mills	11	Chris Wilkinson	72	Alan Platt	4
Adrian Cambriani	10	Alan Platt	27	Russ Gibson	2
Chris Wilkinson	10				
1986-7					
Steve Mills	12	Colin Fenn	65	Kieron Murphy	3
		Huw Rees	7	Chris Wilkinson	3
1987-8					
Dave Gillan	9	Colin Fenn	40	Nick Grimoldby	3
		Steve Guyett	19		
1988-9					
Dave Gillan	14	Steve Guyett	65	Brian Brown	5
		Jeff Coutts	11		
1989-0					
Brett Daunt	12	Greg Pearce	47	Brett Daunt	3
Mick Taylor	12	Steve Guyett	33		
Hussein M'Barki	11				

1990-91

Darryl Pitt	10	Greg Pearce	74	Craig Grauf	2
		Tim Dwyer	27		

1991-2

Shane Buckley	17	Chris Smith	78	None	
Darryl Pitt	12	Darryl Pitt	11		

1992-3

Shane Buckley	16	Chris Smith	61	Paul Fisher	1
Mark Riley	12	Darryl Pitt	12	Mark Riley	1

1993-4

Mark Johnson	43	John Gallagher	157	John Gallagher	2
Mark Riley	30				
Scott Roskell	21				
John Gallagher	17				

1994-5

Scott Roskell	24	John Gallagher	39	Craig Green	2
Mark Johnson	19				
Darryl Pitt	14				

viii   League positions & summary of results season by season

Season	Div	Place	Pl	Won	Dr	Lost	Pts	For	Against
1980-1	Two	3rd	28	20	0	8	40	447	237
1981-2	One	13th	30	9	1	20	19	365	539
1982-3	Two	1st	32	27	1	4	55	699	294
1983-4	One	13th	30	9	1	20	19	401	694
1984-5	Two	8th	28	17	1	10	35	528	519
1985-6	Two	9th	34	16	1	17	33	679	709
1986-7	Two	12th	28	8	2	18	18	461	632
1987-8	Two	17th	28	10	0	18	20	382	559
1988-9	Two	15th	28	10	0	18	20	464	650
1989-0	Two	8th	28	16	2	10	34	496	488
1990-1	Two	7th	28	17	2	9	36	450	338
1991-2	Two	4th	28	14	0	14	28	428	483
1992-3	Two	5th	28	12	2	14	26	534	562
1993-4	Two	3rd	30	21	2	7	44	842	522
1994-5	Two	4th	30	20	1	9	41	732	480

ix   League matches against other clubs

Barrow:	Won: 6	Drawn: 0	Lost: 4
Batley:	Won: 13	Drawn: 0	Lost: 7
Blackpool:	Won: 6	Drawn: 0	Lost: 4
Bramley:	Won: 18	Drawn: 1	Lost: 7
Bradford N	Won: 0	Drawn: 0	Lost: 4
Bridgend:	Won: 2	Drawn: 0	Lost: 0
Cardiff:	Won: 1	Drawn: 0	Lost: 1
Carlisle:	Won: 13	Drawn: 1	Lost: 6
Castleford:	Won: 0	Drawn: 1	Lost: 3
Chorley:	Won: 4	Drawn: 0	Lost: 0
Dewsbury:	Won: 11	Drawn: 1	Lost: 6
Doncaster:	Won: 10	Drawn: 1	Lost: 5
Featherstone:	Won: 2	Drawn: 0	Lost: 8
Huddersfield:	Won: 13	Drawn: 2	Lost: 9
Hull:	Won: 2	Drawn: 0	Lost: 2
Hull KR:	Won: 1	Drawn: 0	Lost: 7
Hunslet:	Won: 8	Drawn: 1	Lost: 5
Highfield: *	Won: 15	Drawn: 0	Lost: 5
Keighley:	Won: 10	Drawn: 0	Lost: 6
Leeds:	Won: 0	Drawn: 1	Lost: 3
Leigh:	Won: 4	Drawn: 1	Lost: 9
Mansfield:	Won: 3	Drawn: 0	Lost: 5
Nottingham:	Won: 2	Drawn: 0	Lost: 0
Oldham:	Won: 4	Drawn: 1	Lost: 7
Rochdale:	Won: 12	Drawn: 0	Lost: 14
Salford:	Won: 3	Drawn: 0	Lost: 3
Sheffield:	Won: 4	Drawn: 0	Lost: 10
Southend:	Won: 2	Drawn: 0	Lost: 0
St Helens	Won: 0	Drawn: 0	Lost: 4
Springfield:	Won: 1	Drawn: 0	Lost: 1
Swinton:	Won: 10	Drawn: 1	Lost: 7
Trafford:	Won: 3	Drawn: 0	Lost: 1
Wakefield:	Won: 5	Drawn: 0	Lost: 7
Warrington:	Won: 1	Drawn: 0	Lost: 3
Widnes:	Won: 2	Drawn: 0	Lost: 2
Whitehaven:	Won: 13	Drawn: 2	Lost: 9
Wigan:	Won: 2	Drawn: 0	Lost: 4
Workington:	Won: 8	Drawn: 1	Lost: 5
York:	Won: 13	Drawn: 0	Lost: 13

* Also includes Huyton and Runcorn Highfield

x   Results 1980-1 to 1994-5, season by season

Opponent	Competition	Date	Home or away	Result

1980-1

Opponent	Competition	Date	Home or away	Result
Wigan	Division Two	14.9.80	H 9,554	24-5
Keighley	Division Two	21.9.80	A 3,027	13-24
Swinton	Division Two	28.9.80	H 5,589	25-11
Blackpool	Division Two	5.10.80	A 906	15-2
Huddersfield	Division Two	12.10.80	H 5,971	30-7
Doncaster	Division Two	19.10.80	A 672	28-16
York	Division Two	26.10.80	H 7,159	23-5
Bramley	Division Two	9.11.80	H 5,405	10-7
Dewsbury	Division Two	16.11.80	A 2,500	9-7
Leeds	JP Trophy 1	23.11.80	H 12,583	9-3
Wigan	Division Two	30.11.80	A 8,100	2-15
Leigh	JP Trophy 2	7.12.80	A 7,606	9-17
Hunslet	Division Two	21.12.80	H 5,629	19-5
Batley	Division Two	28.12.80	H 6,237	15-5
Whitehaven	Division Two	4.1.81	A 4,235	0-6
Rochdale	Division Two	11.1.81	H 6,162	8-24
Bramley	Division Two	18.1.81	A 1,750	21-11
Huyton	Division Two	25.1.81	H 5,805	25-4
Hunslet	Division Two	1.2.81	A 1,842	12-11
Swinton	Division Two	8.2.81	A 3,550	9-13
Wakefield T	Challenge Cup 1	15.2.81	H 15,013	5-9
Blackpool	Division Two	1.3.81	H 4,715	8-0
Keighley	Division Two	8.3.81	H 5,285	24-3
Huyton	Division Two	15.3.81	A 500	19-3
Dewsbury	Division Two	22.3.81	H 5,258	16-4
York	Division Two	29.3.81	A 7,351	10-15
Whitehaven	Division Two	5.4.81	H 6,707	15-0
Batley	Division Two	12.4.81	A 3,250	8-10
Rochdale	Division Two	16.4.81	A 2,750	19-5
Huddersfield	Division Two	19.4.81	A 2,435	3-8
Doncaster	Division Two	20.4.81	H 5,867	37-11

1981-2

Swinton	Lancashire Cup 1	16.8.81	H 3,200	32-15
Salford	Lancashire Cup 2	23.8.81	A 3,642	3-19
St Helens	Division One	30.8.81	A 7,000	4-35
Warrington	Division One	6.9.81	H 5,057	28-9
Hull	Division One	13.9.81	A 16,049	5-21
Featherstone	Division One	20.9.81	H 4,881	17-36
Barrow	Division One	27.9.81	A 4,300	13-6
York	Division One	4.10.81	H 4,477	33-10
Widnes	Division One	11.10.81	H 6,777	12-15
Warrington	JP Trophy 1	17.10.81	A 2,500	15-24
Leeds	Division One	25.10.81	A 5,226	12-12
Whitehaven	Division One	15.11.81	A 2,500	10-2
Wigan	Division One	22.11.81	H 5,762	14-15
Warrington	Division One	29.11.81	A 3,817	8-16
Castleford	Division One	6.12.81	H 4,675	7-19
Leigh	Division One	3.1.82	A 4,500	11-18
Wakefield	Division One	24.1.82	H 3,948	13-12
Widnes	Division One	27.1.82	A 3,750	12-33
Castleford	Division One	31.1.82	A 2,239	14-26
Barrow	Division One	7.2.82	H 3,571	5-18
Hunslet	Challenge Cup 1	14.2.82	H 3,392	14-4
Hull KR	Division One	17.2.82	A 7,281	3-20
Hull KR	Division One	21.2.82	H 3,851	10-31
Hull	Challenge Cup 2	28.2.82	H 9,481	5-11
Bradford N	Division One	7.3.82	H 3,862	5-15
Whitehaven	Division One	14.3.82	H 2,512	25-14
Wakefield	Division One	17.3.82	A 2,033	13-18
St Helens	Division One	21.3.82	H 3,546	2-17
Featherstone	Division One	28.3.82	A 2,000	10-35
Leigh	Division One	4.4.82	H 3,572	11-10
York	Division One	9.4.82	A 2,592	22-13
Wigan	Division One	12.4.82	A 5,614	4-19
Hull	Division One	18.4.82	H 4,227	17-12
Leeds	Division One	25.4.82	H 4,055	20-24
Bradford N	Division One	28.4.82	A 3,957	5-8

1982-3

Doncaster	Division Two	22.8.82	H 2,715	30-10
Bramley	Division Two	25.8.82	A 1,000	10-2
Hunslet	Division Two	29.8.82	A 3,000	26-15
Swinton	Lancashire Cup 1	5.9.82	H 2,796	20-8
Rochdale	Division Two	10.9.82	A 831	20-5
Wigan	Lancashire Cup 2	15.9.82	A 6,054	15-4
Wakefield	Division Two	19.9.82	H 3,855	18-12
Salford	Division Two	26.9.82	A 2,494	26-13
Warrington	Lancashire Cup SF	30.9.82	3,356 *	8-17
Dewsbury	Division Two	3.10.82	H 3,325	23-18
Cardiff	Division Two	10.10.82	A 2,004	15-10
Blackpool	Division Two	17.10.82	H 3,075	8-15
Swinton	Division Two	24.10.82	A 1,799	23-7
Whitehaven	Division Two	31.10.82	H 3,079	18-0
Dewsbury	Division Two	7.11.82	A 900	13-7
Australia	Tour match	14.11.82	H 10,432	5-22
Rochdale	Division Two	21.11.82	H 2,714	14-13
St Helens	JP Trophy 1	27.11.82	A 4,000	5-17
Huyton	Division Two	5.12.82	A 300	50-5
Batley	Division Two	19.12.82	H 2,163	36-10
York	Division Two	2.1.83	A 2,742	18-7
Huddersfield	Division Two	9.1.83	A 842	22-7
Huyton	Division Two	16.1.83	H 2,848	41-2
Blackpool	Division Two	23.1.83	A 840	28-5
Doncaster	Division Two	30.1.83	A 576	10-4
Salford	Division Two	6.2.83	H 3,681	17-9
Rochdale	Challenge Cup 1	16.2.83	A 750	24-4
Bramley	Division Two	20.2.83	H 2,864	12-18
Bradford N	Challenge Cup 2	27.2.83	H 4,977	4-11
Hunslet	Division Two	6.3.83	H 2,476	25-25
Whitehaven	Division Two	13.3.83	A 1,908	6-0
Wakefield	Division Two	20.3.83	A 3,982	25-15
Keighley	Division Two	3.4.83	H 2,479	29-0
Batley	Division Two	10.4.83	A 739	21-5
Swinton	Division Two	12.4.83	H 1,050**	34-2
Huddersfield	Division Two	14.4.83	H 499 **	35-3
York	Division Two	17.4.83	H 2,856	21-13
Keighley	Division Two	24.4.83	A 1,094	11-17
Cardiff	Division Two	6.5.83	H 3,321	14-20

* Wigan ** Widnes *** Chelsea FC

Wakefield	Division One	21.8.83	A 2,254	14-18
Leigh	Division One	24.8.83	A 3,638	8-22
Featherstone	Division One	28.8.83	H 2,401	21-11
Salford	Lancashire Cup 1	4.9.83	A 1,986	15-16
Whitehaven	Division One	11.9.83	H 2,010	24-6
Oldham	Division One	18.9.83	A 3,222	12-30
Hull	Division One	25.9.83	H 3,838	29-24
Warrington	Division One	2.10.83	A 3,093	9-29
St Helens	Division One	9.10.83	A 3,129	14-18
Leeds	Division One	16.10.83	H 2,972	10-44
Wakefield	Division One	22.10.83	H 1,570	16-14
Bradford N	Division One	30.10.83	A 4,377	2-21
Featherstone	JP Trophy 1	6.11.83	A 1,767	10-12
Hull KR	Division One	13.11.83	A 6,200	10-42
Oldham	Division One	20.11.83	H 2,437	21-4
Castleford	Division One	4.12.83	H 2,515	6-6
Hull	Division One	11.12.83	A 10,045	11-36
Bradford N	Division One	18.12.83	H 2,482	6-16
Leeds	Division One	26.12.83	A 5,944	6-30
Salford	Division One	2.1.84	A 1,847	6-4
Hull KR	Division One	8.1.84	H 3,037	18-38
St Helens	Division One	22.1.84	H 1,967	0-30
Swinton	Challenge Cup Prelim	29.1.84	H 1,680	14-4
Castleford	Division One	5.2.84	A 3,131	7-26
Whitehaven	Challenge Cup 1	12.2.84	A 1,638	17-10
Wigan	Division One	19.2.84	H 2,293	22-10
Widnes	Challenge Cup 2	26.2.84	H 3,591	10-12
Whitehaven	Division One	4.3.84	A 1,116	0-18
Wigan	Division One	18.3.84	A 7,237	18-38
Widnes	Division One	21.3.84	A 3,417	16-14
Leigh	Division One	25.3.84	H 1,464	12-24
Salford	Division One	8.4.84	H 1,622	10-12
Warrington	Division One	15.4.84	H 1,639	32-58
Featherstone	Division One	22.4.84	A 1,961	18-38
Widnes	Division One	25.4.84	H 1,146	25-13

1984-5

Sheffield	Division Two	9.9.84	A 1,145	18-14
Swinton	Lancashire Cup 1	16.9.84	H 1,545 *	18-25
Swinton	Division Two	23.9.84	A 1,459	10-31
Runcorn	Division Two	30.9.84	A 360	16-22
Carlisle	Division Two	6.10.84	H 2,300	18-47
Huddersfield	Division Two	13.10.84	H 1,800	26-8
Whitehaven	Division Two	21.10.84	A 1,745	18-28
Blackpool	Division Two	28.10.84	H 1,100	4-8
York	Division Two	4.11.84	H 1,100	22-20
Salford	Division Two	9.11.84	A 1,504	12-28
Hull	JP Trophy 1	18.11.84	H 2,324	14-36
Wakefield	Division Two	25.11.84	H 750	13-12
Bramley	Division Two	9.12.84	A 750	12-11
Salford	Division Two	16.12.84	H 650	13-19
Southend	Division Two	1.1.85	A 504	16-14
Huddersfield	Division Two	3.2.85	A 748	24-8
Halifax	Challenge Cup 1	10.2.85	H 1,095	4-17
Blackpool	Division Two	3.3.85	A 300	22-25
Bridgend	Division Two	8.3.85	H 400	23-8
Rochdale	Division Two	10.3.85	H 620	19-16
Wakefield	Division Two	17.3.85	A 1,385	12-34
Rochdale	Division Two	20.3.85	A 222	25-0
Runcorn	Division Two	24.3.85	H 650 **	17-16
York	Division Two	31.3.85	A 1,285	20-36
Southend	Division Two	5.4.85	H 720	24-17
Bridgend	Division Two	8.4.85	A 173	32-8
Whitehaven	Division Two	14.4.85	H 780 ***	10-10
Carlisle	Division Two	17.4.85	A 850	14-10
Sheffield	Division Two	21.4.85	H 720	40-30
Bramley	Division Two	28.4.85	H 650 ***	22-20
Swinton	Division Two	3.5.85	H 1,047 ***	19-26

* At Swinton ** Chiswick *** Wealdstone FC

1985-6

Blackpool	Division Two	1.9.85	H 1,008	6-2
Doncaster	Division Two	8.9.85	A 282	14-11
Wigan	Lancashire Cup 1	15.9.85	A 8,943	13-24
Wakefield	Division Two	18.9.85	A 1,449	10-18
Batley	Division Two	22.9.85	H 1,036	22-41
Bramley	Division Two	29.9.85	A 1,050	42-24
Whitehaven	Division Two	6.10.85	H 992	21-17
Rochdale	Division Two	13.10.85	A 1,464	6-12
Wakefield	Division Two	20.10.85	H 1,233	4-18
Barrow	Division Two	27.10.85	A 2,339	8-40
Leigh	Division Two	3.11.85	A 3,072	13-42
Bramley	Division Two	10.11.85	H 831	18-20
Workington	Division Two	17.11.85	A 574	28-24
Warrington	JP Trophy 1	24.11.85	H 1,493	13-20
Sheffield	Division Two	8.12.85	H 801	28-21
Carlisle	Division Two	15.12.85	A 591	14-13
Runcorn	Division Two	22.12.85	H 751	44-2
Leigh	Division Two	5.1.86	H 1,001	18-22
Keighley	Division Two	12.1.86	A 645	6-18
Workington	Division Two	19.1.86	H 815	36-8
Rochdale	Division Two	26.1.86	H 910	26-12
Barrow	Challenge Cup 1	26.2.86	H 1,220*	14-26
Blackpool	Division Two	2.3.86	A 410	22-12
Whitehaven	Division Two	9.3.86	A 1,130	8-18
Huddersfield	Division Two	16.3.86	A 406	8-14
Doncaster	Division Two	6.4.86	H 902	12-14
Runcorn	Division Two	16.4.86	A 300	8-26
Sheffield	Division Two	20.4.86	A 700	12-23
Hunslet	Division Two	23.4.86	A 283	20-14
Huddersfield	Division Two	27.4.86	H 803	26-26
Carlisle	Division Two	2.5.86	H 875	22-41
Barrow	Division Two	5.5.86	H 586	18-50
Mansfield	Division Two	7.5.86	A 243	42-16
Mansfield	Division Two	10.5.86	H 370	43-20
Batley	Division Two	11.5.86	A 725	13-28
Hunslet	Division Two	16.5.86	H 472	34-28
Keighley	Division Two	18.5.86	H 505	27-14

* Wigan

Whitehaven	Lancashire Cup 1	14.9.86	A	1,602	6-72
Sheffield	Division Two	21.9.86	H	680	14-68
Mansfield	Division Two	28.9.86	A	364	18-32
Keighley	Division Two	5.10.86	H	658	44-12
Rochdale	Division Two	12.10.86	A	756	12-20
Batley	Division Two	19.10.86	H	812	23-24
Hunslet	Division Two	2.11.86	H	867	4-16
Sheffield	Division Two	9.11.86	A	510	8-17
Dewsbury	Division Two	16.11.86	H	647	16-6
Bramley	Division Two	23.11.86	A	649	10-18
Castleford	JP Trophy 1	30.11.86	H	1,374	24-34
Dewsbury	Division Two	7.12.86	A	532	26-30
Blackpool	Division Two	14.12.86	H	678	30-12
York	Division Two	21.12.86	H	625	18-16
Swinton	Division Two	26.12.86	A	1,700	10-50
Huddersfield	Division Two	4.1.87	H	578	12-18
Kells	Challenge Cup Prelim	22.1.87	A	2,310	4-4
Huddersfield	Division Two	25.1.87	A	379	24-16
Kells	Challenge Cup Prelim Replay	27.1.87	H	370	22-14
Halifax	Challenge Cup 1	1.2.87	H	1,562	10-38
Blackpool	Division Two	8.2.87	A	410	28-48
Bramley	Division Two	15.2.87	H	661	24-20
Swinton	Division Two	22.2.87	H	745	15-15
York	Division Two	1.3.87	A	1,183	19-21
Runcorn	Division Two	8.3.87	H	572	19-2
Hunslet	Division Two	15.3.87	A	1,107	4-30
Whitehaven	Division Two	22.3.87	H	668	8-8
Whitehaven	Division Two	29.3.87	A	1,900	14-32
Keighley	Division Two	4.4.87	A	216	9-22
Batley	Division Two	5.4.87	A	502	15-8
Mansfield	Division Two	12.4.87	H	625	12-20
Rochdale	Division Two	17.4.87	H	766	16-33
Runcorn	Division Two	20.4.87	A	202	9-18

1987-8

Sheffield	Division Two	30.8.87	H	686	12-20
Runcorn	Division Two	6.9.87	A	383	16-23
Salford	Lancashire Cup 1	13.9.87	A	1,644	4-58
Keighley	Division Two	20.9.87	H	605	34-6
Workington	Division Two	27.9.87	A	736	14-22
Doncaster	Division Two	4.10.87	H	822	12-17
Bramley	Division Two	11.10.87	A	650	26-18
Featherstone	Division Two	18.10.87	H	774	19-16
Dewsbury	Division Two	25.10.87	A	503	10-32
Papua New Guinea	Tour match	1.11.87	H	1,216	4-12
Oldham	JP Trophy Prelim	8.11.87	A	3,197	8-36
Bramley	Division Two	15.11.87	H	531	16-8
Huddersfield	Division Two	22.11.87	A	453	14-52
Sheffield	Division Two	29.11.87	A	550	6-16
Workington	Division Two	6.12.87	H	565	2-12
Keighley	Division Two	12.12.87	A	766	10-33
Dewsbury	Division Two	20.12.87	H	564	24-0
Mansfield	Division Two	3.1.88	A	391	6-18
Runcorn	Division Two	10.1.88	H	635	22-20
Springfield	Division Two	17.1.88	A	532	0-17
York	Division Two	24.1.88	H	603	4-36
Mansfield	Challenge Cup 1	31.1.88	H	712	4-16
Featherstone	Division Two	7.2.88	A	1,655	0-14
Wakefield	Division Two	14.2.88	H	551	12-28
Huddersfield	Division Two	6.3.88	H	561	10-17
Wakefield	Division Two	13.3.88	A	1,550	0-32
Batley	Division Two	20.3.88	A	465	34-6
Mansfield	Division Two	27.3.88	H	512	6-32
Batley	Division Two	1.4.88	H	617	40-16
Doncaster	Division Two	3.4.88	A	980	11-6
York	Division Two	10.4.88	A	1,926	13-34
Springfield	Division Two	17.4.88	H	584	9-8

Doncaster	Division Two	28.8.88	A	1,382	12-25
Sheffield	Division Two	4.9.88	H	625	21-20
Huddersfield	Division Two	11.9.88	A	379	28-16
Rochdale	Lancashire Cup 1	18.9.88	A	1,184	14-25
Bramley	Division Two	25.9.88	H	620	20-30
Batley	Division Two	9.10.88	H	488	2-22
Bramley	Division Two	16.10.88	A	627	8-30
Huddersfield	Division Two	23.10.88	H	643	61-22
Runcorn	Division Two	30.10.88	A	350	12-20
Bramley	JP Trophy Prelim	6.11.88	A	989	10-56
Mansfield	Division Two	20.11.88	A	313	4-8
York	Division Two	27.11.88	H	535	8-22
Workington	Division Two	4.12.88	A	690	17-16
Hunslet	Division Two	11.12.88	H	537	10-16
Batley	Division Two	18.12.88	A	683	12-31
Rochdale	Division Two	1.1.89	H	628	10-20
Carlisle	Division Two	8.1.89	A	550	10-52
Whitehaven	Division Two	15.1.89	H	566	16-32
Dewsbury	Division Two	22.1.89	A	520	18-16
Bradford N	Challenge Cup 1	29.1.89	H	1,487	10-28
Mansfield	Division Two	5.2.89	H	585	26-12
Dewsbury	Division Two	12.2.89	H	515	19-9
Whitehaven	Division Two	19.2.89	A	956	0-60
Runcorn	Division Two	26.2.89	H	491	28-4
Workington	Division Two	5.3.89	H	617	21-19
York	Division Two	12.3.89	A	1,877	10-30
Doncaster	Division Two	24.3.89	H	866	20-16
Sheffield	Division Two	26.3.89	A	1,500	16-24
Carlisle	Division Two	2.4.89	H	526	22-26
Rochdale	Division Two	6.4.89	A	701	12-26
Hunslet	Division Two	9.4.89	A	873	21-26

1989-0

York	Division Two	3.9.89	H	774	10-9
Huddersfield	Division Two	10.9.89	A	1,852	8-6
Workington	Lancashire Cup 1	17.9.89	A	702	30-24
Chorley	Division Two	24.9.89	A	442	20-8
Wigan	Lancashire Cup 2	27.9.89	H	3,200 *	4-34
Carlisle	Division Two	1.10.89	H	1,014	50-6
Whitehaven	Division Two	8.10.89	A	1,009	14-15
Rochdale	Division Two	15.10.89	H	1,184	4-18
Bramley	Division Two	22.10.89	H	758	16-6
Hull KR	Division Two	29.10.89	A	4,000	0-44
Whitehaven	Division Two	5.11.89	H	706	24-0
Bramley	Division Two	12.11.89	A	650	17-0
Oldham	Division Two	19.11.89	H	1,440	10-40
Batley	Division Two	26.11.89	A	997	12-10
Halifax	Regal Trophy 1	3.12.89	H	1,542	18-32
Hull KR	Division Two	17.12.89	H	1,009	6-60
Doncaster	Division Two	31.12.89	A	2,211	8-8
Trafford	Division Two	7.1.90	H	652	10-20
Doncaster	Challenge Cup Prelim	14.1.90	H	898	23-16
Rochdale	Division Two	17.1.90	A	2,024	8-42
Batley	Division Two	21.1.90	H	692	17-14
Ryedale- York	Challenge Cup 1	28.1.90	H	856	14-14
Ryedale-York	Challenge Cup 1 Replay	31.1.90	A	2,059	16-12
Oldham	Division Two	4.2.90	A	3,542	4-52
Bradford N	Challenge Cup 2	11.2.90	H	1,665	2-20
Nottingham	Division Two	18.2.90	A	285	34-14
Doncaster	Division Two	25.2.90	H	652	28-12
Ryedale-York	Division Two	4.3.90	A	1,515	14-18
Huddersfield	Division Two	11.3.90	H	804	34-10
Trafford	Division Two	18.3.90	A	400	22-18
Nottingham	Division Two	25.3.90	H	617	44-10
Carlisle	Division Two	1.4.90	A	800	14-2
Dewsbury	Division Two	8.4.90	H	732	14-14
Chorley	Division Two	13.4.90	H	717	38-10
Dewsbury	Division Two	16.4.90	A	742	16-22
Hull KR	Second Division Premiership 1	22.4.90	A	4,308	6-40

* Hendon FC

Runcorn	Lancashire Cup 1	26.8.90	H	628	50-0
Leigh	Lancashire Cup 2	2.9.90	A	2,818	8-40
Workington	Division Two	9.9.90	A	771	4-9
Barrow	Division Two	16.9.90	H	645	22-8
Whitehaven	Division Two	23.9.90	H	600	8-30
Dewsbury	Division Two	30.9.90	A	605	6-16
Bramley	Division Two	7.10.90	H	550	20-6
Keighley	Division Two	14.10.90	A	698	29-22
Runcorn	Division Two	21.10.90	A	500	22-12
Batley	Division Two	28.10.90	H	804	14-7
Trafford	Division Two	4.11.90	A	428	28-27
Ryedale-York	Division Two	11.11.90	H	600	4-9
Swinton	Division Two	18.11.90	A	1,238	4-13
Dewsbury	Division Two	25.11.90	H	515	14-10
Castleford	Regal Trophy 1	2.12.90	H	810	8-14
Doncaster	Division Two	16.12.90	A	1,051	4-0
Trafford	Division Two	6.1.91	H	502	13-6
Leigh	Division Two	20.1.91	H	702	20-23
Ryedale-York	Division Two	27.1.91	A	1,351	4-22
Swinton	Division Two	3.2.91	H	820	26-10
Halifax	Challenge Cup 1	17.2.91	A	4,624	6-46
Chorley	Division Two	24.2.91	A	326	36-2
Leigh	Division Two	27.2.91	A	1,122	12-12
Batley	Division Two	3.3.91	A	758	20-4
Workington	Division Two	10.3.91	H	500	6-7
Barrow	Division Two	17.3.91	A	600	20-8
Whitehaven	Division Two	24.3.91	A	322	20-16
Chorley	Division Two	29.3.91	H	600	28-9
Bramley	Division Two	1.4.91	A	600	8-8
Doncaster	Division Two	7.4.91	H	427	6-12
Keighley	Division Two	10.4.91	H	252	28-16
Runcorn	Division Two	14.4.91	H	354	24-14
Halifax	Second Division Premiership 1	21.4.91	A	4,400	24-42

1991-2

Workington	Division Two	1.9.91	A	2,515	8-12
Rochdale	Division Two	8.9.91	A	1,046	28-26
Wigan	Lancashire Cup 1	15.9.91	H	2,700	10-38
Sheffield	Division Two	22.9.91	H	1,200	22-44
Leigh	Division Two	29.9.91	H	650	20-18
Oldham	Division Two	6.10.91	H	850	20-23
Carlisle	Division Two	13.10.91	A	500	4-12
Ryedale-York	Division Two	20.10.91	H	500	20-10
Workington	Division Two	27.10.91	A	2,145	10-4
Rochdale	Division Two	3.11.91	H	750	14-22
Sheffield	Division Two	10.11.91	H	900	12-29
Oldham	Regal Trophy 1	17.11.91	A	2,165	10-16
Leigh	Division Two	24.11.91	H	600	14-4
Oldham	Division Two	8.12.91	A	3,200	10-0
Carlisle	Division Two	22.12.91	H	500	12-8
Leigh	Division Two	26.12.91	A	2,815	6-13
Ryedale-York	Division Two	5.1.92	H	350	18-6
Rochdale	Division Two	12.1.92	A	2,100	32-12
Rochdale	Division Two	19.1.92	H	750	20-18
Highfield	Challenge Cup 1	2.2.92	A	230	12-12
Highfield	Challenge Cup 1 replay	4.2.92	H	250	24-10
Workington	Challenge Cup 2	9.2.92	A	2,554	2-9
Oldham	Division Two	16.2.92	H	950	8-12
Carlisle	Division Two	23.2.92	A	400	24-28
Sheffield	Division Two	27.2.92	A	1,000	12-36
Workington	Division Two	1.3.92	H	600	28-7
Ryedale-York	Division Two	8.3.92	A	951	14-8
Oldham	Division Two	15.3.92	A	2,500	4-16
Carlisle	Division Two	22.3.92	H	450	20-15
Leigh	Division Two	29.3.92	A	2,500	8-30
Ryedale-York	Division Two	5.4.92	A	706	4-16
Sheffield	Division Two	12.4.92	A	2,000	4-38
Workington	Division Two	17.4.92	H	750	32-16
Huddersfield	Divisional Premiership 1	26.4.92	H	561	14-4
Oldham	Divisional Premiership SF	10.5.92	A	2,893	14-22

Oldham	Division Two	30.8.92	A	2,428	12-27
Rochdale	Division Two	6.9.92	H	500	30-10
Carlisle	Division Two	20.9.92	A	600	46-14
Huddersfield	Division Two	27.9.92	H	850	46-10
Bramley	Division Two	4.10.92	A	800	8-30
Swinton	Division Two	11.10.92	A	600	6-16
Featherstone	Division Two	18.10.92	A	2,000	10-40
Rochdale	Division Two	25.10.92	H	1,000	12-24
Carlisle	Division Two	1.11.92	H	400	18-18
Wakefield	Regal Trophy 1	8.11.92	H	900	30-0
Rochdale	Division Two	15.11.92	A	1,222	16-25
Swinton	Division Two	22.11.92	H	500	20-6
Huddersfield	Division Two	29.11.92	A	1,500	14-18
Leigh	Regal Trophy 2	6.12.92	A	2,000	6-16
Bramley	Division Two	13.12.92	A	1,500	8-16
Featherstone	Division Two	20.12.92	H	850	8-30
Swinton	Division Two	10.1.93	H	350	12-6
Bramley	Division Two	17.1.93	H	450	20-0
Featherstone	Division Two	24.1.93	H	750	6-32
Oldham	Challenge Cup 1	31.1.93	A	3,500	6-34
Carlisle	Division Two	7.2.93	A	1,500	28-14
Featherstone	Division Two	14.2.93	A	2,242	12-58
Bramley	Division Two	21.2.93	H	550	20-12
Rochdale	Division Two	24.2.93	A	726	18-30
Swinton	Division Two	7.3.93	A	500	24-26
Huddersfield	Division Two	14.3.93	H	650	31-17
Oldham	Division Two	21.3.93	A	2,500	27-20
Huddersfield	Division Two	25.3.93	A	1,500	2-17
Carlisle	Division Two	28.3.93	H	650	30-8
Oldham	Division Two	31.3.93	H	500	20-20
Oldham	Division Two	18.4.93	H	638	30-18

1993-4

Batley	Division Two	27.8.93	H	1,010	40-6
Keighley	Division Two	5.9.93	A	3,264	17-14
Doncaster	Division Two	10.9.93	H	890	38-18
Huddersfield	Division Two	19.9.93	A	3,197	10-34
Dewsbury	Division Two	26.9.93	H	1,124	17-42
Barrow	Division Two	3.10.93	A	1,200	12-37
Ryedale-York	Division Two	10.10.93	H	786	24-20
Highfield	Division Two	17.10.93	H	648	62-6
Hunslet	Division Two	24.10.93	H	623	48-12
St Esteve	Regal Trophy 1	31.10.93	H	952	48-16
Workington	Division Two	7.11.93	A	2,000	13-12
Featherstone	Regal Trophy 2	14.11.93	H	1,336	26-12
Carlisle	Division Two	28.11.93	H	711	38-24
Bramley	Division Two	1.12.93	A	421	30-18
Whitehaven	Division Two	5.12.93	A	980	16-16
Ryedale-York	Regal Trophy 3	12.12.93	A	725	42-10
Bradford N	Regal Trophy 4	19.12.93	H	1,818	10-22
Swinton	Division Two	29.12.93	H	602	22-12
Rochdale	Division Two	2.1.94	A	1,068	8-15
Shaw Cross	Challenge Cup 3	16.1.94	H	551	40-14
Doncaster	Division Two	23.1.94	A	1,113	10-20
Featherstone	Challenge Cup 4	30.1.94	H	1,553	14-28
Huddersfield	Division Two	6.2.94	H	1,036	10-24
Batley	Division Two	13.2.94	A	608	18-29
Keighley	Division Two	16.2.94	H	672	13-10
Dewsbury	Division Two	20.2.94	A	992	30-16
Barrow	Division Two	27.2.94	H	605	52-14
Ryedale York	Division Two	6.3.94	A	1,034	22-14
Hunslet	Division Two	13.3.94	A	524	46-22
Workington	Division Two	20.3.94	H	1,479	20-20
Bramley	Division Two	27.3.94	H	514	64-0
Highfield	Division Two	1.4.94	A	280	58-6
Rochdale	Division Two	4.4.94	H	661	28-10
Swinton	Division Two	12.4.94	A	278	20-18
Whitehaven	Division Two	17.4.94	H	836	30-21
Carlisle	Division Two	24.4.94	A	550	26-12
Keighley	Premiership 1	8.5.94	H	1,247	66-12
Doncaster	Second Division Premiership SF	15.5.94	A	2,238	16-6
Workington	Second Division Premiership Final	22.5.94		35,644 Old Trafford	22-30

1994-5

Carlisle	Division Two	21.8.94	A	458	38-16
Hunslet	Division Two	28.8.94	A	520	14-25
Barrow	Division Two	4.9.94	A	780	16-10
Keighley	Division Two	11.9.94	H	1,302	10-30
Highfield	Division Two	18.9.94	A	210	30-8
Batley	Division Two	25.9.94	H	905	30-2
Swinton	Division Two	2.10.94	H	955	40-29
Dewsbury	Division Two	9.10.94	A	1,537	8-23
Bramley	Division Two	16.10.94	H	625	40-12
Rochdale	Division Two	21.10.94	H	1,202	12-3
Ryedale-York	Division Two	30.10.94	H	619	10-13
Carlisle	Division Two	6.11.94	H	570	23-16
Hunslet	Division Two	13.11.94	H	617	40-2
Hemel Hempstead	Regal Trophy 2	27.11.94	H	738	34-16
Salford	Regal Trophy 3	4.12.94	A	2,088	14-16
Barrow	Division Two	11.12.94	H	575	30-6
Leigh	Division Two	26.12.94	A	1,750	10-24
Hull KR	Division Two	8.1.95	A	1,880	4-38
Keighley	Division Two	11.1.95	A	3,895	25-14
Huddersfield	Division Two	15.1.95	A	2,200	8-20
Ellenborough	Challenge Cup 3	22.1.95	H	363	30-10
Highfield	Division Two	29.1.95	H	352	42-4
Batley	Division Two	5.2.95	A	1,106	22-10
Hull KR	Challenge Cup 4	12.2.95	H	905	20-26
Swinton	Division Two	19.2.95	A	768	38-26
Dewsbury	Division Two	5.3.95	H	870	22-16
Whitehaven	Division Two	15.3.95	H	603	18-16
Bramley	Division Two	19.3.95	A	550	38-6
Ryedale-York	Division Two	26.3.95	A	737	12-25
Hull KR	Division Two	2.4.95	H	887	34-22
Huddersfield	Division Two	9.4.95	H	1,360	24-24
Leigh	Division Two	14.4.95	H	902	60-6
Rochdale	Division Two	18.4.95	A	1,017	4-22
Whitehaven	Division Two	23.4.95	A	1,103	30-12
Whitehaven	Premiership 1	8.5.95	H	830	28-1
Keighley	Premiership Semi-final	14.5.95	A	3,627	4-38

Challenge Cup Results

Season	Round	Opponent	Date	Home or away	Result
1980-1	1	Wakefield	15.2.81	H	5-9
1981-2	1	Hunslet	14.2.82	H	14-4
	2	Hull	28.2.82	H	5-11
1982-3	1	Rochdale	16.2.83	A	24-4
	2	Bradford	27.2.83	H	4-11
1983-4	Prelim	Swinton	29.1.84	H	14-4
	1	Whitehaven	12.2.84	A	17-10
	2	Widnes	26.2.84	H	10-12
1984-5	1	Halifax	10.2.85	H	4-17
1985-6	1	Barrow	26.2.86	H *	14-26
1986-7	Prelim	Kells	22.1.87	A	4-4
	Replay	Kells	27.1.87	H	22-14
	1	Halifax	1.2.87	H	10-38
1987-8	1	Mansfield	31.1.88	H	4-16
1988-9	1	Bradford	29.1.89	H	10-28
1989-0	Prelim	Doncaster	14.1.90	H	23-16
	1	York	28.1.90	H	14-14
	Replay	York	31.1.90	A	16-12
	2	Bradford	11.2.90	H	2-20
1990-1	1	Halifax	17.2.91	A	6-46
1991-2	1	Highfield	2.2.92	A	12-12
	Replay	Highfield	4.2.92	H	24-10
	2	Workington	9.2.92	A	2-9
1992-3	1	Oldham	31.1.93	A	6-34
1993-4	3	Shaw Cross	16.1.94	H	40-14
	4	Featherstone	30.1.94	H	14-28
1994-5	3	Ellenborough	22.1.94	H	30-10
	4	Hull KR	12.1.95	H	20-26

* At Wigan

Won: 10   Draw: 3   Lost: 15

John Player and Regal Trophy Results

Season	Round	Opponent	Date	Home or away	Result
1980-1	1	Leeds	23.11.80	H	9-3
	2	Leigh	7.12.80	A	9-17
1981-2	1	Warrington	17.10.81	A	15-24
1982-3	1	St Helens	27.11.82	A	5-17
1983-4	1	Featherstone	6.11.83	A	10-12
1984-5	1	Hull	18.11.84	H	14-36
1985-6	1	Warrington	24.11.85	H	13-20
1986-7	1	Castleford	30.11.86	H	24-34
1987-8	Prelim	Oldham	8.11.87	A	8-36
1988-9	Prelim	Bramley	6.11.88	A	10-56
1989-0	1	Halifax	3.12.89	H	18-32
1990-1	1	Castleford	2.12.90	H	8-14
1991-2	1	Oldham	17.11.91	A	10-16
1992-3	1	Wakefield	8.11.92	H	30-0
	2	Leigh	6.12.92	A	6-16
1993-4	1	St Esteve	31.10.93	H	48-16
	2	Featherstone	14.11.93	H	26-12
	3	Ryedale-York	12.12.93	A	42-10
	4	Bradford N	19.12.93	H	10-22
1994-5	2	Hemel H	27.11.94	H	34-16
	3	Salford	4.12.94	A	14-16

Won: 6   Draw: 0   Lost: 15

Lancashire Cup Results

Season	Round	Opponent	Date	Home or away	Result
1980-1		Did not enter			
1981-2	1	Swinton	16.8.81	H	32-15
	2	Salford	23.8.81	A	3-19
1982-3	1	Swinton	5.9.82	H	20-8
	2	Wigan	15.9.82	A	15-4
	SF	Warrington	30.9.82	Wigan	8-17
1983-4	1	Salford	4.9.83	A	15-16
1984-5	1	Swinton	16.9.84	H*	18-25
1985-6	1	Wigan	15.9.85	A	13-24
1986-7	1	Whitehaven	14.9.86	A	6-72
1987-8	1	Salford	13.9.87	A	4-58
1988-9	1	Rochdale	18.9.88	A	14-25
1989-0	1	Workington	17.9.89	A	30-24
	2	Wigan	27.9.89	H**	4-34
1990-1	1	Runcorn H	26.8.90	H	50-0
	2	Leigh	2.9.90	A	8-40
1991-2	1	Wigan	15.9.91	H	10-38

* At Swinton   ** Hendon FC

Won: 5   Draw: 0   Lost: 11

Divisional Premiership Results

Season	Round	Opponent	Date	Home or away	Result
1990-1	1	Halifax	21.4.91	A	24-42
1991-2	2	Huddersfield	26.4.92	H	14-4
	SF	Oldham	10.5.92	A	14-22
1993-4	1	Keighley	8.5.94	H	66-12
	SF	Doncaster	15.5.94	A	16-6
	Final	Workington	22.5.94	Old Trafford	22-30
1994-5	1	Whitehaven	8.5.95	H	28-1
	SF	Keighley	14.5.95	A	4-38

Won: 4   Draw: 0   Lost: 4

xiv Summary of players appearances

Player	App	Sub	Tries	Goals	D/G	Pts
Abdurahman, Dazi	7		2			8
Aitken, David	19	1	5			20
Aiyede, Bola	0	2				
Alexander, Adrian	3					
Allen, David	102	6	34			107
Armitage, Des	1	1				
Aspey, Mal	35	6	19			57
Colin, Atkinson	40	2	6			24
Bader, Tony	1					
Baker, David	4					
Barker, Bill	1		1			4
Barrow, Norman	36	3	9	10		56
Bayliss, Steve	41		21			71
Beevers, Ben	8	1				
Bermingham, Martin	0	1				
Berney, Gary	6	2	4			8
Best, Tony	1					
Beverley, Harry	104	2	3			9
Bibby Neil	20	13	3			12
Bishop, David	1					
Blackman, Richard	12	1	4			16
Booth, Craig	7		1	28		60
Bowden Reg	116	4	14			42
Bowen, Karl	5	1				
Boyce, Bob	21	3	2			12
Boyle, Wayne	1					
Braniff, Gary	1	1				
Breem, J	0	3				
Briscoe, Phil	11		1			4
Bridge, Russ	109	4	12			48
Brown, Brian	6		1		5	9
Brown, Jeff	2					
Browning, Russell	51	4	8			32
Bryan, George	18		3			12
Bryant, Justin	28	4	6			24
Buckley, Shane	63		33			132
Bullough, David	16	1	9			36
Burke, Mike	1					

Player	App	Sub	Tries	Goals	D/G	Pts
Burridge, Martin	1					
Burrows, Alan	1					
Bush, Peter	3	1				
Butler, John	1	1				
Callow, Steve	5	2				
Campbell, Logan	31	1	25			100
Cambriani, Adrian	119	2	42			146
Camilleri, Chris	6					
Carroll, Bernie	8					
Carter, Scott	31	1	6		1	21
Cass, Peter	4					
Caton, T	0	1				
Chambers, Paul	2	2				
Chatterton, Ian	16	2	1			4
Cheetham, Paul	19	4	6			24
Churchill, Lachlan	30	8	8			32
Collier, Andy	1					
Collis, J	0	1				
Cooper, Dominic	12	6			1	1
Cooper, Tony	2	1				
Corcoran, Colin	9	8				
Coutts, Jeff	46	1	17	21	3	61
Crompton, Kieran	0	1				
Crossley, John	88	3	48			150
Croston, Mark	2					
Cruickshank, David	12	2	3			12
Dalgreen, John	58		9		2	29
Daunt, Brett	26		12		3	39
Davis, Mike	44	1	25		1	101
Deaker, Gary	26	1	5			20
Dean, Martin	1					
Dearden, Alan	41	2	1			4
Diamond, Steve	109		24	305	4	691
Doherty, Joe	93	11	13			42
Domic, Sid	18	1	8			32
Draper, Roger	0	1				
Dray, Matt	37	5	5			20
Driver, David	14	1	8			32
Duffy, Don	52		9			36
Duncan, Darryl	6					
Durham, Keith	0	1				

Player	App	Sub	Tries	Goals	D/G	Pts
Dutton, Joe	11	1	4			16
Dwyer, Tim	21		3	27		66
Dynevor, Leo	13		7			28
Eckersley, David	**85**	**8**	**21**	**6**	**17**	**93**
Ekoku, Abi	**27**		**15**			**60**
Elgar, Nick	6		1			4
Evans, Dave	4	1	3			12
Evans, Lynn		2				
Feighan, Frank	**38**	**6**	**10**			**35**
Fenn, Colin	**50**	**8**	**1**	**107**		**218**
Fisher, Paul	29		6	3	1	31
Fiso, John	1	1				
Flashman, Brian	**5**		**2**			**8**
Francis, Hugh	**8**	**4**	**2**			**8**
Gallagher, John	**51**	**0**	**19**	**196**	**2**	**470**
Ganley, Chris	**55**	**5**	**13**			**40**
Garland, Ernie	6		2			8
Garner, Steve	**33**	**3**	**7**			**28**
Garside, Brett	4	2				
Gibson, Russ	**13**	**5**	**5**	**6**	**2**	**34**
Gilbert, Bernie	**18**	**4**	**2**			**8**
Gillan, Dave	**97**	**4**	**38**			**152**
Glover, Mick	24		2			8
Gould, John	0	1				
Gourley, Tony	**125**	**6**	**2**			**6**
Graham, Mike	1					
Grauf, Craig	29		7		2	30
Green, Craig	35		11	9	2	64
Green, Gavin	1					
Green, Ken	**13**	**13**	**1**			**4**
Green, John	1					
Grimoldby, Nick	**45**	**5**	**4**	**3**	**3**	**25**
Guyett, Steve	**74**	**6**	**12**	**117**	**3**	**289**
Haggath, Glen	18		3	2		16
Halafihi, Nick	**39**	**10**	**8**			**32**
Hanson, Chris	0	1				
Harvey, Dave		1				
Heisner, Ross	2					
Helg, Albert	2	2				
Henley-Smith, Gary	18		8			32
Henney, Harold	**37**	**2**	**8**		**1**	**33**

Player	App	Sub	Tries	Goals	D/G	Pts
Herbert, Justin	0	1				
Herdman, Martin	71	21	14		1	45
Heugh, Cavill	29	5	4	23		62
Hoare, Sean	61	29	16			54
Hodson, Mark	1					
Hogg, Tim	1					
Holderness, Kevin	1	5				
Hudson, Roger	2	5				
Hull, David	49	1	6			22
Hulme, Steve	1					
Hunter, Brian	6		2			8
Hutchinson, Mike	61	4	3			12
Jackson, Bob	8		1			4
Jennings, Scott	16	1	1	2		8
Johanneson, Lawrence	24	13	2			8
Johnson, Mark	73	0	66			264
Johnson, Nick	0	1				
Jones, Charlie	94	22	16			63
Karalius, Tony	20	2	2			6
Keating, Noel	36	16	2			8
Kelly, Shane	13	4	3			12
Kennedy, Eric	21		6			24
Kerapa, Jason	5	1	2			8
Kete, Ivan	9	3				
Key, Andrew	23	3	4			16
Kimaingatau, Alan	3					
Kimberley, Mick	1					
King, Dave	20	7	10			40
Kinsey, Tony	131	25	18		10	74
Knight, Bob	24		1			4
Koehner, M	10					
Lane, Gary	12		3	1		13
Langer, Kevin	21	1	6			24
Lawrie, Geordie	19	5	2			8
Lee, Mark	26	2	9			28
Leslie, Roy	41	9	8			32
Lester, Roy	28	19	4			12
Liddell, Peter	25	5	2			8
Looker, Tony	47	1	9			36
Luxon, Geoff:	1	10	1			4
M'Barki, Hussein	148	15	74			265

Player	App	Sub	Tries	Goals	D/G	Pts
MacCorquodale, Iain	28		6	75	3	171
Mann, Warren	6		2			8
Manning, Kevin	**20**	**5**	**2**			**8**
Mansfield, Glenn	26		9			36
Manthey, Greg	16		5			8
Masa, Santi	9		2		1	9
Massey, Luke	19	5	2			8
Matautia, Ben	0	1				
Matthews, Frank	**17**	**4**	**4**			**16**
Matthews, Ian	17	4	4			16
Mayo, John	6					
McFadden, Frank	2	3				
McMullen, Gerry	0	1				
McCabe, Red	18		8			32
McCarthy, Ray	1	1				
McIvor, Dixon	**17**	**13**	**4**			**16**
McKenzie, Grant	2		2			8
Meachin, Colin	0	1				
Mellors, Ian	**41**	**16**	**4**			**16**
Michalski, Darren	**23**	**14**	**2**			**8**
Mighty, Andrew	**25**	**1**	**7**			**28**
Miller, Craig	**29**	**1**	**4**			**16**
Millington, Wayne	**9**		**1**			**4**
Mills, Steve	**100**	**8**	**50**	**3**		**199**
Mitchell, Simon	3	2				
Mohr, Sean	5	2	4			16
Mordell, Bob	5	3				
Moss, Graham	2					
Mulkerin, Danny	**40**	**4**	**2**			**8**
Murphy, Kieron	**105**	**14**	**24**		**3**	**99**
Nissen, Glen	18	2	4			16
Noble, Mick	**15**	**3**	**3**			**12**
Noel, Tony	1					
Noonan, Derek	18		4			12
O'Brien, Gary	3		2			8
O'Doherty, Pat	18	1	7			28
O'Riley, Paul	**16**	**3**	**5**			**20**
Olsen, Ben	27	3	3			12
Ovens, Ray	4		1			4
Parkes, Brian	5					
Pearce, Greg	**47**	**3**	**8**	**121**		**274**

Player	App	Sub	Tries	Goals	D/G	Pts
Peart, Barry	1	1				
Perryment, Ian	2	2	2			8
Pitt, Darryl	95	20	47	24		232
Plath, John	15	2	4			16
Platt, Alan	27		5	27	4	78
Platt, Billy	2					
Pram, Jason	2	1				
Pratt, Greg	16		1			4
Prendergast, Paul	1					
Radbone, Carl	36	2	9	4		35
Rea, Tony	12		2			8
Rampling, Darren	2	7				
Ramsey, Neville	44		11		1	49
Rees, Huw	51	7	15	12	2	86
Reinsfield, Peter	28	6	4			16
Rendell, Brian	11	5	2		8	
Render, Andrew	2	4			1	2
Rex, Ian	5	2				
Riley, Mark	79		54		1	217
Rippon, Andy	4		2	7		22
Risman, John	18	2	3			9
Roach, Jason	11		5			20
Roberts, Steve	5	5				
Robertson, Karl	3	2	1			4
Rochford, Paul	13		4	14		44
Rolls, Frank	2	3				
Roskell, Scott	88	1	55			220
Rosolen, Steve	110	1	16			64
Rotheram, Dave	114	36	14			56
Rugless, Troy	15		4			16
Sada, Adam	3		1			8
Sanchez, Wayne	21		3	9		30
Scott, Conrad	11	8				
Scott, Gary	1	1				
Scourfield, John	7		5			20
Shaw, Andy	2	2				
Shaw, Darren	33	2				
Simpson, Kevin	4	5				
Simpson, Ian	11	2	1			4
Smith, Chris	72	18	7	146		320
Smith, Martyn	4	1				

Player	App	Sub	Tries	Goals	D/G	Pts
Snowden, Ian	1					
Sokolov, Andre	1	1				
Souto, Peter	**51**	**20**	**9**			28
Spencer, Adrian	**5**		**1**	7		18
Stevens, Paul	9	1	1			4
Stewart, Sam	**70**	**2**	**8**			32
Stockley, John	3		1			4
Stockley, Trevor	**39**	**1**	**14**			56
Stoop, Andre	15		9			36
Stringer, Harold	6		1			3
Tabern, Ray	7		1			4
Tawera, Takura	15					
Taylor, Craig	**41**		**3**			12
Taylor, Mick	**84**	**3**	**19**			76
Timms, Victor	8	5	3			12
Tinsley, Eddie	5	3				
Tolcher, Ken	1					
Townsend, Glen	**15**	**7**	**3**			12
Trembath, Dennis	1	1				
Trialist (S. African)	3			3		6
Tuffs, Neil	**48**	**12**	**6**	**0**	**2**	20
Van Bellen, Ian	20	2	4			12
Walker, Jason	17		6			24
Walker, Paul	15		1			4
Walsh, Michael	2	3				
Ward, Jimmy	**2**	**2**	**1**			4
Webster, Duncan	11		2			8
White, Peter	22	1	7			28
Whiteley, Chris	**28**	**9**				
Whittaker, John	1					
Why, Adrian	**0**	**3**				
Wightman, Ian	**11**	**3**	**1**			4
Wilby, Tim	**24**	**4**	**1**			4
Wilkinson, Bernie	**41**	**4**	**8**			32
Wilkinson, Chris	**69**	**4**	**17**	**141**	**13**	363
Williams, Brett	26	1	1			4
Winborn, Doug	**5**	**6**	**1**			4
Wing, Jason	**13**		**2**			8
Winstanley, Chris	**24**	**3**	**3**			12
Wood, John	**57**	**8**	**11**			33
Woodcock, Martin		1				

Player	App	Sub	Tries	Goals	D/G	Pts
Worgan, Graham	2	1				
Workman, Glen	25	17	1			4
Wright, Rob	7	4				
Yates, Mal	0	1				
Zillman, Andrew	37	1	2			8

Bibliography:

Introduction:

Trevor Delaney   Rugby League on Tyneside, *Code 13 no.4*, August 1987
    A History of Manningham RFC, *Code 13 no.5*, December 1987
Raymond Fletcher
& David Howes   Rothman's Rugby League Yearbook 1982-3, *Rothman's Publications*, London 1982
Robert Gate   Rugby League, An Illustrated History, *Arthur Barker*, London 1989
Vince Karalius   Lucky 13 Stanley Paul London 1964
Keith Macklin   The History of Rugby League Football, *Stanley Paul*, London (revised edn 1974)
Huw Richards   Reflections on a Past Decade, The British Coal League Yearbook 1990-1, *Kingswood* London 1990
    A Bit of a Dream, really, British Coal Rugby League Yearbook 1991-2, *Kingswood*, London 1991
David Smith &
Gareth Williams   Fields of Praise, *University of Wales Press*, Cardiff 1980
Gareth Williams   1905 and all That , *Gomer Press*, Llandyssul 1991
Graham Williams   Midland Manoeuvres: A History of Northern Unionism in Coventry, *Code 13 no.2*, December 1986
    A Capital Idea - The First proposed Club for London , *Code 13 no.6*, March 1988
    If At First You Can't Decide - A History of South Shields , *Code 13 , Nos 15 & 17*

The International Matches:

Les Bettinson   In the Lions Den , *Kingswood*
Ray French (Ed)   The Match of My Life, *Headline*
Robert Gate   Rugby League Fact Book, *Guinness*
Robert Gate   The Struggle for the Ashes, *R. E. Gate*
Robert Gate   An Illustrated History: Rugby League , *Arthur Barker*
David Hodgkinson
and Paul Harrison   The World of Rugby League, *Allen and Unwin*
David Lawrenson   Offiah: A Blaze of Glory, *Methuen*
Keith Macklin   The Story of Rugby League, *Stanley Paul*
Adrian McGregor   Simply the Best, *UQP*
Steve Roach
& Ray Chesterton   Doing my Block , *Ironbark Press*
Eddie Waring   On Rugby League, *Mullen*

The 1930s Clubs, and Fulham, London Crusaders & London Broncos period:

Ian Clayton
& Michael Steele When Push Comes to Shove, *Yorkshire Arts Circus*

Brigadier-General
A. C. Critchley Critch! The Memoirs. 1961

Trevor Delaney The Grounds of Rugby League

Robert Gate George Nepia, *Code 13*

Dave Hadfield Playing Away, *Kingswood*

Simon Inglis The Football Grounds of Great Britain , *Collins Willow*

John M Jones The History of London Highfield, Acton & Willesden, Streatham & Mitcham Rugby League Football Clubs 1933-1937

John M Jones London Highfield - Twenty Years ahead of their time, *Open Rugby*

Michael Latham Leigh Rugby League Club A Comprehensive Record 1895-1994, *Mike RL Publications*

Malcolm MacDonald An Autobiography (as told to Jason Tomas), *Arthur Barker*

Tom Mather The London Experience, *Open Rugby*

Tony Pocock (Ed) British Coal: The Rugby League Yearbook 1991-2, *Kingswood Press*

Huw Richards Getting Worked Up Watching Bambi, in XIII Winters edited by Dave Hadfield, *Mainstream Publishing*

Tom Stenner Sport for the Million, *Sportsmans Book Club*

Laura Thompson The Dogs, *Chatto & Windus*

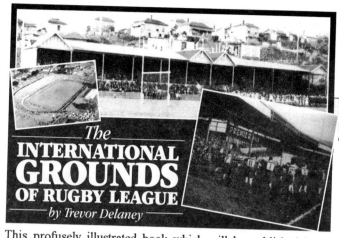

The **INTERNATIONAL GROUNDS OF RUGBY LEAGUE**
by Trevor Delaney

This profusely illustrated book which will be published in time for the game's centenary in August 1995, is an ambitious companion to the widely-acclaimed *The Grounds of Rugby League*. Apart from all the major English grounds, *The International Grounds of Rugby League* will also cover every ground where international and test matches have been played by the game's leading International Board countries over the last century - over 100 grounds in total. There will therefore be specific sections written by an expert on that particular country or region. The page format of this (approx 208 pp) softback edition will be 198 mm x 210 mm; and there will be a full-colour cover and an 8 page full-colour section.

****

London Calling!
The Independent London Broncos Fanzine

are proud to support London League Publications in their latest endeavour

Read us every month of the season for:
* Interviews with notable club and Rugby League figures
* Independent news, views & comment, including news of local amateur clubs
* Home and away match reports
* A fantasy Rugby League competition (the only fanzine to have one)
* For not being the match programme!

On sale at home matches, by subscription and at Sportspages in London and Manchester. *London Calling! - Simply the best and still only £1*

45, Estella Avenue, New Malden, Surrey, KT3 6HX. Tel: 0181-942-3063

Your local supporter.

We wish you every success and are delighted to offer our support to your publication.